Deep Inside the Underground Economy
How Millions of Americans Are Practicing Free Enterprise in An Unfree Society

by Adam Cash

Breakout Productions
Port Townsend, Washington

Deep Inside the Underground Economy

How Millions of Americans Are Practicing Free Enterprise in An Unfree Society

© 2003 by Adam Cash

Published by:
Breakout Productions
PO Box 1643
Port Townsend, WA 98368
Phone: 360-379-1965

ISBN 1-893626-49-0
Library of Congress Card Catalog Number 200310037

Contents

Dedication

*To the freedom of economic acts between consenting adults;
and to all Guerrilla Capitalists everywhere.*

"To seek the redress of grievances by going to law, is like sheep running for shelter to a bramble bush." — *Dilwyn*

"Men seldom, or rather never for a length of time, and deliberately, rebel against anything that does not deserve rebelling against." — *Carlyle*

"That government is best which governs least." — *Jefferson*

Introduction

Since the first version of this book appeared almost twenty years ago, there's been a greater interest in guerrilla capitalism because of the increasing difficulty in earning a living while playing by the government's rules. During most of this century, Europeans have complained about the invasion of American culture, leading to the "Americanization" of Europe. The opposite flow, leading to the "Europeanization" of America, has received much less notice. This country is no longer "the land of the free," as big government becomes bigger in the European fashion and plays a more intrusive role in our lives. America is no longer "the home of the brave," since most Americans have become docile conformists, too timid to do anything but follow the crowd and do exactly what they're told.

This country is no longer "the land of the free," as big government becomes bigger in the European fashion and plays a more intrusive role in our lives.

Some Americans have protested openly, with some success. Various "tax revolts" in states have shown that many people are tired of being taxed to death. California's Proposition 13 was a well-known example of this. Many other Americans consistently vote down bond issues when they have the opportunity. During the last few years, we've seen tax cutbacks in various states and even a tax refund by the Bush administration in early 2001. It's pretty clear that the majority of voters and taxpayers are tired of high taxes, especially when they see how the government often wastes money on questionable projects. There also exists in this country an underground movement of people who love freedom and are not afraid to live free lives while their neighbors abjectly accept economic slavery.

Many Americans work as "wage slaves," the worst situation of all. They wait for their weekly paychecks, accepting that the government will amputate part of their earnings before they even see them. They know and accept that the Internal Revenue Service knows every cent they earn, and that they have absolutely no choice in the matter. They commute to work without compensation or even being able to deduct the cost of commuting. Perhaps worst of all, they live under the shadow of the ax, wondering if and when they'll be "down-sized."

The real entrepreneurs, however, are the free-thinkers, the guerrilla capitalists.

Next in the gradient are the self-employed. As small business owners, they know that they can keep a greater proportion of their earnings because they have many more deductions open to them. Business expenses are deductible, and the smart small business owner takes full advantage of every legal deduction. The real entrepreneurs, however, are the free-thinkers, the guerrilla capitalists.

Free-thinkers know that freedom exists for those who are bold enough to bend and even break the rules. They know that true freedom begins inside one's own mind — which the government cannot invade — and that it's impossible to be free without free-thinking. Free-thinking means not being bound by mindless conformity, and it means daring to be different, without worrying what unimaginative and timid friends and neighbors do or think. Free-thinking means learning how to break the rules for a higher purpose, not just for the sake of rule-breaking.

Free-thinking Americans are self-reliant and don't depend on the government to provide everything for them, because they're sophisticated enough to understand the truth of Ralph Waldo Emerson's words:

Deep Inside the Underground Economy
How Millions of Americans Are Practicing Free Enterprise in An Unfree Society

2

"For every benefit you receive a tax is levied." Their reply to offers of government "generosity" is, "Thanks, but no thanks."

Free-thinking people will always be more free than those who expect the government to protect their freedom, because they create their own freedom.

These free-thinking people will always be more free than those who expect the government to protect their freedom, because they create their own freedom, instead of passively waiting for someone else to do it for them. Anyone who waits for someone else to make him free will always be beholden to his liberator.

The real freedom-lovers know better than to accept the politically correct news and views contained in the mainstream media, designed to lull and stupefy credulous people in their audiences. They reject the world-view spouted by the "talking heads" on TV. These skeptical people are the guerrilla capitalists.

The guerrilla capitalist has always been on the cutting edge of free enterprise, especially in tightly regulated economies. Even in World War II Europe, when price and wage controls, rationing, and even employment were enforced more severely than in the United States, guerrilla capitalists formed black markets, even in totalitarian countries. This was despite severe sanctions by the secret police. The opportunity to earn and spend more than was allowed by totalitarian governments seduced even the officials assigned to enforce economic regulations, and bribery was one common way of easing around onerous laws.

Guerrilla capitalism involves activities that have traditionally been perfectly legal and honorable ways of earning a living.

Guerrilla capitalism isn't essentially criminal. As we'll see, it involves activities that have traditionally been perfectly legal and honorable ways of earning a living. The problem is not with the guerrilla capitalist, but with government and its relentless propensity to exercise more control over its citizens. Brewing alcoholic beverages has never been illegal until recent years, during the ill-advised "prohibition" era. Before prohibition, the government taxed alcohol, and the Treasury Department's "revenooers" raided stills operated by those who did not pay taxes on their prod-

ucts. Even after repeal of prohibition, the government resumed imposing special taxes on alcoholic beverages, and anyone involved in making, distributing, or selling drinking alcohol without paying the government its due is a criminal.

Likewise, gunsmiths were reputable tradesmen until the government began regulating their activities. Today, it's illegal to manufacture a firearm without a special license from the Bureau of Alcohol, Tobacco, and Firearms, the regulatory agency that demonstrated its special talent for law enforcement at Waco, Texas, in early 1993.

The Coming Electronic Prison

Some governments make it policy to track their citizens throughout their lives, monitoring their employment and their residences. These are not only totalitarian governments, but governments of what we call "Western Democracies," such as France and Switzerland.

In this country, today we face the prospect of having our economic lives regulated to an extent impossible in the wartime Europe of fifty years ago, because computers make it possible for the government to track every resident literally from birth to death. Laws requiring the reporting of every birth everywhere in the country are the basis of universal registration, already existing in fact, if not in statute. Children are subjected to mandatory education, where their intellectual, emotional, and social lives are scrutinized and documented by teachers and school "counselors."

Selective Service registration has tracked males of military age since World War II. Even today, all males age eighteen and over are required to register, although this country has not had conscription since the early 1970s. All members of the work force have been registered for decades through the benign-seeming "Social Security" laws, which require withholding a portion of wages for retirement pensions. Income tax laws on the federal, state, and local levels ensure that these governments have computerized records of everyone working for a salary. Even self-employed people, formerly free of the practical effects of such laws, are coming under increasingly tight scrutiny as the computer allows tracking of vast amounts of data. Today, anyone performing "contract labor" for a business has his income reported on Form 1099, and the Internal Revenue Service can match these to individuals and obtain a good estimate of yearly earnings.

Many don't yet take it seriously, but children are assigned Social Security numbers at an early age. New laws require a parent to register his child with the Social Security Administration in order to use that child as an exemption. This number stays with the child throughout life, giving the government a precise accounting of above ground employment and the amount earned.

Laws designed to impede money laundering also work to make everyone's financial transactions more visible to the IRS and other government police agencies.

On the pretext of pursuing drug money, various federal agencies have been scrutinizing our financial transactions more closely than ever before. Laws designed to impede money laundering also work to make everyone's financial transactions more visible to the IRS and other government police agencies.

There's worse to come. The terrorist attacks of September 11, 2001 have led to new laws designed to tighten security by restricting our freedom. One proposal has been for a national identity card containing a magnetic stripe with digitized information about the bearer. Federal police agencies already have received enhanced powers to eavesdrop on telephone calls and e-mail. There is even a developing technology of electronic chips implanted under the skin to trace the whereabouts of people who have committed no crime.

More government agencies are becoming involved, directly and tangentially, in extracting money from Americans. Business owners must buy business licenses from local bureaucracies. Retailers are required to buy a license to collect sales taxes on behalf of the state or municipality. Many professionals, such as doctors, attorneys, and accountants, must pass state-mandated proficiency examinations, paying a fee for the privilege, to practice their skills for pay. Even firearms dealers, already heavily-regulated, must now pay more for their licenses, the result of the Brady Bill's misguided effort to combat crime.

Another intrusion by tax collectors has been the "eye in the sky" programs put in place by city and county building inspection departments. Today, some jurisdictions buy aerial photographs of their areas to detect those who erect buildings or make additions to existing buildings without obtaining building permits. This makes it harder for the guerrilla capitalist who wants to build a shop in his backyard.

Governments use motor vehicle ownership as another means of registering and tracking individuals. Although the United States has not adopted the common European practice of requiring any citizen to notify police upon change of address, anyone with a driver's license or motor vehicle registration must notify the appropriate agency when he moves. This, in practice, provides government authorities with up-to-date information about your residence. Police can use the radio or a mobile computer data terminal in the patrol car to call up your driver's license and motor vehicle registration in seconds. New licenses have magnetic stripes containing your personal information and the officer can retrieve it by swiping your card through a slot on his on-board computer.

Recreation is also under government scrutiny and taxation. While hunting and fishing licenses have been in place for decades, in most locales the owner of a small boat must register it with the state and buy a license for it. State and national parks and campgrounds have user fees and parking fees, and in many places it's no longer possible simply to park an RV at the side of the road or in a field for the night.

Many states, such as Arizona and New Mexico, impose sales tax on the most basic need of all: food. Unless you grow all your own food, you're forced to pay taxes just to eat.

Today we see an increasingly greedy government reluctant to give up any of its taxing and spending powers, despite the end of the cold war.

Today we see an increasingly greedy government reluctant to give up any of its taxing and spending powers, despite the end of the cold war. Rather, the government is seeking new enemies around the world to justify large military spending. Federal, state, and local legislators devoted to the "tax and spend" philosophy of management are imposing new taxes and increasing old ones. This follows the trend pointed out by Elbert Hubbard, the self-taught philosopher and advocate of self-reliance: "Government is a kind of legalized pillage." One reason for this trend is that legislators realize it's possible to extract more from wage earners with the aid of new methods of data processing. Formerly paper trails were necessary, but

Deep Inside the Underground Economy
How Millions of Americans Are Practicing Free Enterprise in An Unfree Society

4

today's electronic technology has opened up more ways of finding who earns and spends what.

The wide use of credit and debit cards ensures that such transactions leave an electronic trail, accessible to government agents. Personal and business checks document other transactions. Bank records are open to inspection, making it difficult for enterprising individuals to conceal assets. The bottom line is that anyone who wants to keep more of his earnings than the government allows faces an increasingly difficult task.

Is it worth it? Is the extra effort involved in keeping part or all of your economic life underground bringing rewards large enough to justify it? The answer depends upon your outlook and willingness to go that extra mile.

Breaking Free

If you can operate a lucrative underground business, earning far above your minimal needs, you have the opportunity to build up a respectable nest egg for retirement.

If you're in the lowest economic bracket, an extra hundred or two hundred dollars per month makes a big difference in your disposable income, that is, what you have left over after paying rent, food, and other basic living expenses. Earning those few extra bucks is safest, because the IRS doesn't scrutinize carefully the lives of the poor and unknown.

If you can operate a lucrative underground business, earning far above your minimal needs, you have the opportunity to build up a respectable nest egg for retirement. In fact, if you're outstandingly successful, you'll be able to escape the rat race by early retirement.

What Do YOU Want?

What are your needs? What are your wants? Some people really don't earn enough to make ends meet and welcome the chance to earn extra money, not necessarily in the underground economy, but any way they can, even if they have to pay extra taxes on the extra income. Others resist paying taxes because of a profound conviction that the government wastes their money. These people often hold full-time jobs

and pay taxes on their incomes, but want to earn extra tax-free money.

Some want "pin money," or "mad money," to buy luxuries that they could not otherwise afford. Some want to develop a skill or a business to supplement retirement income. This need not be something that is done only after retirement, as it's best to acquire a resource before the actual need for it.[1]

Others, with a hard-core survivalist orientation, feel that the economy will sooner or later crash, and they want a way of earning a living that is inflation- or depression-proof. They may also seek to put away supplies for survival. These can range from freeze-dried foods through silver coins to guns and ammunition.[2]

Yet others simply resent paying taxes, and want to be able to keep all of what they earn. There are other motives, and other needs, and one person can have two or more reasons at the same time. The main point is to understand your motives and needs, and to assign priorities.

- Are you interested in extra income, regardless of whether or not you have to pay taxes on it?
- Do you distrust the Social Security system so that you feel the need to assure your retirement income?
- Are you apprehensive about the economy so that you feel you need to provide for surviving economic collapse?
- Do you object to paying taxes or feel that you're being tapped for more than your share? Are you willing to take risks to avoid taxes? If so, how big?
- Do you just like to "get away with something," as many of us faced with a crushing economic situation and an oppressive society do?
- Are you greedy or do you like to conspicuously show off what you own?

Only you can answer these questions. Answer them honestly, because only accurate answers will enable you to plan to meet your needs. Be aware of your weaknesses, such as greed or the need to show off, because these can be dangerous liabilities if you enter the underground economy.

What Level for You?

Rather than try to promote or dictate a certain inflexible technique of earning money in the underground economy, let's examine the possibilities.

While the facts about the economy are fairly clear, those about underground workers are not. This is because people vary so much in skills and personalities. They vary in willingness to change their lifestyles, and willingness to take risks. Let's examine some of the checkpoints along the road to the underground. Identifying these different levels of involvement will enable you to select what best suits your skills, personality, and life situation.

Level I: Dipping your toes into the water.

This basically means exploiting the opportunities in your regular occupation, something that many people already do. If you're self-employed, you have the chance to skim off some of the receipts without declaring them on your tax return. A doctor, for example, still occasionally gets paid in cash, and if he's discreet, he can pocket some of it without making waves, or even ripples. A plumber also gets cash jobs, as does a repairman, lawn care specialist, etc.

There are, however, two main points to keep in mind in this effort: First, don't skim so much that it shows conspicuously. If you deprive your business of too much visible income, the experienced examiners at the IRS may note the imbalance and wonder how you can afford to incur so many business expenses or occupy such a large building, with so little income. The corollary to this is to watch your deductible expenses and not deduct more than is appropriate for the income you declare.

Tax examiners have carefully worked out guidelines that tell them what the normal proportions of expenses are in relation to income. They've had years of experience examining many tax returns, and they've worked out averages for almost every sort of deduction. For example, they have computed what proportion of income goes for church contributions in different income brackets. They know what the average figure is for supplies in various types of businesses. If your tax return seems out of proportion, it will suggest to the examiner that he should seek out unreported income.

Don't get greedy and try to skim off too much. Start slowly and build it up. At some point, you may be called in for an audit. This is your early warning, which tells you that your declared expenses are arousing suspicion.

The other main point to keep in mind is to watch your lifestyle, and don't flaunt your wealth. We'll get more deeply into this aspect in Part III.

Level II: Extra hours, extra work.

This is moonlighting without a visible income. Many people hold part-time jobs, collect paychecks, and suffer through withholdings. Moonlighting for cash or other untraceable income is a safe step forward into the underground. Other untraceable income can come from bartering your skills and accepting payment in hard goods or in reciprocal services, as many do. For example, one engineer, who was also a skilled cabinetmaker, traded some handmade furniture to the midwife who delivered his wife's baby.

Level III: Operating a business without declaring the income.

Normally the business must be a sideline, because trying to live without a visible means of support can lead to problems, both with the IRS and with nosy neighbors. A mail-order business is one type of enterprise that is easy to disguise or even totally bury, because of the nature of the business.

Level IV: Living underground.

This is the radical step of establishing a nomadic existence, suitable mainly for those who so much detest paying taxes that they're willing to adopt a totally different lifestyle in order to avoid paying them. It means taking a job under a false identity, falsifying the withholding form with a claim of extra dependents and a spurious Social Security number, and moving on before any detailed investigation occurs. (Career criminals of various types often live nomadic lifestyles, but they're outside the scope of this book.)

This is very difficult to do, and requires a special type of personality. It's possible to earn a lot of money this way, and to salt it away in Swiss accounts, but it's not very likely. In practice, almost the only legitimate jobs open to people who can't tolerate a background check are menial ones, those with "no questions asked" and low pay.

Choosing the Right Way

This book contains a survey of different ways of earning money as an underground worker. Not every way is for you. You'll have to assess your skills and preferences realistically to find what's best for you. It's vital to avoid the mind-set that tells you that you can do anything you want to do. Few of us are so gifted that we can succeed at everything we try. In most fields, few people make it to the top. Anyone who tells you that you can succeed at anything sim-

Deep Inside the Underground Economy
How Millions of Americans Are Practicing Free Enterprise in An Unfree Society

6

ply by following his plan is merely blowing smoke at you. There's no substitute for hard-core realism.

It's vital to avoid the mind-set that tells you that you can do anything you want to do.

The best way is to build on what you've got. For example, if you've got a good language skill, and can write clearly and concisely, you might start a resume-writing service. If your skills are mainly manual, if you can fix almost anything even though you have a hard time explaining just how you do it, you might consider appliance repair. Whatever skill you may have, the simplest thing is to use what you've got by applying it to earning money in the underground.

Of course, if you want to do something for which you think you have the talent but are not quite prepared, you may have to invest in education to improve your skill.

The hardest and riskiest way is to branch out into something with which you're totally unfamiliar, however attractive it might seem. You don't know if you'll be able to do it, you'll have to spend money to get training, and you run the risk of crashing, or finding that your effort was a waste because you don't like it after all. You may also discover that you can't earn enough at it to justify the money you laid out to learn.

This tells you to beware of many promises by various training schools that you can earn "big money" in electronics, or air conditioning repair, or whatever, if you pay them to train you. Unless you're already somewhat acquainted with the field, you have no way of knowing what you'll earn, whether you'll be able to find work, or even if you have the native ability.

If you own your own home and have an assortment of tools because you do your own repairs, you have a head start at setting up a repair business, which, incidentally, is often a cash business.

All in all, it's best to start out with something that requires the least investment. In many instances, you can get off to a flying start by using what you've already got, without having to sink more money into a fledgling business. For example, if you own your own home and have an assortment of tools because you do your own repairs, you have a head start at set-

ting up a repair business, which, incidentally, is often a cash business.

In the following pages, we'll survey some good fields as well as some bad. The purpose is not only to give you a guide to what you might do, but also to warn you of the disadvantages and dangers you might encounter in some areas. There are many of these and unless forewarned, you could find yourself in a sticky situation. Look over the possibilities carefully and then decide how you want to start. It may be easier than you think.

What's Changed during Recent Years

It used to be easier to earn a living outside the regulated economy. During the middle 1980s, for example, the Internal Revenue Service was forced to throw the bulk of the Forms 1099 they received straight into the incinerator, because it did not have the computer power to match all of them with taxpayer names. Today it's different because the IRS has procured new and more powerful computers to track earnings. The IRS tracks everybody's income if there's any sort of paperwork or electronic trail attached to it.

New banking and currency laws require banks and other financial institutions to report large transactions to the IRS. Even traveler's checks are regulated today, and if you buy more than $3,000 worth, a report will go to the IRS.

It's also much harder to drop out of sight today than it was ten years ago. Your name is likely to be in dozens of computers.

It's also much harder to drop out of sight today than it was ten years ago. Your name is likely to be in dozens of computers, many operated by private parties such as credit bureaus, as well as government computers. If you are male, your birth record is on file with the government's dormant Selective Service Board unless you've risked prosecution by not registering. Everyone who has ever held a job or had a Social Security number is on file with the IRS and the Social Security Administration. As we've seen, parents are now required to register their children with the Social Security Administration if they want to receive a tax deduction for them. Your driver's license and motor vehicle registration are on file with the state, and the federal government has access to these records.

Your name and other information are on file in various places. If you've ever filled out an employment application, your life history, including your Social Security number, is on file and accessible to investigators. If you rent an apartment, your biographical and employment data are on file in a rental agent's office, where a credit bureau can gain access. If you've ever bought a house or any sort of real property, you have a financial history on file, as well as your name on file in the county deed office. Some cities, such as Portland, Oregon, have ordinances requiring apartment managers to run criminal background as well as credit checks on applicants, to ensure a "crime-free" environment. The telephone company asks for personal information when you apply for telephone service.

To earn money without being taxed today, you have to work at a regular job, as cover employment, while earning hidden income by other means.

All of this chokes off opportunities to operate totally underground businesses, which is exactly what all of this information gathering was designed to do. To earn money without being taxed today, you have to work at a regular job, as cover employment, while earning hidden income by other means. Even organized crime bigwigs today have "legitimate" businesses set up to provide them with an ostensibly "legal" source of income to avoid prosecution by the IRS.

Today, you have fewer legitimate deductions available to you when you fill out Form 1040 because of sweeping "reforms" by Congress. There are fewer loopholes to exploit, and you have to tread carefully to avoid an audit. If you do have a disagreement with the IRS, you begin at a greater disadvantage than ever before. The U.S. Supreme Court slammed the door on "Fifth Amendment Filers" about two decades ago. You are required by law to provide information against yourself on IRS forms.

What This Book Will Do for You

This book explores the economic problems of getting along in the United States today in friendly, conversational terms, avoiding technical language. Within these pages, you'll find clear and understandable explanations regarding why earning a living is so tough these days, and how you can make it easier by reducing the tax bite.

It will show you some of the ways in which the government wastes your hard-earned tax money and then asks you for more. It will show you how to save more of the money you do earn, both on direct expenditures and on taxes, and how to take some little-noted and little-used deductions on your income tax return.

Obviously, not all of these methods will be for everyone. No single individual could use all of them, at least not all at once. However, there is a wide enough variety presented here to give you some choices.

This is basically a self-improvement book. But unlike many other entries in this genre, it does not pretend to provide any "secret" formula for quick and easy riches. There is no easy way to become rich, except by inheritance, and few of us are lucky enough to enjoy that. You are not likely to become rich, and certainly not by reading a book.

However, by reading this book, and acting upon the information that is relevant to your needs, you can improve your situation. You still won't be rich, but you will be better off than before.

This book is about the underground economy. It's about the guerrilla capitalists who have simply quit paying all or part of their taxes. It is not about above ground tax protesters. It is not about drug dealers, loan sharks, prostitutes, and others who evade taxes on illegally derived income, although we'll discuss their methods of operation to provide perspective.

The guerrilla capitalist can be anyone, even people you know. The guerrilla capitalist can be of either sex, any age, and in any occupation. The guerrilla capitalist could be your babysitter or your dentist. The guerrilla capitalist could be the waitress in the coffee shop where you eat breakfast, or the guy who picks up your trash. It could even be you.

If you resent the many ways our several levels of government take and spend your money, this book will outline ways to combat this.

If you resent the many ways our several levels of government take and spend your money, this book will outline ways to combat this. You'll learn how to put part or all of your earnings out of sight of government snoops. If you're a wage slave, you'll see ways to supplement your official, documented in-

Deep Inside the Underground Economy
How Millions of Americans Are Practicing Free Enterprise in An Unfree Society

8

come by underground methods, on and off the job. You'll discover ways to keep the assets already earned under the surface, invisible to an audit by revenue agents. You'll find means of using the system's weaknesses against it, taking advantage of legal loopholes and seams in existing laws.

In this book, we'll cover in vast detail the whole phenomenon of guerrilla capitalism. We'll consider what types of businesses are best suited for the guerrilla capitalist, and discuss ways in which practicing guerrilla capitalists evade taxes. We'll provide dozens of capsule descriptions of actual underground businesses, and longer case histories, to lead you step by step through the everyday business of the underground economy.

We'll discuss the pitfalls of using banks, and why underground workers are very guarded about keeping their money in banks. We'll show you how guerrilla capitalists fiddle the books, how they keep their income off their tax returns, and what they do with their unreported income. We'll study how the IRS can discover underground income, and what guerrilla capitalists can do to protect themselves from discovery.

This isn't just a text, it's a workbook. In these pages you'll find checklists and survey forms to help you outline ways to earn extra money, and to keep more of what you earn.

In Part I, we'll begin with several overviews of the underground economy, and how you may find a place in it. We'll get into tactics for fudging your tax return, and diddling your books. We cover the uses and abuses of receipts, deductions, and many more methods of reducing your tax bite.

Part II discusses the crux of the matter: making all or part of your income invisible to the tax authorities. There are many ways to do this, from "skimming" from an above ground business to barter, and we'll cover the entire range.

Part III deals with the many ways to enjoy your unreported income without attracting the attention of the tax authorities by conspicuous consumption. This is truly important if you don't want to give yourself away by obviously spending above your overt means, because many underground workers have been caught through this sort of carelessness.

Do you want to be more fiscally fit? If you do, then read on.

Notes

1. Dr. Gary North, *Government By Emergency*, American Bureau of Economic Research, Fort Worth, TX, 1983, pp. 1-49. This gives a clear and convincing explanation, for anyone who hasn't been following the news, of why the Social Security system is in deep trouble, and getting in deeper. It's frightening enough for those old enough to be retiring soon, but the uncertainties of a distant future are particularly serious for those who won't be retiring for many more years.

2. *Ibid.* Dr. North, along with many other survivalist authors, explains that not only is the Social Security system in trouble, but the whole economy is a house of cards. His view contradicts the consensus of the acknowledged experts in economics, but the experts have been wrong enough times, and about enough questions, to suggest that they are not infallible. On page 41, he describes a book published after the onset of the "Great Depression," which quoted many "experts" who said, all through the 1920s, that it couldn't happen.

   Of course, we've recently seen many examples of how experts can be wrong. Since the September 11, 2001 attacks it's been politically correct to predict that the American economy is on the rise again. Both experts from the government and private analysts have cited statistics, such as consumer spending, to "prove" that the economy is getting back to normal, but anyone watching the stock market, especially during the week of April 22, 2002, can see that the economy is still very shaky. Nobody really knows the future of the American economy, and it's best to take optimistic predictions with a grain of salt.

Part One
Why Go Underground?

Why are we taxed so heavily? Why are we taxed at all? The answers depend on who you ask. Some of the answers are very disturbing, and we'll delve into them in Chapter One.

There are basically two approaches you can use to keep more of the money you earn, and to keep your extra assets out of sight of the Internal Revenue Service. Each has a degree of risk in proportion to rewards. The first to consider is operating entirely underground, reporting no income, and paying no taxes. This is how many people engage in criminal activities such as prostitution or drug traffic, because they have no choice. It's awkward to file an income tax return listing your occupation as a "bank robber," "drug wholesaler," "prostitute," etc. If you're involved in overtly illegal activities, filing a Form 1040 is just a nuisance, and you can easily ignore it. In any case, being prosecuted for income tax evasion is the least of your problems.

If you earn your income in something illegal, you can afford the additional risks of directly ripping off the Internal Revenue Service. There are several ways of doing this, which we'll discuss in Appendix Three.

The second strategy is to lead an above ground existence, with an obvious and legal source of income, and use this as a front to keep your underground activities deeply buried. There are two basic ways of doing this, depending on whether you're a wage slave or self-employed.

First is to hold a salaried job as your overt source of income, while earning extra, unreported income on the side. You may have opportunities to earn extra, unreported income on the job, if you're alert.

There are some practical, legal measures that the employee can take to increase his income and not pay taxes on it. With a reasonably cooperative employer, he can improve his position, and avoid the taxes that ordinarily would follow. Some practical ways are:

1. *Ask for fringe benefits, not wages.*
    An increase in the paycheck usually bumps the employee into a higher tax bracket, but if the extra money goes into fringe benefits, it's not taxable. A medical plan, extra days off, shorter workdays, etc., all help the employee without penalizing him through taxation. Unions, knowing this, have for years asked for more fringe benefits than outright pay increases.
2. *Take compensation in trade or goods, not money.*
    Jose[1] was a chef at a top-rank hotel, known for the quality of its dining room. In dollars, his pay was low, but one of the perquisites of employment, for chefs and dishwashers alike, was food. Not only did the kitchen serve free meals to those who worked in it, but the employees got to take some home, too. The reason was that, as a high-quality dining room, there was a policy of "no leftovers." A roast or ham would not be served the next day if the traffic didn't wipe it out on the day it was cooked. Rather than throw it out, the management let the employees have it. The same rule applied to bread and rolls, as freshly baked goods were the stock-in-trade of the hotel. With the variety of the menu, there was always ample food for each employee to take home to his family, and while doing so, they helped themselves to other perquisites, such as butter and cheese. The result was that Jose for many years fed his family the same first-class food the wealthy guests ate, and his wife spent very little at the local market.
    Jack, an electrician, often worked overtime, but had an arrangement with his employer that was convenient, although not quite legal. In compensation, he'd take electrical supplies for his own sideline, instead of overtime pay. This

Deep Inside the Underground Economy
How Millions of Americans Are Practicing Free Enterprise in An Unfree Society

10

suited them both very well, because his employer didn't like paying time-and-a-half, and Jack didn't want to be in a higher tax bracket, which would have eaten up the overtime rate.

3. *Keep an eye out for scrap*.

Frank was a printer, and in the commercial shop in which he worked, there was a lot of waste, scrap paper that was useless because it was left over from runs, and went into the dumpster. Frank collected this scrap with his employer's blessing and sold it on the side to friends who needed small amounts of paper. It wasn't much money, but he kept what he made.

4. *Work at a sideline, such as those suggested in this book*.

The income tax return you file is simple and straightforward, listing only your salaried employment, and the normal proportions of exemptions and deductions. Your sideline and the extra benefits you gain from it remain totally off the books. We'll examine the benefits and perquisites of being a hired employee in this section.

The second way is possible if you're self-employed, and is more complicated. At the outset, you divert some of your income, not reporting it. There are several ways of doing this, which we'll consider in detail later. The other aspect is to keep as much of your reported income as possible for yourself by inflating your deductions.

Many people are doing this, and the IRS knows it. In 1987, for example, 14 million taxpayers shorted the IRS by 24.3 billion dollars. This is an average of $1,736 each.[2]

Keep in mind that you absolutely cannot avoid paying some taxes. Sales taxes take a piece out of every dollar you spend. You pay a fee whenever you obtain a driver's license or register your motor vehicle. This is the price you pay for living during the 21st century. It's like breathing: You cannot take a breath without inhaling some smog.

Planning for a Grim Future

The massive layoffs of the 1990s showed working people that giving their loyalty to an employer means nothing.

Americans are caught in a crunch. On one side, good jobs are becoming scarcer. The massive layoffs of the 1990s showed working people that giving their loyalty to an employer means nothing, that employers will ruthlessly cut jobs for higher profits, and that loyalty is a one-way street in the business world. American companies exported jobs to undeveloped countries to save on labor costs without giving much thought to the earning power of Americans who are supposed to be their customers.

On the other side of the crunch, existing jobs are more heavily taxed than before, in terms of real dollars adjusted for inflation. While "income" taxes have dropped somewhat, the Social Security "contribution" has increased dramatically, providing a huge Social Security trust fund for Congress to raid when it wants to spend more money.

This is an important point. Many good jobs, as well as lower-level ones, have disappeared, either abolished or exported by companies seeking higher profits. Between the summers of 1990 and 1992, 1.8 million nonfarm jobs disappeared.[3]

Forty-nine percent of the vanished jobs in the transportation industry, for example, were supervisory ones. Middle managers are feeling the bite as well. Meanwhile, the officially listed number of jobs increased, but most of these were low-paying ones, such as hamburger flipper.

The net result is that many people who formerly held what they considered to be good, well-paying jobs, have had to settle for much less. "Junk jobs for chump change" has become both a popular expression and a way of life for many Americans. This phenomenon, ignored by the government — especially politicians seeking re-election on the basis that they "created jobs" for their constituents — is the "hidden depression."

We see this in reports of average earnings, after adjustment for inflation. The average weekly earning for a nonsupervisory employee fell from $261 per week in July 1990 to $255 per week two years later.[4]

You don't need official or quasi-official statistics to see the hidden depression at work. Ask your relatives, friends, and neighbors. John, a former airline employee who earned $14 per hour and many benefits, now works for an air freight company and receives $8 per hour and fewer benefits. The ex-trucker who lost his $20 per hour job had to accept a warehouse position paying half that. Count the number of people you know who changed jobs recently and note whether they traded up or down.

Official unemployment rates include only those who are collecting unemployment benefits or who are registered with state employment agencies.

Considering the run-around job-seekers receive from state employment agencies, it's understandable that many don't keep returning. One 1992 estimate was that an additional 1.1 million "discouraged workers" were not on the rolls, having given up the search after their benefits expired.[5]

Today, even if your income is entirely from tax-free municipal bonds or even entirely underground, you cannot avoid paying taxes.

Compounding the problem of earning a living is the grimly repressive tax structure. Today, even if your income is entirely from tax-free municipal bonds or even entirely underground, you cannot avoid paying taxes. As a start, there are sales taxes, which apply to almost everything you buy. Sales taxes take a bite out of earnings when the taxpayer tries to spend them. Other taxes have hidden impacts. Corporate taxes, while ostensibly aimed at corporations, actually hit the small taxpayer because corporations simply pass the tax increases on to their customers. These are the hidden taxes that are impossible to avoid today.

There are yet more avenues for federal, state, and local governments to take their bites out of peoples' earnings. Most states have state income taxes. New York City even has a city income tax. There are excise and luxury taxes, entertainment taxes, property taxes, motor vehicle taxes, and many others imposed by state and local governments. This makes it practically impossible to drop out and avoid paying taxes in some form.

Even underground living today is becoming more difficult. Right now, it's still possible to lead a totally underground existence, but the prospects are vanishing. Although living a nomadic life is possible, unless you're determined to subsist at the lowest level, you have to register with the government. If you don't believe this, try driving a car or motorcycle without license plates!

The Internal Revenue Service is taking advantage of the best features of electronic information processing and electronic banking. A modernization plan revealed in June 1990, stated that tax collectors were getting ready to use a Cash Management System (CMS) to substitute electronic processing for paperwork. This is to speed up the collection and digestion of information about tax collection and those who owe taxes.[6]

Electronic tax tracking and people tracking is technically possible today, and the only restraint is the difficulty of "selling" the idea to the American people. However, government bureaucrats are very adept at getting what they want by packaging it in a nonthreatening way and presenting it as another step in the "war on crime," "war on drugs," or some similar program for our protection.

Although Americans have resisted government registration, it's creeping up on us. As we've seen, children now get Social Security numbers to make them eligible as exemptions on parents' tax returns. If a federally operated medical plan becomes law, you'll need a registration card to obtain medical care. Driver's licenses are now de facto official I.D., and many states now issue "nondriver's licenses" for blind people, cripples, and other nondrivers who need a universally accepted identification card.

It may become impossible within our lifetimes to live outside the system, just as it's difficult now. The government will not allow you to "drop out" of the system. Today, anyone who simply takes to the woods to live off the land will soon run afoul of game wardens and discover that he can't even hunt to eat.

In Idaho, one dropout tried to live a basic hermit-like existence in the woods, but state game wardens hassled him, making it impossible for him to live. They were so persistent that one confrontation resulted in a gunfight, leaving two game wardens dead. The dropout today can no longer pitch his tent on public land without buying a permit, and if he camps on private land, the owner may charge him with trespassing. The era of the mountain man is over.

It's Getting Worse

The economic trials of the 1990s were merely precursors for worse news. In 2000 and 2001, the economy was worsening even before the terrorist attacks. Industrial production kept dropping, and in May 2001 there were 124,000 manufacturing employees laid off. Between July 2000 and May 2001 the total manufacturing jobs decreased by 670,000.[7]

There is a definite reason for this. Manufacturers are moving their operations to other countries to reduce costs and increase profits. Emerging countries such as China are grabbing a larger proportion of formerly American jobs. One effect is that only five out of twenty-three major American industries have

Deep Inside the Underground Economy
How Millions of Americans Are Practicing Free Enterprise in An Unfree Society

12

been increasing production, and this was before the economic catastrophe of the September 11 attacks.[8]

The terrorist attacks dealt a nasty blow to our already faltering economy. Literally overnight, the travel and hospitality industries slumped because of the sharp drop-off in commercial flying. Airlines laid off thousands of employees immediately, and hotels, restaurants, resorts, and cruise lines followed. One small airline closed its doors in the wake of the attack. Only Southwest Airlines did not impose layoffs, although Southwest delayed delivery of eleven airliners it had previously ordered. Airplane manufacturers such as Boeing found that orders for new aircraft dropped, and they laid off thousands of employees as well. So did European aircraft manufacturers such as Airbus Industries. The many subcontractors who make parts for airliners also saw a sharp decline in orders.

During 1998-2000, the number of layoffs had hovered around 600,000 a year. In 2001, layoffs had reached 1,400,000 by the end of September.

Layoffs had become a fact of life in America even before September 11. During 1998-2000, the number of layoffs had hovered around 600,000 a year. In 2001, layoffs had reached 1,400,000 by the end of September.[9]

The layoffs produced a new caution in the retail market, and retailers reported an average decline of 2.4 percent in sales in September following the attack. The stock market dropped sharply in the aftershock of the events, and it hasn't yet recovered despite several reductions in the interest rate by the Federal Reserve Board. The only benefit to Americans during this period was that oil and gasoline prices dropped because of reduced demand.

The Crystal Ball

In 2002 we've seen contradictory articles in the media regarding the current recession. Some tried to judge its extent. Others were optimistic despite the known facts, leading to a suspicion that they were planted, because they stated that there were economic indicators that the current recession is ending. We have no way of knowing how accurate these crystal ball articles are, because only time will tell. Let's not forget that the Great Depression of the 1930s ended only after the United States got involved in World War II. Right now we're involved in a low-grade war

against terrorism, but this doesn't seem to be ending the recession.

There's an old cliché that states: "If your neighbor gets laid off, it's a recession; if you get laid off, it's a depression." This is a very pragmatic point of view and worth remembering.

If you're already earning your living illegally, the additional risks of being officially out of the system aren't excessive.

These grim facts dictate strategy. If you're already earning your living illegally, the additional risks of being officially out of the system aren't excessive. If, on the other hand, you're a wage slave, you'd be sacrificing a lot to live like a fugitive. Instead, use underground activity to earn an extra, undeclared income, while you ostensibly earn your living from your above ground job, while you still have it. This is the extra benefit to having a sideline, according to noted authority Jordan L. Cooper. It's a good hedge against being laid off, a real prospect these days.[10]

Notes

1. All names have been changed.
2. Chambliss, Lauren, "Cheating Hearts: The IRS is Zeroing in on the Taxpayers Who Tend to Fudge the Most on Their Returns," *FW* 159, no. 11, May 29, 1990, p. 60.
3. Memmott, Mark, "Job-Seekers' Wild Goose Chase; Thousands of Good Jobs Gone For Good," *USA Today*, August 21, 1992, p. 1B.
4. *Ibid.*
5. *Ibid.*
6. "The IRS Moves Into the '90s With CMS (Cash Management System)," *Corporate EFT Report*, 10, no. 12, June 13, 1990, p. 3.
7. Kurlantzick, Joshua, "Not Made in America," *U.S. News & World Report*, July 2, 2001, p. 32.
8. *Ibid.*, p. 34. There's also worse news. Even before September 11, employers were looking to eliminate 1.6 million more jobs, according to an article by Kim Clark, "You're Laid Off!" *U.S. News & World Report*, July 2, 2001, p. 50.
9. "Snips, Snips, Oops!" *The Economist*, October 13, 2001, pp. 59-60.
10. *How To Make Cash Money Selling At Swap Meets, Flea Markets, Etc.*, Jordan L. Cooper, Loompanics Unlimited, Port Townsend, WA, 1988, p. 8.

Chapter One
Taxes, Taxes, and More Taxes

To understand the basics of the guerrilla capitalist, we have to look at the dynamics of taxation and its effect on behavior. This is basic economics, very simple to understand and very clear in its implications. In theory, taxes are the price citizens pay for living in a civilized and industrial society. As originally laid out by the Constitution, the federal government was empowered to collect certain excise taxes to support its minimal activities.

The world has changed since the Constitution was ratified. Over two centuries have passed and we've seen government grow until it intrudes into areas of our lives that were left alone in bygone years. The phrase "big government" has come into common usage, and today is a cliché.

Big government requires big money to support it and it gets this money by taxation. In some countries, the official tax rate is nothing less than fierce. In Israel, for example, the government calculated that its citizens pay seventy-one percent of their gross income in taxes. Many other countries have tax rates approaching this.

Governments are greedy. This sounds sacrilegious to those who have a worshipful attitude toward the government, but it's true for the simplest of reasons. Big government is run by small men and women, such uninspiring figures as Jimmy Carter, Spiro Agnew, Bill Clinton, Margaret Thatcher, and Tony Blair, politicians who promise much and deliver little.

Some people have great respect for the law. While laws may be necessary for the smooth running of society, it's important to remember that laws are made by people, and are therefore as imperfect as the people who make them.

Tax laws are often even more silly and incomprehensible than other laws.

Tax laws are often even more silly and incomprehensible than other laws. While most of us understand and recognize the need for laws against murder, robbery, and the like, it's hard to see the wisdom of a set of laws that taxes the residents of one state at one rate, while the citizens of another pay a different rate. Liquor and cigarette taxes are perfect examples. It's also galling to see a millionaire whose income is from tax-free municipal bonds pay less in taxes than his chauffeur, whose income is earned and reported on a W-2 form to the IRS.

The tax parasites try to create a feeling of guilt in the person who evades paying taxes by telling him that his "fair share" will have to be paid by someone else. This spurious reasoning is baloney. First, it assumes that the government has the right to spend as much as it possibly can, and then it's up to the rest of us to pay "our share" of its debts. In this country, the government is supposed to be the "servant of the people," and therefore should be willing to get along on whatever the people voluntarily provide. Secondly, just because one person doesn't pay his taxes doesn't mean that someone else has to pay more. Just the opposite could be the case. During the War between the States, Lincoln imposed the first federal income tax, but so few people paid it that the government had to abandon this plan. The obvious conclusion is that, contrary to government propaganda, people who don't pay their "fair share" can actually cause everybody's taxes to be reduced.

With the current cost of the "war on terrorism," the national debt will go up again, beyond the ability of American citizens ever to pay it.

Finally, exactly what is everybody's "fair share?" The government runs up fantastic debts, so much that the national debt is a mind-boggling figure that may

Deep Inside the Underground Economy
How Millions of Americans Are Practicing Free Enterprise in An Unfree Society

14

never be paid off. Divided among the people of this country, it runs into hundreds of thousands of dollars per person. The debt reduction that came with the end of the Cold War was short-lived. With the current cost of the "war on terrorism," the national debt will go up again, beyond the ability of American citizens ever to pay it.

Dan Bawly, Israeli accountant and commentator, takes the view that big government and big taxes are evils in themselves.[1] Jerome Tuccile points out that high taxes are incentives to evasion, because low tax rates are not worth the trouble of evading.[2] He supports his case by citing the examples of West Germany and Japan, which during the post-war era dropped their taxes and consequently had few problems with tax evasion.

Why Government Spending Won't Decrease

Nowadays, few can fail to be aware that the government wastes their tax money, but the true extent of this waste is astonishing — and even worse is how waste is actually built into the system! We have read how the Department of Defense has paid hundreds of dollars for such items as screwdrivers and hammers, which are available in any hardware store for a few dollars each. Government spending goes up every year, and the deficit grows every year. Let's look at the government debt explosion over the last 40 years.

Harry Truman added $45.4 billion to the debt from 1945 to 1953. Dwight D. Eisenhower added $19.2 billion from 1953 to 1961. John F. Kennedy and Lyndon Johnson added $60.5 billion from 1961 to 1969. Richard M. Nixon and Gerald Ford added $190.1 billion from 1969 to 1977. Jimmy Carter added $182 billion from 1977 to 1981, and Ronald Reagan added $547 billion from 1981 to 1985. All Presidents since have followed the pattern, right to this day, as we'll soon see.

For an overview of what's happened to the National Debt regardless of which administration was in power, let's look at how the national debt has risen during the last half century to get an idea of how it's become increasingly burdensome. The following figures come from the U.S. Treasury web site:

1950	257,357,352,351.04
1960	290,216,815,241.68
1970	389,158,403,690.26
1980	930,210,000,000.00
1990	3,233,313,451,777.25
2000	5,674,178,209,886.86[3]

It's continued to increase during the new century. According to the U.S. National Debt Clock, the national debt stood at $6,280,853,473,526.26 on November 17, 2002.[4] Another way of looking at it is that the national debt has increased an average of $1,140 million each day since September 28, 2001.

We can already see how the current situation with the war on terrorism will add more military spending. This is the second largest single item in the budget, with Health and Human Services leading.

Reagan, who talked more about "balancing the budget" than any other president, ran up triple the debt that "free spending" Jimmy Carter did!

It clearly doesn't matter which party is in power. Reagan, who talked more about "balancing the budget" than any other president, ran up triple the debt that "free spending" Jimmy Carter did! Even with George W. Bush, a self-proclaimed conservative, there is no end in sight.

With the end of the Cold War, the first President Bush promised us a "peace dividend," but somehow that promise has evaporated, both because of the Gulf War and its aftermath, and because of increased spending on social programs. True, there were budget surpluses announced during several years. In Fiscal Year 1998, the surplus was supposedly $70 billion, and the Fiscal Year 1999 saw a surplus of $124,360 billion. The government announced a surplus of $236,993 billion for 2000, and one of $127,021 billion for 2001. However, the government also spent money "off budget," which accounted for the rise in our national debt during those years. Let's examine some of these figures in detail:

Year	Budget Surplus	National Debt
1998	$70,039 billion	5,526,193,008,897.62
1999	$124,360 billion	5,656,270,901,615.43
2000	$236,933 billion	5,674,178,209,886.86
2001	$127,021 billion	5,807,463,412,200.06

Let's note that, whatever the government has told us about how much money it's saved or how large the budget surplus is, the bottom line at the end of each fiscal year is that the national debt has been larger every time! This process is what some cynics call "creative accounting."

How do we enjoy a budget surplus while the national debt keeps rising? The answer is simple. The government plays a sneaky game with the figures in a bold and outrageous manner that would put Arthur Andersen and Company to shame. Enron, by comparison, is playing with nickels and dimes.

Put very simply, the candidates on both sides tell the same tired lies year after year and many voters still believe them. It's not exclusively an American problem, either, as voters in France, Britain, and other Western countries repeatedly elect the same sort of politicians that we Americans do.

The real problem is deeper than the mediocre quality of our elected officials. Despite strident accusations by some, these are for the most part not inherently evil men, intent on worsening the lot of the people who put them into office. Instead, they are marginally competent men, unable to understand the large issues, lost in the mass of immediate details, and trying to find a compromise between conflicting needs.

Let's look at "defense" spending to get an insight into why our "national security" threatens to destroy our economy with its voracious appetite for ever more expensive weapons.

This is the most powerful industrial nation in the world, but it is still not quite able to produce both guns and butter, despite the assurance of various presidents that it can.

A common slogan is, "War is good for business." This is true in the sense that the need for large numbers of weapons and support items do bring large government contracts and create jobs in the areas where the factories producing these weapons are located. However, the basic fact is that our national resources are limited. This is the most powerful industrial nation in the world, but it is still not quite able to produce both guns and butter, despite the assurance of various presidents that it can. The old Soviet Union found that it could not sustain the pressure of providing both copious armaments and lavish consumer goods indefinitely. Something had to give, and it did, which is why the Soviet Union is history.

Money spent on weapons has to come from somewhere, and this means one or more of these sources:

- Taxpayers, who pay higher rates. This absorbs a lot of the overtime pay that defense industry workers enjoy.
- Diverting from other government projects, such as building and maintaining our highway systems. One result of this is the increasing deterio-

ration of our roads, which has become critical despite a large road improvement program during the last couple of years.

- Printing more money. This causes inflation, as we've seen over the decades.
- Borrowing. The national debt is out of hand, has been for several decades, and despite the promises of our current President, plans for reducing it are mostly fantasy. The needs of the "War on Terrorism" have pushed plans for saving money into the background.

A good example of why our defense spending keeps increasing is the B-1 bomber. The last version of the B-17 "Flying Fortress" heavy bomber produced in WWII cost $276,000 each. Since then, bombers have become more "sophisticated," which is "governmentalese" for complicated, and their prices have gone up to the sky.

When the B-1 was first proposed, over a decade ago, the projected price was about $20 million apiece.[5] This was to be the most sophisticated, versatile, and capable weapons system in our arsenal and, of course, it had its price. The price, in relation to what it could do and the costs of other, already existing systems, did not seem like a very good deal to President Carter, and he cancelled the program in 1977, after the projected price of each aircraft had gone to about $90 million.

President Reagan took another look at it and decided that the Air Force should have it, but the price in 1981 was at $200 million apiece. By 1983, when the bomber was included in the procurement budget, the price had gone up to $553 million each.

The Northrop B-2 "Stealth" Bomber, made of exotic materials, is more expensive by far. At $20 billion a copy, it's much more costly than any other airplane ever built, although the end of the cold war suggests that the "Stealth" bomber no longer fills a need. We can't blame inflation or union demands for all these price increases. The reasons lie in the method of procurement and the nature of technology itself. We'll find the same pattern in most new weapons systems, such as the Air Force's new F-22 Raptor.

Each armed service must compete with the other services for a share of the defense dollar. The service chiefs try to present attractive pictures of their needs and understate the costs.

Deep Inside the Underground Economy
How Millions of Americans Are Practicing Free Enterprise in An Unfree Society

16

Each armed service must compete with the other services for a share of the defense dollar. The service chiefs try to present attractive pictures of their needs and understate the costs. For example, when an Air Force general quotes a price for the B-1, he's likely giving the price of the airplane alone. This figure doesn't include the cost of new bases and other facilities needed to service the plane, the costs of training the people who will fly and maintain it, the costs of ancillary weapons systems it will carry, and the cost overruns which he anticipates. The eventual cost of each B-1 aircraft exceeded one billion dollars, when you counted all the expenses that went with it. However, there's worse.

We occasionally buy "interim models" — weapons that are not really suitable for the job. Sometimes this is simply due to a mistake. More often it's deliberate policy, which is hidden from the voters and taxpayers. Not counting the prospects of bribes to generals and admirals[6] and the expense-paid trips that companies lavish upon them, there is a serious purpose to buying inferior models of weapons. The purpose has to do with research and development and lead times.

It is impossible to build a modern, complicated weapon from scratch. In order to procure the weapon, the Pentagon has to buy it from a company that can make it. There has to be a design team and a factory with the proper equipment. If a company does not get enough government contracts to keep it going, it will go out of business. The skilled workers will find employment elsewhere and perhaps be lost to the industry as a whole.

Normally it takes ten or more years to design an aircraft and get it into production. This is with an established company that is a going concern. It would take even longer if the project came into the hands of a company that had to start from zero to assemble a team of engineers, design the weapon, and build a manufacturing facility. This is why it's in the Pentagon's interest to keep the various companies that comprise the "defense industry" alive and well, even if it means buying inferior models.

A cutting-edge weapon today will be obsolete as soon as the competition brings out a new model.

Another factor is the increasingly rapid pace of technological advances. The slogan, "If it works, it's obsolete," is not just a joke. Better weapons are always on the drawing boards. This means that a cut-ting-edge weapon today will be obsolete as soon as the competition brings out a new model. Often a new airplane is not practical because of the huge cost involved. It's cheaper to "upgrade" the existing model: tack on some improvements that will give it the ability to do a better job. This, too, costs money, and it's impossible to anticipate the cost when ordering the original model.

The attacks of September 11, 2001 have given the government carte blanche for increasing military spending, as well as spending on federal police agencies and federal intelligence agencies. The president stated publicly that we were at war, and that it would be a long war with perhaps no definite end, though the U.S. Congress did not declare war on anyone or any country.

Now we come to that dirty word that pervades Washington politics, "pork." This means including carefully rationalized expenditures to benefit the representative's constituency. According to Arizona Senator John McCain, this year's budget contains about $9.6 billion in pork. Surely this is an underestimate, because it doesn't even come close to accounting for the increase in our national debt. However, let's look at a few items buried in other appropriations bills:

- $2 million were appropriated to restore Birmingham, Alabama's Vulcan Statue. This amount would pay for 35,000 doses of Cipro, used to treat Anthrax and other serious bacterial infections.
- Fairbanks, Alaska, got $2.25 billion to develop "winter recreation alternatives," and this amount is more than enough to buy two cruise missiles.
- California's Lancaster National Soccer Center will receive $740,000, which is more than enough to pay for 18 "Sidewinder" missiles.

Another kind of pork consists of delaying or canceling the closing of unnecessary military bases, which are scattered around the country in the constituencies of most of our congressmen.

Another kind of pork consists of delaying or canceling the closing of unnecessary military bases, which are scattered around the country in the constituencies of most of our congressmen. Take Albuquerque's Kirtland Air Force Base, for example. During and after World War II it was important to the Air Force because, among other reasons, it had one of the only two runways that would accommodate the giant B-36 bomber. Kirtland also held the country's largest storage area for nuclear weapons. The Manzano Mountains, adjoining Kirtland, held a large and elaborate bunker designed to accommodate the president and his staff deep under the surface in case of nuclear war. With the end of the Cold War, these needs have evaporated.

The Air Force declared Kirtland surplus in 1995 and it was on a tentative list of bases to be closed. However, Kirtland contributes about one billion a year to the economy of Albuquerque and the surrounding area, and New Mexico's congressional delegation struggled powerfully to keep Kirtland open. Each member of Congress has his own favorite pork projects, and in order to obtain support must trade favors with other pork-minded members. As a result, Kirtland has been kept off the short list of bases scheduled for closing.

These are only a few of the examples that fall into the category of "government waste." There are other expenses that are much harder to correct because they're built into the very fabric of our system of government.

Multiple Levels of Government

We must remember that the very structure of our tax system and the agencies which collect the money are redundant and wasteful. To give a simple example, a resident of New York City pays federal income tax. He also pays New York State income tax. On top of this, he has to file a New York City income tax return. Here we have three redundant bureaucracies doing the same basic job, collecting income taxes.

We have, by law and by tradition, a system of local governments because of the states' rights provision in the Constitution. We say we shun a strong central government, even though that's what we have today. Actually, we have the worst of both possible worlds. To see how this works in practice consider one function of local government: the police:

Americans say they don't want a national police force. We like to keep our police forces local and under local control. What we get is a complex system of competing and overlapping jurisdictions, each with its own police force, each following its own laws and procedures.

Typically, a criminal is arrested by a town police force for violating the state's criminal code. He's housed in the town jail until arraigned in the state court by a county prosecutor. During the trial he's the responsibility of the county sheriff, who keeps him in the county jail. If he's convicted and the violation is a major one, he then goes to the state prison to serve his sentence.

We have police forces on all levels doing the same job. One example is the "war on drugs." The federal government has the Drug Enforcement Administration (DEA). State police forces have their drug squads, as do county sheriffs. Local police forces also have narcotics bureaus or squads. In some areas they overlap, setting up "area drug task forces," with members from all agencies in the local area.

Take another example, a simple traffic accident. Two cars collide on a street, the centerline of which is the boundary between the city and the county. A city police officer arriving at the scene determines that since the cars have come to rest in the county, it's the responsibility of the sheriff's office, and he radios for a deputy to come do the paperwork. He stands by, redirecting traffic, while the deputy is on his way. When the deputy arrives, he pursues the investigation and cites one of the parties for violating a state traffic law, and causing the accident. As a routine part of his investigation, he radios for a "10-29," a routine check to determine if either of the parties is a fugitive from justice. His dispatcher sends a request to the state crime computer and one to the National Crime Information Center, run by the U.S. Department of Justice in Washington, D.C., to see if there are any interstate warrants on them.

The cost of inefficiencies in our government can't be measured only in money.

These are normal, routine, bureaucratic complications. They involve a lot of overly complicated paperwork, which costs money. Thus, we see that the cost of inefficiencies in our government can't be measured only in money. The problem is far more serious than that. The net result is that, although we pay more for government than ever before, we are not getting what we're paying for.

Our various levels of government increase in size and cost, but not in effectiveness. In fact, as long as they continue to be organized the way they are, they'll continue to be less effective with each passing year. Less effective and more expensive. That is the hard reality of the "system." That is why government

Deep Inside the Underground Economy
How Millions of Americans Are Practicing Free Enterprise in An Unfree Society

18

spending will not decrease, regardless of the promises of politicians.

How Some People Avoid Taxes

In the United States there is a subculture of people who make serious efforts to avoid paying taxes. Knowing that they cannot evade paying taxes altogether, they use various legal stratagems to avoid paying some taxes.

Jeff, who lived in California, bought a new Ford Explorer through the Internet. He flew to Texas to the dealer who had offered him an attractive price, and the salesman met him at the airport. He drove him to the state motor vehicle bureau, where Jeff registered his new vehicle and obtained a Texas driver's license. This was to establish him as a resident of Texas, which has no personal income tax, and thus he was able to avoid paying the California state income tax. Jeff customarily keeps driver's licenses from several states, obtaining them through a clever stratagem. He obtains a duplicate license in each state, claiming he's lost the original. He uses the original to obtain a license in another state, as most states require applicants to turn in their previous licenses. Thus, he can prove he's a resident of whatever state seems most convenient for his purpose.

Others lead a nomadic existence, living in motor homes and traveling around the country. These people are either retired or high-grade migrant workers employed in well-paying occupations, such as the construction industry. They establish legal residence in states with no personal income tax, such as Texas or Nevada. They rent a mail drop address as their "legal residence," and obtain vehicle insurance and driver's licenses in those states. There are mail drops specializing in the needs of these nomadic people and they use street addresses instead of postal box numbers to make it appear that the mail goes to a residence. The mail drops forward their mail regularly to wherever they're staying for the moment. To reduce the amount of other taxes, they learn where sales taxes are either lower or absent. The state of Oregon, for example has no sales tax, and they plan so that they make their major purchases in that state. These tactics allow them to avoid paying some of their taxes, and saves them a considerable sum each year.

It's common sense that people will make great efforts to evade burdensome taxes. Where taxes are light, it's simply not worth the trouble. Now let's examine how the rich avoid paying taxes.

How the Fat Cats Avoid Paying Taxes

Middle-class people can avoid some taxes, but the ones who avoid paying millions of dollars are the rich, mainly because they have such huge incomes. We've all heard stories of millionaires who pay less in taxes than their chauffeurs. Some might be exaggerations, but they definitely have a basis in fact. The "movers and shakers" who run the system have a lot of hidden influence over the law for several reasons.

The expression "the best legislators money can buy" is not a meaningless slogan, because the rich can afford large campaign contributions to influence legislators.

Part of being rich is making the best use of the huge amounts of money available. The expression "the best legislators money can buy" is not a meaningless slogan, because the rich can afford large campaign contributions to influence legislators. Even the Presidency is for sale, as we saw during the Clinton Administration, when a night in the Lincoln Bedroom had a price tag.

Bribery in the sense of a briefcase full of money is outdated. The modern way to bribe a legislator is through "campaign contributions." This device permits truly huge bribes to be made, above board and perfectly legally. Anyone who makes such a payment wants something in return. It's naive to think that someone who contributes a huge sum to a candidate's election campaign fund does it because he's practicing good citizenship. He always wants special consideration, although he may not have a specific "favor" in mind at the time.

Rich people don't become rich by doing other people favors for nothing. Rather, they manipulate other people and use them, their talents, and their assets for their own benefit. One who makes a campaign contribution, even if he requires no "quid pro quo" at that moment, is making an investment in the future. Once the candidate accepts a contribution, he becomes beholden to his benefactor. He's accepted a favor that will be called in someday. That's how American politics works.

Another way to bribe a public official is more common in the West than in the East. Typically, under the "city manager" system, the mayor is not the actual chief executive, but acts more in the role of President of the City Council. He and the other councilmen are usually business owners, and someone who wants a "favor" can bribe them by "throwing business their way."

We see examples of this when a city council lays out a "downtown redevelopment" plan, often aided by federal funding through the Department of HUD. While the selection of the contractors is supposedly rigorously controlled by a system of sealed bids, it's not the same with the laying out of the plan. The corrupt official can make the specifications such that his favorite company is the only one that can bid on it, or at least can bid lower than the others and yet earn a huge profit.

Another way is a stock "tip." The public official, or more often a member of his family, will buy stock following a "tip" from the owner or chief executive of the company issuing the stock, say, just before a three for one split. This again is an above-board bribe, which is difficult to prove. It's a violation of SEC rules, but the difficulty of proof is overwhelming, and we see very few prosecutions for this.

The official who is the subject of this "favor" doesn't face the problem of accounting for a sudden large deposit of cash, and doesn't have to worry about "laundering" it. The bribe comes prewashed, which makes it not only very convenient, but extremely safe. If he's the least bit prudent, he keeps the transaction above-board, paying the required taxes on it, and thereby avoids any problems with the IRS. The IRS doesn't concern itself with the source of income, as long as the recipient pays taxes on it.

The Internal Revenue Code didn't write itself. It was originally devised by legislators, and has been much modified since its inception. Most of the changes were not to make paying income taxes easier for the average taxpayer, or to make the rules and forms easier to understand, but rather to create loopholes for the wealthy who "own" the legislators who make the laws.

With their wealth, they can hire the best lawyers and accountants to help them avoid taxes. The rich don't have to forge paperwork to reduce their tax burden. They can, upon the advice of specialists, take advantage of existing loopholes in the law, many of which existed long before they were born, for the benefit of a previous generation of millionaires.

Having high-priced talent available makes a huge difference if there's a disagreement with an agent of the IRS. The working-class taxpayer, if he finds himself required to go for an audit, has to take time off from work, thus losing pay, and brings his records for the scrutiny of an IRS examiner who is a "pro" at extracting taxes from the little guys. Inevitably, the small taxpayer feels anxious and victimized, and with good reason. He doesn't know the ins and outs of the tax laws. If the examiner disallows something, chances are the small taxpayer doesn't know the mechanism by which he may appeal the ruling, or even that he has the right to do so.

By contrast, the millionaire doesn't bother to attend a meeting with the tax examiner, if ever his return comes under scrutiny. Instead, he has an accountant or a tax lawyer in his employ to attend to this nuisance. In this way, he's in a much better position to defend himself than the small taxpayer.

The tax lawyer walks in for the confrontation. Typically, he's got a degree from Big Time U, while the examiner attended Podunk State and earns much less money as well. It's an unequal contest from the start. The rich man's agent does the intimidating, not the tax examiner. The IRS agent is really on the defensive, as he'll have to substantiate every point he wishes to make, knowing that if there's any doubt, any ambiguity, the tax lawyer is ready and able to appeal his decision.

The wealthy person is free to rearrange his lifestyle to avoid taxes. The small taxpayer can't do that. He may be free to change jobs, or to move to another city, but not to make a basic break. In any event, his income is so low that he can't save much money even by the most rigorous steps he might take. The millionaire, however, can take advantage of a few provisions in the tax laws, the famous "loopholes."

Income from municipal bonds isn't taxable. Income from the sale of stocks is taxable at a lower rate than is earned income. The working-class type who collects a paycheck each week hasn't really got these options. Almost every cent he makes has to go to put food on the table and shoes on his children's feet.

Having a residence outside the United States provides exemption from paying U.S. income taxes. The very rich do this as a matter of course, and indeed own homes in various countries for this purpose. When we read of a millionaire motion picture star making his home in Switzerland, we can be sure that he chooses the place for a more substantial reason than simply enjoying the scenery or the quick access to ski sites. It's a convenient and utterly legal way of avoiding paying taxes on a substantial income.

Deep Inside the Underground Economy
How Millions of Americans Are Practicing Free Enterprise in An Unfree Society

20

Another way is to form a foreign corporation in a country that caters to this sort of traffic. Liechtenstein and Monaco are two that are very receptive to sheltering corporations, because their tax laws give the greatest concessions compared to American laws. This is completely legal and available to the wealthy entrepreneur who seeks a safe haven. Again, the "working stiff" doesn't have this choice open to him.

Taking advantage of the special loopholes that favor business owners is another way the rich avoid the ravages of the IRS. There are so many of these loopholes that it would be impossible to close them without scuttling the whole Internal Revenue Code.

The business executive often uses company-owned facilities, materials, and supplies for personal purposes. This is a course open even to the smallest business owner, but the flagrant, high dollar-volume abuses occur in the largest companies.

Most large corporations have company aircraft, supposedly for ferrying their executives to "business conferences" around the country. Typically, there's a company pilot on call and he spends part of his time ferrying around the owner and his family for various personal purposes.

There's no law to forbid a business meeting from being held at a resort such as Las Vegas or Aspen, and it's legal to mix business with pleasure.

There's no law to forbid a business meeting from being held at a resort such as Las Vegas or Aspen, and it's legal to mix business with pleasure. After the "meeting," which may be perfectly legitimate, the executives take a tour, or go to a nightclub with the company picking up the tab. The time spent attending to "business" during such a junket can be small compared to the number of hours spent seeing the sights.

Even close to home, the company picks up the tab for entertaining clients. The owner or chief executive often attends these shindigs, and the company pays for the cost of his entertainment, too. Often, an executive will invite a client to dinner at an expensive restaurant, and ask him to bring his wife.

The "hospitality suite" is another way of avoiding paying taxes on entertainment, or declaring it as income. Large corporations maintain such "hospitality suites" year-round at luxury hotels in the area, for the accommodation of visiting business owners. Often, however, the suite is vacant, which provides a convenient accommodation for the executive and his wife who want to "get away from it all" for a few days, while living at company expense. A hospitality suite also provides a convenient place for an illicit affair outside of marriage.

On a larger scale, some corporations maintain private resorts, often at vacation spots both within and outside the country. It's slightly easier to keep a resort going in another country, such as Bermuda or the Cayman Islands, because the IRS has a harder time tracing the exact use the resort gets. The owner or executive can claim that he flew there with his family for a "conference," and the IRS can't subpoena records to determine whether personnel from a client corporation actually attended.

While the small business owner gets away with some fudging, in proportion it's "nickel and dime" compared to the actions of the large corporations.

While the small business owner gets away with some fudging, in proportion it's "nickel and dime" compared to the actions of the large corporations. The difference in scale is staggering.

The restaurant owner who appropriates food for his personal use gets away with perhaps a couple thousand dollars' worth a year. One family can eat only so much, and nobody feasts on caviar and champagne every day. Similarly, the gas station owner can only take so much labor and materials for his personally-owned vehicles.

A corporate jet can easily cost several million dollars. The cost of fuel, maintenance, pilots' salaries, hangars, and other associated expenses can easily amount to several hundred thousand dollars per year.

On a smaller scale, a "hospitality suite" at a luxury hotel can easily cost five hundred dollars a day, and often more. Even with a substantial long-term discount rate, this comes to fifty or one hundred thousand dollars a year. This is for the suite alone, not including additional fees for meals and room service when someone is in residence.

Many lavish dinners pass as "entertainment for clients." The bill for a modest party for four at a medium-priced restaurant is easily one hundred dollars, including drinks and tip. Such executives don't ever take their clients to a fried-chicken or hamburger stand. The cost of a dinner can escalate rapidly, depending on the restaurant and the number of people involved.

We see from this that there's one rule for the little guy, and another for the big boy. It's hard to take seriously any system that not only allows this, but has it written into its laws.

The ones who benefit the most from our government pay the least to support it. The main burden of taxation falls upon the ones who can least afford to pay, and this gives the little guy a strong incentive to join the underground economy. Simultaneously, he can look for loopholes of his own while running an above ground business.

Can Loopholes Work for You?

There's a never-ending search for loopholes, by both small and big business owners, because dealing with the IRS has the characteristics of a game in which the object is to get away with as much as possible without being caught. The people who play this game don't worry much about the "morality" of paying taxes, or the "immorality" of avoiding them. It's a competitive sport. The end: to minimize the tax bite; the means: shielding sources of income within the arcane wording of the law. Many high-priced tax lawyers and accountants make cushy careers out of this.

In seeking loopholes, one piece of advice we sometimes see is to be sure to have a "letter of opinion" from a lawyer or accountant.[7] Let's look at this in perspective. Such a letter is a "cover your ass" device only. It does not make a loophole legal. The IRS may still disallow it. The letter merely shows that the taxpayer was following respectable and qualified advice, and not trying to perpetrate a criminal fraud. It's a device to avoid criminal prosecution, nothing more. Having such a letter does not exempt the taxpayer from paying back taxes if the IRS disagrees with its contents. It's not a shield against paying interest on any tax owed. It does not even forestall an IRS tax auditor from imposing a penalty payment.

Criminal prosecution is usually unlikely. As long as the claimed loophole is documented and the taxpayer sets on paper his income and expenditures, the IRS will only go after his money, not his hide. The loophole is merely a point of disagreement, not a peg on which to hang a prosecution.

The single most important fact about tax loopholes is that they're not for the average taxpayer. Most of them are special laws passed because of machinations behind the scenes by rich and "influential" people who have enough money to buy congressmen.[8] Another point about loopholes is that they're like quick-

sand, because the Internal Revenue Code changes every year, and what's legal one year is not the next, and vice versa. This makes it very important to keep abreast of new developments.

The most discouraging aspect of most of these tax loopholes is that they apply mainly to people who have large investments. like investment credits, depreciation rates, stocks, oil royalties, foreign assets, and real estate.

The "new" Reagan tax package was really nothing new. It followed in the old pattern of giving tax advantages to business owners, with the biggest concessions to the biggest wheelers and dealers. This principle, having big business take all the concessions and sticking the small salaried wage-earner with the bulk of the tax bill, has been the guiding principle of taxation in this country for generations. The Bush tax refund of early 2001 was also a gimmick to attain popularity in the ratings, while the government went ahead and pillaged the Social Security Trust Fund.

While theoretically the law in this country applies equally to all, in practice this is not so. We see this flagrantly in tax laws, because many of the tax relief provisions, although legally applying to every citizen, are simply not accessible to everyone. We don't all own huge tracts of real estate, or oil wells, or have money invested overseas.

Some provisions, however, can be helpful in certain cases. Anyone with money to spare can put it in an "All-Saver" tax-free account, and earn $1000 of tax-free interest. A married couple who wants to salt money away can earn twice that amount. This has to be money the person won't need for a long time, and if it's a married couple, they'd better not get divorced. The catch with this is that the individual can't touch the money for a year.

Changes in the laws regarding depreciation rates can be useful for the small business owner. There's a new "Accelerated Cost Recovery System" which enables the taxpayer to take more "front end" depreciation. This is useful for those who buy and sell property fairly quickly; as they can take more than normal depreciation for the time they own the property.

There's an additional loophole if the property is leased to another party. Under certain conditions, it's possible to depreciate it again. This is typical of the fictions of the Internal Revenue Code.

A slight concession to people over 55 comes with the sale of a house. Formerly, the first $100,000 of the sale price was tax-free, but now it's $125,000. A quirk in this law applies it only to married couples,

Deep Inside the Underground Economy
How Millions of Americans Are Practicing Free Enterprise in An Unfree Society

22

and if they get divorced they each qualify for that $125,000 exemption.

A business owner who needs many deductions for a certain year can choose between depreciating capital expenditures or writing them off in one lump sum. This is called "expensing." There used to be a rule of thumb that only small dollar volume items were allowable as full deductions. The cash value of these depended upon the accountant figuring the tax form, and hovered between $250 and $300. This is another example of a fiction incorporated in the Internal Revenue Code.

A tool costing less than that value could be written off entirely the year of purchase, even though its useful life, in common-sense terms, would justify depreciating it over several years. However, to avoid excessive paperwork, this fiction of instant depreciation has long been part of the law.

Now there are some new guidelines, and the dollar amount may be higher for certain categories. This is a fairly safe ploy to try. It involves a murky aspect of the tax law and an examiner may not pick it up. "Expensing" a computer, for example, can easily pass. The only risk is having it disallowed, having to depreciate it, and not getting the full deduction for that year. However, experience has shown that this is a very small risk, as small business owners regularly do this for their desktops.

There's a little-known provision in the IRS code that allows tax-free gifts to employees of up to $400. This need not be in cash, but could be in some other form. This is a useful way to provide bonuses, and deduct them, too.

For certain types of businesses, it's possible to hire minority group members and get a twenty-five percent tax credit on their earnings. This rule goes further than ethnic minorities, and includes recent college graduates and others on a list of "target" groups. This is worth a look, and can provide a loophole for the small business that can use it.

Incorporation seems very attractive to the small business owner, especially because the tax rates on corporations are currently lower than those applying to wage-earners and unincorporated proprietors. Superficially, this appears to be a fine advantage, but there's a catch. Everything depends on the size of the business. It costs money to incorporate, and this can wipe out any savings. The money involved is not only the initial lawyer's fee and the fee for the state charter, but the extra cost for a more complicated tax return each year.

For example, Tom and Ida decided to incorporate. Tom worked as a freelance artist and Ida sold real estate for a local agency. Their combined income was not high and no tax savings were possible, even though they foresaw long-run savings. They paid their fees, filed the papers, and listed themselves as employees of the corporation. They paid themselves small salaries, had the corporation pay for their medical insurance, and put their vehicles in the name of the corporation. The net result was that they lost money the first year. This was not surprising, and they counted on long-term savings.

They soon ran into some problems. To make use of their earnings, they had to collect larger salaries, which were subject to the individual tax rate. They also found that medical insurance was deductible anyway, whether paid by the corporation or individually. The new IRS code stipulates that whatever personal use they make of their corporate vehicles now counts as personal income, and they had to keep logs of their trips and enter their personal miles. As for their grandiose aspirations, they were "a day late and a dollar short."

Butch, the owner of a growing business, states flatly that a sole proprietorship is the only way for him. After long discussion with his accountant, he decided that unless his business becomes much larger than it is now, incorporating simply wouldn't pay.

Marriage can be a good loophole. If one spouse has a high income, and the other a low one, filing a joint return averages their income and yields a lower tax bite. A business owner who hires members of his family can distribute the total income among several individuals,[9] which results in lower net taxes for the family.

Bob runs an above ground business out of his house, so part of his plan was to buy a bigger house. This immediately gave him high interest payments to deduct, and large parts of his utility bills as well. Bob is an audiophile, and under cover of his business, he has purchased an assortment of very expensive recording equipment. He legitimized this by making and selling self-improvement tape cassettes via mail order.

Bob needs help in running his business and has solved this problem by putting his family on the payroll. Their pay is taxable to them, of course, but it is still family income that is taxed at a lower rate than if Bob reported it all on his own tax return.

Bob wants to keep his business above board, so he has hired a full-time bookkeeper to maintain his records. Actually, her job takes about two hours a day, and she is Bob's girlfriend. So Bob doesn't have to "keep" his mistress with an apartment and an allowance, European-style. Bob does it the American way by giving her a soft job and generous salary.

Bob has his fingers in a lot of pies and is always looking for things to "invest" in, so he writes off a lot of "business" trips. He dabbles in real estate and deducts an expensive car, which he allegedly uses to impress clients.

Bob is particularly creative when it comes to medical expenses, disdaining the doctors in his own city. He prefers to go to a fancy clinic in a West Coast resort town for his annual check-up, which enables him to deduct his entire vacation each year.

We could go on and on some more about how Bob does it, but you get the idea. Bob's creative way of arranging his affairs enables him to maximize his deductions without too much risk. Bob is constantly studying and reassessing his situation and keeps developing new wrinkles to minimize his tax bite by maximizing his deductions.

Individual Retirement Accounts (IRA) for employees and Keogh Plans for the self-employed offer ways to defer taxes that are accessible to some people in the lower-income brackets.

Individual Retirement Accounts (IRA) for employees and Keogh Plans for the self-employed offer ways to defer taxes that are accessible to some people in the lower-income brackets. So do the more recent "Roth" IRAs. The catch is that this requires good money management. Unfortunately, debt seems to be part of the American lifestyle, and not many people can handle this. Anyone who has some money to spare can take advantage of these savings plans with tax-free interest. According to the law, anyone can deposit up to $2,000 per year for an individual, and $2,250 for a married couple. The interest earned is tax free, but there are some catches. There are no withdrawals permitted until age 59½. Anyone wishing to withdraw money from these accounts before then must pay a penalty which more than likely wipes out the earnings. The theory behind the IRA is that the individual gains because his taxes are deferred until retirement, when he'll presumably be in a lower tax bracket.

Practically, this means that "spare cash" must be exactly that, money which the taxpayer doesn't need for current expenses, doesn't need to pay off debts, and doesn't foresee needing as part of an "emergency fund" for the near future. Anyone interested in such a savings plan must calculate very carefully how much cash reserve he should keep on hand in a conventional or money market account to take care of emergencies. A major car repair or medical bill can wipe out a savings account quickly. If there are no ready cash reserves and it becomes necessary to dip into the IRA account, the taxpayer will be much worse off than if he'd never started.

Another obvious fact is that anyone with a substantial debt should not start any such account. With the high lending interest rates, it's better to pay off the debt, as even the deductions allowed for interest payments are only a fractional saving, and the interest is still an out-of-pocket expense. The tax-free status of an IRA doesn't even begin to make up for this.

There's another catch involved with IRAs and Keogh plans. The tax rate in years to come may be much higher. While it's true that the present administration has introduced income "indexing" to reduce the inflation creep that puts people in higher tax brackets every year, this is something we can't take for granted. We can't predict the future, and those of us who are still far from retirement may find some unpleasant surprises down the road.

Notes

1. Dan Bawly, *The Subterranean Economy,* McGraw-Hill, NY, 1982, p. 1.
2. Jerome Tuccille, *Inside the Underground Economy,* New American Library, NY, 1982, pp. 125-26. This book, like many others cited in this volume, is out of print. However, you can often find them in libraries or used book stores and some have a limited availability on Amazon.com. This means that you enter the name of the book in their Web site and sometimes they can find it for you.
3. "Historical Debt Outstanding: 1950-2000," *Bureau of the Public Debt Online,* Internet, www.publicdebt.treas.gov/opd/opdhist04.htm, 17 November 2002.
4. Ed Hall, "U.S. National Debt Clock," *Ed Hall's Home Page,* Internet, www.brillig.com/debt_clock, 17 November 2002.
5. Tobias et al., *The People's Guide to National Defense,* William Morrow, NY, 1982, p. 346.

Deep Inside the Underground Economy
How Millions of Americans Are Practicing Free Enterprise in An Unfree Society

24

6.   It's surprising how many military officers find cozy jobs in the defense industry upon retirement. These jobs are partly rewards for past performances in helping the companies that hire them, and partly because they know their way around the Pentagon, as their former service buddies are still in top jobs there. This inside influence is valuable for a company selling to the military.

7.   *Bill Greene's 101 New Loopholes*, Harbor Publishing, San Francisco, CA, 1983, p. vii.

8.   *Ibid.*, p. 2.

9.   W. Charles Blair and John K. McGill, *Employing Family Members in Your Business: A Tax Bonanza!,* Taxwise Publications, 1983.

Chapter Two
Coping With the Internal Revenue Service

The Internal Revenue Service (IRS) is a branch of the U.S. Department of the Treasury that has grown from a very modest start into a bureaucratic monster. It began in 1862, when President Lincoln appointed a Commissioner of Internal Revenue to collect the first income tax to finance the Civil War.[1] The income tax was unpopular, and was repealed in 1872. Most of the federal government's revenue was from taxes on alcohol and tobacco products. In 1914, after income tax was reinstated, a person with $20,000 in taxable income was taxed at one percent, and someone with $500,000 in taxable income was liable for a whopping seven percent. During the year 2000, the IRS collected over $2 trillion from Americans. In 1914, the IRS had 4,200 employees; today it has 100,000 and a budget of $9.4 billion. The IRS claims to be increasingly efficient, stating that it spent thirty-nine cents for each $100 it collected during the year 2000.[2]

As with any bureaucracy that has gotten out of control, its rules and procedures are arbitrary and unfair. For example, in the area of deductions, you can deduct the cost of doctor's fees, but you cannot deduct the price of a health spa to help keep you in shape. If you sell your house at a profit, that profit is taxable unless you buy another house within a specific period. However, if you sell it at a loss, you cannot deduct the loss at all. Birth control pills are deductible, but not maternity clothes. A working man who goes out to lunch with his foreman or shop buddies cannot write it off, but a "business owner" who takes his "business associates" to a "business lunch" can. Toothbrushes and toothpaste, to keep your teeth healthy, are not deductible, but if you get a cavity, the cost of a dentist is.

Every now and then the government has a tax reduction. In 1965, the basic rate went down from 20% to 14%, while in the top bracket, the rate dropped from 95% to 70%. More recently, the rate for the top incomes dropped from 70% to 50%, a full 20-point reduction. If the IRS were consistent, the 20% bracket people should now be tax-free, but we know they are not. In any event, tax rates fluctuate with the whim of Congress.

While income tax rates have dropped over the last fifty years overall, the Social Security rate has increased tremendously.

The government has been playing a devious game with taxpayers. It "gives" with one hand and takes back with the other. While income tax rates have dropped over the last fifty years overall, the Social Security rate has increased tremendously. We've been hearing recently that, because of Americans' increasing life expectancy, the Social Security system will go broke within a few years. This has served as a pretext for increasing Social Security rates. The truth is that the "Social Security Trust Fund," the repository for Social Security payments, has been used as a slush fund by Congress, and Congress has repeatedly raided the fund to pay for its spending bills.

The IRS depends heavily on what it terms "voluntary compliance," which means that most taxpayers send in their taxes without overt coercion.

The IRS depends heavily on what it terms "voluntary compliance," which means that most taxpayers send in their taxes without overt coercion. However, many simply don't have a choice. In 1943, Congress passed the "Current Tax Payment Act," which required withholding of taxes by employers. The net result was that employees no longer received their full pay, but the balance after an estimated tax was amputated. The main reason for this was the govern-

Deep Inside the Underground Economy
How Millions of Americans Are Practicing Free Enterprise in An Unfree Society

26

ment's convenience: Many people did not file Form 1040, the official paperwork, and did not send in their payments. The IRS would have been strained to chase down these nickel-and-dime taxpayers to collect their money, and the withholding ensured that the IRS got its money first.

The IRS is still plagued with what it euphemistically calls "late filers," people who do not file returns for that year, and persist in not filing returns. This is why the IRS has been conducting a program to "bring them back into the system."[3]

We can go on looking at statistics for many pages, but that will take us only so far. The most important information for you, or for any taxpayer, is the dynamics of tax collection, how it works in practice. Only by looking closely at the system is it possible to analyze the weak points and determine how to lessen the tax bite.

The IRS Myth

It's popular in some circles to refer to the Internal Revenue Service as "the American Gestapo." This is a bad comparison. The IRS simply is not as efficient and capable as the Gestapo was. Making such a comparison exaggerates the proficiency of the IRS and makes it seem a much more formidable opponent than it is in real life. To show the difference, let's first take a quick look at the Gestapo, as it really was.

The Geheime Staats-Polizei, the Gestapo, was an agency for internal security and counterespionage. Contrary to the image presented in films and television programs, it was not composed of jack-booted sadists recruited from prisons and mental hospitals. Gestapo officers were experienced criminal investigators, recruited from the best of the country's police forces. Mueller, the Chief of the Gestapo, came from the Karlsruhe Criminal Investigation Department. Others were recruited from among the brightest university graduates, many with advanced degrees.

The Gestapo got a bad image because of the activities of people such as Adolf Eichmann. Actually, this was one small part of the Gestapo's efforts, and the sub-section assigned this duty was staffed by lackluster people such as Eichmann. The much-publicized Eichmann trial showed the sort of person he was: a clerk. Despite his rank of Colonel, he was simply a clerk in his function, a colorless figure who performed a routine job. The picture he presented on television was unimpressive: an unimaginative person doing a dull job. Rounding up and deporting ci-

vilians, including women and children, was not a demanding task compared to running down skilled enemy agents, and the Gestapo did not assign their best people to it.

The intrepid and imaginative investigators handled the hard jobs: intercepting agents' radio transmissions, code-breaking, tracing networks of spies, arresting and "turning" them, and deception operations. Contrary to Allied propaganda, the Gestapo did not arrest agents and immediately beat them up to force confessions. It wasn't in their best interest to do so.

Instead, they first tried a soft approach, persuading their captives that they had more to gain by cooperation than by resistance. This is exactly the technique used by criminal investigators throughout the world. A captive who cooperates, who talks and turns in other members of his organization, is much more useful to a police force, including the Gestapo, than one who keeps silent and goes to his execution without talking.

The Gestapo, like other security forces, turned many of their captives into double agents, who pretended to be still working for the Allies while really obeying Gestapo orders. One of the most ignored stories of World War II is how successfully the Gestapo did this. Producing propaganda about sadistic tortures attracts more readers than telling a true story about the patient and diligent efforts that produce more rewarding results in the end. It's also self-serving to portray an enemy as ruthless and sadistic instead of admitting that he's very clever and capable.

The Gestapo was feared, not because it was composed of criminal sadists, but because it was so effective. At the time, it was one of the best security police forces in the world, possibly the very best, and even today there are not many security organizations that equal it.

Now let's turn to the IRS and see it as it really is. Despite its sophisticated computers, it still depends on human material for its tasks. Instead of daring and intrepid investigators, we see bureaucrats in three-piece suits, more concerned with fringe benefits and retirement than with doing their jobs well. There has been falsification of their skills. Remember the TV series *The Untouchables*, with Elliot Ness as the courageous hero who took on the mob? Actually, although the real-life Ness was a treasury agent, he did not handle all the cases presented on TV, and most of his work was not as exciting as the series portrayed.

Physically, an office of the IRS looks very much like the Social Security Administration, the State

Corporation Commission, or the Office of Management and Budget. We see the same desks, the same clocks on the wall (avidly watched by the paper pushers), and the same file cabinets. In fact, we see basically the same people. Only the names are different. The term "paper pusher" is accurate and descriptive, because these people's work is ruled by endless reports, forms, regulations, procedural guidelines, and schedules. Their method of operation depends on the framework laid out in their operations manual.

The main motivation is a package of salary, perquisites, and fringe benefits that goes with the job. Many of them spend more time worrying about their fringe benefits than doing their jobs. Another serious concern is abiding by the multitude of regulations that rules their lives and not falling into a trap in which they'll be liable for blame, thereby endangering their chances for promotion, their retirement benefits, and even their careers.

This leads to the "CYA" (cover your ass) mentality. An employee will strive to avoid taking any risks, even in pursuit of the agency's objectives, because taking risks, especially if they're outside the guidelines and rules that govern him, are dangerous to his occupational health. There is no spirit of bold entrepreneurship in the IRS, only a dull and plodding adherence to procedures.

Much of what we hear and read about the IRS is propaganda, news slanted to give a false impression and exaggerate the IRS's effectiveness. We read about massive central computers recording every detail of everyone's finances and armies of agents and examiners poring over tax returns and masses of other forms to put together their picture of tax evaders.

Occasionally we read of IRS participation in the various "Organized Crime Strike Forces" that crop up in various parts of the country. These titles give an impression of massive effectiveness, but the reality is quite different. A "strike force" peopled by agents in three-piece suits is laughable. It is mostly ineffective, because its method of operation is chasing paperwork instead of chasing lawbreakers. Although we read that Elliot Ness and his crew put away Al Capone, his mob and its descendents live on. In Chapter Three, we'll look at the story of Al Capone in more detail.

Organized crime today is stronger than ever, despite the many millions of man-hours of enforcement effort, and the mass of publicity. Arresting and convicting a few men with Italian surnames does not put the Mob out of business.

If the IRS can't "get" the big operators, then what can it do? It can catch the inexperienced and unwary, who don't know how to take simple precautions to protect themselves. The small evaders, just starting out, and the naive ones are its victims.

It's true the IRS has computers, but anyone who has had a foul-up on his computer-generated utility bill has an idea of the limitations of computers.

It's true the IRS has computers, but anyone who has had a foul-up on his computer-generated utility bill has an idea of the limitations of computers. Anyone who has a legitimate tax refund coming understands that the IRS computers don't cope well with even routine work. Anyone who has had to endure the frustrations of a home computer knows that these machines are often fallible, and some models don't work well at all.

Computers can only do what their masters tell them to do. Dull and unimaginative people will operate their computers in dull and unimaginative ways.

This is why a person can take an above-ground job, giving a false Social Security number and falsifying his W-4 to have nothing withheld, and the IRS won't catch up to him for months or years. All this information goes into a computer, which operates with the speed of light, yet what do the human operators do with it? Drowning in paperwork, they move at a snail's pace.

Unfortunately, it's true that you can't win a confrontation with the IRS. They have the law and the manpower on their side. If you stand up to fight them, they'll knock you flat.

Is this always true, though? Aren't there some instances of people who have fought and won? Yes, there are, but it takes a lot of money and a good lawyer, and the risks are great. You don't have to win in court, though. There are other ways of winning.

As noted before, keeping a low profile is one way of winning. The best way to win is not to have to fight, and if the IRS never sees you, it can't take what's yours, and you win.

As we stress in this book, part of keeping a low profile is being one of many. Small business owners, who don't have the power and influence to get the special tax breaks of the rich, generally underreport their incomes by fifteen or twenty percent. This costs the government billions of dollars. In its "official"

Deep Inside the Underground Economy
How Millions of Americans Are Practicing Free Enterprise in An Unfree Society

28

figures, the IRS tries to underplay this because it doesn't want to let out how truly inefficient it is.

> **A federal judge in Montana stated that if one thousand people in that state were to file falsified withholding forms, it could "destroy" the system.**

These figures are frightening to the people in government. Money isn't the only problem; widespread disobedience of the tax laws is another. A federal judge in Montana stated that if one thousand people in that state were to file falsified withholding forms, it could "destroy" the system. In that case, the defendants were five men. Probably they were the only five who'd been caught!

There are two ways of interpreting such news. One is the "rotten apple" interpretation, in which we consider the ones being prosecuted as just a few rotten apples in the barrel. The other is the "tip of the iceberg" theory, which leads us to believe that those who have surfaced are only a few of the many who have jimmied their W-4s.

It doesn't take much insight to decide which is the correct interpretation. The evidence is overwhelming that many more people are involved in tax avoidance than the IRS wants to admit. Despite its propaganda line that tax cheaters are just a few isolated criminals, it's evident that there are many. Consider just one category, migrant workers. There's reason to believe that tens of thousands of them file false W-4 paperwork. Some of these are in the construction industry and others are farm workers.

The huge number of violators results in saturation of the IRS. It simply does not have enough investigators to audit every tax return filed by every self-employed person in the country, nor to track down every person who has filed a falsified W-4. Despite threats of prosecution by the IRS, their chances of catching violators are slim: first, because of the complexity of the legal system. It's possible, by pleading "not guilty," to delay the trial and sentencing for months or years, even if one is actually guilty. Second is the limited manpower of the various public prosecutors. Even in criminal cases, very few defendants come to trial. Most cases resolve themselves by plea agreements.

> **The major task for which the IRS exists is to collect money.**

The major task for which the IRS exists is to collect money. If the IRS catches a middle-class homeowner short on his taxes and he is unwilling to pay up, it can slam the iron fist of repression down on him and seize his house, his car and other property, attach his wages, and confiscate his bank accounts.

> **Possibly one of the biggest secrets the IRS keeps is that it can do almost nothing against tax evaders who are poor.**

Possibly one of the biggest secrets the IRS keeps is that it can do almost nothing against tax evaders who are poor. They own only the clothing on their backs, or perhaps a second-hand car. If the car is not paid up, the IRS has very little to grab.

The IRS justifies its existence by collecting money from taxpayers. Rumor has it that a tax examiner has to fulfill a quota of one hundred dollars per hour to satisfy his supervisors. In that regard, it simply doesn't pay for the IRS bloodhounds to chase down the lowest economic class of tax evaders, because they can't squeeze that much money out of them. It seems, therefore, that poverty or near-poverty is a sort of protection against the IRS examiners; it hits them right where they live.

Consequently, it is possible to "win" against the IRS, under certain circumstances. "Winning" does not necessarily mean open defiance, but just getting away with not paying taxes.

If the underground worker understands the IRS and how it operates, understands its few strengths and great limitations, and makes good use of this information, he'll be able to tailor his effort to his needs and avoid the mistakes that trap the unwary. With proper information and proper use of that information, he'll be able to earn money and keep what he earns.

The Everyday IRS

The basic process for the taxpayer is this: Declare your income, subtract your deductions, and pay tax on the balance. For the purposes of this discussion, we will not differentiate between deductions, exemptions, and tax credits. They all accomplish the same thing, lessening your tax bite.

All of the tax books tell you the same thing: Minimize your income and maximize your deductions in order to pay the least tax.[4] This is conventional wisdom, and it's true. It is what they don't tell you that's even more important to the beleaguered taxpayer.

The big weakness in the IRS's system for collecting taxes is in income reporting.

The big weakness in the IRS's system for collecting taxes is in income reporting. Former IRS Commissioner Jerome Kurtz, in his testimony before Congress,[5] says those who earn money in a conventional job, with withholding and W-2 forms, report 97% to 98% of their income. By contrast, those who are self-employed report only 60% to 64% of the total. The chances of concealing income are much greater if you are self-employed than if you work for wages that leave a paper trail.

This leads to the most important point of all: In your dealings with the IRS, the burden of proof is upon them regarding your income, but it's upon you regarding your deductions.

While in theory you are required to list all of your income, they can't make you do it unless they can catch you underreporting. To take deductions, on the other hand, you must list them and have the receipts and other paperwork available to support them if you are ever audited. If you cannot prove a deduction or if you can't show that an expenditure falls within the allowable categories, the IRS can and will disallow it.

We can see from this why many wage-earning taxpayers feel the tax burden hits them especially hard. Their employers record and report every cent they make to the government, while others who earn their incomes differently can play games with the IRS and get away with it, if they are discreet.

Wages

With the paper trail this sort of income leaves, there are not many chances for anyone to get away with not paying taxes on it. There is one method that is useful only to the person who chooses to live totally "underground." If such a person assumes a totally false identity with false I.D. papers and lists enough exemptions on his W-4 when he takes a job, he will have very little withheld from his wages[6]. For this to work consistently, the person must be able to move on to a new job each year or two, before the IRS catches up to him. Some people play this game with great success for many years.

Illegal immigrants sometimes work a variation of this scheme. They will borrow a relative's Social Se-

curity card or fill in a totally false Social Security number on the W-4. They normally live a nomadic existence, and in many cases are caught by the Immigration Service and deported before the IRS can call them in for an audit.

If you hold a regular job, you could fill in a fake Social Security number, confident that the IRS would not catch up to you for several years. However, this won't work in your favor if it's your regular career because when tax collection agents finally get to you, they'll hit you for any back taxes you owe. The basic point here is that a moving target is hard to hit.

Cash Payments

This is the basic form of concealed income. The person who receives payments "under the table" can easily neglect to report all or part of this income, because cash is untraceable.

Many people still get away with underreporting income by check when it's not wage income.

Payments by Check

Incredibly, many people still get away with underreporting income by check when it's not wage income. Even though checks leave a definite paper trail, and banks microfilm every check they handle, the fact is that this information is not available to the IRS unless the IRS audits you. If the IRS audits you and the auditor feels your bank records are worth a look, he can subpoena them, and that's the end of the game for you. With only a small percentage of tax returns being audited and an even smaller proportion subjected to close investigation, the odds against this happening are comforting.

Even in this day and age, it's possible to get along without a checking account, although it might be inconvenient. It's still perfectly legal to pay your bills in cash or by money order. It's also legal to have someone else cash your checks for you, if you have a customer who pays you by check. If you are a plumber, for example, and you do a little moonlighting after hours, your supplier may be willing to have you sign over second-party checks if he knows you well.

Rents, Royalties, and Other Income

This is the broadest category of all, and contains many sources of income that are capable of concealment. The IRS is tightening up its controls, now re-

Deep Inside the Underground Economy
How Millions of Americans Are Practicing Free Enterprise in An Unfree Society

30

quiring that a Form 1099 be sent in for many of these payments, but there are still many gaps. Banks report interest on savings, and some restaurant workers' tips are now subject to withholding, but rents are not under such tight controls. Income from capital gains on coins, stamps, and precious metals are still basically out of reach of the IRS, although the IRS now requires stockbrokers to report their clients' earnings with a Form 1099.

Many middle-class people feel the major part of the tax burden is on their shoulders, and unfortunately, the facts bear them out. Those on welfare, with no income, obviously pay no taxes, and the wealthy can afford to hire high-priced lawyers and accountants to find the tax loopholes that often result in their paying a ridiculously low amount of tax on an enviably high income.

Enforcement and Coercion

The IRS fosters a climate of fear by barking a lot, but as we shall see later, its bite is not as terrible as some believe.

Anyone who does not pay the taxes that the government says he owes runs the risk of being forced to pay or, in extreme and unusual cases, criminal prosecution. The IRS fosters a climate of fear by barking a lot, but as we shall see later, its bite is not as terrible as some believe.

The first thing to make clear is that the IRS's principle goal is your money, not your life or freedom. They send few people to prison because a taxpayer behind bars cannot earn money, and the government, instead of taking part of his earnings, has to pay his room and board. In 1979, only 1,820 people were formally prosecuted for tax evasion.[7] During 1999, 2,952 people were prosecuted. In 2000, the number dropped to 2,424, and in 2001, it dropped further to 2,335. Slightly over eighty percent of these went to prison.[8] This is a tiny proportion of the people audited, and an even tinier part of all those who evaded taxes and were never caught.

Even if the chances of being criminally prosecuted for tax evasion are small, and the chances of being convicted smaller still, there are other consequences that you'll have to endure. You'll have to hire a lawyer, attend court on your own time, lose pay from your job or business, and have both the worry and the inconvenience of fighting a prosecution. By contrast, the IRS special agent and the U.S. attorney don't care

about these things, because it is all in a day's work for them. It is what they get paid for, and win or lose, the case will not upset their lives. It will not cause them to lose sleep, lose pay, or have to pay expensive legal fees.

How to minimize or eliminate the tax bite is a problem we all share, but we are not all equally equipped to fight this battle. Much depends on our station in life. A contract killer, dope wholesaler, or stickup artist doesn't care about the Internal Revenue Code. Beating the tax laws is one of his lesser problems. Someone risking the death penalty or twenty years in prison isn't going to be impressed by the IRS bureaucrats; a six-month sentence for failure to file doesn't worry him much.

Basically, the IRS requires you to report your own income and tax owed. Sometimes you are locked in, as when you work for wages and your employer withholds taxes and files a W-2 with the IRS. The IRS can pursue nonfilers who have paperwork indicating income but who fail to file a return. It will certainly pursue tax rebels who openly proclaim themselves as such.[9]

Even today there are tax protesters who refuse to file or pay as a protest against the government's policies. Some are opposed to military spending in general, or are protesting our involvement in Afghanistan, for example. Others protest the government's funding of animal experimentation or other programs. These are not true guerrilla capitalists, because their tax evasion is a political statement and they don't seem to care that they risk prosecution.

The IRS has a checklist, known as the "Discriminant Function System," which they use to pick out returns that are likely to contain major errors or reflect attempts at evasion...

Many people file tax returns that provoke the IRS to take a closer look at them. The IRS has a checklist, known as the "Discriminant Function System," which they use to pick out returns that are likely to contain major errors or reflect attempts at evasion, enabling them to zero in on people who can be coerced into coughing up more taxes. The Discriminant Function System is a list of ways in which tax returns differ from averages the IRS has worked out over the years. It also reflects the IRS's experience in picking out certain categories that suggest the filer is concealing something. Some specifics are:

1. Outstanding discrepancies, such as claiming no children one year and ten the next, or an income that is completely out of line with your occupational category, e.g., a lawyer that earns only five thousand dollars a year.
2. Deductions much larger than average. The IRS will want substantiation or they will disallow it. A table showing some average deductions for different levels of income is useful to every accountant and necessary to every taxpayer who wants to be on solid ground.[10]
3. Returns showing heavy travel and entertainment deductions. Experience has shown that many abuses occur in these categories.
4. Those claiming exemptions for other dependents besides wives or children.
5. People who list a hobby as a deduction, claiming it as a business. For this to work, the "business" must occasionally show a "profit."
6. Returns from people who, by the nature of their work, have the greatest opportunities to cheat. This includes doctors, lawyers, and anyone who deals largely in cash. During recent years, though, doctors have been absorbed into health insurance plans that create a paper trail, and therefore have fewer opportunities to cheat.

This last point is worth a close look. A person who earns less than $10,000 a year and is subject to a W-2 form has to face a 1 in 143 chance of being audited.[11] A self-employed person with an income of over $30,000 annually has a 1 in 17 chance of being audited. Someone earning W-2 reportable wages that total over $50,000 a year has a 1 in 9 chance of facing the auditor. Experience has shown that those who are self-employed and deal in cash have the opportunity to conceal income, and that will be the main direction of an audit. Those with large W-2 salaries, on the other hand, are likely to be business owners who are creative in devising large deductions. The IRS will approach them from a different direction.

The IRS also has a small program of spot-checks, in which returns are selected at random in what it calls the Taxpayers Compliance Measurement Program. This is like being struck by lightning. It probably won't happen to you, but if it does, the auditor will go over every detail of your return, while in a conventional audit he'll question only the areas that have attracted his attention.

The IRS has two methods of auditing the return: direct and indirect. The direct method involves gathering and examining the paperwork related to the return — the W-2, the Form 1040, receipts to support deductions, etc. This is the method it uses to knock down returns that are fudged with inflated deductions.

A person who owns a yacht and claims income of only $10,000 a year is plainly living beyond his reported means and will have a lot of explaining to do.

The indirect method is more sophisticated and it is the one the IRS uses to check on unreported income. IRS investigators can — and do — subpoena bank records, business ledgers, invoices, and other paperwork to verify the accuracy of the reported income. Sometimes it is obvious. A person who owns a yacht and claims income of only $10,000 a year is plainly living beyond his reported means and will have a lot of explaining to do.

Sometimes it's more subtle than the previous examples. A business owner who claims a rate of profit lower than the norm for his type of enterprise may be concealing income, and the examiner may check his bank records to determine his cash flow, constructing a picture of how it adds up for the year. He may use sophisticated accounting methods, such as deriving a figure for net worth, checking inventory at the start and the end of the year, totaling cash register tapes, etc.

You, as a citizen and taxpayer, may feel outraged that the IRS can dig into your private records in its search for additional taxes. Nevertheless, it has the law on its side. Bank records, which normally require a court order to make them available to another party, are vulnerable to what is colloquially known as a "pocket summons," which an IRS agent can whip out and fill in on the spot to compel your banker to open your records to him.[12]

The picture is not all black. Although the IRS has some very heavy artillery that it can use, it rarely does so, and if you are wise and keep a low profile, your chances of being bombarded with a full-scale investigation are small. Let's look at ways to avoid an audit, and to cope with one if it happens to you.

Keep Off the IRS's Radar Screen

The basic principle of success as an underground worker is that avoidance is better than confrontation. That is why it's wise to keep a low profile. There have been some people who have ignored this principle and found it very costly. Some years ago on the

Deep Inside the Underground Economy
How Millions of Americans Are Practicing Free Enterprise in An Unfree Society

32

TV program *Sixty Minutes*, several tax evaders boasted how they had fooled the IRS, possibly without realizing IRS people watch that program, too. The result was predictable. They all were called down for some uncomfortable sessions with tax examiners.

Lucille Moran, a prominent tax protester, steadfastly refused to file a return for years. This resulted in a running legal battle with the IRS. A man named Irwin Schiff became involved in a long struggle with the IRS by filing a "Fifth Amendment Return." This is one on which the taxpayer writes his name and address, and the statement that he declines to answer the other questions under the protection of the Fifth Amendment. The IRS sees this as an affront to its authority, and prosecutes those who do this. The tax protesters appeal their convictions,[13] but a long, drawn-out legal contest is inevitably expensive. In any event, on April 19th, 1983, the U.S. Supreme Court ruled that citizens may not claim Fifth Amendment protection to withhold information from the IRS.

Another open defiance of the IRS is starting a "church," a right guaranteed by the first amendment of the Constitution. Unfortunately, those who have tried this have found that the IRS is not stupid, and have had to fight legal battles to maintain their status. Again, this is expensive, and even if the protester wins, he might find that it has cost him dearly.

It's difficult to find a needle in a haystack because it is so small, yet it can be done with a metal detector. However, finding one particular strand of hay, which looks exactly like millions of others, is almost impossible.

The successful guerrilla capitalist wants to avoid a fight with the IRS. He does this by keeping a low profile, blending in with millions of other citizens. The analogy of trying to find a needle in a haystack gives a basic insight into how this works. It's difficult to find a needle in a haystack because it is so small, yet it can be done with a metal detector. However, finding one particular strand of hay, which looks exactly like millions of others, is almost impossible. The idea is to look just like all of the other strands of hay in the haystack. You should not draw attention to yourself by claiming deductions so large they seem unreal. You must not make a spectacle of yourself by openly confronting the IRS. For the IRS to harass you, they first have to notice you, and you must make that as unlikely as possible.

We have seen what the IRS looks for in selecting returns for audit. Avoiding the features of such returns is one means of prevention, and prevention is better than cure.

How to Cope With an Audit

Every guerrilla capitalist, if he is wise, will consider the possibility that he may be "called down" by the IRS for an audit or a more extensive investigation. We have already seen that an audit may come about routinely, or it may come because the IRS has noted a feature of your tax return that suggests noncompliance with the tax laws.[14]

If you have the misfortune to be selected for an audit... this is your golden chance to strike hard if you are clever.

If you have the misfortune to be selected for an audit, you'll probably receive a notice giving you the time and place of the audit, and telling you what documents to bring. This is your golden chance to strike hard if you are clever.

Keep in mind that the IRS is in operation to collect money, and they have to do this with limited means. Former IRS Commissioner Mortimer Caplin liked to boast that the IRS collected five dollars for every one spent on enforcement of the tax laws. The right tactics can put a crimp in that figure.

Each auditor has to work his way through a heavy caseload, and has to meet a quota. An unofficial estimate is that each auditor has to produce $100 in additional taxes per hour he works. Your goal is to reduce his productivity by wasting his time, which you can do easily and tactfully if you are smart and discreet about it.

The first step is to phone your assigned auditor to break your appointment, the same day if possible. Tell him you have an emergency (doctor, dentist, car broke down, etc.) and ask if you can meet him at the same time the next day. Show willingness to come in as soon as possible after the original appointment, to maintain the appearance of cooperation.

If you have to lose pay from your job because of this, be sure that you remember that more than a few hours' pay is at stake here. If your boss is a decent fellow and feels the same way you do about the IRS, he can alibi you for the broken first appointment.

When you do go in, be on time, again to demonstrate good faith. It will count against you if you are late, and you may risk being labeled a wise guy. When you meet the auditor, be polite and don't try any of the cheap tricks they have all encountered before, like being "buddy-buddy" with him or her, or screaming about your "rights." They are used to these tactics, and will not be impressed. Adopt a low-key manner and don't antagonize the examiner.

Bring the documents requested with you, but be sure to bring only those requested. Have them arranged neatly so you can find them quickly. Don't make the mistake of bringing in a shopping bag full of receipts and dumping them on his desk. He has seen that before, too, and if he gets angry with you, he might go after you whatever the cost.

Some investigators may try to force the pace by snapping questions at you, to induce you to snap an answer back without thinking.

Be polite. Answer questions simply and directly, but — and this is an important but — don't rush. Think out your answers very carefully before you open your mouth. Some investigators may try to force the pace by snapping questions at you, to induce you to snap an answer back without thinking. Avoid this at all costs, but be open about it. Tell the investigator frankly that you want a minute or so to think about your answer, or you want to look at your receipts to refresh your memory. Remember that he has his appointments closely scheduled, and has only so much time to devote to your case. When he asks you to produce a document, do it, but do it slowly and carefully, without making it obvious you're out to waste his time. If you need more time to think, ask to go to the bathroom. That is a request the examiner cannot refuse and it will buy you several minutes time.

If you're the nervous type and easily get flustered under pressure, admit your weakness to yourself and have your tax accountant accompany you to the session. You may want to do this anyway as a routine precaution. Your accountant is a pro, accustomed to dealing with the IRS. The examiner will not be able to bulldoze him as he might an unpracticed and unsophisticated taxpayer. IRS auditors have been known to employ unfair tactics and try to bluff taxpayers when they feel the taxpayer does not know all his rights.

If he asks you to produce a document that was not listed on the form you got (bring the form with you, to show him), say, "I'm sorry, but you didn't ask for that. If I'd known, I would have brought it."

If he asks you to provide any information that is not dealt with in the documents you have, don't answer it. Tell him you don't remember, but you'll be glad to go home and get your checkbook, rent receipts, etc., and bring them next time.

One of the most common traps is the cost-of-living statement that an examiner will ask a taxpayer to fill out when there is difficulty in finding documentation of his income. This is an indirect method of establishing income and is loaded with traps. It is in your best interest to minimize your expenditures, for obvious reasons, and you should be very careful with your answers. This is a golden opportunity to stonewall him, but only if you do it correctly. Be modest about it and soft-spoken. For example: "I don't know exactly what we pay for rent. My wife makes out the checks. I'll be glad to go and get them, though."

If he tells you to give him an estimate, refuse absolutely. "I can't be sure that what I would tell you would be right. I have to sign that paper, and I don't want to risk perjury." If he tells you that there is no risk of perjury, reply that you would prefer to give him accurate information, and the records to support it are at home. Be tactful, but firm.

Remember you are playing for time, and trying to waste his and make him work for every penny he squeezes out of you. If you can present yourself as a poor but honest soul, he might even decide there is not much to gain in spending more time on the investigation, and drop it at that point. This may let you off the hook.

If, however, he tries to bulldoze you, and tells you he is going to disallow a certain deduction because you don't have the supporting documents there, dig in your feet. The gloves are off. If you really have the documents at home, insist on speaking to his supervisor. Tell him, politely of course, that you can prove your point and you want to come back with the paperwork. If he tells you to mail them, tell him you have recently lost some important papers in the mail and you'd prefer to hand-carry them.

The tax auditors are so overloaded that even a few people practicing delaying tactics will jam up their systems.

Deep Inside the Underground Economy
How Millions of Americans Are Practicing Free Enterprise in An Unfree Society

34

These tactics might seem petty, but they will result in wasting the examiner's very limited time. Each hour he spends on you he will not be able to use to pursue another taxpayer. His backlog of cases will continue to pile up. The tax auditors are so overloaded that even a few people practicing delaying tactics will jam up their systems.

So if you find yourself called down for an audit, you can keep your wits about you and inform yourself properly before you go to the IRS office. There is excellent published material on how to handle an audit.[15] There is also good advice on what not to do in order to handle an audit properly and avoid the attention of the IRS.

Be prepared for traps and trick questions. Never forget these examiners interview people all day, every day, and are skilled at drawing out vital information with seemingly trivial questions.[16] It's critically important, and worth repeating, that you must participate in the interview in a careful and deliberate manner, for your own protection.

As part of your low profile, don't try to act as if you're a tax expert. You aren't and probably never will be. Today's Internal Revenue Code consists of 17,000 pages, and even IRS examiners don't know it all.[17]

Today the IRS audits those earning between $25,000 and $100,000 a year more often than those beyond these limits. The IRS audited 0.4 percent of those earning less than $25,000 per year in 2001. This contrasts with the 0.58 percent audit rate for all taxpayers.[18]

All in all, keeping your head down is the best basic tactic. Not giving the IRS reason to investigate you will avoid many problems with them, and if you're called for an audit, giving an impression of being an honest and typical taxpayer will help disarm their suspicions.

Fighting Back

For good reasons, many people feel helpless against the bureaucracy of the government. They may write to the local newspaper or to their congressman, but in their hearts they know this will do nothing meaningful. They also know if they try to fight the IRS openly, they will get their heads knocked off or be involved in aggravating litigation that can go on for years.

However, there are ways of fighting back without being singled out and getting hurt, ways to throw monkey wrenches into the complicated machinery of the IRS without becoming a martyr.

The IRS operates more and more with computers in an effort to cope with the mountains of paperwork they must process each year. It also has to work within a budget, with limited resources and manpower to pursue its cases. One consequence of this is that the IRS sends out preprinted, specially coded envelopes to many taxpayers along with their Form 1040 and booklet. If you get one of these packages, remember the IRS is not providing you with a pre-addressed envelope because they're nice guys. The envelopes are coded to go through a computerized sorting machine to speed up processing. Returns that come in other envelopes must be sorted by hand, which consumes manpower. Therefore, do not use the envelope or peel-away label the IRS sends you unless you expect a refund and want to speed up the processing of your return. Make them sort it by hand to degrade their efficiency.

If you have some time to spare one day and are in a good mood, get some Form 1040s and some blank W-2s, fill them out with fictitious names, and send them in. An interesting twist is to use names and addresses of people who have died recently, as seen in the obituary columns. For the accompanying W-2, fill in the name of a real company you have reason to dislike, such as an auto dealer who sold you a lemon. To make sure the return gets the IRS's attention, fill it out to show the taxpayer owes money. The IRS will make every effort to track the person down to collect, diverting manpower they otherwise might have used to harass you.

For more ways of striking back at the IRS, see Appendix Three.

The Future

What are some possible changes that might affect you as an underground worker? We have to consider these prospects, even though the government seems to be addicted to the present inefficient system of collecting taxes, because although changes appear unlikely, the situation could deteriorate enough to force the government into new ways of thinking.

One possibility is a value-added tax, or VAT, which is used in Great Britain and other countries.

One possibility is a value-added tax, or VAT, which is used in Great Britain and other countries. This is a tax imposed on goods and services, not income. This would, essentially, be a tax on expenditures, not income. If the federal government abolished income tax and adopted a VAT you wouldn't have to worry about concealing income, but you'd get hit hard on every cent you spent. One countermeasure would be to rely even more on barter, trading your skills and products for those of others. This would require a major change in your lifestyle. You'd be buying less from established companies that paid the VAT, and more from other underground workers who relied on barter, to avoid the official paperwork.

Another possible change is the flat tax, as proposed by former presidential candidate Steve Forbes. The flat tax is simply a uniform tax rate applied against your income, without the deductions, exemptions, tax credits, and other complications of our present tax code. One country that has adopted this system is Russia, a country that has suffered much from being top-heavy in its bureaucracy. In 2001, President Putin persuaded the Duma to pass a flat tax rate; this simplification has resulted in more Russians paying tax, and has lowered the tax rate. Personal income tax revenue went up by forty-seven percent, according to official Russian government figures.[19]

However, a flat tax would not solve all problems, and might not necessarily reduce the burden on taxpayers. Even in Russia, people still have to pay sales tax, VAT, property tax, and many others.[20] In this country we have several levels of government, and states, counties, and cities impose their own taxes to meet their expenses. An underground worker still has to pay these if he buys goods and services and owns property. The flat tax would apply, obviously, only to income the government could trace, and the underground worker would still have plenty of leeway to conceal income. Coping with sales taxes would still be possible through the barter system.

The flat tax would apply, obviously, only to income the government could trace, and the underground worker would still have plenty of leeway to conceal income.

The future may bring some surprises, and this is why it's important for the underground worker to remain mentally alert and flexible to meet changing tactics by government tax collectors. It's important to recognize that, despite our government's history of being inflexible, changes might come about, and these would require new techniques of beating the tax collector.

The Ethics of Tax Evasion

Questions of ethics and morality are impossible to answer in a way that everyone will accept. Morality, like the law, varies from place to place, time to time, and person to person. Sexual morality, for example, has undergone a significant change in America during the twentieth century. Each person, has his own code of morality that may or may not be consistent with the law or with a particular religion.

Whether to go into the underground economy, and how far to go, are questions each of us must answer for ourselves. If you're thinking of doing it, you must be aware that, although many people do it, and successfully, it is technically illegal to avoid paying taxes, and you might get caught and be forced to cough up the money the IRS says you owe. There is a possibility of a fine, as well as interest on back taxes, along with a slight chance of criminal prosecution and a prison sentence.

As a start, you need a firm conviction that what you're doing is right and moral, even though it conflicts with the law.

As a start, you need a firm conviction that what you're doing is right and moral, even though it conflicts with the law. You also need the emotional stamina to sustain your effort, and the technical know-how to enable you to do it smoothly, elegantly, and without risking discovery. Finally, you must accept that there is a risk, however slight, of getting caught and having to face reprisals by the government.

The main reason the government is having so much trouble getting everyone to conform scrupulously to its way of assessing and collecting taxes is that many people feel that they're doing nothing wrong by withholding cooperation. People who are law-abiding in other ways feel that their earnings are none of the government's business. Although they may not be able to articulate it in these terms, many feel that there's something illegitimate in the government's amputating a portion of their income and wasting it on useless projects, boondoggling, and

Deep Inside the Underground Economy
How Millions of Americans Are Practicing Free Enterprise in An Unfree Society

36

pork-barrel expenditures. The government calls these people "cheaters," but who, really, is being cheated?

Is it cheating for a person to want to keep the fruits of his own labor? Is it cheating for someone to believe that he can better spend his own money than a bunch of politicians and bureaucrats? In reality, it's the government who really cheats.

Popular mythology says that the government consists of "representatives" elected by a "majority." However, in most cases, this is simply untrue. In reality, elected officials comprise a tiny minority of the government. Most officials are political appointees put in place by the elected officials. The head of the Internal Revenue Service, for example, was appointed, not elected. The auditor who grills you over your tax return never got his job by winning votes.

Many of these political appointees got their jobs, not because they're particularly qualified for them, but because they're cronies of the person who appointed them. How many secretaries of state, for example, worked their way up through the State Department? Almost none. How many Secretaries of Defense are former generals? Few. How many Secretaries of Agriculture are former farmers? They might be lawyers, political hacks, or simply wealthy people who were able to purchase their jobs, but rarely farmers.

Often high political appointees got their jobs as a payback for generous campaign contributions. Some of the top jobs are ambassadorships to countries such as France and England. These posts are usually held by people with no experience in diplomacy, people who never worked for the State Department, and who often can't even speak the language of the country to which they're appointed.

It's really the entrenched bureaucracy that runs things in Washington and they don't "represent" anything but their own interests.

Government actually consists mostly of politically appointed bureaucrats, parasites who never won an election. It's really the entrenched bureaucracy that runs things in Washington and they don't "represent" anything but their own interests. Even those "elected" by "majority vote" can claim no real mandate. Only about half of our country's population is eligible to vote. Fewer than half of these voters turn out for most elections. The presidential election brings out the greatest proportion of voters, while elections for gov-

ernor and mayor bring out fewer. So a politician winning with fifty percent of the vote can claim to be "representing" about 12.5 percent of the people at best. Some win by even smaller margins.

President Clinton, for example, got elected by about forty-three percent of the voters, because there was a third-party candidate who absorbed votes. Yet he claimed a "mandate" from the American people. George W. Bush won the Presidency in the Electoral College, although he had a smaller amount of the popular vote than his opponent, Al Gore. This hotly contested election caused a constitutional crisis and had to be settled by the Supreme Court, leaving many people feeling that Bush was not elected legitimately.

Although by their very nature ethics are very subjective and open to interpretation, we can make a few blanket statements about ethics and laws.

Cash's First Principle states that a law must be judged reasonable and fair to be acknowledged and obeyed by the majority of people. Most people agree, for example, that rape, robbery, and murder are wrong and live their entire lives without raping, robbing, or murdering anyone.

New laws covering financial and administrative matters don't have the moral force of traditional laws based on the Ten Commandments, English Common Law, and other historical and traditional codes of behavior.

Cash's Second Principle states that new laws covering financial and administrative matters don't have the moral force of traditional laws based on the Ten Commandments, English Common Law, and other historical and traditional codes of behavior. People can and do violate them without feeling that they're doing anything wrong, because government leaders have created exceptions and loopholes in the laws so that they may break them without fear of sanctions. It's as if "Laws are for little people," as stated by Leona Helmsley.

Cash's Third Principle is that if the people do not recognize a law's legitimacy, enforcing it will require certain and harsh punishment.

Cash's Fourth Principle is that there are not enough police officers and/or government agents to enforce laws that most people ignore or flout. Prohibition provided a good example. The "war on drugs" is another. It would be necessary to lock up a significant proportion of the country's population to suppress illegal alcohol, illegal drugs, or the underground economy.

Cash's Fifth Principle states that people are not as stupid as their leaders think. They make poor choices at the polls. They grudgingly accept poor government as their lot in life. However, although they may not be able to express it clearly, they understand that government leaders have hidden agendas, and that the welfare of their constituents is low on their list of priorities.

This leads us to Cash's Corollaries.

Cash's First Corollary: Only laws that make sense, such as those against rape and murder, are worth following.

Cash's Second Corollary: If government leaders don't obey the law, they have no right to expect common citizens to obey.

Cash's Third Corollary: Stealing from the government is all right, but stealing from a private citizen is wrong because real people get hurt.

Cash's Fourth Corollary: Tax evasion is all right, because it's only stealing from the government that makes the laws that discriminate against little people.

Cash's Fifth Corollary: The only thing wrong with tax evasion is getting caught.

Notes

1. "Historical Highlights of the IRS," *Internal Revenue Service Digital Daily*, Internet http://www.irs.gov/newsroom/display/0,,il=42&genericId=230 99,00.html, 11 March 2002.
2. *Ibid.*
3. *Ibid.*
4. Howard Fishkin *Taxpayer's Survival Manual*, Book Promotions Unlimited, Flushing, MI. Also see J.R. Price, *In This Corner, The IRS,* Dell Publishing Co., NY, 1981.
5. U.S. Congress, *Hearing Before The Joint Economic Committee,* 96th Congress, 1st Session, November 15, 1979.
6. A good guide to obtaining fake I.D. is: *The I. D. Forger*, John Q. Newman, Loompanics Unlimited, 1999.
7. *In This Corner, The IRS*, p. 234.
8. "IRS Criminal Investigations Division: Fiscal Years 1999, 2000, and 2002," *United States Department of the Treasury*, Internet. http://www.ustreas.gov/irs/ci/numbers/docthree.htm, 11 March, 2002.
9. Jerome Tuccille, *Inside the Underground Economy*, New American Library, 1982, pp. 11-43.
10. "X," C.P.A., *How To Cheat On Your Taxes*, 1040 Press, p. 33.
11. *Tax Avoidance*, Anonymous, privately printed, p. 7. This book is out of print.
12. *How to Determine Undisclosed Financial Interests*, Loompanics Unlimited, Port Townsend, WA, 1983.
13. *Inside The Underground Economy*, pp. 11-48. This is an excellent discussion of the aboveground tax protestors and how the IRS has followed an active campaign against them.
14. *In This Corner, The IRS,* pp. 54-69.
15. See *Churchification: Incorporate Your Own Church Without a Lawyer*, Church Liberation League, 1983. See also *Survival Manual*, Howard Fishkin, pp. 46-49 for a summary of ways to behave at an audit, and, *In This Corner, The IRS*, pp. 54-69 and 208-31, which gives insight into IRS objectives and how it views this issue. The author is a former IRS agent, knows his material, and gives detailed information on how the IRS works.
16. *In This Corner, The IRS*, pp. 54-69 and pp. 208-231; How to Cheat On Your Taxes, pp. 102-103. This is a very good list of "don'ts" for those who want to avoid trouble with the IRS. See Taypayer's Survival Manual, p. 49, for a short discussion of traps in the interview.
17. Curt Anderson, "Fed Tax Burden Drops," *Albuquerque Journal*, 15 April 2002, p. A1.
18. *Ibid.*
19. Eric Englemen, "Flat-Tax System Works for Russians," *Albuquerque Journal,* 15 April 2002, p. A4.
20. *Ibid.*

Chapter Three
Tax-Fudging Tactics

There are only two basic ways of ducking taxes: minimizing income and inflating deductions. If you're operating an above ground business, you need to become familiar with ways to screw the IRS on your tax return by exaggerating your deductions, thereby reducing your taxable income. If you're operating totally underground, you don't need this information because you don't file a return.

Tax-fudging tactics are useful against state and local taxes as well. One of the best fudges is taking advantage of tax loopholes. Let's highlight a few that we'll discuss in more detail later.

Smart Operators Use Loopholes to Avoid Taxes Legally

Washington, D.C., home of the "Beltway Bandits" and some of the sharpest operators in the nation, has a set of tax loopholes all its own. It's easy to avoid real-estate transfer taxes, for example. Owners don't buy or sell real estate, but shares in the limited partnerships that are the owners of title. Another loophole frees building owners of taxes if a building they own isn't "under roof" at the end of the year. This loophole is large enough to pass a regiment of storm troopers, and building owners simply delay finishing building roofs while renting space on lower floors. Congress, as we might expect, is the worst offender, because it has sole discretion regarding the amount it forks over to the District of Columbia to help run the city. Predictably, Congress takes care of itself, but chronically shortchanges the District.[1]

Fortunately, the range of deductions allowed by law is so wide that only the most unimaginative tax filer would fail to see opportunities for fudging.

Deductions

Deductions are the happy hunting ground for just about everyone, not only guerrilla capitalists, because they offer many interesting opportunities for retaining income. Fortunately, the range of deductions allowed by law is so wide that only the most unimaginative tax filer would fail to see opportunities for fudging.

Save all receipts. Stoop to pick them up off the floor in a store. All receipts can be valuable at tax-filing time. Who's to know that the vacuum cleaner you bought for your country home isn't really for your office? Anyway, small-dollar items slip by without question, because IRS agents are after the big money, as we've seen. They won't audit nickel-and-dime stuff.

Church Contributions

Unless you're a militant agnostic or atheist, you can claim a few hundred dollars as church contributions without presenting any receipts. The IRS routinely accepts this deduction, because it's so small and disproving it would require staking out the taxpayer's home each Sunday morning for many weeks.

Double Duty Deductions

One way to double the number of documents supporting deductions is to work with a partner to pay each other's deductible expenses. It's a simple system: You have a bill from your doctor. Your partner goes to the doctor's office, explaining that he's paying the bill for you, writes a check on his account, and asks the receptionist to mark the bill "Paid." This generates a receipt, which you keep, and a canceled check, which he keeps. You settle with him in cash and return the favor when he has a medical bill.

Deep Inside the Underground Economy
How Millions of Americans Are Practicing Free Enterprise in An Unfree Society

40

Doubling Your Reimbursed Expenses

If you work for an employer who reimburses some or all of your out-of-pocket expenses, there's a simple way to generate double receipts so that you can have your cake and eat it, too. Pay by check and turn in the receipt for reimbursement. Your check will serve as documentation for deducting the expense on your tax return.

Overpaying on an Order

This involves writing a check for more than a large item actually costs, including shipping, and cashing the refund check. Let's say you need a left-handed widget for your workshop or office, and these are available mail order for $299 plus shipping. You overestimate the shipping and the vendor writes you a check to refund the excess. You cash the check instead of depositing it and throw away the invoice. If ever audited and questioned regarding the invoice, you simply state that it got lost. A few of these slips are normal in any business, and you'll get away with it as long as you don't run up incredible totals.

How Small Businesses Fiddle Their Books

Mr. Joe Wage-Earner gets it in the neck: his income tax is taken out of his pay before he even receives it! Not much chance to do any "fiddling" there. Withholding is the Internal Revenue Service's way of collecting its taxes up front, before the taxpayer ever sees a paycheck. This saves IRS agents the tiresome task of pursuing small accounts and is one reason why the salaried employee is truly a "wage slave."

Since the small business owner reports his own income, he can greatly reduce his tax liability by "adjusting" financial figures.

Having one's own business, on the other hand, opens up a lot of opportunities for creative accounting. Since the small business owner reports his own income, he can greatly reduce his tax liability by "adjusting" financial figures.

Skimming is one such opportunity. Skimming simply means taking cash off the top of the sales and not reporting this money as income. Nearly any retail business receiving a decent proportion of its sales in

cash can do this. If you took in $200 today, take $25 and put it in your pocket. Report $175 as sales on your taxes. It's as simple as that. However, you have to be wary of audit trails. If the business owner reports his sales from his cash register tapes, he will just simply leave the cash drawer open and not ring up any sales for the last couple hours or so of the day.

Skimming is best kept within reasonable bounds. It is best done by taking just a little, say ten to twenty percent off the top, and still deducting all expenses. If you start skimming more than that, you are going to encounter a problem. The profit margin on your business will be lower than "normal," and this is one thing an income tax auditor looks for. What some do to get around this is to hide expenses as well as income. They literally keep two sets of books.

If a business owner is skimming fifty percent off the top of his receipts, he knows that if he deducts all his expenses, his tax return will appear very abnormal. Consequently, he covers this by hiding half of his expenses, that is paying them in cash. Therefore, no record appears in his bank account, and then he just throws away those receipts. In this case, he is actually conducting half of his business off the books. This can get pretty tricky, but is fairly common.[2]

It is the opinion of this author that a person is better off hiding only income, instead of both sales and expenses, but you must weigh the consequences and then choose your own tactics.

There are other ways of taking cash out of a business. Even if you get paid with a check or money order, you can still avoid reporting the income on your taxes in a couple of ways. You can simply take the check or money order to the bank it is drawn on and endorse and cash it right there. Postal money orders can be cashed at the post office. Another way is to endorse checks or money orders and use them to pay bills — a "second-party check."

Another thing that you can do is to deposit all the checks in your bank, but get cash back when you make the deposit. You fill out the deposit slip, listing all the checks, and then at the bottom, request a cash withdrawal directly on the deposit slip. Some deposit slips have a place especially for this purpose.

This way, a smaller amount is listed as the total deposited, and it is the net amount of the deposit that appears on your bank statement. This is risky, because if the IRS were really out to get you, it could subpoena the bank's copies of all deposit slips, but the IRS seldom does that because it's very tedious. On nearly every audit, the normal IRS procedure is to add up the deposits from your bank statements and then compare the total with the income you reported on your income tax return.

You should make sure that all these returns reconcile with each other, since it is a common audit practice to examine returns other than the one being audited, to make sure that income and expenses are consistent.

This is a good place to talk about consistency in your tax returns. If any of your business at all is on the books, you will be filing several different tax returns. You should make sure that all these returns reconcile with each other, since it is a common audit practice to examine returns other than the one being audited, to make sure that income and expenses are consistent. For example, if you deduct for "labor expense," the figure for labor on your income tax return should be exactly the same as the amount on your state unemployment tax return, your state income tax return, your form for paying state withholding, your workmen's compensation return, etc. Likewise with your income: The amount reported on your income tax return should be exactly the same as the amount on your state sales tax return, and so on down the line. A set of books that is internally consistent has a much better chance of getting through an audit than a set riddled with contradictions.

Now let's look at some ways of fiddling those tax returns.

One way is inventory adjustments. Due to the way "income" is figured for purposes of federal income tax, small business owners are forced to pay taxes on their inventory. Stock on hand at the year's end is considered an asset of the business, and money spent on this inventory is not deductible until the stock is sold. Thus, the small business owner spends his income on inventory, and still has to pay taxes on that money, even though he hasn't sold the stock yet. The lower the inventory at the end of the year, the smaller the tax liability will be. Business owners are supposed to perform an actual physical count of their inventory at the end of the tax year, but some provide an "estimate." As long as the "adjustment" is within reason, the chances of being caught are almost nonexistent. For example, a well-stocked convenience store may have $90,000 in inventory — or maybe it is only $75,000, instead. By the time an auditor appears on the scene, how could he tell the difference?[3]

Another technique is "extra" cash paid-outs. This is an easy one that can add up over a period of time. Most supermarkets and many other stores now have cash registers that print on the register tape exactly what it is you bought, so this one won't work with receipts from those stores. But if you go into the local mom and pop grocery and buy a six pack of beer, a package of cheese, and a Sunday paper, the receipt you'll receive will have only the prices and total listed, with no indication of what it was you bought. Therefore, you put this receipt in your business paid-outs, after first scribbling "ballpoint pens, tape, and stamp pad" or something similar on it. You then deduct this as an office expense on your income tax. Some have even been known to purchase receipt books and pads of invoices at an office supply store and fill them in with "cash paid-outs." Every little bit helps.

Yet another way is recording personal expenses as business expenses. This is very similar to the technique discussed above. Let's say you go to the supermarket to buy household items, such as window cleaner, toilet paper, hand soap, vacuum cleaner bags, etc., for your home. The supermarket receipt will list these items, but it doesn't itemize their end use. An auditor won't know that this material wasn't for the office. This can also work with magazine subscriptions, stereo equipment (music system for your office), building supplies, camera equipment, etc. Even meals in restaurants can be deductible if they were "business" meals.

We have covered here only a few of the more likely ways you can fiddle your books. In practice, what you can do is limited mainly by your imagination and willingness to take risks.[4]

Making the Most of Receipts

Receipts are the heart of any deductions you claim on your tax return.

One often-overlooked method of maximizing deductions is using receipts. Receipts are the heart of any deductions you claim on your tax return. The Internal Revenue Service demands substantiation for any deductions, and this usually means having a piece of paper to show. Maximizing your deductions can bring you untaxed income you otherwise would not have had, even if your business is completely above ground, which is why many business owners do this.

Deep Inside the Underground Economy
How Millions of Americans Are Practicing Free Enterprise in An Unfree Society

42

Receipts take many forms, sometimes being just scrawled notes, but they look better if they're printed, preferably on a cash register. A hand-written receipt on a printed form will also do very well.

An interesting thing about receipts is that there's no standard format, either by custom or by law. There's no law requiring that a receipt be itemized, or that it list the nature of the item in the transaction, although many do. This is especially true today, as supermarkets and chain stores scan purchases and print out receipts listing the items purchased as a method of inventory control. This prevents you from using a receipt for food as a "business lunch." However, there are many ways around this limitation.

The following example shows how manipulation of receipts will often cover a person's need, whether regarding tax deductions or collecting on an expense account.

Nick took a trip to Atlanta for his company. He was allotted a per diem and would be reimbursed for anything above that if he could turn in a receipt. He wanted to make a side-trip to see an old friend, but knew his company would not reimburse him for this personal business. He took the trip anyway and his friend treated Nick to dinner at a restaurant called "The Tillerman." When the check came and his friend paid, Nick noticed that the stub, which served as a receipt for those who had expense accounts, did not state the nature of the establishment, and furthermore the amount was blank. Restaurants often avoid filling in the amount, as the proprietors know this is an accommodation to the business owner who wants to falsify his accounts, and will indirectly bring in a few extra customers. Nick asked his friend for the stub, filling in an amount that would cover his extra air fare, and passed it off as a motel receipt when he turned in his expense sheet.

Paul was a branch manager for an insurance company. On vacation, he met with several friends for dinner at a restaurant. He offered to pay for the dinner with his credit card and asked his friends to pay him their shares in cash. This produced a receipt for the entire cost of the dinner for Paul, and he listed it in his deductions.

It's important to write on the receipt the date, the names of the people "entertained," and the purpose of the "business lunch," because the IRS requires it.

Today it's important to write on the receipt the date, the names of the people "entertained," and the purpose of the "business lunch," because the IRS requires it. Failing to do so can result in the auditor's questioning the purpose of the meal and disallowing the deduction.

It's sometimes possible to produce duplication of receipts to pad the expense column. Jack had to mail several items, and was able to deduct the postage as a business expense. One of the items had to go by Express Mail. At the Post Office, he made out the multi-part Express Mail form and got back his copy, which he would use as a cash receipt. As he was mailing other items too, he asked the clerk for another receipt to cover the entire amount, which the clerk willingly gave him. He paid this by check. Now Jack had a receipt for a different amount, paid by check. Jack had his cake and ate it, too.

Warren, a plumber, often bought at a hardware store where his friend was manager. His friend would give him discounts, but write up a receipt for the full list prices. Warren usually paid in cash. For large purchases, he paid by check. His friend would provide a receipt for the items at list, and Warren would write a check for the discounted price, plus sales tax. The receipts were undated, being simply strips torn off an adding machine, and with the store's stamp at the top. This made it possible for Warren to list his cancelled check as an expense, and also deduct the receipt as a cash paid out, as the amounts differed and there was no date on the receipt to bring suspicion.

For these methods to work, the receipt and the check should show different amounts, which an auditor will take to mean that they cover different purchases. This will help even if they're dated the same day, as many business owners make more than one purchase from the same source on the same day. Having the receipt undated helps even more. Putting on your own dates with a date stamp can be worthwhile, too.

Using cancelled checks as receipts is a conventional and accepted practice.

Using cancelled checks as receipts is a conventional and accepted practice. There are many businesses that don't issue receipts, and this means the cancelled check is often the only record of an expense being paid. It's conventional to "vouch" a cancelled check, to staple it to an invoice or purchase order, but many small businesses don't do this, because there's no legal requirement for it. This omission lends itself very well to doubling up on checks and receipts, because it makes the transactions virtually untraceable. There are several ways to do this, in addition to the examples cited above.

1. The business owner post-dates his checks by a day or two, on the pretext that he's waiting for a deposit to clear. This method provides a receipt and a check with different dates, which makes it hard to prove they're for one and the same expense.

    One possible problem arises if the supplier writes on the receipt both the date and the check number. An examiner, finding this correlation, will easily disallow the extra deduction. If this happens, the taxpayer can simply claim he made a mistake, and forgot to vouch the two. This is an easily acceptable excuse.

2. Another way is to write the check for a different amount. One excuse to tell the supplier is that there's not enough money in the checking account to cover the bill, and to obtain his agreement to partial payment on that day, and the balance a couple of days later. Most suppliers, if they have regular dealings with the customer and have done this in the past, will allow it. We now have two checks, neither of which matches the amount of the receipt, and only a very astute examiner would catch this subtle point and discover the doubling-up.

3. Yet another way is to write a check for more than the receipt, asking for the difference in cash on the pretext of being short of pocket money. This has a twofold effect. First, it obscures the relationship between the receipt and the check, enabling doubling-up on deductions. The second effect is to provide money for personal use, yet have it officially listed as a business expense.

Making the most of receipts takes judgment and discretion. Some may be tempted to forge receipts or to alter genuine ones. This is foolish, because with a little bad luck, it provides documentation of intent to commit fraud. There are exceptions to every rule, though, and let's look at the ones for this.

The first point is to take the overall view. It's possible, by injudicious use of deductions, to claim expenses that are way out of line. A tax examiner auditing a return will immediately notice if claimed business expenses are so great they don't leave the claimant enough to live on.

Any deductions must be approximately within average guidelines, in order not to attract attention.

IRS auditors have guidelines, tables of average deductions and expenses for various categories of businesses. This gives them clues when claimed deductions are questionable, and a lever with which to probe further. Therefore, any deductions must be approximately within average guidelines, in order not to attract attention.

We have to note several characteristics of receipts, because there are some pitfalls for the unwary. First, they must be credible. A receipt from a liquor store can pose problems, if the store name and/or type of business shows on it. It will then be necessary to "backstop" the receipt by claiming "entertainment" deductions, which means that it's essential to show a need for entertaining clients, or at least that it was necessary to give liquor as Christmas presents to some clients. Fortunately, this is common practice in many businesses, and the only point to watch is that the date on the receipt, if there is one, should be shortly before Christmas.

Another important point is the printing on the receipt. Some department stores code their receipts with a key for each department. This is for their internal accounting purposes, not to help the IRS, but a sophisticated IRS examiner can make use of this if he knows the codes, which are not secret and easy to find out with a phone call. Some department stores print the appropriate letter codes right on their price tags, for the cashier's benefit, and an IRS examiner can simply walk in and note the type of merchandise sold under each letter code.

For example, if a business owner buys liquor at such a store, and each department has its own letter code, this can trip him up. If he writes on the receipt, "tools," and the slip has the letter "H" alongside the amount, it will cause him a problem if "H" stands for "liquor." Perhaps the hardware department has the letter "P," and the business owner must be aware of this to make his receipts internally consistent.

Questioned documents examiners have various ways of differentiating inks, such as photographing them through filters, and using ultraviolet and infrared light.

Deep Inside the Underground Economy
How Millions of Americans Are Practicing Free Enterprise in An Unfree Society

44

One dangerous practice is to forge receipts. The risk depends on the method. Some try to alter a receipt, something that can be hard to do. A cash register receipt is almost impossible to alter, because changing the amount will mean inserting another printed number, and this is very difficult. A handwritten receipt is easier to alter, at least to pass a superficial examination. It's possible to change a figure from $50 to $150 by inserting a numeral "1" before the "50," but only if the numbers aren't closely spaced. This does, however, bring up several problems.

The type of writing must be the same. The ink and the type of pen must match, for a start. Under close scrutiny by a "questioned document" examiner, any difference in type of ink can show up, even though they may seem to be the same color. Questioned documents examiners have various ways of differentiating inks, such as photographing them through filters, and using ultraviolet and infrared light.

Actually, few receipts turned in to the IRS ever wind up on the desk of a questioned document examiner, but this is a possibility that the business owner must keep in mind, because there are easier ways of fudging receipts.

Outright forgery is safer, because it does not present any incriminating evidence on its face. Business persons who have dealings with other businesses have many opportunities to pick up copies of invoices from them. It's as easy as taking a few off a pile on a desk. The preferable type of invoice is the one that is not serially numbered, because this makes it harder to disprove. Serially numbered invoices are always correlated with other documents in the company's internal accounting. An invoice for a service call, for example, will lead to a listing on a servicer's route sheet, where he lists all the calls he makes each day. It's usually one component of a multipart form, with several duplicates floating around in the company's files. An invoice for a shipment will correlate with a shipping memo, a purchase or work order, and other documents. A persistent investigation will reveal any such claims that are not backed up in the company's files.

Fortunately for the small business owner, many companies don't have rigorous internal accounting methods, and this precludes the IRS examiner's proving a claim spurious by failing to find a trace. Many receipts are written on cheap pads from the local stationery store, and don't have serial numbers. Many small businesses don't bother to have invoices with

their company names printed. This makes forgery easy.

An IRS examiner will be mainly interested in disallowing deductions, not starting a prosecution.

This is very important as a safeguard against prosecution. An IRS examiner will be mainly interested in disallowing deductions, not starting a prosecution. Failing to find substantiation of a deduction simply means that he disallows the deduction. On the other hand, providing him with a forged document that he can trace and prove false gives him proof that there was a deliberate attempt to defraud the government, and this can lead to serious consequences.

This is a critical point. Failure to list income can be explained as "forgetting," and many examiners will accept this, although they suspect it's an outright lie, because they're more interested in collecting tax money than spending public funds to keep a delinquent taxpayer in prison. It's also possible to explain many bookkeeping irregularities as errors, but an outright forgery is beyond explanation. It's documentary, prima facie evidence that many examiners will not ignore.

Backstopping: a Vital Point

It's possible to forge everything from a birth certificate to a driver's license, complete with color photograph.

The term "backstopping" is one we hardly ever see outside the professional literature of forgery, yet it's vital to understand it and to use the concept, because otherwise we risk serious problems. Various books have dealt with forgery of many types of documents. It's possible to forge everything from a birth certificate to a driver's license, complete with color photograph. However, a totally forged driver's license, no matter how perfect, will not stand up to examination for a very good reason.

If the person carrying it is stopped by a police officer, even for a minor traffic violation, the routine radio check with the state driver's license bureau will disclose that there is no record of that license being issued. If the forgery is an adaptation of a license already issued, with the name and photograph changed, it will be immediately apparent that it was issued in another name.

The point is clear: There must be supporting documents to "backstop" the forgery and they have to be consistent with the forgery in order not to arouse suspicion. This is also relevant to people who try to forge documents to support an effort to evade taxes. Sometimes a lack of backstopping will reveal the forgery during an investigation, even though the forgery itself may be perfect.

An example is an invoice from a nonexistent company. It's easy to have anything printed, including invoices. However, a suspicious Internal Revenue agent who decides to make a phone call will soon find that such an invoice is spurious. It doesn't necessarily take a phone call. A quick check of the Yellow Pages will show no listing for the spurious company, and this will prompt a more intensive investigation.

One device that will reduce the risk is to search through previous editions of the Yellow Pages for companies that have gone out of business. Printing paperwork purporting to be from one of these companies is fairly safe, because it's not at all easy to check out, even for the most suspicious investigator. Verification would require tracing the former executives of the defunct company and trying to obtain a sample of their paperwork, which may have been destroyed. Even then, if the forgery isn't clumsy, it may remain impossible to prove.

However, asking any former owner or employee to remember whether a single invoice was actually issued is beyond reason, especially if the records no longer exist.

Any employee of the defunct company might be able to say that the company letterhead or logo did not look like the forgery, if the forger did not take the elementary precautions of reproducing the genuine article. However, asking any former owner or employee to remember whether a single invoice was actually issued is beyond reason, especially if the records no longer exist.

As we've seen, it's possible to "lift" some invoices from a company while visiting. Often, it's as easy as taking a few off a pile on a desk. Depending on how involved the company's accounting system is, this can be a help or a time-bomb waiting to explode upon the slightest investigation. If the invoices are serially numbered, it will be impossible to produce any-

thing that will stand up to even the most casual investigation. Unless the IRS examiner accepts it at face value or the company no longer exists and the records have been destroyed, tracing the invoice to prove it is a fake will be very easy.

Having an accomplice inside the company will help, but even with this, the built-in controls of the accounting system may make backstopping the invoice difficult or impossible. It's always possible to insert a copy of the invoice and even a supporting purchase order and shipping record, but at the yearly internal audit the discrepancy will show up because the internal auditor will find no record of payment to match with the other paperwork.

One significant exception is a going concern that has recently had its records destroyed by fire. This doesn't happen often enough to make it a serious prospect. Although there are many fires each year in American cities, the coincidence of having one at a company whose paperwork might be useful for supporting tax deductions is not very common, and in any event, it would first be wise to find out if the company normally microfilms its paperwork to guard against such an eventuality.

Getting paperwork to support claimed deductions is not as easy as it might seem, and the opportunities are limited.

We can see, therefore, that getting paperwork to support claimed deductions is not as easy as it might seem, and the opportunities are limited. Certain conditions are absolute disqualifications and merely provide a government prosecutor with documentary evidence of intent to defraud. Nevertheless, there's a lot of paperwork that can be useful:
1. Cash register receipts.
2. Invoices without serial numbers.
3. Restaurant receipts and stubs, especially if they're not numbered and the cashier fails to fill in the amount.
4. Cancelled checks, especially if they duplicate actual payments. These are often very safe to use.
5. Documents issued by a business with a friendly owner who is willing to help actively and falsify his records in a way that will stand up to investigation.

We see that backstopping is not necessary for many pieces of paperwork, because they're not part of a strictly controlled system. However, failure to backstop when it's required can lead to disaster.

Deep Inside the Underground Economy
How Millions of Americans Are Practicing Free Enterprise in An Unfree Society

46

Saving Receipts

The sophisticated business owner keeps any and all receipts he collects, saving them in a shoe-box for convenience, because he knows he may need one or more of them to help him with his deductions. Many will be unsuitable, for various reasons. Some will be coded, showing the department of the store, which will perhaps cause him difficulty in assigning the deduction. Many will have the store or business' name printed, which again can make it difficult to use them for deductions. Supermarkets, for example, don't carry many items that are needed to run a business, which makes this category of receipt questionable.

Not always, though: Dave owned a block of apartments, and did all his shopping at a department store which had a supermarket as well as other departments. He saved all his receipts, because at the time, this department store did not code its receipts, having only the store name and the prices printed on the cash register receipts. This enabled Dave to include food and liquor purchases in his "business expenses," claiming them as paint, hardware, and other supplies he used for maintaining the property. Cleaning supplies Dave bought for personal use also provided receipts that he used as deductions, claiming they were for cleaning apartments.

One serious limitation comes from dated receipts. Each year's tax form allows listing only that year's expenses, and many receipts from previous years become useless.

The "Tax Party" and Other Advanced Techniques

People often are caught in the audit net the IRS sets out. Sometimes it's because of stupidity; other times, it's just the normal course of affairs, as in the case of anyone who is self-employed and in one of the higher income brackets, which tend to attract attention from the IRS.

What can the individual do to protect himself? Let's listen to "Jerry," a self-employed printer who has had a lot of experience with the IRS. Jerry understands the way the world really works, and is realistic. He doesn't try any bizarre antics, either to earn money or to keep it, just common-sense measures that enable him to keep a greater share of his profits than the IRS would like:

I've been audited each year for the last three years. The IRS knows I'm self-employed, which gives me the opportunity to play a few games with them, and they do not like that at all. I know they can only audit me once a year, so I take advantage of that. The IRS man has to show something for his audit, and I let him have something. In return, I get something.

When I get a notice that they want me for an audit, I call all my friends and hold a tax party. They bring all the cash register receipts, invoices, and other paperwork they can, and we have a big party while doing it. We all have our tax parties and help each other out.

When the time comes for me to see the IRS man, I work it one of two ways. I let him question the deductions he wants, and watch while he takes them off my return. Say he takes off five hundred dollars' worth. Then I pull out my envelope and say: "While I was getting my papers together for this meeting, I ran across another five hundred dollars' worth of deductions I'd forgotten to include. Here they are."

This puts me back on the track again. Sometimes, though, I work it differently, because I know the poor guy has to meet his productivity quota, and I don't try to stonewall him. He takes off the amount of deductions he wants, and I write a check to cover the additional taxes. Then I file an amended return, a Form 1040-X, adding the new deductions based on what I collected at the tax party. I send this in, and the IRS sends me a refund.

When I need some invoices to support some deductions, I pull them out of my file of blanks and fill them in, or have a friend fill them in.

Because I'm a printer, I get a chance to obtain a lot of forms and invoices that wouldn't otherwise come my way. I do a lot of jobs for businesses, and I keep a few of each one I print. I also have a crackerjack typesetter who'll fix me up with anything I ask. When I need some invoices to support some deductions, I pull them out of my file of blanks and fill them in, or have a friend fill them in. I have a "paid" stamp, and I stamp them, and that's that.

The reason this works is the IRS people are paper happy. They don't care what it is or where it comes from, as long as it's on a piece of paper. It's a cover-your-ass thing, and it doesn't matter who is being audited. The only thing that counts is that piece of paper. They never check it out.

This is why any sort of receipt works for me. I can have a receipt from a motel and include it as business entertainment. I keep my supermarket receipts — maybe they'll be good for something, someday. Just about anything at all can go, if you use a little imagination with it. It's hard to believe what you can get away with. Any piece of paper will do.

A friend of mine owns a bunch of rental properties. He has to maintain them, and in doing this he gets a lot of receipts from plumbers, electricians, and hardware stores. The IRS doesn't know whether the receipt is for work on his personal house or his rentals. The receipt doesn't give the address of the property. Hell, he even goes and saves the receipt when he buys liquor at the supermarket. The receipt doesn't say "Liquor Department," not where he buys it. He then marks it as "faucet" or something like that, and turns it in.

The guy who put in my pool, he wanted to do it under the table, and so did I. We worked it out. There was no paperwork at all. First, I paid him cash, but also gave him a trade-out. I got him five-hundred dollars worth of printing, letterheads, envelopes, invoices, and such, and he took this as part payment. He gave me a nice discount for cash, and that resulted in my getting the pool half-price.

I got a new air conditioner put in with no money at all changing hands. First, I paid for part of it in printing for the guy. Next, I had another customer who wanted to pay me for a job with a solar unit, which his company makes. I didn't want the unit, but I wondered if the air conditioning man might be interested. He looked at the set-up, and decided that he could sell it to another customer of his, and get paid for the installation, too. He took it, and that's how I got my air conditioner for nothing.[5]

This is a refreshing point of view from a successful business owner who faces the IRS without anxiety, because he knows what works and what doesn't work. Jerry is an above ground business owner who has an underground side. His business gives him the "cover" he needs for his other activities, which include not only the extra deductions we've seen, but also a bit of "skimming."

It helps to be a middleman, and to have lots of contacts. Contacts are the key to the sort of barter deals that Jerry uses, and also the key to cooperative acquisition of paperwork. With the right approach, it's possible to handle the tax problem without fear.

So the small taxpayer is not utterly helpless before the IRS. While big businesses have their sophisticated methods of avoiding paying taxes, the small taxpayer can defend himself too, if he uses his brain and knows how to make the most of his receipts.

The IRS and Selective Enforcement

The IRS tries to present itself as an incorruptible federal agency, applying the law evenly and fairly to all citizens. This isn't quite true. While most of the rank and file of IRS personnel are guilty of nothing worse than being too limited in talent to find work in the private sector, some are corrupt enough to allow themselves to be used for essentially political purposes.

In theory, every citizen is equal under the law, but anyone even slightly acquainted with law enforcement knows that theory and practice are not the same.

The term "selective enforcement" has become popular in recent years. In theory, every citizen is equal under the law, but anyone even slightly acquainted with law enforcement knows that theory and practice are not the same. At the most elementary level, the police will make more of an effort to catch a child killer than a prostitute. This is in keeping with the values of the community, and we can't complain about it. Sometimes police executives will decide to enforce one category of laws more rigorously than the others in response to public pressure or for other reasons. A demand to "clean up" the downtown area of a city, for example, often results in a short-term drive against hookers and transients. A few months later, when the heat's off, everything returns to normal.

Selective enforcement also makes sense in minor offenses such as traffic violations. In cities where the

Deep Inside the Underground Economy
How Millions of Americans Are Practicing Free Enterprise in An Unfree Society

48

purpose of traffic laws is to protect the public, not generate revenue, there is selective enforcement. Police officers will ignore minor offenders, such as those who don't come to a full stop at a stop sign, if there's no traffic coming. Instead, they'll concentrate on the dangerous offenders, the reckless drivers and the drunks, who cause many serious accidents.

On the larger scene, however, "selective enforcement" has become a tool to preserve political power. One flagrant example was during the Nixon administration, when the White House used the FBI, IRS, and CIA to harass those on its "enemies list."[5]

This was the climax of years of imaginative effort by the IRS to get into regular law enforcement. The story of Chicago during the 1920s and 1930s presents a good view of how this came about. The official version claims that during the late 1920s the Chicago police were almost impotent against Al Capone and other mobsters, because the organized bands had very effective methods of protecting themselves. Mobsters corrupted police officers, prosecutors, and even judges to keep out of jail. They had their "bought" legislators who helped pass laws that favored organized crime and resisted measures designed to curb it.

Enter the federal government. We've seen on TV the remarkable and romanticized exploits of Elliot Ness and his "Untouchables," who broke up the Chicago mobs with little help from local police, according to the TV version. However, Al Capone remained free because he used his organization to insulate himself from prosecution for his crimes. Whenever any gangland murder took place, it was always by a Capone subordinate, and the Big Boss himself was always miles away, establishing an alibi.

At the time, Elmer Irey was chief of the intelligence division of the Internal Revenue Service, and he played a major role in sending Capone to Alcatraz. The key was income tax evasion. Big Al simply had not filed tax returns that accurately declared his income, and this left him open to prosecution under federal law. Big Al was convicted and sentenced to prison.

That's the legend, and fairly true as far as it goes. Now let's look at the rest of the story.

Chicago was corrupt long before the gangs of the 1920s. The political machine, with its rigged elections and patronage system, had the city in the palm of its hand. When the Italian, Irish, and other immigrants came on the scene and started moving in, the "establishment" saw this as an encroachment on their power. By this time the original corrupters were liter-

ally and truly the establishment, owning the banks and the large corporations. They didn't have to break the law; they made the law.

However, they'd become soft from easy living, and they couldn't prevent the pushy, aggressive newcomers from starting to build their own empires. The law enforcement officials, whom they thought were in their pockets, soon changed loyalties, siding with those who made bigger payoffs. Moreover, the new arrivals dealt in the sort of consumer goods and services that have always been popular: alcohol and prostitution.

The establishment had connections in Washington that the immigrants lacked and was able to obtain help from the federal government. At the time, federal law enforcement agencies were staffed by bright and ambitious young men. The "young Turks" of the Treasury Department saw a golden opportunity to hone their skills and earn some good public relations by playing the role of "gangbusters," whereas before they'd been the "damned revenooers." Al Capone was the key. Since prosecution of a noted gangster under an obscure statute was a new field, they were able to build up a case before Capone knew what had hit him.

Not to be outdone, J. Edgar Hoover of the almost unknown Federal Bureau of Investigation decided to attain some recognition. He had tried to make a name for himself during the "Palmer Red Raids" of 1919, and thereafter beat the drum to warn people about "subversives." During the prosperous 1920s, however, nobody was interested in the "communist threat," mainly because it almost didn't exist. The United States was prosperous and the American government was stable, which is why the communist and other radical parties had very few members and practically no influence during those years. The FBI languished, almost unknown to the American public.

The gangster era provided an alternate route. Although there were enough federal laws on the books to keep the FBI busy, these were not the sort that attracted headlines. Spectacular shootouts across the American countryside did, however, and this is what J. Edgar Hoover sought.

Carefully choosing his targets, Hoover did not go after organized crime, because it was obvious that if the mobsters were buying off local officials, they could also corrupt FBI agents. Instead, Hoover chose small-time hoodlums, such as John Dillinger and a few others, unconnected with organized crime. By building these people up in the headlines as "public enemies," Hoover gave them formidable stature and persuaded the voters and taxpayers that his agents were facing a monumental task.

This is the basic story of how Hoover, Irey, and their small staffs managed to turn American history around in midstream. Up to that time, there'd been great mistrust of a too powerful national government, and especially a national police force. With clever public relations, these hitherto obscure Washington bureaucrats were able to persuade people to be more receptive to the idea that federal enforcement agencies should have more power and, of course, bigger budgets.

> **With clever public relations, these hitherto obscure Washington bureaucrats were able to persuade people to be more receptive to the idea that federal enforcement agencies should have more power and, of course, bigger budgets.**

Selective enforcement is still with us. Anyone who's had a run-in with the IRS knows this is true. A tax protester, for example, may not infringe the law, but simply exercise his constitutional right of free speech. However, the IRS doesn't see it that way. The IRS has the right to investigate anyone, and this power can fall heavily on the subject of its attention. The IRS can, and does, use its investigative power to punish, without a trial or a chance for defense, anyone whom it wishes.

In certain cases, there's some reason, as in the example of an informer. The "turn in a friend" program is still with the IRS, and anyone can inform on anyone else. The agent to whom he tells his story will, if it seems plausible, fill out a "Form 211" and have the informer sign it, in order to be eligible for a reward.[7] However, not all such "tips" are valid. Some arise out of malice. A spiteful, jealous, or vengeful person can send in an anonymous "tip" and thereby harass his enemy. While at first sight this might seem absurd, the fact is the IRS will investigate if the tip seems plausible. It's merely necessary to sound convincing on the phone to cause trouble for an enemy with the IRS.

"The power to tax is the power to destroy" is such a well-known principle that we needn't discuss it further. What is not as obvious is that the power to investigate is also the power to destroy. Let's look at a hypothetical individual, "Smith," to see what can happen to him if the IRS gets on his case.

Smith receives a summons for an audit. This means he must report to the local IRS office with whatever supporting documents and receipts the examiner requests. Smith realizes he'll lose time and pay from work, and phones to find out if he can arrange an appointment during the evening or on a weekend. He finds out that the IRS keeps normal business hours, and he must report during those hours. How he arranges this, and the consequences to him, are not their problem, but his problem.

When he arrives, the examiner questions him about his return, and asks for documentation of his deductions. Smith finds out that this is not like a criminal prosecution in which the defendant is innocent until proven guilty. Instead, the burden of proof is upon him, and he must defend himself against what seems to be a presumption of guilt.

The examiner decides Smith owes another five hundred dollars. Smith disagrees, and knows enough about his rights to understand that he has the option of an appeal. However, to do this, he has to make an appointment for another session, during business hours of course, and lose another half-day's pay. Five hundred dollars is a large enough amount to make it worth the effort, and he asks for another appointment.

The appeal turns out against him, and the result is that he gets a tax bill for five hundred dollars. The examiner, friendly and sympathetic, tells him afterward that he might have won his appeal if he'd had a tax lawyer or an accountant with him, as a professional would have been better able to present his case.

Smith knows that not being satisfied with the verdict, he has the right to another level of appeal, and that for this he'd better be prepared. He sees an accountant, and finds out that the fee for representation will be one hundred dollars. He'll have to count on losing a full day's pay this time, because the session promises to be lengthy.

Let's leave Smith now to tally the cost to him. Smith earns fifty dollars a day. The accountant's fee is two days' of Smith's pay. He'll have to pay the accountant one hundred dollars, win or lose.

> **Win or lose, the IRS will not reimburse him for time lost from work or the cost of his defense.**

In fact, he's already lost. At least, he's going to have to lose two hundred dollars that he had not foreseen. If he loses the appeal, he'll have lost seven

Deep Inside the Underground Economy
How Millions of Americans Are Practicing Free Enterprise in An Unfree Society

50

hundred dollars. Win or lose, the IRS will not reimburse him for time lost from work or the cost of his defense.

What can we learn from this? This is not a spectacular case. There was no animosity involved, nor a purposeful persecution for Smith's political beliefs. Smith is not a tax protester, nor a gangster — he's just an ordinary citizen who was the target of a routine examination by the IRS.

Let's now look at "Brown," who is having a more serious run-in with the IRS. Brown's tax return is in dispute. He's done absolutely nothing wrong, and is only guilty of sloppy bookkeeping. He failed to save some receipts to substantiate several large deductions. When Brown comes in, losing half a day's pay, the examiner tells him that he's going to disallow some of his deductions, and that Brown will have to pay another thousand dollars. Brown protests. The examiner is firm, explaining in a reasonable manner that's the way it is, and Brown's going to have to pay. Brown, now angry, tells the examiner that he'll fry in hell before he pays anything he doesn't owe, and stomps out of the office.

The next day at the bank, Brown finds out that his savings account of five hundred dollars has been attached by the IRS, and that he can't withdraw any money from it. On payday, his employer tells him he's not getting a paycheck, because the IRS has garnished his pay, and he won't get another cent until the "debt" is paid off. When he gets home, a neighbor tells him a government investigator has been asking about him.

We can stop here. This is enough to show what can happen. We don't have to get into what the IRS can do to a tax protester, or someone's political enemy. The point is that this can happen to anyone.

The FBI has been accused of many abuses[8] but not of persecuting a set number of innocent people each year to fill a quota. The IRS has the power, and uses it, to punish summarily many thousands of its "clients" each year.

Part of the reason is deterrence, or more impolitely, terrorism. Sending a message out to the people that the IRS may, without provocation and without warning, call them in for an audit is a way of telling them the iron fist of repression may descend upon their heads at any time. The IRS feels this "keeps them honest." Not so.

We've seen that the underground economy is huge, and so scattered and pervasive that even the government, with all its computers, millions of tons of paperwork, and armies of agents, cannot get even a close approximation of its size. This suggests that "deterrence" doesn't work.

Further proof is available almost next door. Anyone who has a close and trusted relationship with a small business owner might, if the business owner really trusts him, get an earful of how he "beat the Feds" on last year's return. The situation is much like that which faced Treasury agents during Prohibition. There are so many people doing it that the agents can't even find them all, much less arrest and prosecute them.

What Can You Expect From Your CPA?

Will your CPA (assuming you have one) be very helpful in setting up your underground business? Will he help you devise strategies for evading taxes?

The answer is "No" in most cases. This may seem surprising, but a look at the CPA's situation will help us understand why. We can start by considering the case of Ben, an accountant and tax preparer who got into deep trouble with the IRS a few years ago, and spent time in prison on several charges.[9]

Ben had a busy practice, and was the accountant and tax preparer for many individuals and businesses. He was very sympathetic to his clients' needs and his philosophy was to decide in favor of the client in doubtful instances. He felt the IRS agents could always disallow a deduction if they saw fit, and that it was foolish for a taxpayer to disallow it himself.

Some of Ben's clients falsified information blatantly enough to get caught, and the discrepancies were enough for a criminal prosecution.

His clients were happy with his services, but the IRS wasn't. Ben had given them enough trouble to motivate them to watch any returns prepared by him very carefully, seeking an opportunity to "get" him. This watchfulness paid off. Any tax preparer must use the information that his client provides, and some of Ben's clients falsified information blatantly enough to get caught, and the discrepancies were enough for a criminal prosecution.

The IRS holds the tax preparer equally responsible for the return; this gave them an opening to prosecute Ben personally and he was sentenced to prison. When he got released on parole, he was so angry at the IRS agent who set him up that he tried to hire a contract killer to get his revenge. The "contract killer" Ben dealt with turned out to be an undercover agent and this led to prosecution for attempted murder.

Let's look at each aspect of this dreadful case to understand what happened and why. First, we see that the IRS does not like to lose. Its agents don't like a smart accountant who knows the rules better that they do and helps his clients beat the system. They prefer a compliant accountant who defends his clients' interests, but not too much. The situation is like that of defense attorneys in the old Soviet Union. There, as in the U.S., attorneys were "officers of the court," but in the Soviet Union their role was much more limited than the role of criminal defense attorneys here. Their purpose was mainly to negotiate a settlement between the accused and the court, to persuade the judges that the defendant was momentarily overcome by capitalist greed, or whatever, but now sees the error of his ways, repents, and asks for mercy. Any Soviet attorney who tried to go beyond this and make a serious effort to defend his client American-style, risked being prosecuted himself as a coconspirator.

IRS Reprisals

The IRS takes the same view as the old Soviet courts. An overly zealous accountant who gives them several black eyes will go on their revenge list. Thus, they exert very strong pressure on CPAs to "sing along with Mitch." They consider this to be deterrence, and it works. So don't expect too much from your accountant.[10]

Accountants are especially vulnerable to reprisals for several reasons. They're the concentration points for any effort to fight the IRS. An accountant handles many returns. Each taxpayer handles only one, his own. There are many more taxpayers than there are accountants, and this makes it much harder for the IRS to give each taxpayer the same degree of attention.

Most taxpayers "cook" their returns in one way or another. One estimate of this number runs as high as ninety percent.[11] The IRS undertakes a few prosecutions of these errant taxpayers, and makes sure they get as much publicity as possible. It carefully plays down how tiny this proportion is. Only 2,251 convictions occurred in 2001.[12]

Accountants feel the pressure more. If a citizen is prosecuted, most people in the area don't know him. Accountants, as members of a small and tightly knit occupational group, tend to know each other from meetings of professional associations, and even socially. When bad things happen to an accountant, they all hear about it, and the fear hits home. An accountant who doesn't play along can have some or all of the following happen to him:

1. The IRS will pay special attention to all returns he prepares.
2. If their desire to harass him is strong enough, they'll audit everyone who goes to him. If any ask why they're being audited, it's easy for the examiner to slip in a comment that this accountant is known for fudging, and that anyone who employs him can expect an audit. The language will be subtle, the hint obscure, but the message comes across: "You will be audited if this guy prepares your return!"
3. Auditing each return he prepares will cut into his time, which cuts into his business, since every hour he spends at the IRS office is an hour he can't devote to another client.
4. The IRS will seek to prosecute him, using a faulty return as a lever.
5. In an extreme case, the IRS will send in an undercover agent to set him up. Undercover agents are in more widespread use by the IRS than many people realize. An agent will pose as an ordinary taxpayer and have him prepare a fraudulent return. This opens the way for a prosecution.

Undercover Agents

The undercover agent may be an IRS employee or a "turned" taxpayer caught with a return that leaves him open to prosecution. In such cases, if the IRS needs a fresh face for an undercover job, the delinquent taxpayer is confronted by an agent who says, "Let's make a deal!" The taxpayer, wanting to avoid prison, has little choice. Under IRS instructions, the delinquent goes to the targeted accountant and sets him up for the IRS to catch.

The activity of undercover agents has not come to light so far, except in the case of prosecutions of mobsters. Among accountants, this danger is well known.

Deep Inside the Underground Economy
How Millions of Americans Are Practicing Free Enterprise in An Unfree Society

52

Although instances of IRS agents' tapping telephones, confiscating Social Security checks of old ladies, and other excesses have been documented in congressional hearings, the activity of undercover agents has not come to light so far, except in the case of prosecutions of mobsters. Among accountants, this danger is well known, which is one reason why they're reluctant to go too far with a client. They simply don't know if the client is on the level or an undercover agent seeking to set them up. Even a long-term client may have gotten into trouble and been "turned."

Law enforcement agencies have a tendency to exceed their authority and go far afield on "fishing expeditions." This is why there are constitutional safeguards against unreasonable search and seizure, and why a warrant is required for an arrest. Otherwise, police officers would be searching and arresting people merely on suspicion, or randomly, just to see what would turn up.

Undercover operations, being secret, are outside the reach of the constitution. Theoretically, this shouldn't be, but it's very hard to invoke the protection of the Constitution against unseen danger.

We have no way of knowing the precise extent of IRS undercover operations. Are they directed only against targeted accountants? Is there a program to "spot-check" all accountants regularly? We can't answer that confidently.

This is a heavy burden for the CPA to bear. He knows the IRS is literally looking over his shoulder. This is an inducement to refrain from pursuing his clients' interests too enthusiastically. Yet, some do it. Why?

Some are ideologically motivated, as Ben was, feeling big government is trampling the rights of small citizens. Others, by virtue of their positions, have near immunity to prosecution. These are the full-time employees of large corporations, who can arrange their employers' affairs, secure in the knowledge that they're not being set up by walk-in traffic. Others are independent, but service only a few major accounts. The same applies to them. They know their accounts, do not deal with unknown walk-ins, and this gives them a feeling of security.

The small business owner or wage-slave who goes to a tax service or an accountant with many small clients, can expect only routine processing.

These high-powered, high-priced accountants are simply unavailable to the small taxpayer. The small business owner or wage-slave who goes to a tax service or an accountant with many small clients, can expect only routine processing. Experience shows that they will not go out of their way to suggest tax havens to their clients, even when they're completely legal and above board.

We see from this that the small taxpayer is on his own, and the best strategy for him to follow is to escape notice. The IRS is much more adept at crushing the small delinquents it manages to catch than it is at enforcing the tax laws on the big-buck boys.

Notes

1. Henry Jaffe, "The Gravy Train," *Regardie's Magazine 10*, no. 6 (February 1990), p. 32.
2. Zay N. Smith and Pamela Zekman, *The Mirage,* Random House, NY, 1979. This book has an excellent chapter on skimming.
3. "X," C.P.A., *How to Cheat on Your Taxes,* 1040 Press, 1983. This book contains an excellent section on inventory adjustments.
4. *Ibid.*
5. Information developed from a 1987 conversation with an underground entrepreneur and personal friend of the author.
6. Bill Greene, *Win Your Personal Tax Revolt,* Harbor Publishing, San Francisco, CA, 1981, p. 12.
7. *Ibid.*, p. 343.
8. Fred J. Cook, *The FBI Nobody Knows.* Macmillan, NY, 1964.
9. Ben was the author's accountant, until his difficulties with the law landed him in prison. This account is partly based on publicly available information, partly on an interview with Ben, and partly on reconstruction of what happened.
10. Greene, *Win Your Personal Tax Revolt*, p. 350.
11. "IRS Criminal Investigations Division: Fiscal Years 1999, 2000, and 2001," *United States Department of the Treasury,* Web site, www.ustreas.gov/irs/ci/numbers/docthree.htm, 11 March 2002.
12. *Ibid.*

Chapter Four
The Myth of the Steady Job

Most of us have been programmed to believe that the way to economic security is a steady job with a large company and the benefits of a regular paycheck with many fringe benefits, including retirement plans. We're indoctrinated into this fallacy in school and by our parents, as well as by propaganda in the media.

A steady career with a large company is usually neither rewarding nor secure.

The reality is quite different. While there still are some people who "hire on at 18, retire at 65," they are a tiny minority. A steady career with a large company is usually neither rewarding nor secure.

Anyone who hasn't been asleep during the last twenty years has seen the news of one large, "respectable" company after another either going bankrupt or laying off many employees. The term "downsizing" is now part of our everyday language. We've also seen major companies "exporting" our jobs, building plants in other countries where wages are lower than ours and employee benefits are few or nonexistent. The auto industry, once considered the mainstay of the American economy, is a perfect example of both. Technological obsolescence, foreign competition, and an unhealthy economy can cause a disaster for the employee of a large company.

Some large companies have hired many part-time employees to do the work of a few full-timers because they don't have to provide fringe benefits to part-timers.

When a large company either fails completely or has a massive layoff, the prospects of the laid-off employee are especially bleak, because he'll face intense competition from many other former employees in seeking a new job in that area. When several thou-sands are suddenly out of work, they saturate the market, and the individual will either be out of work for a long time or have to take a job that pays much less. A mass layoff makes it suddenly a "buyer's market" for employers. Prospective employers know that they have many desperate applicants for every opening they offer, and they can be ruthless in setting wages and skimping on benefits. Some large companies have hired many part-time employees to do the work of a few full-timers because they don't have to provide fringe benefits to part-timers.

The security the individual seeks by working for a large company just isn't there. A pension plan seems appealing on paper, but most of them require a certain period on the job before the employee is "vested," that is, entitled to the benefits. If he's laid off before then, he simply gets back what he paid into it, and he's literally out on the street.

Executives of many large companies, especially the ones that have regular layoffs, cynically set the "vesting" period just long enough so that the majority of the employees will be caught in a layoff before they become vested. This enables the company to offer very appealing paper benefits without having to pay off on them for most employees. Many excellent examples of this practice occur in the "defense" industries, where production follows the awarding of government contracts and mass layoffs come at the end of the contracts. We've also seen employers requiring their employees to invest in company stock, which eventually becomes worthless when the company dies. Meanwhile, the company's executives have dumped their own stock before it became worthless.

The few people who manage to hold on to their jobs through the recurrent storms of layoffs find themselves in other binds.

Deep Inside the Underground Economy
How Millions of Americans Are Practicing Free Enterprise in An Unfree Society

54

The few people who manage to hold on to their jobs through the recurrent storms of layoffs find themselves in other binds. Most of us have heard the term "wage slave" and know what it means. An employee who feels trapped, who works for years at an unrewarding job, is a wage slave. He counts the days to retirement, knowing that if he leaves his employment he'll lose his pension. This is a device used by employers who want to keep some of their employees without offering additional pay in proportion to their skill and experience.

In practice, the employee who wants better pay and benefits will usually find it by seeking another job.

The long-term employee is more often victimized than rewarded for his loyalty. Managers, instead of seeing them as exceptionally loyal workers, view them as dull plodders who lack the initiative to seek anything better. Accordingly, they hold back pay increases, feeling that the employee is too powerless or weak-willed to protest in the most effective manner possible: finding another job. In practice, the employee who wants better pay and benefits will usually find it by seeking another job. This is one important reason why there's so much turnover in the job market.

The Search for Security

The key word is "diversification," a term often used in business. A large company tries not to put all its eggs in one basket and seeks to avoid the threats of overwhelming competition and technological obsolescence by entering different areas. Similarly, an employee can find security more quickly and effectively by following the same plan.

The single-paycheck employee, if he loses his job, will be out in the cold very quickly and very suddenly. The person with several sources of income stands to lose only part of it at one time. This is why many people hold more than one job or keep portfolios of stocks and bonds. It's still possible, but extremely unlikely, to be wiped out all at once when there are multiple incomes. Diversification pays off! It's a simple and obvious idea, but one book presents it as a "secret."[1] It's not a secret at all, but a simple principle followed by employers and employees alike.

This is why many people "moonlight," not just for the extra income or to avoid paying taxes. In one important sense, moonlighting above ground, which means paying extra taxes, is still beneficial because it brings extra security. Underground moonlighting means tax-free income. A part-time job, overt or covert, is valuable when the employee's company lays him off without warning. It can hold things together for a while, and can even work into a full-time job if the opportunity and timing are right.

The laid-off employee with a sideline, something unconnected with his regular work, finds that with extra time on his hands, he can expand his business to earn more money, and with persistence and a little luck can even make it his main income.

On the Job

If you're a wage slave, you may be reluctant to give up your steady employment for a try at underground life for several reasons. The uncertainties of making a new start can be daunting, especially if you have a family to support. Another reason is benefits. Underground, you have to provide your own benefits, while they come as part of the compensation package in many jobs. Another good reason is that you're probably comfortable in your present job, or at least not so uncomfortable that you want to make a total break.

Ethics

This often-neglected topic is worth a close look, because people like to feel good about what they're doing, to feel they are moral persons. There is a lot of counterfeit morality, though, which often misleads people into seeking less for themselves than they might if they had more realistic views of the real world of business.

An employer often expects his workers to be loyal to an unrealistic degree, while offering nothing in return.

An excellent example is company loyalty. An employer often expects his workers to be loyal to an unrealistic degree, while offering nothing in return. He expects two weeks notice when an employee quits, but lays off or fires people with no notice at all.

Related to company loyalty is the problem of "conflict of interest." An employer expects that his employees will not work in competition with him. One who runs a plumbing shop, for example, may demand that his employees not moonlight, either for themselves or another company, in competition with him, although he employs several people and tacitly sets them up in competition with each other.

This is a subtle point, and many employees don't realize that they're being set up in competition with each other. When business slows down, for example, the employer will tend to lay off the least productive worker. Pay increases usually go to the employees whom the boss considers most valuable. The employer who awards promotions on the basis of ability forces his employees to compete among themselves for the slot.

As a wage slave, the odds are that you're being cruelly exploited. If you're not exploited now, you soon may be as companies continue to downsize, eliminating employees and piling their workloads on fewer remaining workers. Downsizing is a modern economic version of the ancient Roman Empire practice of "decimation," executing every tenth person. The modern version isn't designed for punishment, but for economic gains: to save on salaries and to provide the survivors with incentive to work harder.

The "Kleenex Employee"

The working drone, treated like a slave, soon realizes that he's a throw-away, a "Kleenex employee," to be discarded the moment he's served his purpose or the moment it's expedient or convenient. If you're a Kleenex employee, it quickly becomes obvious.

You and fellow employees notice that your employer is progressively eliminating high-salaried workers such as yourself and replacing them with entry-level people earning half or a third of what you make. If you face this sort of situation, you know the feeling of being whipsawed: You could be on your way out the door, and even if you're not, you'll be forced to pick up a share of the work of the one who does go. You are one of those provisional survivors that management consultant Dale Dauten characterizes as "Gaunt but not forgotten."[2]

You also have the nagging feeling that you have to work even harder to prove your value to your employer so that you're not the next victim.

You also have the nagging feeling that you have to work even harder to prove your value to your employer so that you're not the next victim. Meanwhile, your fellow Kleenex employees are in the same bind, competing with you for a decreasing number of jobs.

Some not-yet-downsized workers have reported morale at an all-time low, with employees "at each other's throats."[3] The emotional strain puts stress on families, dissolves already weak marriages, and generally leaves everyone involved very unhappy and anxious. Anticipating the next decimation isn't a happy prospect, because you know that either you or one of your fellow expendable employees will be on the street soon. Management/labor relations become very tense.

This sometimes happens because some supervisors get too far into the spirit of treating their subordinates as expendable. They treat them worse than peons, displaying demeaning and abusive attitudes towards them. In extreme cases, corporate brutality has led to workplace violence, with downsized employees returning to wreak vengeance on former supervisors.

Complaining doesn't help. Employers fundamentally don't care except when an over-wrought employee shoots up the workplace. One supervisor's handbook advises: "Salary complaints should be handled the same way as any other employee complaints. Let the grumbler talk... There is a good chance that the employee will 'cool down' in a week."[4]

Employees' rights and employees' privacy are irrelevant. During the last decade, employee privacy rights have been steadily destroyed.

In other words, employees' rights and employees' privacy are irrelevant. During the last decade, employee privacy rights have been steadily destroyed. Workplace urine testing is common, to weed out those who use drugs, including tobacco, even off-duty. Some major companies, such as Lockheed, have announced policies of not hiring smokers at all.[5]

E-mail, used to send messages within and without the workplace, is a happy hunting ground for company snoops. The Electronic Communications Privacy Act of 1986 does not cover workplace eavesdropping.[6] Although your boss may feel that he's got the right to monitor your e-mail or your telephone extension to uncover disloyalty — such as transmitting his company's secrets to a competitor as in the Bor-

Deep Inside the Underground Economy
How Millions of Americans Are Practicing Free Enterprise in An Unfree Society

56

land International case — it's more complex than mere corporate security. To uncover illicit transactions, your boss has to listen in on many, many other communications, including conversations with your spouse or friends.

Arguing with the boss is always a losing effort. Even when the issue strikes at the employee's vital interests, a bitter argument can have severe repercussions later, because an employer's good references are helpful in finding other employment. It's necessary to suffer in silence unless you're willing to suffer the consequences.

Some employers expect their workers to put in extra hours without compensation. This is, bluntly, stealing the employee's time. While the payment of overtime is usually regulated by state labor laws, the worker who is victimized finds it hard to bring a grievance, because he faces the day-to-day problem of putting bread on the table, and is afraid of losing his job. A court victory in several years' time will not feed his family tomorrow.

According to one authority, "There are as many ways to steal from an employer as there are kinds of businesses."

With employee morale down in the cellar, apathy sometimes sets in, with employees no longer caring about their jobs because of the fatalistic realization that they're doomed. Some steal the employer's time by taking excessively long breaks. According to one authority, "There are as many ways to steal from an employer as there are kinds of businesses."[7]

The ethics of acquiring unofficial perks on the job are clear. Common experience shows the low-level employee that everybody's doing it, and that the biggest perk-gatherers are the employers themselves. Another point is that the cruelly overworked and underpaid employee is merely taking what's rightfully his.[8]

One group of underpaid paralegals burdened with heavy workloads worked out a way to supplement their incomes, taking advantage of their employer's laziness. Their law firm specialized in personal injury cases, and a small proportion of their clients became "MIA," Missing In Action. These were plaintiffs who had broken off contact with the law firm because they had died, moved away, or simply lost interest in pursuing litigation. Insurance companies were trying to settle the cases one way or another, but the firm could not do so without authorization from these missing clients. The paralegals were able to forge their clients' signatures, collect the settlements, pay off the doctors and lawyers involved, and divide the remainder among themselves.[9]

A liquor company was about to move from Boston to Louisville, and employees and managers knew that their jobs would evaporate with the move. Not surprisingly, employees began accidentally breaking cases of liquor and consuming the contents. Supervisors also participated. They tallied each month's shrinkage, which they informally called "drinkage," and went on their way. As the closing date approached office equipment and furniture began to disappear. On closing day, shipping department personnel arranged for their own severance bonuses, loading 200 cases of booze on a truck for themselves and other employees.[10]

Others take more drastic action. One sawmill employee telephoned bomb threats to the company on glorious spring afternoons, which forced the evacuation of the plant until police determined that the threat was a hoax.[11]

The Revenge Motive

One employee programmed his company's computer so that if ever his name were missing from the payroll account, the entire memory would erase.

Other employees in key positions have taken steps to ensure that if they become downsizing casualties, the company will be in a world of hurt. For computer technicians, the "logic bomb" is one way. One employee programmed his company's computer so that if ever his name were missing from the payroll account, the entire memory would erase.

Another put a timed logic bomb with a fail-safe feature into the programming. If he didn't punch in a code word every thirty days, the computer would erase both its program and database. The company did terminate this employee, and company officials were horrified to find millions of dollars' worth of data erased.[12]

Many private employers abuse their power by punishing all employees for real, imagined, or potential misbehavior. If one employee steals a piece of equipment, the boss may begin a policy of searching all bags and briefcases at the plant gate. A recent trend is to force all employees to submit to periodic urine testing because a few have used illegal drugs. The contrast with the powers of the police is striking. Police officers cannot routinely search all apartments in a building because one tenant is a drug dealer or has been convicted of receiving stolen property.

Punishment at times becomes even more petty than the minor infractions that provoked it. When one third-shift employee began writing graffiti on the bathroom walls in a department store, management responded by putting locks on all bathroom doors. From then on, employees had to obtain the key from a manager to use the bathroom.[13]

Articles are planted in the media by public-relations departments of companies who claim to provide assistance in finding new employment for their layoffs. For most employees caught in this process, however, the outcome is short and vicious. One article in *USA Today* states it simply: "Layoffs reflect lean, mean times in the corporate world, with an emphasis on mean. Cuts are quick and brutal, with little or no severance and no help in finding a new job."[14]

Downsizing is often sudden and tactless. One sales manager cited by Dale Dauten in his weekly syndicated business column, received a call on his car phone to report to his company's personnel office. He was told that he was being entered into the "Mobility Pool for Decruitment." This is an example of "clownsizing," according to Dauten.[15]

In some companies, the moment of departure is particularly ignominious and humiliating, because company policy is to treat the terminated employee as a suspect. A security guard escorts the new ex-employee from the personnel office as he cleans out his desk, and then escorts him to the parking lot.

Once you've been liquidated as part of a downsizing operation, you may find yourself in the reverse situation: hired as a low-end replacement for highly-paid employees. You may find yourself in the lower half of a two-tiered salary and benefit system, doing the same work as more highly paid old employees in your new company for half the pay and fewer benefits.

Even while still employed, you may become aware of another example of the double standard in ethical behavior. One employee of a New York commercial bank read the booklet on employee banking ethics he'd received when he was hired. Among other points, it prohibited discussing the bank's business, or information about any account, outside the bank and/or using such information for personal profit. He thought it odd, because it was common knowledge that bank and brokerage executives routinely used their "inside information" for personal profit.[16]

X Dollars a Week and All You Can Steal

The naïve employee may see his employer as a mentor and father-figure, but the employee is merely a unit of production to his boss, a totally expendable production-line cipher.

At this point you may be exasperated and feel that your employer is not returning the loyalty you gave him for many years. As we'll see repeatedly, between employer and employee, loyalty is not a two-way street. The naïve employee may see his employer as a mentor and father-figure, but the employee is merely a unit of production to his boss, a totally expendable production-line cipher.

Furthermore, there are increasing signs in the workplace that your boss doesn't trust you. Not only are there guards at the exits, but telephones and computer terminals are monitored, ostensibly to keep track of employee production, but also as pipelines into private correspondence. Some businesses place "Stealth Security and Asset Tracking Tags" on pieces of equipment in your office. These tags are thin, business-card-shaped electronic devices that activate an alarm when they pass through special electronic gates at exits. These are very much like the tags put on items in department stores as countermeasures against shoplifting. Some employers make extensive use of company spies and undercover agents.

This is when you begin to think of creating your own fringe benefits. This is the constructive approach compared with workplace violence, which that is counterproductive because it's so unprofitable. Learning to work the angles as a way of getting back what's rightfully yours is worthwhile because it's profitable. Many employees have done this successfully.

Lina, a typesetter, used the company's equipment to do work for her own client list, sometimes for cash and other times for barter. For example, she has traded typesetting for haircuts for years.[17]

Christian, an executive assistant, worked the angles several ways. He came in early to work to use the office photocopier to copy information that he smuggled out to use as source material for publishing his

Deep Inside the Underground Economy
How Millions of Americans Are Practicing Free Enterprise in An Unfree Society

58

own magazine. He also expropriated miscellaneous office equipment, such as staplers, which he sold at yard sales.[18]

Lucien, an underpaid shipping clerk for a manufacturer of sewing notions, resented both his substandard pay and his loud-mouthed, abusive supervisor. He'd noticed that inventory control was so poor that it was practically nonexistent. During coffee breaks, he'd go out to the parking lot for a smoke, always with a box of folding scissors, tape measures, or sewing machine needles in his pocket. He'd sit in his car smoking, while slipping the purloined goods under the seat. He passed the material to his wife, who sold it to fellow employees at the paper cup factory where she worked.[19]

Some supervisors enjoy bullying their staffs and this leads to high turnover, especially if the job is not a particularly good one.

Some supervisors enjoy bullying their staffs and this leads to high turnover, especially if the job is not a particularly good one. One convenience-store clerk, burdened both by knowing that he was working at a "junk job for chump change" and by a malicious supervisor who kept a chip on her shoulder, learned quickly how to take advantage of this. Knowing that at least one hundred employees had gone through this store in the previous year, he took a lot of merchandise for his own use during the night shift. He timed the shrinkages so that most took place immediately after the supervisor had done her monthly inventory, which increased the number of ex-employees she could suspect. Meanwhile, he was careful to do his work conscientiously and well, leaving the place "spotless" after he'd finished his shift. He stockpiled supplies so successfully that the supervisor never suspected him.[20]

Employees with their eyes on the door take eight times as much in unofficial "fringe benefits" as those planning to remain.

You, too, can profit from your job by supplementing your income at your employer's expense. One good reason is to build a nest egg. The hard fact is that the best time to begin thinking about your retirement is before your boss does. If you do, you'll be following a common survival pattern. According to

one anonymous survey, employees with their eyes on the door take eight times as much in unofficial "fringe benefits" as those planning to remain.[21]

As an insider, you have legitimate access to much more property than a visitor or customer. This makes it easier to steal and reduces the chances of getting caught. For example, a bank robber runs terrible risks for little reward, but the bank vice-president who siphons from customer accounts for years often gets away with it. As an insider, you know how the system works and what targets are most vulnerable and most profitable. This is why employers have known for years that employee thefts are more costly than losses from shoplifters, robbers, and burglars.

Some supervisors share in their employee's take-homes, reasonably viewing them as perks of the job. One hotel chef and his staff regularly took home leftover food at the end of each workday, because this hotel dining room would not, on principle, serve leftover food to guests. The hotel management lost nothing, because otherwise the day's leftover food would have gone into the garbage.[22]

Perks of the Job

Some jobs have built-in perks, or opportunities wide open to exploitation. Some are legal, while others are not. Doctors, for example, can earn thousands of dollars a year under the table through kickbacks. The family practitioner has an agreement with a specialist, who "kicks back" a part of his exorbitant fee for each referral. Cash payments, of course, are tax-free.

Purchasing agents are notorious for collecting kickbacks from vendors. The gratuity can range from a free lunch to a car or boat, depending on the value of the contract awarded. Again, these gratuities never appear on the purchasing agent's tax return.

Police officers are conspicuous examples of those who take advantage of perks. One example is the free meal, or the "police discount" at restaurants. To a restaurant owner, the possibility of a stick-up is an ever-present threat, and having police officers on the premises provides a powerful deterrent to thugs deciding which establishment to rob. Some owners offer free or deeply-discounted meals to police officers to encourage them to take their lunch breaks there. Other merchants offer police officers deep discounts on other goods, from auto parts to clothes and appliances, as a quid pro quo. The merchant receives immunity from parking tickets, and the beat cop doesn't hassle trucks double-parked in front of the store to deliver merchandise.[23]

Creating and Exploiting Perks

There are several ways to increase real, on-the-job income without paying taxes on it. One way is to refuse raises. What? Is this man mad? Refuse a raise when I can't get along with what I'm earning now?

If you get enough of a raise, you will find yourself in a higher tax bracket, which will eat up more of what you earn.

Okay, okay, calm down, and let's look at the problem with raises. If you get enough of a raise, you will find yourself in a higher tax bracket, which will eat up more of what you earn. If you're right on the borderline between two tax brackets, it may leave you with less take-home pay than before. This has happened to enough people to make raises bad risks, unless they're very generous.

Labor unions know this. So do employers. That's why there's so much emphasis on fringe benefits today; they're not taxable. When the time for a raise comes around, try to get another fringe benefit instead. You'll like it, and the boss, who has to pay proportionally on your income to Social Security, will like it, too. There are several fringe benefits that you might consider.

Medical insurance

Many employees don't have medical insurance. If you don't have this as a fringe benefit, you have to do without or provide your own from the money you get after taxes. Oh, yes, it's "deductible," but that does not mean the IRS will refund you the money you spend on it, or on any other medical expense. A deduction is not the same as a tax credit. A tax credit means you take what you're allowed directly off the tax you owe. A deduction means that you take it off your taxable income, and if you're in the thirty percent tax bracket, you only get thirty cents on the dollar. Persuading the boss to buy you medical insurance can save you a lot of money, because it's not taxable at all, and he can deduct it on his tax return just as he does your pay and other business expenses.

Vacations

This doesn't put any more money in your pocket, but it does give you more free time, during which you can work at something else, unless you feel you really need the rest and recuperation. If you get a one week vacation per year now, ask for more, unless there's something else you'd prefer.

Lunch

Many companies have cafeterias where employees can buy their lunch at moderate prices. In effect, these are nonprofit restaurants run by the employers. A benefit you might request is a free lunch instead of a raise. Put it to the boss this way: It costs him at least $20 a week per person to run the cafeteria. If you're up for a $40 a week raise, he can instead provide free lunches and pocket the difference. Everybody benefits.

Company Car

This privilege, usually reserved for executives, might apply to you if you're a trusted blue-collar employee. Ask your boss if, instead of a raise, you can take the truck home each night, bringing it back in the morning.

To persuade him to do this, you have to be reliable, with an excellent record of attendance. He'll need that truck in the morning, and if you don't bring it in, even if you have a legitimate excuse such as illness, he'll be seriously inconvenienced.

This can save you big bucks. Have you considered what your car costs to run per mile? A figure of fifty cents a mile is low. If you drive to work ten miles each way, a reasonable figure, you spend an extra $10 each day to do so. It multiplies out to $50 a week. This means $50 after taxes, which means that you have to earn more than that in gross pay. Suggesting to the boss that letting you have the vehicle will be equal to a (roughly) $70 per week raise will be appealing, especially as he won't have to lay out that much cash. Sweeten the pot by promising to keep it washed.

This last point brings us to a discussion of negotiation. Successful negotiation is the key to coming to an agreement. Many people forget this. We see a number of books dealing with techniques of negotiation on the shelves. Whoever the author might be, and whatever approach, the basic principle is the same: both parties must get something out of the deal.

Deep Inside the Underground Economy
How Millions of Americans Are Practicing Free Enterprise in An Unfree Society

60

One foreman complained, "These people come in here and it's always the same: 'Stick 'em up!'" He was somewhat emotional about it, but his point was clear. He resented his employees' asking him for raises without offering anything in return. The company didn't earn unlimited income, and the front office only gave him a certain budget within which to work.

When you negotiate with your employer, decide beforehand how to present your proposal so he sees immediately that he gets something out of it, too.

When you negotiate with your employer, decide beforehand how to present your proposal so he sees immediately that he gets something out of it, too. Make it a trade, not a one-way demand. Even if he refuses, he'll be more likely to give you a good reason, or even come back with a counterproposal that you might find acceptable.

Employers pay close attention to an employee's attitude. They like one who thinks of the company's welfare as well as his own. They resent those who seek only what they can take from the company. Employers have their blind spots. They often see themselves as very generous and view their employees as ungrateful wretches. This is why you should make it a firm rule to offer your boss something in return when you ask for anything. The message you'll get across to him is that you're looking out for him, too.

Trade-Outs

This is an often-unexplored way of getting extra compensation without giving the IRS a chance at it. What does your company make? Can you use any of it, and would you accept some instead of a raise?

This can work anytime, not just when you feel you're up for a raise. A good example is overtime. Employers hate overtime. Suggest to your employer that he might pay you for overtime in trade. This gives both sides several advantages, the first one being that it keeps the transaction "off the books."

Even if both sides charge each other "full list," with you expecting goods equivalent to what you accrue at time-and-a-half, and he charges you what he charges his customers, not his cost, you both benefit. It'll work especially well for you if he's a manufacturer, distributor, or wholesaler, not a retailer.

If, for example, your employer deals in food, it's obvious that you can use some for yourself and your family. There might be a problem, though, if he deals in hard goods such as binoculars. Although he might be willing to trade you a pair or two in return for some labor, if you ask for more than that it will occur to him that you're selling them to your friends, and have set yourself up in competition with him. He'll find that unacceptable. If he manufactures or deals in controlled substances, such as explosives or certain drugs, a trade-out might not be possible, and could even be illegal.

Employers sometimes ask some of their employees to take on tasks that are out of their regular work. This is a good opportunity to ease into contract labor.

Breaking Away

Some employees use their regular jobs to build their own client bases for above ground or underground work.

The employee who leaves and starts dealing with his former boss's customer, in direct competition with him, will arouse the anger of the employer.

The employee who leaves and starts dealing with his former boss's customer, in direct competition with him, will arouse the anger of the employer. He'll accuse him of "stealing," or "pirating" his accounts. Yet many business owners take over the accounts of others, and may even have started in business by "pirating" the account of someone for whom they once worked.

Jack was a salesman for Irving, an employer whom most people described as "paranoid," or "unstable." Irving had a violent temper and brooding personality, and even his most loyal employees didn't stay for more than three years. Jack decided to start his own company in direct competition with Irving and was extraordinarily successful. Not only did he take with him most of the best accounts, but also Irving's most productive workers. Within a year, Irving had filed for bankruptcy.

Future Prospects

We've already seen that the American economy took a nosedive after September 11, 2001. The bottom line appears to be that, despite optimistic stories planted in the media, it's not getting much better.

Whatever the stock market may do in a short-term rally, employees are still being laid off, and those totally dependent on their paychecks are the most vulnerable because they don't have a fallback. This is why the underground economy is more appealing than ever.

Notes

1. Jay Conrad Levinson, *555 Ways to Earn Money,* Holt, Rinehart, and Winston, NY, 1991.

2. Dale Dauten, "The Corporate Curmudgeon," *Albuquerque Journal*, 24 April 1994, sec. G, p. 4.

3. Mindy Fetterman and Julia Lawler, "Out of Work and Scared: Fears Often Leads to Tears for Hot-Line Callers," *USA Today*, 15 November, 1990, p. 1A.

4. Jack Horn, *Supervisor's Factomatic,* Prentice-Hall, Englewood Cliffs, NJ, 1967, p. 167.

5. "Smokers Need Not Apply," *Albuquerque Journal*, 25 April 1994, p. 2.

6. Miranda Ewell, "Is the Boss Reading Your Mail?," *Albuquerque Journal*, 25 April 1994, Business Outlook section, p. 3.

7. Harry Bacas, "To Stop a Thief," *Nation's Business* (June 1987). p. 16.

8. Stuart Henry, *The Hidden Economy: The Context and Control of Borderline Crime,* Loompanics Unlimited, Port Townsend, WA, 1980, pp. 48-51.

9. Martin Sprouse, ed., *Sabotage in the American Workplace,* Pressure Drop Press, San Francisco, CA, 1992, p. 58.

10. *Ibid.,* pp. 128-29.

11. *Ibid.*, p. 55.

12. Pierre Dubois, *Sabotage in Industry,* Pelican, London, 1976, p. 25.

13. Sprouse, ed., *Sabotage in the American Workplace*, p. 106.

14. Julia Lawler, "The New Unemployed: Stopped in Executive Tracks," *USA Today*, 18 October 1990, p. 1B.

15. Dauten, "Corporate Curmudgeon," *Albuquerque Journal*, 17 April 1994, sec. H, p. 5.

16. Related by an acquaintance of the author.

17. Sprouse, ed., *Sabotage in the American Workplace*, p. 64.

18. *Ibid.*, pp. 60-61.

19. Related to the author by Lucien, who earned enough doing this to take his wife out nightclubbing each weekend.

20. Sprouse, ed., *Sabotage in the American Workplace*, pp. 12-13.

21. David Altaner, "Employee Theft," *Fort Lauderdale Sun-Sentinel*, reprinted in *Albuquerque Journal*, 11 April 1994, Business Outlook section, p. 3.

22. The author's uncle was the chef in this case.

23. Henry, *Hidden Economy*, p. 50.

Chapter Five
Basics of the Underground

Most successful underground workers follow certain basic guidelines so they can augment their incomes with the fewest hassles. The guidelines are simple common sense.

Keep a Low Profile

Do not brag of your success or your methods. Do not display any open defiance of the IRS and don't give them any cause to single you out for special scrutiny. That's it. It's simple but not always easy. Many people engaged in illicit activities make the mistake of indirectly advertising it by leaving trails or leading opulent lifestyles. These are major mistakes because they attract unwanted attention.

Traditional advice for the undergrounder has been to keep no records and to use cash for all transactions. This is not as easy as it used to be.

Traditional advice for the undergrounder has been to keep no records and to use cash for all transactions. This is not as easy as it used to be, in part because of new laws passed supposedly to facilitate the government's "war on drugs." Today, anyone paying for a car with a suitcase full of greenbacks is no longer viewed as an eccentric, but a drug dealer or some other kind of organized crime figure. We'll discuss cash transactions in detail later in this chapter.

Avoiding a paper or electronic trail is one requirement for benefiting from your extra income. Leading a low-profile lifestyle is another. People who forget this can bring big trouble down on themselves, especially if they're engaged in something more serious than guerrilla capitalism. Jerry Whitworth, associate of notorious U.S. Navy spy John Walker, was also a petty officer in the Navy. He spent one weekend with his wife in the most ex-

pensive hotel in town, and was chauffeured around town in a rented Rolls-Royce. This level of spending for a navy petty officer earning $23,000 a year was very indiscreet and risked attracting attention.

This point is especially true if you work for any level of government. If you're a clerk at city hall and run an upholstering business from your garage on weekends, don't become a big spender or you may fall under suspicion of corruption.

If you enjoy having a fine car, do not buy an opulent model. A Chevrolet, Mitsubishi, Saturn, or Honda can give you good service for years without advertising "big spender." If you make a point of parking a Cadillac, Lexus, or Ferrari in your driveway, you're bound to attract attention from your neighbors. You also risk having it stolen.

Likewise for clothing. You might enjoy wearing an Armani suit, but avoid the temptation. If you must, remove the label from inside your jacket, so that when you hang it up at work, there won't be an obvious red flag. Better yet, sew in a "J.C. Penney" label. If anyone asks, you can get away with the story that you happened to find a suit that fit you perfectly in a discount shop. Only a tailor might suspect you're lying.

If your friends and neighbors begin to notice you going to a hundred-dollar spot one or two nights a week, the gossip will begin.

If you want to spend your extra earnings at expensive restaurants or nightclubs, do it away from home. If your friends and neighbors begin to notice you going to a hundred-dollar spot one or two nights a week, the gossip will begin. Be discreet and take the time to drive to the next town.

If you wish to buy costly consumer goods, keep them out of sight. If swimming pools are few in your

Deep Inside the Underground Economy
How Millions of Americans Are Practicing Free Enterprise in An Unfree Society

64

neighborhood, don't be the only one on the block to boast one. If you enjoy a big-screen, projection TV, keep it in the basement recreation room or the bedroom, not in the living room where any casual visitor will see it. Likewise, if you want a super sound system with electrostatic speakers, keep it out of sight and don't play it at top volume.

Other ways of avoiding advertising your special status are merely common sense. Don't have custom license plates on your car to tell the world what an important person you are. If you own a business, don't keep a reserved parking place for your vehicle in the company lot.

A more subtle point is to not have an unlisted number, because it suggests that you have something to hide, or have some sort of special status. Hide in plain sight, like a needle in a needle factory, lost among the millions of Joe Blows who have listed numbers. A listed number suggests that you're not important enough to scrutinize with special attention.

Rat-holing Money

Once you earn underground income, discretion requires keeping it out of sight of the tax collectors. Despite our having been indoctrinated from childhood that a bank is the safest place for savings, the moment you deposit any of it in a bank account, you create a paper trail. Without getting into the technicalities, American bank "privacy" laws merely make it easier for the IRS to snoop into your accounts. Today, the decision is easier to make than it was several years ago, because bank interest rates have plummeted and there's truly little financial incentive to keep your money in a deposit account.

Don't try to be clever and keep your secret gains in a safe deposit box, especially not a box rented from the same bank in which you keep any savings or checking accounts. A safe deposit box is a tip-off to auditors that you have something to safeguard and it excites a burning curiosity. The other danger is that, if the safe deposit box is in your name alone, current law requires the bank to seal the box upon your death until government auditors can examine its contents. Although you may be young and live a healthy lifestyle, if you go up in flames on the freeway, the IRS gets first peek.

The Trouble With Banks

Today most banks ask for not only a Social Security number, but formal I.D. when a new customer opens an account.

A bank is one possible place to put unreported income and many people do it, but the practice is dangerous. Years ago, it was possible to open a bank account under an assumed name. There was no requirement for I.D. and a slush fund could be stashed openly in a savings account, collecting interest for years. Today, with the new law requiring withholding of a portion of the interest earned, most banks ask for not only a Social Security number, but formal I.D. when a new customer opens an account.

The reason some people are able to get away with stashing unreported income in a bank account is that the IRS audits so few returns, and carries out major investigations of even fewer yet. The fact that so many people get away with it can lead to a feeling of complacency, and this can be dangerous for you.

With the proliferation of computers, bank records are increasingly available to the IRS. Now the IRS has access to the information regarding the interest you earned. From this, it can infer your income level, and, more importantly, compare your figures with the averages. Anyone showing above-average bank balances will run the risk of special attention, just as anyone who exceeds the norms for certain deductions is singled out.

Recognizing that banks generally require I.D. of their new customers, some underground workers choose to use false I.D. Banks require not only a Social Security number, but a driver's license, passport, or other form of official I.D., preferably with a photograph of the owner. For the person who has to live completely underground, false I.D. is part of his lifestyle. For the person who is moonlighting but otherwise above ground, false I.D. may be too much trouble.[1] While the underground worker may accept the fact that a certain portion of his interest income will be withheld, the paper trail that a bank account leaves in regard to his other income may be unacceptable.

There are other ways to use banks as hiding places for undeclared income. The most obvious is the safe deposit box. This is a trap, however, and many people fall into it. The law permits the fee for rental of a safe deposit box to be deducted, and many do. The purpose behind this piddling allowance is obvious. Anyone who claims such a deduction tells the IRS that he has a safe deposit box,[2] and this is one of the first things the IRS looks for in an investigation. Consequently, sophisticated underground workers avoid having safe deposit boxes in banks, although some do rent them in assumed names, using false I.D.

Some banks have noninterest-bearing accounts available to their depositors. The most common form is a checking account, although many checking accounts today do pay slight interest. If there is no interest paid, the bank does not send a Form 1099 to the IRS, but it still requires I.D. The reason for this is "recourse," a term which means the bank must know whom to contact to make good on a check. The problem of bad checks is serious, and banks want to know with whom they are dealing.

A noninterest-bearing account is slightly less dangerous for you than one that pays interest, in that the bank does not automatically advertise the account's existence to the IRS.

A noninterest-bearing account is slightly less dangerous for you than one that pays interest, in that the bank does not automatically advertise the account's existence to the IRS, but in an investigation, it may be forced to reveal it.

Another problem with banks is that the government requires them to keep microfilm records of every check you write and every check you deposit. A little thought will reveal just how easily a person's financial transactions for any period can be reconstructed with this information. It is evident that it's best to use banks as little as possible for your unreported dealings.

A better choice is a private vault, operated by a company whose only business is renting private safe deposit boxes and who therefore remains out of the purview of banking laws. The problem is that the IRS knows this too. As we've already noted, any employee of a company that rents you a private deposit box will be welcome if he walks into the IRS office with a list of his employer's clients.

The best choice is one that does not produce any documentation at all, at least not in this country. The exact method you use will depend on your income level. Let's look at several profiles so that you can choose the best one for your situation.

Profile A: You earn about $1,000 extra cash a year from odd jobs, and you find yourself spending the money taking your wife to an occasional expensive dinner. With this income level and spending pattern, there's no need to take any special precautions, except don't leave a paper trail or blab about how smart you are to fool the government.

Profile B: Your off-the-books income is about equal to your above ground salary, and while there's no paper trail to endanger it, you worry about where to keep those stacks of hundred-dollar bills. You plan to spend a modest amount and save the bulk of it to supplement your Social Security upon retirement. In this situation, it's worth burying money in a waterproof container in your back yard or building a hiding place in your home.[3]

Do not take the simple-minded solution of simply burying all of your money until you need it.

This is enough income to worry about, but not enough to justify extreme measures. Do not take the simple-minded solution of simply burying all of your money until you need it. If ever the government decides to revise its currency, requiring everyone to turn in whatever cash he has for new bills, you'll be stuck.

Do not invest in stocks and bonds, because these, too, leave a paper trail. Instead, diversify and buy collectibles with part of your underground income. Silver coins are very worthwhile in this respect, because they have value for their precious metal content, but in an extreme situation you can spend them like the currency they are. Silver ingots are far less worthwhile because you leave a paper trail upon purchase. Stamps are worth considering, but keep in mind that rare stamps are not redeemable except with stamp dealers or collectors.

Profile C: You earn over $100,000 annually in hidden income, enough to justify going a few extra miles to safeguard your earnings by stashing some of it offshore. There are several ways to do this, and you can use more than one method in conjunction.

The Cayman Islands, Switzerland, and Liechtenstein are noted for welcoming discreet bank accounts, and they make safe places to store part of your copious hidden income. Getting there normally leaves a paper trail a mile wide, but there are ways to get around this.

Deep Inside the Underground Economy
How Millions of Americans Are Practicing Free Enterprise in An Unfree Society

66

Keep in mind that at the moment, travel into Mexico requires no passport, and there's no record kept of your crossing the border. Establish a credit or debit card account in a Mexican bank, using a mail drop in Mexico as an address. When you establish your Mexican persona, make sure to fudge your birth date and Social Security numbers, if required, by a couple of digits. This will break the electronic trail if the Mexican bank uses a system also used by American banks, such as VISA. Your Mexican account allows you to pay for airline fares and other travel expenses without leaving an obvious trace within the United States. However, this may change in the near future, because of the extra security measures prompted by the September 11 terrorist attacks.

You need a legitimate passport to enter another country, even if your flight begins in Mexico. Obtain a passport under your real name from the U.S. State Department. Don't try to forge one, since customs agents have computer terminals with which they check the validity of passports at the port of entry. In any case, it isn't necessary, because you don't need deep cover.

When applying for a passport, you have to fill in a line for your destination. A simple way to fill in this line is to list a Latin American country for which you need a passport to visit. Keep in mind that the cost of visiting a Latin American country is far less than visiting Europe. Go overseas to establish your secret bank accounts in the name of your Mexican identity. Depart from Mexico and return to Mexico, thereby keeping your travels out of the U.S. Customs computer system. You don't want your passport, ostensibly obtained for visiting Argentina, to produce a trail leading to Switzerland. In any event, you might have trouble explaining to an IRS agent how you were able to afford a $10,000 trip while earning only $30,000 a year.

Once you have accounts set up, and a method for funneling extra cash into them without creating a paper trail, your next problem is destroying the evidence, which exists in the pages of your passport in the form of entry and exit stamps. There are several ways of doing this.

One is simply to burn your passport and allow it to expire if you don't plan to make any more overseas trips. This is the simplest and safest, but it restricts your movements.

Another method is to drop into the U.S. Embassy in Mexico and report your passport lost or stolen. You'll have to fill out an affidavit to secure a new passport. The advantage of this method is that you can still get home in case there's any hang-up about your report. The disadvantage is that it will leave a trail that you were in Mexico, and you might not want this documented.

If you have small children or a pet dog, simply rip out the pages with visas and bring the remains of your passport to the local passport office, explaining that your toddler or pooch destroyed several pages in your passport. Turn in the mutilated one and you will be issued a fresh one in a few weeks.

Starting Up

Planning is important, because if you do not plan, you'll be making decisions by default, and these might not be the best.

There are a few basic decisions you have to make before you take in your first payment. Planning is important, because if you do not plan, you'll be making decisions by default, and these might not be the best. It's a serious mistake to let the tide carry you along, possibly in a direction you don't want to go.

The first choice is whether to work out of your home or to have an office or shop. Most likely, you can work out of your home, but if your sideline involves manufacturing or heavy equipment, you may have to buy or rent premises.

Working out of your home is more low-profile, with one exception. If your underground business involves a lot of walk-in traffic, the number of people visiting you is sure to attract attention and curiosity from neighbors. In the worst case, your neighbors might think you are a drug dealer. In such a case, a rented office or shop is safer.

Throughout this book, we'll present case studies of how some people have established underground operations following the principles laid out here. We'll study in detail how they began, how they sought out clients, and how they kept their earnings secret from the tax collectors. Let's begin by looking at a couple of brief examples of how some guerrilla capitalists set up their operations, and the reasons why.

Ann and her husband have two daughters. She has both an electric typewriter and a word processor in her home, and operates a typing service during the time she has left over from being a housewife and mother. The equipment is inconspicuous, quiet, uses little power, and it's never occurred to her to apply for a business license or check with the city's zoning board. Her income supplements what her husband earns as a deputy sheriff.

Frank has a comfortable arrangement with his boss, the owner of a print shop. His boss allows him to use his equipment after hours for his own work. His boss does not consider Frank a competitor, since he runs only small jobs on the side, and if one of his customers has a big job for him, he'll refer him to his boss. This amicable arrangement saves Frank the trouble and expense of renting his own premises and buying his own equipment. It's also the perfect cover, because Frank operates under the surface of an existing business, using the equipment only after hours.

The Outside Shop

Commercial premises make you much more visible, and certain cities pursue an active and aggressive policy of surveillance of existing businesses.

Setting up an office or shop outside the home is more complicated because it puts you above ground. Commercial premises make you much more visible, and certain cities pursue an active and aggressive policy of surveillance of existing businesses to make sure the city gets its cut in taxes and license fees. Clerks compare lists of licensees against the Yellow Pages to verify that all businesses have the proper licenses and pay taxes. In some cases, city inspectors prowl business parks, office buildings, and other commercial areas to compare the companies physically present against lists of license holders. Others have even more aggressive policies. At least one conducts physical inspections of all businesses to levy a tax on all equipment.

Tax and licensing agencies often have cooperative arrangements, exchanging lists of "clients" and other information. The thoroughness of this practice varies widely, since there is a lot of information to process, but it's unwise to expect them to overlook you. For example, if you have a sales tax license, you're required to file periodic returns showing your gross receipts and send in the sales tax you collect. The city or state agency will be happy to share this information with the IRS, which means that your federal tax return must be consistent with your local paperwork.

If you need a special license from the city or state due to the nature of your business, your name will be on a list circulated to other city and state licensing agencies, where clerks will check to ensure that you're also on their lists. There are some subtleties to this that can work against you if you're not careful. If you use a truck for your business, you have to buy license plates from the motor vehicle bureau. Unless it's a small pick-up, a truck usually has commercial plates, and your name is on a list that is available to other state agencies. Likewise motor vehicle insurance. One of the questions you have to answer when insuring a motor vehicle is whether the main use will be for personal errands or business. If you can run your business using a sedan or pick-up truck, you can get away with applying for personal insurance. However, if your vehicle has commercial plates, you can't.

If you can run your business using a sedan or pick-up truck, you can get away with applying for personal insurance.

This leads you to another decision, whether to operate your business totally underground or to skim from an above ground business. In many cases, you can't operate totally underground, and instead must run your sideline in tandem with your regular job or business, perhaps skimming off the top, or conceal your irregular income while declaring and paying taxes on the rest. If you decide to skim, you'll have to be careful in the way you do it. If you own a bar, liquor store, or other retail business, some of your business will be in cash, and skimming a small percentage will be easy. However, you'll have to watch your expenses and stock purchases to keep them consistent with the income you declare.[4]

If you moonlight as a plumber, some customers will pay you in cash while others will give you checks. This makes the decision easy; you skim the cash payments. The fact that you have an above ground occupation will help cover the skimming, although an IRS auditor will always have his suspicions. You'll have a declared income to explain how you're earning a living. However, in this case, it's important to avoid setting a pattern. Declare some of the cash income, since listing only accounts paid by check would set a very visible pattern.

One recent myth is that of the "cashless society." This view, laid out in many magazine articles in recent decades, proposes that with the widespread use of computers and credit cards, nobody will use cash in the near future. The paycheck will go into the em-

Deep Inside the Underground Economy
How Millions of Americans Are Practicing Free Enterprise in An Unfree Society

68

ployee's account, and he will pay for all his purchases with an electronic card, with the amount instantly deducted from his account by means of a computer linkage.

This system has many benefits, according to the mythmakers: There will be no need for cash, making robbery obsolete. The computer will make bad checks impossible, because it will provide an instant survey of the payer's account to determine whether or not there are enough funds to cover the purchase. The individual's bookkeeping will be done for him by computer and this will make the filling out of tax forms easy.

There are several things wrong with this idea.

1. It will make government surveillance of any person's finances easy, a necessary prerequisite for total taxation. With computerized records, the IRS will be able to trace nearly every cent earned and every cent spent by nearly everyone in the country.

2. Such a plan, if implemented, would knock the bottom out of a lot of the underground economy, which is probably the main idea behind such an expensive and far-reaching step.

3. It simply doesn't work. The people aren't buying it. Proof of this is given in a study by Professor Peter Gutman, in the *Financial Analysts Journal*, Nov./Dec. 1977, in which he states that there is a large amount of cash circulating, despite the growth of the checking and credit card industries. In a statement to Congress,[5] Gutman said that in 1976, there were $480 in cash circulating for each person in the United States. He added that we are not becoming a "cashless society," but using more cash.

The IRS confirms this, stating that on April 1, 1979, there were $100 billion dollars in general circulation.[6] This trend is continuing. A recent U.S. Treasury report showed that on September 30, 2001, there were $612 billion dollars in circulation.[7] It is obvious that not only is there a huge underground economy in this country, but that, logically, the people involved deal mainly in cash.

A check must be redeemed, and leaves a record in at least two places: the payer's checking account and the records of the person who cashes or deposits the check.

The reasons are obvious. Cash is basically untraceable. A check must be redeemed, and leaves a record in at least two places: the payer's checking account and the records of the person who cashes or deposits the check. Bank records, while supposedly private, can easily be subpoenaed by the IRS. They provide documentation to an IRS investigator who is trying to establish unreported income.

Cash is the way to go for the guerrilla capitalist. The IRS proves this in their report dealing with unreported income,[8] where they show that those who gain income through salaries involving W-2 forms are able to understate their incomes far less often than those who are self-employed and deal in cash. The lesson is clear. The guerrilla capitalist can "forget" to report income in cash, but should include on his tax return income which he receives in checks, because they are traceable if the IRS starts digging.

If you do get paid by check, there are a couple of things you can do to minimize traces in your own bank records. Rather than depositing the check in your own bank account, endorse the check to someone else and use it to pay a bill of your own. For example, Tom, the underground trucker, gets a check from a contractor for cleaning up a building site. Instead of depositing the check, Tom endorses it over to a garage and uses it to buy gas and oil for his truck and van.

Another way to bury a check is take it to the bank where it was drawn and cash it right there. This keeps it out of your own bank records.

You might find that very few customers pay in cash, and one way to encourage this is to offer a discount for cash, but only to regular customers you know.

Now let's look again at the decision regarding whether to deal in cash, checks, or both. The best way is to deal in both, for obvious reasons. However, you might find that very few customers pay in cash, and one way to encourage this is to offer a discount for cash, but only to regular customers you know. The reason is that your next customer might be an IRS agent, for they live in the same communities the rest of us inhabit. Waving a red flag to a dedicated IRS type could lead to problems.

If your business is your sole source of income, you obviously have to show you make a living at it, and you can't declare a profit that is too small to support your living standard. This limits your potential, but brings us right back to one of the fundamental rules: Don't get greedy. Greed can lead you into a trap of your own making. We'll cover this more thoroughly later in the chapter.

Tim, a repairman, has a few accounts on the side. His total income from this comes to less than two thousand dollars a year, almost all of it in checks, which he deposits in his bank account. He knows he leads a modest lifestyle, and in any event he doesn't earn enough side income to allow him to spend conspicuously. He knows that although the checks leave a paper trail that would be visible to a full-scale investigation, he's probably below the IRS's radar screen. His income, lifestyle, and tax return are very ordinary, and not apt to arouse the curiosity of an IRS auditor. This is why he's gotten away with this for years. As we'll see throughout this book, others also leave paper trails and get away with it because they're not conspicuous enough to attract unwanted attention.

Advertising is another topic for a decision. An above ground business often must advertise, if only to keep up with the competition. As an undergrounder, you're not locked into a certain volume of business. The exception is if your business carries enough overhead to require that you do enough business to remain solvent. In that case, you'll have to be partly above ground, since overhead usually comprises rent on premises, license fees, and other expenses not directly tied in with your volume.

The successful undergrounder usually depends on word-of-mouth advertising.

This is why the successful undergrounder usually depends on word-of-mouth advertising. This happens in several ways. One customer can recommend you to another. You can, if you hold a regular job, troll for customers yourself.

This ties in with the "hidden job market," a pool of jobs that are never advertised or listed with the state employment service. Estimates vary, but many people agree that many employers fill jobs by means of the hidden job market, which is mainly word-of-mouth. There are several reasons for using the hidden job market.

1. Advertising an opening or listing it with the state employment service, brings a lot of unqualified applicants to an employer's door. This is a waste of time. To avoid legal hassles, it becomes necessary to document why each unqualified mope did not meet that company's standards, and this ties up the employer's time.

2. Using the hidden job market enables an employer to zero in quickly on the person he wants. Many employers know their competitors and their competitors' employees. At times, they wish they had a particular person in their employ. Word-of-mouth allows an employer to make a quiet job offer, without formalities, and often outside normal channels or practices.

3. An employer might want to hire a competitor's employee only part-time to help out during a busy period. It's much easier to do this informally than to advertise for a part-time employee.

Ben, a former butcher now working as a meat salesman, mentions to some of his accounts that he's available for a few hours a week off the books to help them through peak periods. As a salesman, his hours are flexible, and he finds the time to work for cash during normal business hours.

Another way to advertise is to "cold canvass," calling on potential customers to let them know that you're available. This usually means many unproductive hours, as many prospects will turn you down, but on the other hand, you're only looking for a few accounts.

At times, the regular job and the guerrilla business are totally unrelated, yet they dovetail. Nicholas, a machinist, operates a small retail coffee and cake concession on his company's premises, with the full approval of management. He earns extra income by selling coffee and rolls to his fellow employees during breaks. He deals only in cash, charges no sales tax, and rents no shop or office. He gives the managers free coffee and pastries in return for being allowed to operate, and of course, does not declare his considerable extra income.

By planning your business, you'll be able to run it smoothly and avoid awkward and last minute decisions. You'll also be better able to avoid the risk and embarrassment of getting caught.

Some Underground Economy People

Bill operates an above ground janitorial service handling commercial customers. Some of his clients — bachelors, widowers, and divorced men — asked him if he could take on private accounts. Bill decided to do these clients after hours and pocket the income without running it through his books. Bill is running his underground business under the cover of his

Deep Inside the Underground Economy
How Millions of Americans Are Practicing Free Enterprise in An Unfree Society

70

above ground business. Expenses for supplies for his private clients are buried in with his commercial accounts, while none of the income gets reported. Bill has been doing this for years now.

When Harry was first making a business out of his fishing hobby, he found that to sell to a seafood store required a license and no store owner would buy from him without it.

Harry, a retired lumber executive, lives in a seacoast town, has a small boat and loves to fish. He goes out each morning and catches more fish than he or his wife can eat. Harry makes extra cash income by selling his fish to local restaurants. When Harry was first making a business out of his fishing hobby, he found that to sell to a seafood store required a license and no store owner would buy from him without it. When he canvassed a few restaurants, he found that a license to sell was required here, also, but he discovered two restaurant owners who were willing to buy from him for cash, since they were tired of being held up by local licensed fishermen. The deals are safe for Harry. Restaurant owners pay him under the table in cash and ignore his lack of a license because they get a good deal from him. Harry sells only fresh fish, caught that morning. His prices are low because he has no overhead. Harry has been doing this for three years now, ever since he retired. He has never reported any of this income. Sometimes he barters his fish for a nice meal for him and his wife.

Amanda, a former beautician, works her old trade underground. Now married and unable to hold a full-time job because of the demands of home and children, she supplements her husband's income by doing her friends' and neighbors' hair in her home. She uses her old equipment, which was paid for long ago, so she needed no capital investment to get her little sideline started. The cash she collects makes a useful, tax-free addition to the family income. She also saves the family money by cutting her husband and kids' hair. Amanda doesn't report any of her income, which is mostly in cash. Sometimes she barters for babysitting, home-grown garden vegetables, etc. Her friends and neighbors appreciate the low prices Amanda charges, much lower than a licensed establishment could charge, and this also provides free word-of-mouth advertisement.

The owner was glad to get some honest, hard-working, part-time help without the taxes and record-keeping requirements of on-the-books employees.

Joey is a college student who moonlights off the books as a bartender at a local nightclub. Joey's dad used to own a bar, so Joey knows all the angles of his underground occupation. Joey works the "Happy Hour" five afternoons a week. How he got the job was simple. He scouted likely bars and approached the owners with his proposition: He would work for minimum wage, in cash, with no taxes taken out. Of the four bars he scouted, two offered him jobs, and he accepted one. The owner was glad to get some honest, hard-working, part-time help without the taxes and record-keeping requirements of on-the-books employees. And Joey was glad to get a job he could do well, and the hours he wanted to work. Joey is such a good bartender that his tips usually exceed his pay. He does not plan to ever report any of this income. He knows other bartenders who have similar arrangements — in fact, he got the idea from his dad, who often had part-time help off the books.

Lorraine is a widow with a ten-year-old boy and lives in a two-story, three-bedroom house. Her husband left her in debt when he died and she desperately needs to supplement her meager income as a sales clerk. So she rents out her spare bedroom to a college student. Feeling that she simply cannot afford to pay income tax on this extra money, she does not declare it. Her house has a garage, and since Lorraine does not own a car, she rents the garage also. Both her renters pay her in cash, and she leaves this income off her tax return.

Pedro and Juan drive a sanitation truck for the city. From their truck, they run an underground salvage business. The valuable items people throw out with their trash amaze them because they regularly pick out appliances they can recondition, furniture that needs only minor repairs, and lots and lots of books, records, and clothes, as well as other salvageable items. Twice a day, they stop by one or the other of their garages, depending on where that day's route has taken them, and unload the recyclable stuff they have picked up. The city doesn't expect any of its employees to move very fast, so the small amount of extra time their sideline takes them is easily absorbed in their breaks. On weekends, Pedro and Juan dispose of their repaired "trash" at second-hand stores and garage sales. They have never reported any of this income. They know plenty of other city employees doing similar things.

His brother-in-law is a bank officer and helps Don to launder the checks he receives, enabling Don to totally avoid taxes on his profitable sideline.

Don trains dogs as a sideline to his regular job. As a dog handler in the Army, he received a solid background in training dogs for obedience and guard work. Don raises guard dogs in his back yard and trains them himself. He can sell a trained guard or attack dog for about three thousand dollars. Don usually has two or three dogs going at once and sells about ten dogs a year. His brother-in-law is a bank officer and helps Don to launder the checks he receives, enabling Don to totally avoid taxes on his profitable sideline.

Janice is a housewife and the mother of two preschool children. During the day, she runs a profitable business caring for the young children of working couples. She currently has ten preschool children in her charge, and the income from this adds a useful sum to her husband's salary. Most of her clients pay cash, and the few checks she gets she endorses over to the local supermarket, where she is well known. She advertises mainly by word-of-mouth, and sometimes with notices on local bulletin boards. Most of her clients are neighbors who know her to be a reliable person who cares about children. They see her not as a businesswoman, but as simply a person trying to earn a few extra dollars by helping out her friends. None of her income has ever appeared on a tax return.

Ralph is an apartment house owner. This is too above ground an occupation to not report the income, so Ralph has found other ways to avoid paying taxes. Ralph is his own manager and repairman for his small apartment complex, and when he does his taxes, he includes plenty of cash receipts for groceries and liquor and other personal expenses, marking them "Supplies" or "Cleaning Materials" or "Repairs." His favorite shopping place is a department store that sells hardware, building supplies, groceries, and liquor under one roof, and whose cash registers produce receipts that are not itemized. Ralph manages to "pad" his "deductions" by a comfortable amount each year, saving him considerably on his taxes. He knows other landlords who do the same thing.

Red is a welder who cuts hair on the side. He learned barbering in the Air Force. His haircuts are short and simple. They are also cheap. He works at home in the evenings and on weekends, sometimes in the kitchen, at other times in the back yard. His customers are mostly buddies from work and neighbors who don't want to pay the ridiculous prices charged by licensed barber shops. Red will accept nearly anything in payment: cash, boxes of .38 caliber ammunition, home-canned food, and even a six-pack of beer, which, as often as not, he shares with his client after the haircut is over. Sometimes the beer drinking starts during the haircut, and a good time is had by all — tax free, of course.

Most of his customers pay him in cash, but when Sam gets a check, he simply takes it to the bank it is drawn on and cashes it there.

Sam is a retired newspaper publisher with an artistic bent. His hobby was calligraphy (fancy hand lettering) and upon retirement, Sam began supplementing his pension and Social Security by doing calligraphy on the side for cash. He gets his business by word-of-mouth, and sometimes puts up cards on bulletin boards in supermarkets, laundromats, etc. Most of his customers pay him in cash, but when Sam gets a check, he simply takes it to the bank it is drawn on and cashes it there. All his customers are local, so this is easy to do. Sam has never reported any of his calligraphy income.

Lisa is an underground childbirth instructor. There is a trend away from hospital-centered birth in this country because of the expense and other drawbacks involved. Women are becoming increasingly aware that pregnancy is not an illness and are rebelling against the abuses that occur in obstetrics. Obstetricians often induce labor with drugs to conform to their schedules, not the mother or the baby's. They also use an excessive amount of drugs, which can have serious effects on both babies and mothers.

After giving birth to her first child in a hospital Lisa decided there had to be a better way. She studied and learned and her next two children, a boy and a girl, were born at home. Both were born with so little difficulty that she decided to teach others about this alternative to the medical establishment. This is different from being a midwife, who actually delivers babies. Lisa advertises by word-of-mouth, and with notices on bulletin boards. She uses lectures, video-

Deep Inside the Underground Economy
How Millions of Americans Are Practicing Free Enterprise in An Unfree Society

72

tapes, and printed material in her lessons. She collects in cash or sometimes in barter. Her husband has a full-time above ground job, so Lisa does not report her underground income. She has met other childbirth instructors who are doing the same thing.

Frank works in a gun store. He also teaches shooting on the side. Although not a top competitive shooter, he's more than good enough to teach people the basics of armed defense, which has little to do with competitive shooting, anyway. He seeks his prospects among his customers and convinces novices who buy firearms for home defense that owning the weapons is only half the story. He and a partner take small, informal groups out to a deserted area each weekend and give them a basic course in how to handle and fire their weapons. Payment is usually in cash, and the few checks they receive they "launder," either cashing them at the banks they were drawn on or endorsing them to others to pay off bills.

Ellen decided to earn extra money by taking in washing, saving her customers the trouble of taking their wash to the coin-operated laundry and having to wait for it.

Ellen lives in one of the "old neighborhoods" in an Eastern city. Most of the people in her neighborhood live in apartments, and are "business couples," with both husband and wife working. Ellen decided to earn extra money by taking in washing, saving her customers the trouble of taking their wash to the coin-operated laundry and having to wait for it, then fold their laundry and repack it. She inquired door-to-door, and the response was enough to get her started. She then put up a card describing her services in the local market, and even on the bulletin board of the coin-operated laundry on the corner! Since Ellen lives in a house, with a washer and dryer in the basement, she finds it easy and profitable to work her business in with the rest of her housework. On particularly busy days, she employs her oldest boy to deliver to and pick up from her customers. She offers same-day service at no extra charge. If the customer delivers his or her laundry to her before eight in the morning, on the way to work, it's ready for pickup at five the same day. Ellen usually gets paid in cash, but she passes the occasional checks at the local market. The owner has known her for years and accepts her third-party checks without hassle or questions. This is a largely immigrant neighborhood and many of the

residents distrust and fear the authorities, which means that she has no reason to fear being denounced to the IRS.

In reality, the main emphasis in executive protection is avoidance, not gun battles, and Perry arranges for his clients' schedules and movements so as to minimize the risk of encountering a threat.

Perry, a retired U.S. Secret Service agent, has a generous government pension and earns money on the side by providing "executive protection," the current term for bodyguarding, to select clients. Most of his assignments are short-term, guarding people who have received threats until their fears subside. He gets his business both by word-of-mouth and through referrals from a friend, another retired Secret Service agent who runs a private guard agency. When his friend gets a request that his "rent-a-cops" can't handle, he calls in Perry. As most of the clients pay by check, Perry "launders" these through his friend and they split the profits. Perry gets many fringe benefits through these contacts. Many of his clients travel extensively, taking Perry with them. Perry knows that in most cases the threats are only imaginary and feels safe visiting foreign places with the clients paying the fare. Since the executive protection agent must stay close to the protectee, Perry gets the benefits of staying in expensive hotels and eating at the same expensive restaurants his clients do. This sideline pays for some travel that Perry otherwise wouldn't be able to afford. The risk isn't as great as readers of sensational popular novels would believe. In reality, the main emphasis in executive protection is avoidance, not gun battles, and Perry arranges for his clients' schedules and movements so as to minimize the risk of encountering a threat. In his career, both in the Secret Service and in private practice, he's never had a shootout. He feels confident of living to a ripe old age.

Madame Yvonne is a part-time underground seamstress catering to the Park Avenue trade, and she works out of her home. In New York there are many custom dressmakers, skilled people who build dresses from scratch or alter store-bought ones, and they operate from locations with heavy overhead, as we'd expect from a high-rent district. Madame Yvonne learned her trade in France, where she was born, and her distinctive French accent gives her a prestigious aura with her clients. The prices she charges are significantly below those charged by the high-overhead custom tailors, and she keeps it all, tax-free. Using her young son to make pick-ups and deliveries, she turns over enough business to make it all worthwhile.

Mike owns his own garage and repairs foreign cars. With his partner, Steve, he also restores old and badly beat-up foreign classics. He gets spare parts at mechanic's discounts, which makes the proposition more attractive, and he doesn't even have to do all the work himself. He uses the old car projects as "fillers" when business is slow, and puts his mechanics to work on them. He gets discounts on painting, which he's not equipped to do. He already had a going business, and all his tools and facilities are written off as part of the business. For him, it's pure profit.

Janice, a housewife, had to give up her job as a pet groomer to take care of her new son. This requires her to stay at home all day, except for shopping and visiting, when she takes her son with her. In the search for extra cash, she had an easy start. In her job, she'd built up many personal contacts and had a clientele that liked her work. Many clients, bringing their pets for grooming, would ask specifically for her. Janice planned ahead. She built up a list of names and telephone numbers of clients who liked her work. When she was pregnant and ready to leave her job, she had some business cards printed, giving her home address. During her last weeks, she handed them out to her list of clients, adding verbally that she'd give their pets the same care for less money. She could afford to do this because she anticipated no overhead. Planning to work at home, she already had her personal set of tools. Not having to rent a store, she has practically no expenses. Her husband, George, built her some holding pens in the back yard, where she keeps pets waiting for her care or for their owners to pick them up.

Rich and Ron own an exterminating business. They have made a comfortable living from it for years. One reason they find it comfortable is that they also have some clients on the side. They bill their big commercial clients in the normal way, sending an invoice at the end of the month. Some of their private clients, however, get a special deal. These are friends to whom they make the offer: "Pay us cash, keep it off the books, and we will give you a good discount for your trouble."

Fred was an early retiree, made his "pile" legitimately, and had many tens of thousands in the bank. Realizing that inflation was eating up most of what he earned in interest, and taxes took the rest, he looked around for another way of investing. His nephew was a bright young man who wanted to open a fried-chicken franchise, but lacked the money. The nephew was eating his heart out as an "assistant manager" of a similar franchise, and slaving away as a counter clerk for almost no money, despite the title. Fred, knowing the nephew was both capable and experienced, approached him with this offer: He'd give him the money to buy into a franchise. The money was a gift, not a loan, and there would be no paperwork recorded. In return, he simply wanted a percentage of the take. The nephew would be able to earn enough to pay this percentage without strain every month, giving Fred a steady, untraceable retirement income. Fred found this worked so well that he did it with several other bright young business types he knew, and soon had a totally underground income that gave him a better lifestyle than he could have earned otherwise.

Jerry operates a tire store, and he saves the wheel weights that come off customers' rims. Instead of selling them to a scrap dealer, he sells them to several friends who are into reloading and cast their own bullets using wheel weights as a base. He gets more money from his friends than he would from a dealer and his friends don't have to buy carload lots as they would at a dealer. They pay cash and Jerry doesn't enter the sales on his books.

Len is a farmer who collects extra income during the hunting season. He charges hunters a small fee for hunting on his land.

Len is a farmer who collects extra income during the hunting season. He charges hunters a small fee for hunting on his land. The hunters pay it willingly, because Len's farm is conveniently close to the city and they know they have a certain amount of protection while on Len's land. The game wardens don't patrol private property in the same way they oversee state land, and minor violations usually go undetected. Len, of course, doesn't report the fees on his tax return.

Rick works as a photographer for a large and prestigious New York City art museum. Museum pay is not the best, and Rick has a sideline, using the barber training he picked up earlier in life. He cuts hair for his fellow employees during lunch and breaks, doing a fairly good, but not fancy job at less than the

Deep Inside the Underground Economy
How Millions of Americans Are Practicing Free Enterprise in An Unfree Society

74

going rate in barbershops. His investment in tools was minimal, since he had them left over from when he'd worked as a barber. He is able to use a straight-backed chair in his darkroom, and sweeping up the hair afterwards is not a serious problem because of the tile floor. Payment is always in cash, which he pockets, undisclosed to the IRS.

Ron is a homosexual and owns a two-bedroom house. He rents his spare bedroom, finding tenants through a gay roommate service. Although he doesn't have personal relationships with his "roommates," he finds it comfortable to have people like him renting, because it avoids embarrassment. The extra unde-clared income helps him sustain the lifestyle he likes. He thinks that, although he's a city worker and not underpaid, the tax bite on his official salary is large enough.

These underground workers make use of skills they've learned during their regular employment, or as a hobby, or learned especially for their new occu-pations. They demonstrate various ways of conceal-ing their income, either by being completely under-ground, or by concealing their underground activities in the shadow of an above ground business. You can learn by studying their methods and finding those that will be applicable to your situation.

Cautions for the Undergrounder

Anyone practicing underground economics must use good judgment and follow several cautionary guidelines. Failure to do so is ignoring common sense, and can cause you complications.

Obviously, this book is about how to avoid paying taxes, but there's no getting away from it, the gov-ernment will tax you one way or another, and when it's got you, you must pay up or face real trouble. Never send in a tax return that states that you refuse to provide information because it might incriminate you. It's an old story by now, but "fifth-amendment filers" got their noses bloodied by the U.S. Supreme Court almost twenty years ago. Don't try this if you want to stay out of jail.

Another aspect of paying taxes is that the government forces you to be its tax collector under certain conditions.

Another aspect of paying taxes is that the govern-ment forces you to be its tax collector under certain conditions. If you sell goods, local governments will oblige you to collect sales tax. If you have employ-ees, you'll have to withhold income taxes and Social Security taxes and turn them over to the government periodically. Some states, such as New Mexico, have a "gross receipts tax" that amputates a portion of a business owner's income right off the top. However, do not think that the taxes you collect are a slush fund from which you can make interest-free loans to your-self.

If you fail to hand over the taxes when they're due, you can get hit with a penalty of ten percent for "fail-ure to deposit," and five percent monthly if you con-tinue to be delinquent. You can ruin your business, but even then you're not off the hook, because you're personally liable for the amounts.[9]

Another potential stumbling block is refusing to pay taxes on principle. Some Vietnam-era war pro-testers still owe the IRS money, and one couple found their house seized and put up for sale by the IRS for the $27,000 in taxes, fines, and penalties they owed. There are other forms of reprisal, such as de-priving people of their livelihoods. Another tax pro-tester, dentist Tom Wilson of Shelburne Falls, MA, stopped paying taxes to the IRS, and then to the state, which then suspended his license to practice.[10]

The lesson is clear: when working your way around the IRS, never stand up and throw down the gauntlet. They'll break your neck. If you despise the IRS, there are other and less risky ways to fight them.

Discretion

You've heard the saying, "Three can keep a secret if two of them are dead." In other words, if you really want to keep a secret, don't tell anyone else. Keeping your own counsel is important for several reasons, all revolving around the basic fact that "what other peo-ple don't know can't hurt you." Once you let some-one else in on your secrets, you give them power over you.

When you tell a person something in confidence, you can't predict how many people will eventually learn your secret once your confidant begins shooting off his mouth.

If you tell anyone how you earn undeclared income or inflate your deductions to retain more of what you've earned openly, you compromise your safety many times over. It's very much like the principle that when you have sex with someone, you're also having sex with all of his or her previous sex partners, especially with regard to exposure to AIDS and other nasty sexually-transmitted diseases. When you tell a person something in confidence, you can't predict how many people will eventually learn your secret once your confidant begins shooting off his mouth.

Letting other people in on your secret provides them with the opportunity to hurt you for financial gain, or just for fun. As we've already seen, the IRS provides financial rewards of up to ten percent of the money recovered to snitches who inform on their friends. This "turn in a friend" program has been running for decades and it has been profitable for the IRS. However, not everyone snitches for profit. Some people get an emotional charge from seeing other people suffer.[11]

Make no mistake about it — some of your neighbors, your fellow Americans, are among the most venal and treacherous people on Earth. Look at the number of people you know, work with, and even number among your family, and ask yourself how many you'd categorize as "back-stabbers," "opportunists," etc. Now look at it the other way: How many would you feel comfortable trusting with your life? Play it safe — if you can't trust someone with your life, you can't trust him with a secret that could affect your life.

This also applies to tax preparers. If you employ one, be very careful regarding what you tell him. Above all, do not brag about how you're screwing the IRS, for two reasons.

1. He might refuse to prepare your return, not wanting to become involved with anything that could result in a prosecution. This becomes dangerous for you, because he might still pass on a tip to the IRS.
2. He might prepare your return, but tip off the IRS about exactly how you're fudging your figures, to collect a reward. After all, you've put him in a perfect position to spill your guilty secrets for profit.

Another motive is jealousy. Someone envious of your superior lifestyle may decide to ruin it for you by snitching you off to the government. If he can earn a few bucks sticking it to you, so much the better.

Historically, estranged spouses have been among the IRS's most prolific informers.

Yet another motive is revenge. Although you'd be very foolish telling a dangerous secret to an enemy, once you tell anyone at all, the news may reach an enemy or rival in a roundabout way. Also, today's friend can turn into tomorrow's enemy. Be especially wary of the estranged spouse, who might do anything for revenge. Historically, estranged spouses have been among the IRS's most prolific informers. Some have even falsely accused their husbands of child molestation during divorce proceedings, so snitching a spouse off to the IRS is small beer.

Still another motive is blackmail by a business rival or estranged spouse. By its very nature, blackmail is one of the most underreported crimes, and many blackmail victims are forced to suffer in silence. Yes, you can report a blackmail attempt to the police, and go as far as prosecution, but it can be a Pyrrhic victory if the IRS steps out from the wings and chops your head off after it's over.

This is why it's smart to handle information on a "need to know" basis. If you have a cash business on the side, your accountant does not need to know about it to make out your tax return. If you and your wife take periodic trips to Las Vegas, there's no need to advertise that fact to your friends and neighbors. You don't have to display your extra income or your extra purchasing power for the world to see.

Noted New Jersey criminal defense attorney Allan Marain put it this way: "Remember — even a fish would not get caught if he kept his mouth shut."

Security Self-Test

Some people are their own worst enemies because they blab too much. We've noted several times how the IRS depends partly on informers for information regarding people who underreport their incomes. Some informers develop their information from their targets' self-revelations. Are you your most dangerous security liability?

Take this little test, adapted from standards used by government security agents, to see if you're a security risk to yourself. Be honest. Don't shade the truth, because you'd only be trying to fool yourself. Don't write down the answers, and of course don't tell anyone. This is just between yourself and the printed page, but it will help you appraise whether or not you

Deep Inside the Underground Economy
How Millions of Americans Are Practicing Free Enterprise in An Unfree Society

76

should be running the risk of doing anything you have to keep confidential.

1. Do you ever wake up after an evening of boozing wishing you had not said something the night before?

This is a sure sign that alcohol loosens your lips too much for your comfort. Either give up booze, or do your drinking alone. At parties, stick to ginger ale.

2. Do you feel the need to top other people's stories during casual conversation?

If you feel compelled to match or eclipse other people's exploits, even by telling of something illegal, unethical, or immoral that you've done, avoid such discussions.

Maybe you have a competitive nature, but this can get you into trouble. If you feel compelled to match or eclipse other people's exploits, even by telling of something illegal, unethical, or immoral that you've done, avoid such discussions. If you shoot your mouth off, even in seemingly innocuous situations, you may live to regret it. Many street criminals have been apprehended because they shot their mouths off and someone reported what they said. The Hollywood Video criminals who killed five people in Albuquerque during a video store robbery were very indiscreet, and an acquaintance of theirs turned them in to collect the $100,000 reward money. Without this snitch, the police would never have caught them.

3. Do you gamble enough so that you're always tight for money?

A pressing need for money, especially when driven by a gambling debt, will warp your judgment. You may be pressed to take avoidable risks just to pay off the debt.

4. Do you have an indiscreet spouse, who blabs your business all over town?

A chatterbox spouse can repeat anything you reveal, so if this is your situation, learn to keep your sensitive secrets to yourself. Also keep this in mind if you talk in your sleep.

5. Does your spouse have expensive tastes, which you're having trouble satisfying on what you earn?

This is another source of problems. Both spies and criminals get into trouble satisfying the needs of a greedy and acquisitive spouse or romantic partner. Love is truly blind, and can lead you to take unnecessary risks to keep your partner happy.

6. Do you have other guilty secrets that someone could use against you?

If you have a secret drug habit, or molest children, you leave yourself open to blackmail. The insistent demands of a blackmailer can drive people to take desperate chances.

7. Do you enjoy or prefer an opulent life-style, wallowing in conspicuous consumption as you tool around town in a Mercedes and with a Rolex on your wrist?

People who obviously live above their means attract attention. Parking a Range Rover in front of your modest townhouse or low-rent apartment is like waving a red flag. Also, driving it to where you work as a shipping clerk provokes questions from fellow employees, and probably your boss as well.

Don't Get Greedy

It's easy to absorb about ten percent undeclared income into your lifestyle without making a conspicuous splash and attracting attention.

You may be in the underground economy to earn the few extra bucks that make the difference between getting along on your overt income and being constantly strapped. Maybe you just need enough to keep up with inflation. Overall, it's easy to absorb about ten percent undeclared income into your lifestyle without making a conspicuous splash and attracting attention. However, an undeclared income equal to your legal one is much harder to consume inconspicuously, and in some instances, much harder to cover.

For example, the liquor store owner who "skims" part of his sales, not ringing them up on the cash register, can easily get away with a small percentage of his gross. However, if he tries to skim half or more, it will be harder to cover. His invoices will show that he purchased a certain quantity of stock, and it will be incredible to the tax auditor that such a large percentage was lost through breakage and shoplifting.

Overdoing it means taking risks. It requires good judgment to calculate the amount you can safely cover up. Going overboard breaks your low profile and makes you a prime target for the IRS.

Stolen Goods

One problem with any sort of underground or flea-market selling is the prospect of receiving stolen goods. If you don't plan to get your hands dirty with theft yourself, it's pointless to take the risk of prosecution for criminal receivership.

Whatever you do, avoid accepting any serial-numbered items from doubtful sources. A crate of binoculars offered to you at a rock-bottom price might have been stolen from a loading dock, and their serial numbers make them traceable. One underground seller during the 1960s bought a consignment of stolen binoculars, and got into deep doo-doo when one of his customers sent in the guarantee card. With this entry into the case, police were able to trace the binoculars back to the seller.

Burglary squad detectives attend flea markets and swap meets, their pockets filled with "hot sheets" listing the makes, models, and serial numbers of recently stolen items.

Another reason for avoiding anything traceable is that burglary squad detectives attend flea markets and swap meets, their pockets filled with "hot sheets" listing the makes, models, and serial numbers of recently stolen items.

Some jobs pay "*X* dollars a week and all you can steal." The nature of some businesses, such as restaurants, construction, etc., make tight inventory control impossible, and employers are resigned to having a certain portion of their stock ripped off. If you sell material taken from your employer, do not, repeat, DO NOT deal with professional "fences," receivers of stolen goods. Professional fences often cheat their clients by conspiring to fix prices or by flimflamming on the count.[12]

Avoiding a professional receiver of stolen goods means limiting your operation, since you probably won't be able to dispose of large quantities of material for cash the way a career criminal can. However, you must make this sacrifice for your own security, for two reasons.

The first is that these sleaze-bags are likely to turn you over if arrested, which is why dealing with a fence is living on borrowed time. Fences have so many channels of criminal contacts that the local police burglary squad is aware of them, and sooner or later will catch them in a "sting" operation. When this happens, the fence, as a professional criminal interested only in saving his hide, will rush to make a deal by informing on others.

The second reason is that you must keep your volume low to remain undetected. As we saw in a previous chapter, Lucien's expropriating of a few boxes of scissors and sewing needles went totally unnoticed because of the tremendous volume of goods pouring through the shipping room. Your employer may be annoyed at the disappearance of a couple of reams of typing paper, and he may worry a bit about inventory shrinkage. However, he'll go ballistic if every computer in his office vanishes one night.

The same caution applies if you're skimming from your own business. Although the material is yours to sell, the fence will assume that it's stolen, and this can lead to an unwanted visit from the police. Although you'll be able to clear yourself of theft charges, you don't need that sort of attention.

Firearms

A firearm may not only be hot, but it may have been used in a crime, which makes its possession very dangerous.

By all means avoid dealing in firearms on the underground market, for several reasons. First, a firearm may not only be hot, but it may have been used in a crime, which makes its possession very dangerous.

Another reason is the tangle of local and federal paperwork needed to deal in firearms legally. If you're a firearms dealer — and the rule of thumb is that if you sell over ten firearms per year you are a dealer — you need a Federal Firearms License, the well-known "FFL" available from the Bureau of Alcohol, Tobacco, and Firearms (BATF). The cost of an FFL has gone up astronomically, thanks to the Brady Bill that went into effect on February 28, 1994. Forget about forging an FFL. They became harder to forge in 1993 with the adoption of specially printed paper.

Yet another reason for staying away from firearms is that undercover cops and BATF agents prowl flea markets looking for stolen goods and illicit firearms deals and dealers. This is such a hassle that many flea market operators do not rent space to gun dealers, even legitimate ones.

BATF agents pose as prospective buyers, seeking to entrap dealers. When they work flea markets, they

Deep Inside the Underground Economy
How Millions of Americans Are Practicing Free Enterprise in An Unfree Society

78

go as far as asking other merchants who are not fire-arms dealers, if they have firearms for sale. If you're merely selling Indian jewelry but you answer that you have a firearm in your truck you'd sell for the right price, they've "Gotcha!"

Stupid Tax Dodges

Several operators in New York's garment district, which is not noted for high business ethics, were fined for selling products at retail sample sales without acquiring the proper state sales tax certificates. Fines were not terribly high — one company was fined only $100.[13] So we see, noncompliance with an easily-enforced bureaucratic requirement produced a hassle. Worse, it's an alert signal to federal agencies such as the IRS to take a closer look at the businesses involved.

Prosecution

The fear of prosecution keeps many employees timid, afraid to seize extra job benefits because of an exaggerated idea of the risks involved. The reality is very different.

Our cultural values affect our criminal justice system, and have resulted in higher penalties for crimes against the person than crimes against property. We see the rapist, murderer, or armed robber as a greater threat to society than the fraud artist or tax evader.

Consequently, street criminals such as muggers and armed robbers take disproportionate risks for little potential reward. A convenience-store robber literally risks his life, often for fifty dollars or less. If caught with a gun in his hand, proving his guilt isn't terribly difficult.

A banker or stockbroker who takes advantage of inside information to swing a favorable stock deal is theoretically breaking the law, but proving it is another matter. The prosecution must prove that the defendant had the inside knowledge with the intent to use it, and this is a very difficult thing to prove because knowledge is intangible.

Guerrilla capitalists are not likely to find the SWAT team surrounding them, even if the roof caves in and their operations are completely exposed to the IRS.

In the same way, guerrilla capitalists are not likely to find the SWAT team surrounding them, even if the roof caves in and their operations are completely exposed to the IRS. There are other ramifications as well. While a murderer or child molester may find it extraordinarily difficult to make bail while awaiting trial, the tax evader rarely sees the inside of a jail and may even secure release on his own recognizance (ROR).

Avoiding Traps

There are pitfalls for both the cautious and the unwary. Some are legalized rackets, while others depend on widely held assumptions that have no basis in fact. A perfect example is the Individual Retirement Account (IRA), or a Keogh Plan. You may be tempted to start one to provide for your retirement.

The way the IRA is pitched to the working American, it's a way to both save for retirement and to defer paying taxes on the income put into the special savings account until after withdrawal. The reasoning is that after retirement, the individual will be in a lower tax bracket because of reduced income. The implicit promise is that tax rates will not increase between now and retirement.[14]

Even when a benevolent-seeming government gives working people a "tax break," it's loaded.

Taxes will increase, whatever the government says or implies. Worse, taxes hit the working poor and middle class worse than they hit the rich, who can afford to pay them. Even when a benevolent-seeming government gives working people a "tax break," it's loaded. When the Johnson tax reduction passed in 1965, dropping the basic tax rate in the lowest bracket from 20 percent to 14 percent, the rich saw their top tax rate drop from 95 percent to 70 percent. In other words, the working poor received a 6 percent tax break, while the super-rich received a 25 percent reduction. On top of that, there was a temporary 10 percent "war surtax" to pay for President Johnson's Southeast Asia adventure.

More recently, tax rates dropped under President Reagan's initiative in 1986. It appeared, at first sight, that the government was actually simplifying and reducing the tax structure. However, what the government gives with one hand, it takes away with the other. At the same time people saw their nominal tax rates drop, they also lost a number of deductions.

Social Security

The only people who came out ahead with Social Security were those at the very beginning, who worked only a few months or years before they qualified by attaining retirement age.

This is another government-run racket that is heavy on promises and low on performance. The theory is that individuals, left to themselves, are so weak-willed that they'll recklessly spend their money without providing for retirement, so the benevolent government will do it for them. In fact, the only people who came out ahead with Social Security were those at the very beginning, who worked only a few months or years before they qualified by attaining retirement age.

It doesn't take a genius to calculate how much interest Social Security payments would earn by depositing them in a simple savings account. Even at a modest two percent rate of interest, the money would accrue at a rate that would provide a healthy amount for retirement.

Retirement Worksheet
How much is the government screwing you by taking Social Security payments from your income? It's not hard to calculate.

Do this exercise for yourself:

Annual Social Security Tax_____

Years until age 65:_____

Multiply what you paid last year by two percent and add the product to the original amount. Repeat this for each year until you reach 65, and see what you have. If you have a financial calculator, you can avoid the tedious task of computing every year's compound interest.

Divide this sum by 10, optimistically assuming you'll live to age 75. Surprised? Match that amount to the highest bracket of Social Security payments today.

Franchises

Many, many people have been suckered into franchises and managed "opportunities" that are only profit makers for their promoters.

Many, many people have been suckered into franchises and managed "opportunities" that are only profit makers for their promoters. Let's look at one managed opportunity first.

One high-rent flea market promoter pushed an extravaganza that promised select location and high returns. The rent for a space was astronomical. Our resident flea market expert, Jordan L. Cooper, turned down the offer and was happy he had declined. The extravaganza turned out to be a flop: Renters were few, shoppers were sparse, and everybody lost their shirts.[15]

Franchises are even worse if your main objectives are to get out from under an employer's thumb and to earn tax-free dollars. A franchise contract allows you to open up a local branch of a nationally advertised firm and to operate it in exactly the way the franchiser dictates. Let's look at the good, the bad, and the ugly.

You sign up to operate a fast-food business, the Tube Steak Frankfurter joints. The contract makes it clear that you're an "independent" business owner, but in practice this means that you take all the risks. The parent company won't bail you out if anything goes wrong.

You must put up tens of thousands of dollars up front, then buy all of your supplies, from frankfurters to printed napkins, from the parent company, although you know that local suppliers carry the same quality goods at lower prices. You must, of course, pay for your business license, tax license, and various other fees for food handling licenses, even before you open your doors.

You're obliged to keep your records in the manner prescribed by parent company policy, and make them available for inspection on demand to ensure that you're not cheating them of any royalties. This makes skimming very difficult. You may have to contribute your "share" to national advertising campaigns. To earn a living, you must work prodigious hours, because your profit margin does not allow you to hire quality help and you have to be there to supervise constantly.

Deep Inside the Underground Economy
How Millions of Americans Are Practicing Free Enterprise in An Unfree Society

80

As for vacations, forget it, unless you can somehow afford to close your shop and give all your hired help time off with pay, during which some will no doubt be looking for better-paying jobs.

You end up realizing that you'll never get rich at this. Your net profit is strictly controlled by the parent company, which perversely may set up another franchiser as your competitor nearby to leech away a proportion of your business. In the end, you've changed from a wage slave to a franchise slave, serving a boss as demanding as the one you'd left.

Notes

1. A good guide to obtaining fake I.D. is John Q. Newman, *The I.D. Forger,* Loompanics Unlimited, Port Townsend, WA, 1999.

2. X, C.P.A., *How to Cheat on Your Taxes,* 1040 Press, 1982, p. 77.

3. Jack Luger, *The Big Book of Secret Hiding Places,* Loompanics Unlimited, Port Townsend, WA, 1987.

4. Zay N. Smith and Pamela Zekman, *The Mirage,* Random House, NY, 1979, pp. 175-82. "Skimming Anyone?" is a primer on the ins and outs of tax avoidance in operating a small business. The techniques explained are in relation to a bar, but are applicable to almost any sort of small operation. The chapter presents the points of view of several experienced accountants who regularly helped their customers skim profits, and their advice regarding keeping things in proportion is worth heeding.

5. U.S. Congress *Hearings before the Joint Economics Committee,* 96th Congress, 1st sess., 15 November 1979, p. 29.

6. U.S. Department of the Treasury, Internal Revenue Service, *Estimates of Income Unreported on Individual Tax Returns, Publication 1104* (9-79) Washington, D.C.: Government Printing Office, 1979, p. 30.

7. "U.S. Currency and Coin Outstanding and in Circulation," *Treasury Bulletin,* December 2001, on *Financial Management Service,* Web site, http://www.fms.treas.gov/bulletin/b41.pdg.

8. Department of the Treasury, *Estimates of Income,* pp. 6-9.

9. Mark Stevens, "Giving in to This Temptation Could Ruin Your Business," *Air Conditioning, Heating, & Refrigeration News* 181, no. 4 (24 Sept. 1990), p. 21.

10. Richard Pollak, "War-Tax Resisters in Massachusetts," *The Nation* 250, no. 23 (11 June 1990), p. 822.

11. The German word for this is "schadenfreude," which means malicious joy at another's distress. There is no English equivalent.

12. Gale Miller, *Odd Jobs,* Prentice-Hall, Englewood Cliffs, NJ, 1978, p. 45.

13. Rich Wilner, "NY State Fines SA (Sports Apparel) Firm over Retail Sample Sales," *Women's Wear Daily* 159, no. 24 (2 Feb. 1990), p. 17.

14. Lauren Chambliss, "Die Hard: Millions of Americans Are Still Putting Money into IRAs Even Though Many Do Not Qualify for Deductions," *FW* 158, no. 2 (12 June 1990), p. 92.

15. Jordan L. Cooper, *Shadow Merchants,* Loompanics Unlimited, Port Townsend, WA, 1993, pp. 131-33.

Part Two
Making Your Income Invisible

The government has made massive efforts to track people and their incomes in order to be more certain of enforcing compliance with its tax laws. Each year brings more restrictions, major and minor, regarding how you may earn money and what you're allowed to do with it. An example is the cash transaction law.

This law, ostensibly passed to close a door to illegal drug dealers, requires banks and businesses to report to the IRS all cash transactions of ten thousand dollars or more. An amendment to that law requires reporting all cash transactions for amounts appearing to circumvent that law. An example is a purchase in the amount of $9,999.

Actually, the long-range effect of this law will be to allow closer scrutiny of how ordinary people, not only illegal drug traffickers, spend their money. Inflation ensures that ten thousand dollars will buy less in goods and services ten years from now than this amount does today. More people will be making $10,000-plus purchases, either by check or credit card, or in cash requiring a report.

Any purchase of traveler's checks in quantities of more than $3,000 total results in a report being sent to the IRS.

More recently, another requirement came about. Any purchase of traveler's checks in quantities of more than $3,000 total results in a report being sent to the IRS.

A more menacing government measure is known euphemistically as the "Value Added Tax," or "VAT." Actually, the VAT is a system of taxing goods and services at every stage of production, extracting the tax before the consumer ever sees the product, so it amounts to a cost-added tax. The VAT, a French invention which has spread through Europe, is actually a "regressive" tax that penalizes low and middle income people most. However, governments of European countries with high rates of tax evasion resort to the VAT as a sure means of extracting taxes from an unwilling population.

The VAT simplifies the problem for the tax collection office, because it means keeping a close watch on perhaps 100,000 businesses instead of many millions of wage earners.

Administratively, the VAT simplifies the problem for the tax collection office, because it means keeping a close watch on perhaps 100,000 businesses instead of many millions of wage earners. A country with the VAT can impose a nominal income-tax rate, while obtaining the bulk of its revenues from VAT.

Such government tax-collection efforts would not be as threatening to us if they were fairly applied. However, they are not. There still exist many loopholes for the rich and the superrich, the "coupon-clippers" who derive their incomes from large holdings of tax-free municipal and public utility bonds, such as Arizona's Salt River Project, while wage earners get sweated for every penny the IRS can take. One minor loophole, bearer bonds, was closed by a U.S. Treasury Department ruling in 1982. Today it's no longer allowed to issue "bearer" or no-name bonds, and all bonds must be registered to the owner to ensure that taxes are paid. Despite the elimination of this loophole favoring the rich, many more exist, but you have to make some of them yourself.

The increasing oppressiveness of taxes has certain consequences. One is loopholes in the laws so the rich can avoid paying taxes. Another is the emergence of the underground economy.

Deep Inside the Underground Economy
How Millions of Americans Are Practicing Free Enterprise in An Unfree Society

82

How Big is the Underground Economy?

By definition, a clandestine activity defies measurement and even the government can come up with only ballpark estimates.

There have been magazine articles and books published on the underground economy, but they all disagree on its size, sometimes by tenfold. By definition, a clandestine activity defies measurement and even the government can come up with only ballpark estimates, which perhaps should more properly be termed "guesstimates." Some figures mentioned in the first version of this book, *Guerrilla Capitalism*, were $700 billion or $542 billion during the 1970s.

From various estimates, several trends appear. The IRS tends to make low estimates of tax evasion because its official line is that the tax system in the United States is just and fair, and most people comply with it. To admit that most people evade taxes if they can would open up a Pandora's box for the IRS, which is why they turn away from the higher estimates. In any event, who can prove them wrong?

"Voluntary compliance" is the official basis of tax collection, but behind this friendly official view is a system of penalties for those who do not comply. It's clear that tax revenue is lower where income is self-reported and there is no withholding tax. This is why the IRS "red flags" tax returns of people who are self-employed, such as doctors.

There are basically two ways of measuring something, whether it be the distance from the Earth to the Moon or the size of the underground economy. One is direct measurement, and the other is indirect. Direct measurement is simple and straightforward, and it's possible to measure declared income and taxes paid simply by totaling the amounts reported on tax returns. Unreported income and unpaid taxes, on the other hand, can only be estimated, as it's not practical to survey people to ask them how much they did not report.

There are several indirect methods. One is to count the amount of money in circulation, multiply it by "velocity" (the number of times the average dollar changes hands in a year) and derive an estimate from that. The errors in this method are obvious.

Another indirect method is the "Exact Match File," a closely-held government survey in which tens of thousands of people were questioned by an outside source to avoid disclosure of IRS involvement, and the data matched with official tax returns. It's important to keep this in mind when filling out a survey form asking for your total income. Some manufacturers' warranty cards include a question about your income, and it's unwise to give away this information. The problems with this method are that it's hard to believe that people would disclose irregular income to strangers asking questions, and it's even more unlikely that big operators, such as illegal drug wholesalers, would answer any questions at all.

Some manufacturers' warranty cards include a question about your income, and it's unwise to give away this information.

Yet another approach is theoretically the most rational one. This uses data derived from the 1972-73 Consumer Expenditure Survey of Labor Statistics.[1] The idea behind this method is that, while the suppliers of underground services may be reluctant to answer questions, the consumers are not. Those conducting the survey analyzed the reported totals of consumer spending on items such as food, babysitting, etc., to try to determine the amounts that went to open suppliers and those to informal ones, such as roadside stands and moonlighters.

At first sight, this seems very rational. However, reading the report carefully shows that its paragraphs are filled with terms such as "probably," "it was decided to regard ten percent" (who decided and why?), "was treated," "believed that as much as 25 percent," "it was assumed," "twenty percent of the residual was assumed," "five percent was allocated to the informal economy," "treated as payments to the informal economy," etc.[2]

Weasel words such as these reveal that the whole exercise was statistical garbage produced by unimaginative bureaucrats, paid for by our tax dollars. Even if the people surveyed answered truthfully, completely, and accurately — and this is doubtful because most of us don't remember every bag of fruit we buy at roadside stands or what we paid the babysitter last year — without knowing the exact status of the parties who received these payments it's impossible to be precise about the total that went into the underground economy.

The National Center for Policy Analysis stated that the United States' Gross Domestic Product is about $8 trillion, not counting off-the-books income.

Let's look at a few more estimates. These are more recent, but apparently no more precise. The National Center for Policy Analysis stated that the United States' Gross Domestic Product is about $8 trillion, not counting off-the-books income. As many as twenty-five percent of Americans earn much of their income off the books. The underground economy is perhaps ten percent of the GDP, but may be more.[3]

The NCPA pointed out that one way of judging the size of the underground economy is by counting the number of $100 bills in circulation. These comprise about sixty percent of the currency in circulation. Most people do not pay for most of their purchases with $100 bills, which creates the suspicion that their main purpose is to finance underground transactions.[4]

IRS Commissioner Charles Rossotti was quoted as saying that the U.S. government loses $195 billion per year in unpaid taxes. The University of Wisconsin's Professor Edgar Feige estimated the underground economy at between $500 billion and $1 trillion in 1993.[5]

Many countries have underground economies. Estimates are that twenty to thirty percent of the economies of Italy, Belgium, and Spain are underground, and that ten to twenty percent of the economies of France, Germany, Ireland, the Netherlands, and Great Britain are underground.[6]

Canada also has an underground economy that causes concern to the government. A summary published by the Bank of Canada admits that estimates of its extent vary between four and fifteen percent of Canada's gross domestic product.[7]

Overall, we can judge the validity of these estimates regarding the size of the underground economy by two criteria:

- Are the estimates consistent with each other? We've seen that they're not.
- Are they consistent with the real facts? Nobody knows. A lot of people are evading a lot of taxes, and feel they're perfectly justified in earning invisible income.

In this part, we'll study ways to earn invisible income. Surprisingly, today there are more roads to invisible earnings than before, despite the best efforts of the Internal Revenue Service.

First we'll study opportunities to supplement your income while working, taking you through a security survey to detect hidden opportunities. We'll then study how to exploit these opportunities for your benefit. We'll also discuss the ins and outs of cash income: how to and how not to handle it. We'll look at one of the IRS's most useful tools, Form 1099, and how to get around it. Finally, we'll look at totally underground earnings, and conclude with a study of barter, which is more common in other countries than here.

Notes

1. U.S. Congress, *Hearings before the Joint Economics Committee*, 96th Cong., 1st sess, 15 November 1979, p. 1.
2. U.S. Department of the Treasury, Internal Revenue Service, *Estimates of Income Unreported on Individual Income Tax Returns: IRS Service Publication 1104* (9-79) (Washington, D.C.: Government Printing Office, 1979), pp. 122-23.
3. "The Unmeasured Underground Economy," *Idea House*, National Center for Political Analysis, Internet, www.ncpa.org/pd/economy-/pd122198b.html 15 March 2002.
4. *Ibid.*
5. "The Underground Economy," Brief Analysis No. 273, *Idea House*, National Center for Political Analysis, Internet, 13 July 1998, http://www.ncpa.org/ba/ba273.html, 11 March 2002.
6. "Unmeasured Underground Economy."
7. Lafleche, Therese, "The Demand for Currency and the Underground Economy," *Bank of Canada*, Internet, Autumn 1994, http://www.bank-banque-canada.ca/en/res/r944b-ea.htm, 11 March 2002.

Chapter Six
A Business Primer

Running a business isn't terribly complicated, apart from the specialized technical knowledge you may require. Obviously, you won't be starting a computer repair business if you know nothing about computers. Most management techniques are common sense, which makes it amazing that universities can puff up the simple principles involved into four-year courses.

The main point is not to make any of the major mistakes, such as hiring incompetent help or getting in over your head financially or technically. Avoid the catastrophic errors, and the rest almost takes care of itself.

Although you have more latitude when starting an underground business, making it profitable requires the same attention to detail as if you were starting an above ground enterprise.

This chapter won't be the equivalent of a Harvard MBA, but it will provide a few fundamental business principles that you can use whether you start an above ground business or an underground one. It's surprising how many people go into business without any understanding of what it takes to make a business work. Although you have more latitude when starting an underground business, making it profitable requires the same attention to detail as if you were starting an above ground enterprise.

Be Realistic

Many small business schemes simply aren't realistic, and neither are the people who promote or follow them. Some promise or expect immediate riches, intoxicated by the prospect of wealth. Others take on clearly impractical or unprofitable lines, destined to be disappointed.

The widely touted "positive attitude" is a scam, pure and simple.

Attitude is important, but it's vital not to exaggerate the role of attitude. The widely touted "positive attitude" is a scam, pure and simple. This is the technique promoters use to browbeat their victims when the schemes don't work out. They tell them that the failure is due to their bad attitudes. This absolves the promoters from any responsibility for the failure.

The proper attitude is that of hard-core realism, understanding the problems involved, and looking for ways to solve them. Some people don't understand this, feeling that anything less than an enthusiastic, "rah-rah" attitude will lead to failure because they're not thinking positively.

There's a big difference between realism and defeatism. Promoters who advertise moneymaking schemes don't want you to realize this. They don't want you to look critically at their schemes, preferring that you accept their claims without any doubts or reservations whatever.

Only by appraising your chances realistically will you get a good start in a new venture.

You must also take the same realistic and critical attitude towards any moneymaking ideas you create. Ask yourself, honestly, if it will work. Is there a market for your goods or services? How do you know? Do you know anyone else who has made this work? If so, why did it work for them? Can you do the same? If it failed, then why? Can you resurrect the idea and make it work for you, avoiding the mistakes the others made? How much will it cost to get started? Can you afford to lose that much if you fail? What are the risks? Only by appraising your chances

Deep Inside the Underground Economy
How Millions of Americans Are Practicing Free Enterprise in An Unfree Society

86

realistically will you get a good start in a new venture.

Estimating Your Market

Market research is a valuable tool for big businesses, for they have to make decisions concerning millions of dollars' worth of investments, and having a rough guide to the potential returns is a planning tool. Some authorities recommend that the small business owner make his own market survey.

The suggested method is to go out and ask potential customers if they need a product or service of the sort you plan to offer. While this method seems very straightforward and attractive, it has some fatal flaws.

Someone who answers hypothetically that, yes, he'd eagerly buy such a product or service may not be willing to shell out the cash when the moment of truth comes.

The biggest one is that many people don't do what they say they'll do. Someone who answers hypothetically that, yes, he'd eagerly buy such a product or service may not be willing to shell out the cash when the moment of truth comes. The promoters of market research don't like to talk about this point, the unpredictability of human behavior.

An excellent example of a market research failure was the Ford Edsel of about forty years ago. Before sinking half a billion dollars into designing and tooling up to produce the Edsel, Ford did market research on the need for such a car. They concluded that the American public, because it had been buying gas-guzzling barges for decades, would willingly snap up more of the same. The rest is history, and Robert S. MacNamara, the author of this catastrophic failure, left Ford shortly thereafter to become the Secretary of Defense under the Kennedy administration, where he applied his methods to the Pentagon.

A better guide than listening to what people say is to observe what they do. This will give you a more accurate idea of whether or not you have something they'll buy. The best guide to people's actions in the future is what they've done in the past, even though conditions change and human behavior changes with them. In this case, the key is that you're changing one of the conditions.

A good example: You're a plumber, seeking some outside work among your friends and acquaintances.

From experience, you know household plumbing sometimes fails, and when this happens, people call plumbers. You also know, from experience and observation, that if people have the opportunity to buy the same grade of product or service for less money, they'll most likely do so. Since you're already in the business and have your own tools, you offer your services, and to your gratification, you find that some people will call on you when the toilet or sink backs up, because you charge them less for the same good job they would get from an established plumbing company.

You'll inevitably find that, of a certain number of potential customers, some simply won't buy when the moment comes.

There's always Murphy's Law, and this will foul up the best estimates, introduce a degree of uncertainty into the calculations, and reinforce the need for caution. You'll inevitably find that, of a certain number of potential customers, some simply won't buy when the moment comes. Some die, some move away, and others simply find a better deal elsewhere. The other side of the coin is that you can also pick up new and unexpected customers, which tends to compensate for the ones you lose.

In the end, it boils down to individual judgment, a lot of which is guesswork. This is why it's smart to minimize your initial effort and investment, because that way you minimize your risk.

Starting out on a Shoestring

It pays to start small, dipping your toe into the water before jumping into the ocean. Unless you're so affluent that you don't need to work in the first place, you're not likely to have much capital to invest initially or operating capital to keep yourself afloat while building up your clientele.

Another reason for starting small is to minimize your risk. The unfortunate fact is that most small businesses fail for a few simple reasons. Many are undercapitalized. Ignorance or poor judgment on the part of the new entrepreneur is another reason, as some people get into the wrong business for their skills, choose the wrong time or place, think the money will just roll in without any effort on their parts, etc.[1]

Without being too negative, another important reason for starting small is to allow you to cut your losses if the business fails. You can abandon the effort without losing your life's savings.[2]

Capital

There are two types of capital, startup and operating. Start-up capital covers the cost of tools and materials you need to launch your business. Operating capital is money you need to pay the bills while your business isn't paying for itself.

The lack of capital needs has been an outstanding criterion of a successful underground business.

Mostly likely you'll start your underground business with minimal capital. Indeed, the lack of capital needs has been an outstanding criterion of a successful underground business. It's worth a very close look at the reasons why this is so, to avoid the traps inherent in using capital.

First, where do you get it? If you sink your life's savings into your new business, you may run into Murphy's Law: "If anything can go wrong, it will." For every story you hear or read about someone who struck it rich in a new business, underground or not, there are many untold ones who failed. You can lose everything.

A greater danger is borrowing money to capitalize your business. You might consider borrowing from a bank, in which case you'll run head-on into the need for documentation. You'll have to show that your business is either a going concern or has a good potential, and this involves paperwork, such as a business license, stationery, a business address, and other encumbering paperwork that is the bane of the undergrounder. Finally, getting a loan from a bank means that you're providing prima facie evidence of your intention to start a business if ever you're audited by the IRS.

Getting a loan from a friend seems more attractive, especially if he's willing to provide an interest-free loan, or one at a lower rate of interest than any bank. However, there's a not-so-hidden danger here, too. By borrowing money, you've bought yourself a silent partner, one who will be looking over your shoulder and wondering when you'll be paying him back.

The cost of the credit figures into your overhead, and we've already seen that one of the advantages of operating underground is the opportunity it gives to eliminate or sharply reduce your overhead, enabling you to offer your goods or services at lower prices than your competition.

Any money you borrow makes your creditor your leech, even if he's your best friend.

In effect, any money you borrow makes your creditor your leech, even if he's your best friend. He'll be riding on your back, and with a small business just starting up, at its most vulnerable point, his weight can be heavy indeed.

Keep in mind that your purpose in joining the underground economy is to free yourself from the burden of taxation. Credit is merely another burden. In effect, it's a system of voluntary taxation, and if you submit to it, you'll give up some of the benefits of operating underground.

The Dangers of Starting Cold

According to the Small Business Administration, eighty-five percent of small businesses fail within five years. There are several reasons for these failures, among them the simple lack of knowledge and ability, failure to assess the market correctly, and under capitalization.

The most common one is becoming overextended, according to the SBA, either through starting out without enough working capital or spending too much through over optimism. A business that takes on too many debts and overhead costs will go broke.

Because of the peculiarities of the underground economy, you can start cold with a greater margin of safety and fewer risks than the overt business owner.

Fortunately, the nature of underground business enables guerrilla capitalists to avoid these dangers. In fact, because of the peculiarities of the underground economy, you can start cold with a greater margin of safety and fewer risks than the overt business owner.

You usually don't have the overhead and additional expenses that a formal business owner has. As you'll most likely operate out of your home, you won't have the overhead of renting a shop or an of-

Deep Inside the Underground Economy
How Millions of Americans Are Practicing Free Enterprise in An Unfree Society

88

fice. Because you start small, you won't have employees, at least not in the formal sense.

Documented above ground employees would compromise your effort to remain invisible to the government. If you have someone working for you, over the table, you have to withhold taxes from his pay and turn them in to the IRS each quarter. This tells them right out that your business exists. You, in effect, become a tax collector for the government, and of course, you want to avoid this.

Managing Employees

The ideal situation, of course, is a business you can operate by yourself. This avoids the problems of screening and hiring competent help, affirmative action laws, and payroll taxes. You also avoid problems with sexual harassment accusations.

This last point is a legal minefield for employers. A stupid and incompetent woman can bring a sex discrimination lawsuit after you award a promotion to someone else, and you can be stuck in a morass of litigation that wastes both your time and the money you'll have to pay a lawyer. Likewise, even ordinary dealings with a female employee can be a hassle because in practice, "sexual harassment" is whatever the woman says it is. If a male employer uses profanity in front of a woman, it's harassment. On the other hand, if a female employee uses profanity in front of her male employer, she's merely demonstrating that she's "liberated."

There's a similar problem with bad minority employees. Such an employee, unable to perform his job properly, might decide he can make more money suing you than collecting a paycheck.

You can really get to know someone when you work with him, and this information is far more reliable than a resume, references, background checks, and various tests some employers use to screen new hires.

This is why hiring is crucial. You can't afford any mistakes, so hire only someone you already know through networking. Since we've previously seen, you can really get to know someone when you work with him, and this information is far more reliable than a resume, references, background checks, and various tests some employers use to screen new hires.

As you're working underground, you're not constrained by equal opportunity laws that push some employers to hire unsuitable or incompetent people to meet an ethnic quota.

Once you hire someone, treat him or her fairly. Be as ethical with employees as you are with customers. Many employers, especially those with a sweatshop mentality, never realize that they're at the mercy of their employees. Bullying, abusing, or underpaying employees can build up a backlog of suppressed resentment that can explode at a moment that hurts you the most.

One incompetent or resentful employee can cause thousands of dollars of damage to expensive machinery.

One incompetent or resentful employee can cause thousands of dollars of damage to expensive machinery. A vengeful employee can also alienate a valued customer by an offensive attitude or poor work. A press operator can announce he's quitting by sabotaging your press just before you run a high-dollar job for an important customer who needs it immediately. A machine service technician can do the same when he goes out to service one of your customer's machines. If your bookkeeper resents you, he can snarl your paperwork hopelessly, then quit without notice. Worse, he can snitch you off to the IRS. A sales manager or customer service representative can lose many customers for you before you discover what he's doing. He might even be building up a customer base for himself and be planning to go into competition with you.

This sort of intangible sabotage is easy to do. A customer service representative or repair technician can tell your customers that you're overcharging for parts and service, and refer your best customers to your competitors. He can also tell them he's going to save them money by short-circuiting the procedures you specified. This can hurt you even more if he's telling the truth.

Exploiting Your Own Knowledge

Using what you learn on the job to promote your own business after you leave is an excellent way of getting out from under the boot of a tyrannical employer. This is a tactic that works well whether your purpose is to set up an above ground competitor or an underground business. It works best if you use information that's not actually an industrial or technical process, thus avoiding a lawsuit. As a practical matter, it's easy to convince a jury that an industrial process may be available only in your employer's plant, but anyone can compile a customer list from a telephone directory.

Lack of skill is an important startup danger. Some people misjudge their abilities, thinking that a certain task is easier than it is, or that they'll be able to pick it up quickly enough to carry them through.

The problem of a market is critical. It's easy to say that you'll start out in what seems a lucrative business, but finding customers is another problem. You'll need a certain minimal selling skill to find potential customers, convince them that you can provide a product or service that they need, and persuade them that buying from you is the best choice for them.

Exploiting Business Contacts

Personal relationships are intangible, and really belong to the individuals involved, not to an employer.

If you're in sales, you may build up enough of a personal relationship with several of your employer's customers to make them your own when you leave to set up your business. Personal relationships are intangible, and really belong to the individuals involved, not to an employer. One print shop owner did not employ salesmen, and made it a point to call on all of his customers regularly to prevent his employees from walking off with any of his accounts. Another employer who used salesmen found that, after a couple of years, his chief salesman was able to start his own company in direct competition with him, and walk away with his biggest account.

Your employer will resent it if you take away some of his customers, but don't let this deter you. Remember, if he takes a customer away from anyone else, that's "free enterprise," and the "free market," but if anyone takes away one of his customers, that's "pirating."

Preparation is crucial. You must be up and running from the day you leave your employer, because if you can't fill customers' needs, they may as well remain with your former employer. Still, you can't survey them to find out how many would be willing to turn their business over to you. The more people you ask, the more chance that one will tell your employer,

and it's only reasonable that he's likely to fire you summarily if he finds you trying to take any of his business. As we've seen many times, loyalty between employer and employee is not a two-way street.

Sometimes the market simply doesn't exist. There are some products and services that just don't sell well. In some fields, there is such intense competition from established businesses that the small undergrounder starting up will be choked off at the outset.

The undergrounder faces many of the risks of the small business starting up. However, he has a tremendous advantage. Because he usually starts his operation as a sideline, without heavy investment and without depending on it for a living at first, he doesn't have to be an instant success. He can afford failure. It won't kill him.

The hard fact is that there is a very good chance of failure. Bearing up under it and recovering is the most important part of failing.

Let's deal with the prospect of failure. The hard fact is that there is a very good chance of failure. Bearing up under it and recovering is the most important part of failing. As an undergrounder, if you start small, don't expect too much, and don't depend on your new business to make you a million bucks the first few months, you'll be able to learn from your mistakes, and do a better job of it the next time.

A Short Essay on Economics

Economics is a deadly dull subject to most of us, and most textbooks, teachers, and politicians don't help the problem at all. They don't explain economics in an interesting and meaningful way, and the result is that many Americans are misinformed and uninformed about such basic ideas as "deficit spending" and "inflation."

This is a short essay, not a major text on economics, and there simply isn't space to lay out all the basic principles. There are several good texts available for anyone who wants to study this further.[3]

An author who has a good track record is much more credible than one who hasn't, or who doesn't make predictions.

Deep Inside the Underground Economy
How Millions of Americans Are Practicing Free Enterprise in An Unfree Society

90

One problem for the individual is that there are many books on crackpot economics in print, including some by "respectable" authorities. It's hard to judge whom to believe. There is a key, though. Many authors make predictions for the immediate future, some of which turn out to be accurate, and others fantasy. An author who has a good track record is much more credible than one who hasn't, or who doesn't make predictions. There are books available that are old enough for their predictions to have been proven and yet recent enough not to be obsolete.[4]

The practical result of widespread ignorance about economics and the lack of interest shown by the majority of people, is that most people give up their right to determine how the government spends their money. Elections have become mere personality contests, and people don't vote on meaningful issues.[5]

"Buy now, pay later" seems to be the American way of life. Most people, unlike their ancestors, feel very free to take on debts without much thought about paying them off. When an individual or a family does this, it's dangerous. When a government does it, it's worse, because it affects the entire population directly or indirectly.

One result is inflation. Not everyone knows what the academic definition of inflation is but everyone feels its effects as dollars buy less and less each year. Almost everyone with a bank account has seen how inflation has at times outpaced the interest rate. Subtract from the interest the income taxes that the government extracts from earnings, and we see that those who try to put away a penny for a rainy day can end up losers. Right now (early 2003), the inflation rate is lower than it was two decades ago, but this won't last. Money market accounts pay very well compared to the inflation rate, but this varies from year to year.

Another obvious result that goes along with inflation is the devaluation of our money, evident to anyone who has noticed that the Treasury Department no longer puts precious metal into our coins. Silver and gold-based coins are worth much more today than their face values, which has led some people to invest in and hoard them as a hedge for a possible economic collapse.

Inflation and deficit spending both put the economic squeeze on the small wage earner, which is a good incentive for the economic undergrounder.

Inflation and deficit spending both put the economic squeeze on the small wage earner, which is a good incentive for the economic undergrounder. An extra, tax-free income is a valuable asset, and a partial solution to the problem of the impact of a sick economy on the individual.

Almost anyone can work for a paycheck. Holding a minimal job and collecting a check from which income tax and various other deductions have already been amputated doesn't require much brains, and little initiative.

Planning how to earn money, and how to keep all of it without surrendering a proportion in taxes requires much more. It requires an understanding of the total picture, and the ability to plan and carry out a plan.

Insurance

Do you need insurance for your business? If so, why?

Let's say you're in the window-washing or painting business. You put up an extension ladder, a strong wind blows it over, and it falls on someone, injuring him. He can sue you. Depending on the seriousness of the injury, what sort of person he is, and what sort of lawyer he has, the suit can be for megabucks. Do you need insurance?

If you own your house, have a couple of cars, and quite a few thousand dollars in the bank, you simply have more to lose than if you rent, own only an old car and the clothes on your back.

Whether you need liability insurance or not depends less on the prospects of your being open to a suit or the inherent danger in your sideline than on the state of your assets. If you own your house, have a couple of cars, and quite a few thousand dollars in the bank, you simply have more to lose than if you rent, own only an old car and the clothes on your back. To give two ridiculously exaggerated examples:

1. You work as an itinerant electrician, and on one of your jobs you accidentally start an electrical fire that destroys a multimillion-dollar building. You're clearly at fault, but your assets consist of an old car worth $500, $100 in the bank, a few clothes, and a TV. You have no insurance. Everything you own amounts to less than two thou-

sand dollars, and you're not in a high-income bracket. How much do you think even the sharpest lawyer can collect?

2. You own a house outright, own a four-plex which you use as rental property, have several cars, fifty thousand dollars worth of savings and stocks, and while working as a weekend mechanic you make a mistake on a client's brake system. This causes an accident and the property damage (no injuries) comes to the value of your assets. Do you think you'll be able to retain any of your property when a smart lawyer gets his hooks into you?

Americans are the most litigious people on Earth. Many thrive on civil suits for things that might seem ridiculous but are valid under a legal technicality. Lawyers are to blame for this; their ethics are questionable at best. Typically they spin out a civil or criminal case with endless appeals as long as the client's money holds out, because the more work they put in on a case, the more they collect.

If ever you're involved in a lawsuit, you'll find that even if you're right, you lose, because of the time and legal fees that accrue.

Insurance adds to the cost of doing business.[6] This is one important reason why established businesses have to charge more than a freelancer doing the same work. In reality, insurance is a form of taxation, but on a private level.

Should you carry insurance? Well, it depends on a few other things, too. How risky is your business or sideline? If you do typing, the odds of becoming liable for damage or injury are very small. Any sort of construction work is far more risky.

If your business is so close to your normal activities that it's covered by other insurance, you may not need it. For example, if you are driving to your "moonlight" job, and you get into an accident, the chances are that you're already covered.

Do you have employees? If so, you may need insurance in case of injury. You will, if they're formal employees, need worker's compensation.

Getting insurance for your business not only adds to your costs, but serves as prima facie evidence that you're operating a business.

So far, the discussion applies to "normal" businesses. If you're an undergrounder, you must always keep in mind that getting insurance for your business not only adds to your costs, but serves as prima facie evidence that you're operating a business. If ever the IRS catches up to you, you won't only be liable for back taxes, but open to criminal prosecution.

The obvious conclusion is that you should not carry insurance for your business if you're operating totally underground. If what you do isn't covered by the normal insurance you carry, don't do it unless you have so few assets that you really risk nothing. If your mode of operation is skimming off your already established business, then you don't have to worry about disclosure, and can carry the insurance you feel you need.

Keeping the Books

Traditionally businesses keep three sets of books. One is for the day-to-day running of the business. One is for the tax collector, showing a pessimistic picture of the profits. And one is to show prospective buyers, exaggerating the profits.

Anyone who operates totally underground, without the IRS even knowing that he's running a business, would be foolish to keep records.

Whether an undergrounder will keep books at all is another question. Anyone who operates totally underground, without the IRS even knowing that he's running a business, would be foolish to keep records. Documentation supplies prima facie evidence of a business's operations, and lays the case right in the lap of a government prosecutor.

An example from the world of crime is the prostitute who keeps a "John list," to aid in keeping track of clients. The list contains all relevant information about a customer: name and address, sexual kinks and preferences, whether he pays well and/or leaves a tip, etc. When vice officers raid a call girl, they always look for a John list because this gives evidence to support a prosecution. The list shows that she is running a business, and the size of that business.

The one who has an underground sideline to his regular business, will of course, keep books, showing exactly what he wishes to show, and no more. This is because he has to maintain a front for the IRS and other agencies.

The one who maintains a home business to provide a peg on which to hang many deductions has to keep books, and they have to be as complete as possible,

Deep Inside the Underground Economy
How Millions of Americans Are Practicing Free Enterprise in An Unfree Society

92

because the better his business is documented, the better case he'll have for justifying his deductions. Someone who, for example, takes work home with him to do in his "office," will need a log of time spent, and a careful collection of all receipts to back up his deductions. He will need copies of his mortgage payment checks, utility receipts, and others so that he can assign a proportion of these bills to his "business expenses."

Keeping the books is only one part of running a business and there are many "management" theories and practices, but college courses in business administration are so insubstantial as to be all but worthless.

Butch, a successful small business owner, had this to say about the technique of running a business: "It's mostly common sense, and avoiding the mistakes some people make. That's it, really, avoiding the big and expensive mistakes. I've seen guys with degrees, but no common sense, make some bloopers that a kid wouldn't make. They get overconfident, and then careless, and they make a mistake that sinks them."

There is some nuts-and-bolts knowledge essential to running a business, and that this depends a lot on the nature of the business. Most of it comes through practical experience — "on the job training."

Butch does acknowledge, however, there is some nuts-and-bolts knowledge essential to running a business, and that this depends a lot on the nature of the business. Most of it comes through practical experience — "on the job training."

The technical end is usually specialized, and each business owner must learn it for himself. Other aspects are somewhat more generalized, such as the field called "personnel." This is merely hiring and directing employees, and most of it depends on the employer's personality. Some people have an intuitive knack for this; others don't, no matter how many courses in interpersonal relationships they have under their belts.

The nuts-and-bolts aspects of bookkeeping aren't very complicated for the small business, and there's no point in rehashing them here when there are many books available on the subject. A superficial knowledge of business law, especially as it applies to taxes, definitely helps, and the rest is already part of most people's experience. Almost everyone knows what a "lien" is, and few don't know what the term "pur-

chase order" means. A college degree in business administration just isn't necessary to run a small business, and most small business owners don't have one.

Making the most of the opportunity to learn at someone else's expense, and then filling in the gaps with brief study, helps to prepare for independence.

Learning the basics is usually part of working for someone else, which is where most of us start. Making the most of the opportunity to learn at someone else's expense, and then filling in the gaps with brief study, helps to prepare for independence.

Common Business Problems

Underground or not, businesses face similar problems, which can often be solved similar ways.

Collection

This is an extremely widespread problem and it's important to note one recurring theme: Businesspeople often try to work with other people's money. The longer they can delay payment, the longer they can keep the funds earning interest for them.

They have a set of priorities based on need. It all depends on who needs whom more. Thus, the telephone bill always gets paid on time. The telephone company won't stand for any nonsense from deadbeats, and their means of retaliation is quick and effective — cutting off service.

The customer who owes you a lot of money has the power to hurt you. Your business may fold if he fails or refuses to pay.

The beginning business owner is insecure and often hesitates to do or say anything that might offend a client, such as asking for payment. After a few knocks, his attitude hardens, and he starts to expect payment within a reasonable time.

One bad aspect of letting a client run up a bill too far is that past a certain point, he's got you. The customer who owes you a lot of money has the power to hurt you. Your business may fold if he fails or refuses to pay. While it's always possible to seek a solution in court, this takes time, and the intentional deadbeat is skilled at spinning out a lawsuit for months, finding one excuse or another not to appear, asking for an adjournment, and using other delaying tactics. Meanwhile, his creditor suffers, because he needs money to operate his business and pay his bills.

Some operators use this as leverage, forcing small businesses to carry them for fear of nonpayment. They'll dole out checks at a slow and measured pace, always staying 90 or 180 days behind, and keep the small business owner on the hook for years, if he lets them.

The remedy is to insist on prompt payment. Getting the leverage to do so is simple. First, diversify your business and have as large a clientele as possible. That way, no major client can sink you. For this and other reasons, many small accounts are better than one or two large ones. The business with only one account is a "captive shop," vulnerable to his client's whims. With many clients, dumping a deadbeat doesn't hurt as much, so making the decision to do so is much easier.

Gaining Customers

This is vital. Without clients, a business can't survive. One intangible factor that's important in building up a clientele is reputation. It's important to build a good one by being honest and reliable. Meeting your commitments will do a lot in this regard. No client is unimportant. He can pass the word and bring you another customer.

Having a number of small accounts helps your sense of security.

Having a number of small accounts helps your sense of security. Inevitably, clients go sour. They move away. They die. They no longer need your services. This is why you have to keep seeking new customers.

However, you can overreach yourself, getting so many customers that you can no longer service them all. This is why it's important to develop a sense of rhythm for your business.

When business is slow, prospect for new clients. When it's busy, service the ones you've got, and don't worry about getting new business that you can't handle.

Keeping Customers

Your reputation, based on the quality of service you provide, is the main ingredient in retaining clients. Unless you're in a one-shot business and follow a policy of hit-and-run, you need repeat business, and you won't get it unless you keep most of your customers happy. This means ironing out problems before they arise and being up front with your clients.

If, for example, you have trouble meeting a schedule because of lack of supplies or a heavy workload, it's better to tell your customer as soon as you become aware of the problem. Kidding him along and then letting him down will arouse resentment. He may well accept the "job," and pay you for it, but won't come back to you if he thinks that you've been dishonest with him. You may offer the lowest price, but if he holds a personal grudge against you, he'll close you out.

You'll find that some customers are very hard to please, and that nothing you can do will keep them happy.

Picky Customers

While it's true that you can't please everybody, this doesn't mean that you shouldn't try to please most of your clientele. That's the basis of your business. Nevertheless, you'll find that some customers are very hard to please, and that nothing you can do will keep them happy.

Some customers are nitpickers. They find fault with everything and ask you to do the work over, perhaps several times. Advertising agency people are notorious for this. One typesetter, who dropped his ad agency accounts, said that they "pick fly shit out of the pepper."

With a problem account, sooner or later you'll have to decide whether you're making or losing money on it. When an unreasonably picky customer bounces your work, you have to do it over, but usually can't collect any more money for it. This can lead to your spending more time on an account than it's worth.

If you're busy, you have to realize that the time you spend servicing such an account takes away from more profitable ones. At that point, you should complete your last commitment to him and leave, not asking for any more business. If he asks you to do another job for him, decline politely.

Dropping Accounts

Dropping an account sometimes requires finesse. The old saying, "Walk out, but don't slam the door," is applicable here. If you do anything to antagonize

Deep Inside the Underground Economy
How Millions of Americans Are Practicing Free Enterprise in An Unfree Society

94

your account, he'll be vindictive and spiteful. You can be sure that he'll tailor the truth to suit himself in telling the story to others. A slow payer, for example, will tell others that the quality of your work was unsatisfactory, never mentioning that he kept you on the hook for an unreasonably long time. These people can hurt you. That's why it's necessary to "massage" them when you cut them off. Tell them that you'd like to continue, but...

The best way to get rid of a troublesome account is to give him very long delivery dates. If he needs his work in a week, tell him, "Gee, I'd like to do this job for you, but I'm already committed to some others and I won't be able to get to it for a couple of months." The hard fact is that some customers can be very troublesome and the best way to handle them is to send them to your competitors.

Stealing

People can and will steal from you. Some may try to steal tangible items, such as products and supplies. Others will steal ideas. Commercial artists steal from each other constantly.

There's some protection against physical theft. It's possible to prosecute. Protection against theft of ideas is much more difficult. Some artists will "adapt" a design, changing a few details in order not to make it too obvious. Writers often plagiarize others' work, calling it "research." By paraphrasing, they can give the illusion of original work. There's no fully satisfactory solution to this. Each protective measure brings new and more ingenious methods of theft.

Bribes

Bribes start with small things, such as giving a customer a present at Christmas. Some customers start to expect such gratuities. Others demand them. Above ground, this is widespread. Fortunately, it isn't common in the underground economy.

A good rule for the small business owner to follow is not to give gratuities of any sort.

A good rule for the small business owner to follow is not to give gratuities of any sort. However, this is almost impossible to practice. It's often necessary to invite a customer out to lunch, which is one way it starts. Keeping it down to a dull roar is the best that most of us can manage.

Normal business problems will always be with us. Coping with them requires some ingenuity, and a little mental toughness. Otherwise, we can lose everything we've built up.

Luck

Despite the claims of various "self-made" men and others peddling get-rich-quick schemes, luck is very important in our lives. Yet most of us don't know exactly what luck is, nor how to make use of it. A clear and concise definition of luck is: the effect of the unknown variables.

Whether we examine a life situation or a card game, we find variables, and usually some of them are hidden.

In every situation there are some variables. Whether we examine a life situation or a card game, we find variables, and usually some of them are hidden. Assuming an honest game, dice may roll and come up in many combinations. The numbers to come are the unknown variables.

In a card game, the dealer presents us with a set of cards, without our knowing in advance what they'll be. These are variables. To continue with this line of thought, once we get the hand, we can play it well or badly, depending on the game and on our skill. Some games, such as chemin-de-fer, are pure luck. Others, such as poker and rummy, depend on both luck and skill.

In most forms of gambling, there are elements of both. An exception is the "numbers" game, in which the winning number depends on the total numbers of bets in races, in various combinations, devised to be absolutely unpredictable.

One important concept we need to examine is that of "odds," the chances of winning or losing. This is important in gambling, but also in business and in life in general. What we call "long" odds are those, which are very much against us, where the chance of winning is small. Many lotteries work this way, selling many tickets but awarding few prizes. They succeed for two reasons:
1. The price of a ticket is small.
2. The prize is very large.

Many people buy tickets, calculating that they can easily afford to lose the money in an effort to get the big prize. Some people are dreamers, relentlessly pursuing the big money even though the odds against them are almost impossible.

In business we find a very confusing combination of luck and skill. Part of the reason that it's confusing is that many people do not deal with it honestly. A get-rich-quick schemer, trying to line you up as a customer, won't tell you that the odds of your getting rich are very small. He'll present testimonials from a very few people who have made it, and pretend that anyone can do it. He'll tell you that it's all salesmanship, that if you fail, it's because you are a failure yourself, not because you attempted something very difficult.

"The difficult we approach with caution; the impossible we do not even attempt."

Further confusing the picture are some slogans, such as "You make your own luck." These have some slight basis in reality, but they're oversimplifications that often lead to misinterpretation. You can, to some degree, make your own luck, but that involves some judgment as to what you decide to try. A good slogan to follow is "The difficult we approach with caution; the impossible we do not even attempt."

It would be unwise, for example, for you to sink your life savings into a business about which you know nothing, and to trust someone whom you don't know well to teach you how to make a success of it. The wise middle course is to assess and balance the risks against the possible return.

The undergrounder that wants to start his own business faces risks. It simply may fail. It may not earn enough money to pay back the investment. Its return may be less than another type of business that he might have chosen instead.

This is why the undergrounder must choose carefully. As a rule, he's not under pressure to produce a certain level of return. He has little or no overhead. His advertising costs are tiny, if he has any at all. If he's smart, his investment is small.

"Moonlighting" at a trade you already know is a good risk, mainly because you already have the knowledge and the tools for the work. You may fall flat on your face, may not be able to get customers, but since you have spent no additional money to set yourself up, you can attempt a riskier business than the conventional business owner who has to sweat out a payroll each week, pay the utilities, taxes, license fees, and all the other costs of doing business.

You can risk failure, but you shouldn't risk much money. If you have to invest a lot, it had better be in something you know is almost a sure thing.

The undergrounder has all of the advantages here. He knows what he's doing. He starts small and works his way up. He risks little and ties up no capital that he doesn't already have. His overhead is small or nonexistent. He can afford to make mistakes that would kill the regular business owner.

This tends to dictate a certain choice of businesses. Capital-intensive businesses are those in which a great investment is required. The purest sort of capital-intensive business is investment in the stock market, where "you let your money work for you." You also put your money in the hands of other people, people whom you've probably never met, and about whom you have no assurance that they won't make a hash of it.

A less extreme course is to invest in your own business. At least the control is mainly in your own hands, although you can't control market conditions.

"Labor-intensive" business is where you invest mainly your time and little money. The time you spend is directly related to the amount you earn. You deal in services rather than goods. There is no possible embarrassing trail of invoices for supplies and materials.

This is how you make your own luck then. Assess the risks and benefits. Assess your skills realistically.

This is how you make your own luck then. Assess the risks and benefits. Assess your skills realistically. Balance the risks against the chances of success: what do you stand to lose if it falls flat? This way, you'll be secure.

Notes

1. *Shadow Merchants,* Jordan L. Cooper, Loompanics Unlimited, Port Townsend, WA, 1993, pp. 11-18.
2. *Ibid.,* p. 5.
3. A list of texts is on pages 323-325 of *Government By Emergency* by Dr. Gary North, American Bureau of Economic Research, 1983. These are all relevant, but some are longer and more involved than others, and are frankly unnecessary for a practical understanding of the subject.

Deep Inside the Underground Economy
How Millions of Americans Are Practicing Free Enterprise in An Unfree Society

96

4. Two excellent books are by Harry Browne, *How To Profit From The Coming Devaluation* and *How I Found Freedom In An Unfree World*, both published by Avon Books. They both date from the early 1970s, but the basics outlined in them are valid today.

5. In the author's home city, about fifty to seventy-five percent of the voters turn out for a mayoral election, fewer than fifty percent for city council elections, and fewer than ten percent for bond elections, the only ones in which the voters have a direct say in what happens to their money. Personality contests attract the most interest, while the important issues meet profound apathy from voters and taxpayers. The result is that the city government, despite the "conservative" image projected by most of the officials, consistently spends more money than it takes in.

6. *The Mother Earth News Handbook of Home Business Ideas And Plans*, Bantam Books, Inc., NY, 1976. pp. 88-89.

Chapter Seven
Getting Started Underground

There are many careers you can follow to earn income out of sight of the tax authorities. In this chapter, we'll cover only a representative sample, because it would take an encyclopedia to list them all. We'll study specific fields, and certain legal and economic factors common to all. For a more extensive list of possible underground occupations, see Appendix One.

Starting Out

There are right ways and wrong ways to get into the underground economy, in the same sense that there are right and wrong ways to change careers. The smartest way is to phase yourself in, beginning with a sideline that requires little capital and equipment.[1]

One person did this as an expedient after being laid off, forced to find a line of work with minimal risk and investment that wouldn't overstrain his limited savings. He quickly found that one weekend's earnings had exceeded his previous monthly salary. This experience isn't unique.

It's vital that you know your field. This may seem so obvious as to be an insult to your intelligence to mention it, but think: how many times have you walked into a store to find that the salesperson knew less about the product than you? How many times did the salesperson appear to be totally ignorant, and unable to operate the equipment you wanted to see demonstrated?

Have you ever encountered an incompetent mechanic, plumber, or even doctor? Other people make this mistake, and lose customers because of their blatant ignorance. Avoid it yourself.

Attitude

Another obvious point, seemingly too basic to be worth discussing, is attitude towards your customers. However, the way you treat your customers is more important than ever, and all signs show that this will become even more important in the future. Let's look at some case studies to see exactly why.

The telephone company used to have a reputation for an uncaring attitude towards its customers, which explains in part the phenomenal success of Lily Tomlin's telephone operator skits on the TV show *Laugh-In* during the late 1960s. Her satire of how telephone operators and "customer service" personnel treated and mistreated subscribers hit many raw nerves, because many Americans had felt slighted by the stonewalling manner in which the telephone company treated them. This collective anger had an influence on the forced breakup of the American telephone monopoly.

Doctors provide another excellent example. Today's arrogant medicos, who make their patients wait and then treat them in an offhand and dismissive manner, inspire resentment. When they goof, resentful and angry patients are less likely to be understanding and tolerant. Instead, they head for a lawyer, and the result is a larger number of malpractice suits than years ago.

If you're still not convinced of the importance of good customer service, recall the frustration you felt when you last had to wait an unreasonably long time in a restaurant, and the waitress passed by avoiding eye contact until you were mad enough to consider leaving. Also think of the times years ago when you called a company, and the receptionist blurted out, "Blank and Company, please hold," before pushing the "ignore" button and leaving you hanging for many minutes. Also think of more recent times, when calling a business puts you in contact only with a tape

Deep Inside the Underground Economy
How Millions of Americans Are Practicing Free Enterprise in An Unfree Society

98

recording, not a human being to help you with your problem.

It's not too hard to figure out that if you've already bought the product and need service or advice, they don't care because they've already got your money. You can't go to XYZ's superior service department if you've bought an ABC. Incredibly, some businesses have automated telephone answering systems for their sales departments, the point of initial contact with customers. You would think that businesses would realize that this type of indifferent treatment drives away customers, who are already fed up with such offhand treatment, and in no mood to tolerate more of the same.

Licenses, Resale Numbers, and Other Business Paperwork

Although we look at these as they apply to particular businesses, an overview is important. In principle, anyone in business is required to have a business license, following the laws of his locale. In practice, some do and some don't. This is how to break it down:

The business owner with fixed premises (store owner, etc.) or who advertises extensively usually has one, because he's out in the open, and local governments check Yellow Page listings, newspaper advertisements, and other sources for violators. He can't avoid being seen, and finds it safer to play legitimately.

In some states, you absolutely must have a business license to sell door-to-door, at swap meets, or to operate any sort of above-ground business.[2] This is an acceptable part of doing business if you're operating above ground and merely diverting some of your income. If, on the other hand, you're running an underground sideline, obtaining a license places you directly in the tax collector's sights.

The underground worker or part-timer who works out of his home often doesn't have to get any license. He gets very little exposure, and the effort of tracking him down is very costly in proportion to the amount of revenue recoverable by the government. As the underground worker tends to operate by word-of-mouth advertising, he runs little risk of detection. He avoids the cost of a business license and the paperwork trail this creates for the Internal Revenue Service, who regularly cross-check these for leads on tax evaders.

Another problem is a "resale number." This is a license issued by the state or local government, which enables a business that buys supplies for resale to avoid paying the sales tax twice. Since he's not the ultimate consumer, he gets the items tax-free, but has to charge his customers tax and remit it to the government. This makes him a tax collector for the government and also establishes a paperwork trail for other tax collectors to follow.

A closer look at the resale number reveals that it has one advantage and several disadvantages. The only advantage is that the underground worker avoids paying sales tax on parts and materials he resells to his customers. The disadvantages are:

1. He must fill out forms to apply for the resale number, which means that usually he must present a business license ("d.b.a.") to establish his legitimacy. This starts a dangerous paperwork trail.
2. When he makes his purchases, he must give his resale license number, which goes into his supplier's records and is open to inspection by tax collectors. Anyone without a resale number can buy his supplies anonymously with cash, thereby avoiding identification.
3. The amount of supplies he buys gives tax collectors a clue to his true income, because they keep informed as to markups and can estimate closely the business's profit.

The underground worker must keep a sense of proportion, and understand that by sacrificing the amount of sales tax, he stands to save more on income taxes.

Likewise for incorporation. There are advantages to incorporating, such as lower taxable income and awarding yourself generous fringe benefits.[3] These apply only if you're operating an above-ground business.

Low-Capital Underground Businesses

The businesses that follow vary as to the skill required, but they all take a minimum initial investment. Some provide excellent opportunities for interim or occasional income, to keep you going while you build a client base in your primary business.

Baby-Sitting
While baby-sitting is a widespread underground occupation, the next step is arranging for baby-sitting services. Acting as a booking agent for baby-sitters,

the broker collects a percentage of the fees. The problem is that brokering requires some advertising and breaks the low profile, thereby attracting the attention of tax collectors.

Busker

This is a sidewalk or subway entertainer, who plays an instrument, juggles, or provides other entertainment while passers-by throw money into his hat or tin cup. Obviously, this is a moneymaker only in populous areas where sidewalk performers are tolerated.

A gimmick helps. One performer used a nondescript mutt he named "Fluffy the Wonder Dog," and he regaled his audience with descriptions of feats the dog could not perform. Another entertainer announced to passersby, "Folks, applause to me is like butter. What I need is bread."[4]

Childbirth Educator

Pregnant women often find that the obstetricians they hire are too busy to provide much education in the complexities of having and caring for a baby. Modern medicine, especially obstetrical practice, is truly assembly-line medicine, high-tech but low-touch. This creates a niche for the childbirth educator, who conducts prenatal classes, has the time to provide individual attention to expectant mothers, and answers the many questions they have about pregnancy, childbirth, and newborn care.

While some childbirth educators are affiliated with hospitals and free-standing birthing centers, many are freelance, getting customers by word-of-mouth. Classes are usually small, with fewer than ten students, and often held in the childbirth educator's home. This provides opportunities for cash fees and bartering for services, out of sight of the IRS. Training is available for this field. For further information, contact:
Informed Home Birth/Informed Birth & Parenting
PO Box 3675
Ann Arbor, MI 48106
Phone: (313) 662-6857

The Bradley Method
Box 5224
Sherman Oaks, CA 91413
Phone: (800) 42-BIRTH

One publication devoted to natural birth is:
Mothering
PO Box 1690
Santa Fe, NM 87504
Phone: (505) 984-8116
Fax: (505) 986-8335

Film Extra

Acting as an extra in a film is occasional work, requiring minimal acting skill but a lot of stamina and flexibility. The problem is that it requires becoming a member of the Screen Extra's Guild, which has a stiff initiation fee.

Flea Market Sales

Selling new or used goods at flea markets can be above ground or totally underground. Organized swap meets, usually held at a parking lot, exhibit hall, convention center, or fair grounds, are very structured, with set fees for table spaces and even season contracts. Organizers require a sales tax license and business card.[5] Although your transactions are under government scrutiny, you can skim or divert some of your earnings. We'll study flea markets in more detail in Chapter Nine.

The other type of flea market is the informal, corner-lot swap meet. In many locales there are empty lots with absentee owners, and almost anything goes. You identify these if you see a row of parked cars with "For Sale" signs, vendors selling seat covers from their vans, and other informal sales operations. Without formal organization, it's first come, first served, and if you can set up shop on a corner lot without incurring the hostility of other vendors who might view you as a possible competitor, you can earn totally tax-free dollars on weekends and holidays.

Street corner operations are another choice. Some operators rent a corner of a store parking lot. Others used abandoned gas stations or convenience stores. Street corner merchants sell as large a variety of goods as flea market vendors. These include furniture, craft items, seat and dash covers, and produce.[6] We'll study street corner operations later in this chapter.

There are several ways of setting up a flea market. Some operators visit garage sales on Saturdays, picking up used household items that they feel they can resell at a profit on Sunday.

One important caution, cited by experienced flea market operator Jordan Cooper, is to walk around the

Deep Inside the Underground Economy
How Millions of Americans Are Practicing Free Enterprise in An Unfree Society

100

site first to survey what others are selling. It's a major mistake to think that, just because a dozen other vendors are selling left-handed widgets, you'll be successful carrying this line. The hard economic fact is that you'll have lots of competition, and this competition leads to price-cutting. Cooper points out that the best profit comes from items for which there is a demand, but no local competition.

One scam used by some vendors is to buy shoddy goods — factory rejects or "seconds" — and hint to customers that they're getting a low price because the goods are stolen. This hustler buys his rejects at rock-bottom prices and sells them for far more than their true value. This is a very safe operation to run, because if the police investigate, the hustler can show sales receipts to prove that he bought his merchandise legitimately.[7]

Furnished Room Rental

This is one of the classic ways to make ends meet. Renting out an extra room in a house you own is a perfect way to collect enough to defray property taxes or mortgage payments. However, it's much harder to sublet an extra room in an apartment, because most rental agreements contain clauses banning subletting.

Gardening

This can be as simple as a high-school student mowing lawns for pay after school, or it can include an otherwise unemployed person regularly servicing lawns for neighbors for periodic fees. Basic equipment includes a lawnmower, shears, and trimmer, but equipment can become sophisticated if the number of accounts justifies the expenditure.

House Sitting

House sitting offers two possibilities. One is collecting a fee for taking care of a residence, which can include feeding pets, watering and mowing the lawn, and other routine work. The other is performing the same work in return for long-term occupancy, which can save you a lot of money on rent. Either way, you can do this while holding a full-time job. Advertising is by word-of-mouth or classified ads.

Masseur

Massages have become more fashionable and more mainstream. All you need to start out is a portable massage table and a small assortment of body lotions and oils. Of course, you must know how to give mas-

sages and you must have a pleasant personality; client relations are all-important in gaining and retaining customers. Many states now require licensing in addition to set school hours completed. A lot of your advertisement will be personal recommendations from satisfied clients, and payment is usually in cash.

Massage can be learned by apprenticeship or attending a school. Further information is available from the

American Massage Therapy Institute
PO Box 1270
Kingsport, TN 37662.

Upscale and trendy people are into more exotic types of massage, such as Japanese "shiatsu." This is "acupressure," and one school for this technique is the

Ohashi Institute
12 West 27th Street
New York City, NY 10001

Yet another trendy technique is "Rolfing," and information on this method is available from

The Rolf Institute
302 Pearl Street
Boulder, CO 80306

Midwife

Growing dissatisfaction with American health care in general, and the American medical establishment's treatment of pregnant women and their babies has sparked a resurgence in childbearing outside the "system." Midwives fill this need, because midwives do not perform the objectionable procedures and treatments doctors often foist on patients, such as drug-induced labor, episiotomies, fetal monitoring, vaccinations, circumcision of boy babies, etc.

There are two types of midwives, nurse-practitioners and lay midwives. While many are affiliated with hospitals and stand-alone birthing centers, others are freelance. Home delivery is becoming popular, which eliminates the need for high-overhead offices and delivery rooms.

The emotional satisfaction is great, and the opportunity for conducting an underground business through cash payments and barter make this attractive. However, in many states it is illegal to practice midwifery without a license. If your patient encounters serious difficulties or even dies, you could be liable for criminal prosecution. Check the laws regarding this profession carefully before you begin to practice. For further information, contact:

Midwifery Today
PO Box 2672-223
Eugene, OR 97402
Phone: (800) 743-0974 or (503) 344-7438
Fax: (503) 344-1422

Pet Care

One home business requiring no investment except a few tools is specialized pet care, such as dog grooming. Some people are willing to pay to have their pets shampooed, groomed, and even boarded while they go on vacation. This is another cash business, with advertising by word-of-mouth or the local supermarket bulletin board.

Resume Writing

This is a solid, low-key personal service requiring little equipment. Basic equipment required is a top-quality typewriter. Stepping up, a computer with a letter-quality printer speeds up the work flow.[8] You can earn more profit by offering 100 copies in addition to the typed resume, and buying a copy machine can pay for itself quickly if you keep at it. This also ties in with typing and secretarial services.

Typing/Secretarial Services

Basic equipment needed is the same as resume writing, but customers are willing to pay for extra services, such as duplicating. Having your own copy machine allows you to sell entire packages, not just basic typing work.

Tutor

Teachers, professors, and students earn extra income by tutoring. Bright students and upperclassmen can tutor less capable students. Teachers and professors, obviously in a good position to tutor weak students, are limited because they have to avoid any impression of impropriety. This is why tutoring a student in one's own home is open to misinterpretation.

Opportunities for Children

Child labor practices have changed over the years. Originally, children were economic assets. Today, parents must support them while they're in school or until they "come of age." In an agricultural society, they were able to help out on the farm from before puberty, boosting the family's economy. The industrial era changed all that, as more people gave up farming and moved to the cities. Child exploitation in unhealthy factories was one of the unpleasant features of nineteenth-century American life.

The effect of these laws was generally good, because there was an increasing need for education to enable a young person to hold his own in the marketplace, where jobs increasingly demanded higher levels of skill and education.

The turn of the century saw the passage of comprehensive child-labor laws to protect young people from economic exploitation. The effect of these laws was generally good, because there was an increasing need for education to enable a young person to hold his own in the marketplace, where jobs increasingly demanded higher levels of skill and education. Restricting the employment of children thus assisted the programs of the public schools, which provided children with minimal education to give them a start in the adult labor market. For most of this century, children have been barred from the labor market with certain exceptions. School-age children have, with government permission, been able to work at certain part-time jobs that did not interfere with their education.

Ambitious young people, however, are not totally unable to earn money except with the government's permission. Only salaried labor is controlled. "Working papers" apply only to formal employment on a regular basis with established businesses. These keep records, withhold taxes, and comply with all of the licensing requirements of the local jurisdiction.

Those wishing to strike out on their own find that young people have special status in the eyes of the law. As a start, the problem of income taxes often doesn't apply to them. This means an almost total immunity from prosecution. Normally, even penalties for violations of the criminal code apply less severely to someone who's under age. In the case of a technical infraction of licensing requirements, or some provisions of the Internal Revenue Code, the young person is very unlikely to wind up in court, as any prosecutor would appear silly coming down hard on a young and minor offender when there are so many mature and flagrant ones unprosecuted.

Another advantage is a practical exemption from licensing requirements and keeping records. While local health officials enforce the health code with restaurants, a kid selling lemonade on the corner won't

Deep Inside the Underground Economy
How Millions of Americans Are Practicing Free Enterprise in An Unfree Society

102

have to cope with this hassle. A child running a business also won't find city or state tax collectors hassling him regarding sales taxes or business permits.

Apart from the law, children have certain advantages over adults in the business world. This results not only from their status as minors, but because most of them live with their parents.

1. They're under little or no pressure to "get a job," as are adults. They don't have bills to pay, food to buy, and all the other burdens adults carry. This gives them the freedom to take their time, select carefully, and not rush into something just because "it's a job and I've got bills to pay."

2. Not being under pressure, they have more freedom to decide that they've made a mistake and give up if an enterprise turns sour. Although Americans like to say they don't give up and they despise "quitters," abandoning an unprofitable pursuit makes more sense than persevering in an unhealthy or unprofitable situation. This is especially important in the case of children. Expecting someone to decide on a career at an early age is unreasonable. Immature people often don't know themselves and their abilities well enough to predict how well they'll do in an occupation. With no work experience, young persons often can't know how they'll make out in a short-term pursuit, and the freedom to make a change is vital.

3. Children living at home and seeking ways to earn money — usually to enhance their allowances — don't have the overhead that adult business owners carry. They don't have to make a certain volume of business per month to keep their heads above water, and they don't have to make heavy investments. Not having a minimum volume, and not having to cope with overhead, they have the freedom to work at almost whatever level of effort they wish. This is very important for the school-age child, who may be serious about his academic work and doesn't want to compromise his chances for an adult career by neglecting his studies.

4. Minimal investment is the common factor among businesses that young people start. Because young people simply don't have the money, they tend towards enterprises they can start on a shoestring. Fortunately there are many of these, giving the beginner a wide choice. In many instances the employer furnishes the tools and equipment, such as for mowing lawns. In others, they can get help from their families.

5. For a young person, a money-making pursuit is the first step towards independence, which many crave. Depending on an allowance is not very satisfying. Earning money independently gives the youngster the emotional fulfillment of not being beholden to parents in this regard.

Avoiding Traps

One of the hard facts of life is that, no matter how many laws there are and how rigorously they're enforced, some of the sharpest minds in the country will be working to circumvent them. Child exploitation is still with us, but in various guises.

One excellent example is newspaper carriers. Newspaper circulation managers, always seeking cheap labor to deliver their papers to subscribers, use a loophole in the law to exploit children. The practice varies from state to state, and certainly in some states delivering newspapers can be worthwhile. In others, it's "the pits."

For the young person contemplating this, a good way to tell is by looking at the advertisements in the local paper. If they constantly advertise for newspaper carriers, it means that they have a high turnover, an unsubtle hint that there's something terribly wrong with the working conditions.

Typically, the carrier is not an employee of the newspaper. He's a contract employee, which means that he gets a certain fee for delivering each copy. In many instances, he's actually a dealer, which in plain language means that he buys the newspapers from the company, delivers them, and is responsible for collecting the subscription money. If he has trouble collecting from an account, the circulation manager isn't interested and the child has to cope with it as best he can. Nevertheless, he's responsible for paying his bill to the newspaper each week to cover the copies he takes to deliver. In climates where weather is inclement, the child has to tough it out or quit.

Other problems come up with some newspapers. Some have erratic press runs, which means that although the papers are supposed to come off the press at a certain time each day, they're often late, and the carrier must wait around for them. As he's an independent contractor, he's not paid for this waiting time, which sometimes is as much as three hours. Basically, since the newspaper managers don't pay the carrier for his time, they don't care. This is important when the carrier calculates whether or not he's earning enough money for the time he invests.

The advertisements for carriers that newspapers run claim this is good training in basic business practice for the young entrepreneur, and that the experience he gains will benefit him in later life. This is merely glossing over the fact that he's on his own, and as an independent contractor under these dictated conditions, he usually gets the dirty end of the deal. In one sense, the experience is valuable, because he gains first-hand knowledge of what it's like to be conned and exploited without the financial damage he would experience in adult life.

An additional problem comes from the attitudes that some adults have towards young people. While they expect, and even demand respect from youngsters, they don't reciprocate, blatantly treating them like second-class citizens. They act as if young people have no rights at all and should be grateful for anything they get. Problem personalities such as these are some of the traps young people can encounter.

The traps usually follow the same pattern. Usually they involve having to report for "work" at a certain hour each day at the same place — a newspaper office or a motion picture theater — having to provide equipment such as a bicycle or a uniform, and uncertainty regarding the number of hours required. Any young person contemplating such a job should first ask any of his friends who work there about working conditions. This highlights one of the most important principles of job hunting, both in the juvenile and adult worlds: "Check out the boss as carefully as he checks you out."

Starting Out

The simplest way to start is by "hustling," which means knocking on doors. A young person seeking part-time jobs without any of the hassles of filling out applications and possibly letting himself in for traps can hustle his neighborhood, going from door to door and asking if the householder needs any work done. Often, this will produce a "hit" very quickly. Almost everyone needs something done for which they're willing to pay a young person. It may be time to mow the lawn, rake up leaves, clean out a storeroom, etc. Many household chores wind up neglected, because the adult doesn't have the time, but more often because it's boring work. This gives the young and ambitious person the opportunity to sell his services on a

one-time basis, with the prospect of repeat business if the outcome is satisfactory.

This "take the money and run" practice may seem insecure, as it is somewhat erratic and depends on finding enough people who need odd jobs done each week, but in reality it has certain advantages. The minor doesn't tie himself down to a fixed job, with the problems that may bring. If he doesn't like it, he can finish off the work that afternoon, collect his money, and not return. It's not a long-term commitment.

An advantage of this canvassing is that the youngster is already known in the neighborhood and doesn't have to present himself to a stranger, or fill out applications.

Another advantage is in collecting for the work. Although taking unfair advantage of a minor is despicable in the eyes of most people, there are some adults who will do it. Some of them simply don't pay, or delay paying. They make excuses, claiming they don't have the money "right now," and tell the minor to come back another day. When he returns, they again plead poverty, hoping that the minor will simply get tired of coming back.

Not many people will "stiff" a child, but if the young enterpriser does find one, he avoids getting in too deeply if his work is a one-shot deal, and he can avoid that person in the future. Meanwhile, he'll be earning money from other, more honorable people, and the loss won't hurt as much.

Jobs With No Investment

Knocking on doors usually means that the employer provides the equipment. A housewife who needs help in cleaning windows won't expect the young person to run home and get his own rags and cleaning fluid. The householder will usually have a rake or lawnmower, and whatever other tools are needed for the work.

Washing windows for a harried homemaker is just one service. Housewives may also need help in other ways, such as carpet beating, hanging washing, shoveling snow, and raking leaves. Some need help in their "spring cleaning," which can keep an energetic young person busy all day.

There are many tasks for which the young entrepreneur can earn money without providing anything but his time and effort. One of these is baby-sitting, in which the parents supply absolutely everything from baby food to diapers, and often even a meal or

Deep Inside the Underground Economy
How Millions of Americans Are Practicing Free Enterprise in An Unfree Society

104

snack for the baby-sitter if the task runs through suppertime.

Similar to baby-sitting is pet walking, for business couples who feel they don't have the time. Again, the client supplies the dog and the leash, and the young hustler furnishes only the labor.

"Wash your car, mister?" can be the start of another investment-free job. Saturday afternoon is the traditional time to canvass the neighborhood for this sort of work.

In many areas, Wednesday and Friday are the big supermarket shopping days. While many supermarkets include carts and even free carry-out service for people who need help in trundling their loads to their cars, those in the city don't always have parking lots, and shoppers have to make their way home on foot. Youngsters who take up posts near the doors of such markets, offering a shopping bag carrying service, can canvass their way to some extra dollars on a busy day.

Laundromats are also sources of extra income. Some housewives need help in stacking the wash, or folding sheets.

Delivering advertising materials is similar to running a newspaper route, but it's usually a one-shot. This is both good and bad. The disadvantage is that it's not steady work. The advantages are that there's usually no time lost waiting for the material to be printed, no customer complaints for missing a house, and no need to collect money. Payment may be by the hour, or by a fixed fee for every thousand delivered.

Investment, Junior Style

There are some occupations that require small investments. The young person may be able to beg or borrow the equipment, or he may have to buy it himself. Parents are often willing to let a youngster use the family lawnmower for working a "route," and anyone offering a window-cleaning service on a regular basis instead of casually can start by scrounging rags and cleaning fluid from his household, replenishing the supply with the money he earns.

Sometimes it takes actual "seed money." In one instance, a boy who got a job delivering telegrams after school persuaded his mother to buy him a bicycle for the task. Relatives often will lay out interest-free loans or an outright gift for the capitalization of the business.

Canvassing the neighborhood, offering a lawn-mowing service, or leaf raking, makes a better im-

pression if the young business owner has the equipment. Trimming hedges likewise requires a special tool, a hedge trimmer, and the one who has the trimmer in his hand and can go to work immediately has an advantage over the one for whom the homeowner must get out the tools. In cold climates, a youngster with his own shovel can pick up work by ringing doorbells after a snowfall.

Shining shoes used to be a popular occupation for young people, but lately, with the increased informality in dress and the widespread wearing of running shoes, there's simply less shoe leather to polish. In some areas, such as a downtown business district, a boy with a shoeshine box may be able to pick up a few bucks catering to the three-piece-suit trade. The minimal investment includes the box, rags, shoe wax, and a couple of brushes.

Selling soft drinks at a public event also requires a minimal investment. Paper cups, ice, and the fixings for lemonade are the minimum needed. Selling to construction crews on hot days can also be worth the time and trouble, unless they're all devoted to beer.

One of the symptoms of an affluent society is conspicuous waste. People throw away items that are still useful, sometimes just because they're several years old and they've bought a new one. Many of these throwaways are worth picking up. Some are appliances, including TV sets and VCRs, that need only minor repairs to make them serviceable. Collecting these and selling them to a second-hand store can bring extra dollars.

In many instances, it's possible to salvage parts from an appliance that's not working. Washers and dryers all have electric motors, and most of them are in running condition. Some repair men strip down old appliances for the parts, which they can install on their own work. Many cities have "stop and swap" second-hand stores that deal exclusively in salvaged material.

Not surprisingly, it's possible to pick up enough serviceable material from people's garbage to start a garage sale. Among the items people throw out are: clothing, cassette tapes, records, books, hand tools, toys, flashlights, kitchen utensils, and ashtrays. This is a very short and incomplete list, but it shows the range of material available. The only investment required is a cart to haul it away.

Recycling in various forms requires a slight investment. This can be on the family level, collecting soda and beer cans, stomping them flat, and periodically persuading a relative to help transport them to a recycling center. This only requires paper or plastic bags to hold the cans.

On a slightly higher level, the young person can seek recyclable items from friends and neighbors. Newspapers and magazines go to paper recycling firms. Metals of various sorts sell, depending on the metal and its application.

An ambitious young person can start a "route" buying or building a cart and making the rounds each afternoon, looking for throwaways. Newspapers and rags are the traditional recyclable items, but aluminum cans have become popular and lucrative during the last decade.

Keeping It All

Most people pay kids in cash. They know that youngsters don't have checking accounts, and don't take MasterCard. This means clean income, utterly invisible, and in any event most young people don't earn enough even to have to file. This means that they are, for all practical purposes, exempt from the tax bite. Starting out in business young is starting out the right way — in the underground economy. The experience will be valuable later.

Unusual Opportunities for Adults

Panhandler

The prospects vary from lucrative to simply awful. Certain locales are terrible for panhandlers, because police officers roust them regularly. Others, such as New York City and other large population centers, have so many people that the pickings can be very good for those who have a well-developed technique.

There are several techniques for panhandling, the most common of which is cultivating the hungry, down-and-out look and approaching prospects with a standard line, "Can ya give a fella a break?" Another is, "I haven't eaten in three days. Can ya help me?" These are transparent lines, and most passers-by will continue to pass by, and the secret of success is to make as many approaches as possible in an hour to catch the few suckers who will hand you money.

One New York legend is of the panhandler, living in an affluent corner of Westchester County, who drove his Cadillac to mid-town Manhattan each morning, changed from his business suit to working rags in the parking garage, and collected enough by intensively working the streets to support his lifestyle. His family thought he was a banker or stockbroker![9]

Prostitution

This has been called the "world's oldest profession," but whatever the characterization, prostitutes are classic examples of self-employed people who deal in services. It may appear redundant and a total waste of space to devote attention to such an obvious business opportunity in a book dealing with the subtleties of guerrilla capitalism. It might surprise you that making a living from prostitution is not as simple as it may appear, and the main point is that today opportunities exist for a low-risk and lucrative subspecialty.

First, let's take a quick look at how not to do it. If you sell your body on the street, your existence will be that of a "poorly paid and highly insecure streetwalker."[10] You will also run a severe risk of catching a sexually-transmitted disease. Another risk is encountering kinky clients who can injure you. There's also a very small risk of encountering a "ripper" type of serial killer who preys on streetwalkers. It's important to note that these dangers apply to both female and male prostitutes.

An extra hazard for streetwalkers is the police. Police officers tend to view prostitutes as conduits for criminal information, and try to induce them to snitch on street criminals they encounter.[11] Snitching can be dangerous, as the subjects of informers tend to take reprisals against those who put the mouth on them.

At best, police officers tend to treat prostitutes in a demeaning manner during arrest, calling them "floozies" and "queers." Some vice officers shake down prostitutes, trading immunity from arrest for sexual services.

The next step up is the "call girl" or "call boy," operating under the auspices of a call ring, which is an underground employment agency for prostitutes. This involves you with organized crime, and both federal and local police are intent on prosecuting these rings. If any of your ring is arrested, the danger of your being sucked in are much better than even, and you face criminal prosecution.

Another way is operating as a semi-freelancer, employed by an escort service. In theory, escort services are perfectly legitimate clearing houses that provide "escorts" for social occasions, any sex between escort and client is strictly a side deal, and the service disavows any knowledge of the sexual side of the service. This thin and hypocritical posturing doesn't fool the cops, and they regularly crack down on escort services.

Deep Inside the Underground Economy
How Millions of Americans Are Practicing Free Enterprise in An Unfree Society

106

The brothel, massage parlor, and photo-modeling studio operate the same way. While the brothel is up front about services provided, the massage parlor and photo studio take the position that they are "legitimate" businesses, with sex taking place as a side arrangement between their employees and clients.[12]

One type of prostitute is the housewife seeking extra money. These "moonlighting mothers" may do street work with all the dangers it entails, or call work for a limited clientele.[13] This practice was the subject of a hard-core X-rated film during the mid-1970s. This flick, titled *Soupe du Jour*, dealt with a small group of suburban housewives who took a minivan into New York City to put in an afternoon's work at a high-class brothel.

Now that we've got the dead ends out of the way, let's see how the successful prostitutes of both sexes do it, with virtually no risk except getting fired. Selling sex for pay safely and without running afoul of the law involves several important principles.

- First is limiting yourself to one partner. This avoids the risks of STD and kinky sex that may leave you injured.
- The second principle is to have regular employment as a cover job, to keep you squared away with the IRS.
- The third is arranging a suitable and safe method of payment.

The typical prostitute is a mistress, or a "secretary" or "administrative assistant" whose duties involve sex after hours. Let's consider the conditions of employment of each type. Let's also note that both sexes are involved in this. There are gigolos as well as mistresses.

The mistress is the classic "kept woman" (or "kept boy") of an affluent married man who maintains his sex partner in the style to which she has become accustomed. The mistress has no visible source of income, but doesn't need any, because she isn't registered with the IRS and doesn't even have a bank account of her own. The man pays her rent, buys her groceries, and provides spending money for clothes and other incidentals. He may even provide a credit card attached to his account. As long as she continues to satisfy him, and he can afford her, the status of the mistress is secure. Her workload merely consists of a few hours in bed each week, and if her source of support doesn't provide full sexual satisfaction for her, she has ample time to obtain sex from another man, or women, according to her tastes.

It's important to acknowledge, not for the sake of being "politically correct" but merely to be realistic, that this can work several ways. The recent examples of homosexual U.S. Congressmen keeping roommates shows that all sexual tastes are involved. One congressman's male housemate even found the time to operate a call-boy ring out of their apartment while his meal ticket was on Capitol Hill legislating!

The "office wife" is the modern version, and this is an even more secure arrangement. The secretary is a legitimate employee, who earns extra perks on her back after hours. This is not to say that she doesn't have genuine job skills as well. In the case of a female executive, the secretary may be a "pretty boy" with a big bulge in his pants as well as a talent with a typewriter or word processor. There's even the homosexual version, as expressed in a classified ad in *Alibi*, a weekly newspaper in Albuquerque:

> Gay White Male, 53, seeks Gay Male, 19-35, for office assistant & companion. Discretion a must. Travel opportunity. Computer skills a plus.

The financial arrangement is especially secure and impenetrable by the IRS, because the office wife may have an expense account. Her boss buys her dinner, takes her to the theater, and even on vacations.

The sexual secretary may not be her employer's mistress, or may have to undertake other sexually related duties for piece-work pay. A $200 or larger "bonus" for an evening's work is not uncommon. One example is the especially attractive woman from the secretarial pool whose duties include "entertaining" the occasional out-of-town client.[14] Her boss may not state explicitly that her job is to provide sexual release for his client, but it's obvious that her job is to keep him happy, whatever it takes, and to put him in a good frame of mind to sign a contract. Employers pay for results, and the successful typist or secretary whose "guests" sign on the dotted line can be assured of more assignments.

Perks for an administrative assistant are even more lavish than for a lowly secretary. The administrative assistant (male or female) may have a company car and a company credit card so that he may charge purchases to his employer. In turn, the administrative assistant may have a special friend (male or female) in the stock room or shipping department.

Yet another type is the nominal jobholder who comes in once a week to collect his or her paycheck. As "office manager," "sales manager," or other executive type, the prostitute has a documented job with a real paper trail, a perfect cover for the real occupation.

The office wife has the best of all possible worlds. There is legitimate employment as a cover job, on which the office wife pays all taxes to keep the IRS happy. The range of perks charged to the company can be mind boggling. Despite the recent changes in the Internal Revenue Code to eliminate or reduce many loopholes, this category of prostitute can benefit from the many remaining perks, including:

- Executive reserved parking
- Free gas and maintenance of the company car
- Free meals in the executive dining room
- Free use of the company "hospitality suite"
- Expense-paid "business seminars" at posh resorts
- Business-related trips of all sorts

As with other sexually-related employment, job security diminishes as youthful good looks fade. Still, the corporate prostitute has years during which to build up a nest egg, and to learn a salable skill to earn a living once the boss seeks a replacement.

Street Trades

"Street trades" is a very loose term that applies to all sorts of street businesses, mostly involving selling products or services. The street trader is mobile, and may overlap with or duplicate the business that operates from a fixed location. Let's look at various kinds of vendors and appraise the advantages and disadvantages of their operations.

We can divide street-corner operators into two types: licensed and guerrilla operators. The licensed operator obtains a business license, finds out who owns the property and arranges to rent it, and obeys all local ordinances. The guerrilla vendor is actually a squatter, setting up shop on a vacant lot or abandoned business on a busy corner and changing his location before anyone thinks to check his business license. Some street peddlers are highly mobile, setting up shop in different locations each day or even choosing a mobile location, such as a subway car.

The guerrilla operator's success will depend as much on local law enforcement officials as on the business climate and product line. Some small cities, especially affluent ones, don't consider street-corner businesses to be sufficiently upscale for their locale. Local officials will relentlessly persecute the guerrilla vendor with the total support of local established businesses who want to drive out the riff-raff. Other localities are live and let live, and the cops realize that they have more important crimes to fight than unlicensed street-corner vendors.

The forms that this sort of business can take are quite varied. Some street workers are simply peddlers, operating out of suitcases and setting up on well-traveled corners or even in subway stations. In some western cities, street-corner flower sellers operate with a basket of flowers, selling bouquets to passing motorists. In cities with a lot of pedestrians, street-corner peddlers sell wind-up toys, small notions and articles of clothing, and other light, durable goods. Another example is the street artist who draws portraits, caricatures, and profiles of clients on the spot, working with paper or canvas, or engraving them onto copper plates.

Others have more elaborate set-ups, such as carts or even trucks in the case of ice-cream vendors. An investment in equipment is necessary for a seller of frankfurters or ice cream.

The operator of a "newsstand," selling newspapers, magazines, candy and tobacco, differs from the store owner only in that he uses a wooden or metal shack erected on a sidewalk instead of renting a store. His premises are more austere, usually lacking physical comforts such as heat, running water, and a toilet. He can't carry much stock because of limited space but he can do as much business as a store owner, even more if he has a good location, and he keeps more of the earnings because his overhead is lower.

Opening up a street business is not a formula for guaranteed success, especially for the guerrilla capitalist. The big advantage is that, because of the nature of the business and the small value of the items, he deals mainly in cash, but there are many disadvantages that can go with it.

One is that, in many cities, the street vendor needs a license, either a "peddler's" license or a business and sales tax license. This immediately creates a paperwork trail, an entry on a list that the state and federal authorities scan regularly to ensure they're collecting from all who are in business. Tax collectors are aware that businesses that deal mainly in cash are hard to audit, and they pay special attention to them.

Despite this, there are many underground street vendors who operate in jurisdictions that require licenses, and avoid the paperwork by not operating from fixed locations. They're highly mobile, working out of suitcases and ready to move on when necessary. They watch for approaching policemen, and can pack up and melt into the crowd at a moment's notice.

Deep Inside the Underground Economy
How Millions of Americans Are Practicing Free Enterprise in An Unfree Society

108

Another disadvantage is that some enterprises, such as selling ice cream, frankfurters, and other foods, require a license from the Board of Health in many jurisdictions. This is an additional expense and also lays a paper trail.

In some cases, such as that of a street artist who sets up shop at a public event, there's an opportunity to earn a lot of money in a very short time. Often, especially if the event is one with controlled access, such as a state fair, he might need a temporary license or permit from the managers of the fair. They may or may not require proof of identity, but usually are only interested in collecting the fees. This means the street worker can surface for a day or two, do his business, and submerge into the depths once he's finished.

The opportunities for street vendors vary widely with the locale, as we've seen, and it's hard to generalize because there are so many special situations.

Tipster

A "tipster" is a low-level intelligence and penetration agent who ferrets out information for criminals. The tipster has access to premises and situations denied to the typical citizen or member of a criminal gang. As a professional observer, the tipster can provide information useful to a burglar or robbery gang. Let's look at some examples of tipsters.

Repair technicians of various sorts gain access to businesses, including highly sensitive areas, while performing on-site repairs. Even in a top-secret area, where the repairman will be accompanied by a security guard, the emphasis will be to ensure that the repair technician doesn't walk off with blueprints, diamonds, or whatever secret or high-value material is available. The tipster, meanwhile, is noting the doors, windows, and security systems, making mental notes of the layout and the types of alarms on the premises.

Delivery men of all sorts, who gain access to homes and businesses, can quickly appraise which contain something worth stealing, and pass the information to their contacts for profit.

Carpet installers are in especially good positions, because they absolutely must work on the premises. While a computer repair technician might find himself working on a defective computer brought out of the high-value area to an anteroom, the carpet installer must have access and remain inside until he finishes. Plumbers and electricians also have direct access to the premises where they perform their repairs.

Mail carriers, while they don't necessarily gain access to the inner sanctums, have an especially good position to assess the economic status of residents, and the types of business conducted in offices. A company keeping a low profile with the uninformative name of "Universal Traders" may receive mail from diamond merchants, pharmaceutical companies, or firearms manufacturers, and this offers the mail carrier a clue regarding the nature of the business.

Secondary tipsters are people in positions to overhear sensitive conversations in the normal course of their work. Barbers and beauticians, bartenders, waiters, and janitors are often privy to the most amazing secrets because their clients treat them as nonpersons, and speak indiscreetly as if they didn't exist.[15]

Taking advantage of these contacts requires personal acquaintanceships with burglars. You don't place an ad in a newspaper, and especially you do not walk into a bar stating that you have information for sale. That might put you right into the arms of a police informer. Only an acquaintance you know who has been involved in burglary is relatively safe as a potential client.

Diverting Income

There are several ways of diverting earned income into your personal pocket, by-passing the normal machinery of reporting. "Skimming" is one, simply pocketing part of your fees. This is easy when you get paid in cash, but you can work it when getting paid by check, as well.

The basic principle is Rank Has Its Privileges (RHIP). It's not a crime if you're the boss, whereas an employee would be in trouble if caught doing it.

Lawyers, doctors, accountants, plumbers, and other self-employed persons, professionals, or tradesmen, sometimes ask their nonbusiness clients to make their checks out to them personally, instead of to their companies. They then simply cash the checks at their banks. They avoid depositing them to break the paper trail.[16]

Income doesn't have to be cash to be diverted. One service technician's scam is to replace parts that don't need replacing, then keep the replaced parts for use on another customer's job. This is a trick to save for customers who give you a hard time, are very late in paying bills, or are otherwise troublesome.

Another way is to rent a car of the same year and model as the one brought in for repair, and exchange parts. Replacing the new battery, carburetor, or even transmission in a rental car entails very little risk of discovery, and the cost of the rental is far less than the cost of the parts bought through legitimate channels.

Case History: Don and Shirley's Underground Used Car Business

Don was a tool and die maker who worked for a small company supplying the auto industry. In 1970, he took early retirement. Don and his wife, Shirley, were both fifty-five years old, and Don had been with the company for over thirty years. They looked forward to traveling and doing the things they had planned for years.

The first two years of their retirement were glorious: the pension checks arrived on time; Don and Shirley bought a beautiful motor home and spent their winters in Florida; and they spent summers at their Illinois home and visiting their two grown children out west. Everything was rosy.

Then tragedy struck, a tragedy so bizarre and unexpected that to Don and Shirley it was like being hit by lightning. The company Don had worked for went bankrupt, and their pension fund was found to be empty. It was like Enron before Enron.

Don consulted lawyers and union representatives and years of litigation followed. They appealed to a U.S. senator to intervene on behalf of Don and other retirees, but in the end, the result was nothing. The company's assets were simply gone, vanished. After the banks and tax authorities took their cuts, there was nothing left for Don and the others who had worked so hard for so long.

This was just the beginning of Don and Shirley's tough luck. Shirley contracted breast cancer, and the treatments were long and expensive. Their medical insurance had come through the bankrupt pension plan, and when the plan went under, their insurance went with it. By this time they qualified for some help from Medicare, but it was not nearly enough. The significant difference had to come out of their pockets. Although Shirley fought and beat the cancer, the battle exhausted their savings.

Six years after retirement, things had never looked worse for Don and Shirley. Without their pension, they were unable to travel. Without their savings, they were unprepared for whatever tragedy might strike next. They had both worked hard for years. They had done everything they were supposed to do. Not only was Don one of the most skilled workers in

the plant, but in over thirty years, he had never missed a day — never even been late. Don and Shirley had given their lives to the system, and they had been screwed by the system — it was as simple as that.

Even worse than the financial devastation they had suffered was the psychological devastation they now endured. All their lives, Don and Shirley had been cheerful, self-confident people in charge of their fate, and eager to see what life had in store for them each new day. Now Don and Shirley felt like helpless victims, at the mercy of forces beyond their control. They couldn't even find jobs, because they were both "too old." They slept later and later each day and awoke with a feeling of dread, afraid of what new tragedy the day might dump on them. With inflation driving up the price of necessities, it was pretty certain they were even going to have to sell their house in order to make ends meet.

And then in their blackest hour, Don was struck with an odd bit of inspiration which was to mean a whole new lucrative career for him and Shirley. This inspiration was to give them back their self-esteem, provide them with a good income and financial security, and return the sense of fun and adventure to their lives. Here's what happened:

Don and Shirley had long ago sold their motor home, and now decided to sell their second car, a Pinto several years old, in order to get living expenses for a few months. Shirley put up a notice on the bulletin board at the neighborhood laundromat. They were asking $1,400 for the Pinto, but actually were willing to settle for far less in order to get some quick cash.

Don was surprised at the number of calls they got — within 24 hours they had received several, and had two people make appointments to look at the car. Don sold the car one morning for $1,200 cash. The other appointment was for the next afternoon, and when Don called to notify him that the car had been sold, there was no answer.

Don walked over to the laundromat to take down the "For Sale" notice on the Pinto, and on the same bulletin board, another person was advertising a Pinto of the same year as Don's! He wanted $1,100. Don stood there looking at that bulletin board. He had $1,200 cash in his pocket. There was a Pinto nearly identical to the one he had just sold which he could buy for $1,100. And there was a guy coming the next afternoon to look at a Pinto Don had advertised for $1,400. If Don could make only $100 out of this

Deep Inside the Underground Economy
How Millions of Americans Are Practicing Free Enterprise in An Unfree Society

110

situation, that money would be pretty important to him and Shirley.

Thus was born an underground used car dealer.

Don quickly took the bus to look at the other car, after calling to make sure it was still for sale. He knocked the price down to $1,000 by offering cash on the spot, got a signed title and receipt, and drove the car home. At first, Shirley was puzzled by what Don was doing, but Don just said, "I want to try something here." The second customer showed up the next day, and after a test drive and some dickering, Don sold him the car for $1,250 cash.

Don could hardly wait to tell Shirley what had happened. He had earned $250 profit in one day for doing practically nothing! Not only that, but the money was in cash! Don and Shirley talked it over, decided to try the same thing again, and it worked just as well the second time. Now they were in business for keeps.

Four years later, Don and Shirley had made a big success of their underground used car business. They traded three or four cars a month, averaging $400 profit on each, for just a few hours of "work." Cash is untraceable, so they paid no taxes on their income. All the money they earned was theirs to keep.

It wasn't easy, though. Don and Shirley worked very hard to learn the right tricks of advertising, buying, selling, and keeping their names out of tax records. It took time, but Don and Shirley had regained control of their lives. Once again they were able to travel, and could even take their used car "business" to Florida or anywhere else! Thanks to the underground economy, these two guerrilla capitalists had rebuilt their lives, and once again were productive citizens, instead of being on the edge of welfare.

How Don and Shirley Worked It

Successful buying is the key to any speculative venture, and Don and Shirley learned many tricks for keeping the buying price down. They purchased cars through many media — bulletin boards at colleges, supermarkets, laundromats, etc., from classified ads, and occasionally even from used car dealers. They knew where they bought was not nearly so important as what they bought.

Since they were looking for fast turnover, they selected only the most popular cars within any category; these cars would resell faster to less sophisticated buyers. They selected mostly smaller cars, such as Pintos, Mustangs, etc. These cars appealed to college students and other young people, they had less

power equipment for a used-car buyer to worry about, and they were frequently purchased by families as second cars.

Don and Shirley selected cars that they could resell for less than $1,500. Most people could pay cash to purchase such a car, whereas they would need to negotiate a loan to buy something more expensive. Don and Shirley were looking for a fast turnover, so any extra time spent by their customer negotiating a loan was money out of their pockets. They found the best thing was to buy no higher than $800-$1,000 so they could resell in the $1,200 to $1,500 range.

They selected cars with popular optional equipment. In most cars, they looked for an automatic transmission, radio, and heater. Other popular accessories were disk brakes, sunroofs, and power steering.

When Don and Shirley looked through the classifieds, they knew which type of cars in which price range and with what accessories to investigate. They especially circled ads which said "best offer" or "must sell" as well as the ones which outright listed a low price. When calling, they always maintained they were private parties, while asking about accessories, dents, upholstery, tires and mechanical condition. They knew if they said, "We speculate in cars," what they were really saying was, "We are trying to make money off your ignorance," which would not encourage the cooperation of the seller.

Don always remembered that he was doing this as a business, and time was money, so he didn't ask useless questions such as, "Have you had much response to your ad?" This would gain Don nothing and give the seller an edge, so Don stuck to the point. A good question was: "It's hard for me to get around since I don't have a car. Can you bring the car by for me to look at?" Frequently the seller would bring the car over, saving Don effort and giving him a psychological advantage in the bargaining session that followed the test drive. In addition, Don would find out if the car wasn't registered or didn't have insurance, and why.

In test-driving the car, Don figured if the engine didn't smoke, it started easily, had full power under hard acceleration, and seemed to be generally sound, it was okay for his purposes. But when he was in his hardass mode, Don would say he heard a "funny noise" in the engine, or brakes, or whatever. He then took the car to the appropriate dealer and had the service department suggest the nature of the problem and estimate the cost of repairs. This was his show.

With the seller in tow, he stopped at muffler shops for muffler questions, and brake shops for estimates of how many miles were left on the brakes. He'd hit a transmission shop for gory stories of how the automatic transmission needed preventive treatment, such as a band adjustment, to save it from major repairs only 5,000 miles from then. Don knew he could elicit the gloomiest predictions by stating that he really didn't know anything about brakes, etc. For example, a good question at the brake shop was, "Why isn't the pedal all the way up?" The answer was always, "Because you need a brake job," even if the car only needed a pedal adjustment.

Sometimes, out of sympathy for the seller, Don tended to get estimates only on "major problems." He knew that if he was more ruthless, a full show would bring him greater success in the bargaining session because:

1. He had presumably collected reliable estimates of the cost of putting the car into safe driving condition — the seller should be willing to accept a price equal to the average "blue book" value minus these repairs; and

2. Don had convinced him that selling cars was a pain in the ass, making him anxious to unload as quickly as possible and get this unpleasant business over with. Don knew every extra effort he made was that much more money in his pocket.

In bargaining, Don started with the average price from one of the "Used Car Prices" guides widely available on newsstands, deducted the cost of repairs, his profit margin, and another $100 or so for horse-trading elbow room, and this was the price he offered for the car.

If the offer was too low for the seller to accept immediately, Don said one of three things:

1. The price you are asking is for a car in great condition. Considering the quotes for repairs on the muffler, transmission, body work, etc., I would be cheating myself to offer more than (another $50).

2. Be realistic. The price you ask may be moderate compared with the other prices in the paper, but everyone knows those prices are intentionally high to make room for horse-trading. Every one of those other cars will sell at a price substantially lower than the price originally asked. My offer, which is a realistic one, is (another $50).

3. You may in fact be able to get what you are asking for the car, but my finances are so tight right now that I can only offer (another $50).

If he haggled to where they agreed on a price, Don then left a deposit, got a receipt for the deposit, and made arrangements to complete the deal. But if the seller was still thinking he could get more for the car, Don didn't give up. He wrote up a little slip of paper (not a business card) with his name, phone number, and price he bid. He handed it to the seller, saying something like this: "Here, put this in your wallet so you can contact me if you decide my offer is a fair price for the car." Even if the seller walked away cursing about how Don was trying to steal his great car, Don found that about one out of three would call him back within a week to accept his offer. (This meant Don only had to look at three cars a week to have a tax-free income of $400 per week.)

When the seller called him back, Don would sometimes say he found out that insurance will be extra expensive so he can only pay $50 less than his previous offer. He knew the seller had tired of the selling process or else he wouldn't have called, and used this knowledge to get an extra discount. Once in a while, a seller would call to ask Don to increase his offer because he had a bid equal to Don's from someone else. In a case like this, Don would usually cough up an extra $50, since his original bid included a margin for such dickering.

Since Don was doing this for a living, he kept accurate records on each car he test-drove, including the seller's phone number and the price he bid. Don found that if he called back a week or so after the test drive, many of the cars would not have been sold, and the seller was much more receptive to his bid.

After buying the car, Don had to get it ready for market. Some minor repairs would contribute to his ability to resell quickly at a decent profit. Most of the things he did required no mechanical ability or knowledge of engines. They were cosmetic work to make the car look better, and therefore be more saleable. In general, he did all of the things that a used car lot would do to make a car presentable.

He washed the car and cleaned the interior. If the upholstery was torn, Shirley would stitch it with upholstery needles and cheap thread from Sears or another department store. Don washed the engine. To cut thick grease, he used gasoline applied with a stiff brush or rag, and spruced up the engine compartment with a spray can of black glossy enamel. Don found that washing the engine was the single most important thing he did to a car. A clean engine in a private party's car says, "This car has been babied," or, "this is a new engine." Many buyers who said on the

Deep Inside the Underground Economy
How Millions of Americans Are Practicing Free Enterprise in An Unfree Society

112

phone that they wouldn't buy without getting a complete mechanical check-up would buy on the spot when they saw a clean engine. Don used Amway clear shoe gloss to make vinyl on dashboards and door panels shine like new and replaced worn floor mats with carpet remnants from a used carpet store. He removed crystallized acid from battery terminals with a solution of baking soda and water, and replaced bald tires with recaps. If the paint was dull or pitted with rust, he got a cheap paint job for $89.95 in a similar, but not necessarily matching, color.

Since Don acquired a small amount of mechanical ability in his years of dealing with cars, he would also give the car a minor tune-up (change or clean the plugs) and adjust the brake pedal. Before he learned how to do these, he would pay a garage to do them. Don stayed away from major repairs. He knew he could sell cars with bad rod bearings and bad clutches just by waiting for the sufficiently naive buyer who always appears when the average popular used car is offered for sale.

In advertising the car for sale, Don learned the most valuable trick is to let local buyers know it was available; most buyers would look first at a local used car rather than one on the other side of town. He knew his best medium was notices on bulletin boards at colleges, laundromats, supermarkets, etc., for which Don had a carpenter's staple gun. In addition to being the best advertising medium, these places had the advantage of being free.

Don used the brightest possible paper to make his ads stand out from the many other ads. These ads were especially effective for selling cars to college students. The little "tear-away" phone numbers were a good idea, too, since the person reading it didn't need to hunt for a pencil and paper to copy down Don's number, and wouldn't remove the entire ad, thereby keeping others from seeing it.

Don always made his ads more creative than so many that said "excellent condition," and he didn't use ambiguous phrases such as "cherry," "loaded," or meaningless phrases such as "cream puff." He didn't take up valuable space with a lot of crap — he used it to describe the good features of the car.

In large block letters (a magic marker was good for this), he would write something like "SAVE $300." Then in the typewritten copy, he emphasized the car's popular features: Sunroof, low mileage, new tires, stereo, or whatever.

Instead of writing something negative such as "dents in body," Don would either write "body fair" or nothing, explaining on the phone that his low price reflected the slight cost of repairing the dents, although the dents could be safely ignored. This way, Don didn't scare off the handyman who wanted to fix it himself or the person who really thought dents were secondary to mechanical condition.

Don made five or six bulletin board ads to a sheet of paper, and Xeroxed them on colored paper, giving him enough ads to place two or three on each bulletin board in his vicinity.

Don and Shirley found their next best advertising medium to be the throw-away classified papers, or "Shopper's Guides," usually given away free at supermarkets, or delivered door-to-door. Not only was advertising cheap in these little papers, but because they're well read, they're good places to sell used cars. Another medium Don and Shirley sometimes used was the Sunday classifieds. In their ads, Don and Shirley used a powerful phrase such as "Super low mileage" or "Super low price," or simply stated the mileage, letting the low figure speak for itself.

Here is a sample classified ad:

> LOW MILEAGE: '76 Pinto. 48,000 miles. Good condition. Ideal for freeways or around town. Worth $1,450, must sell quick for $1,150. 337-9653.

In selling the car, Don knew the most important thing was to appear as a private party, not a dealer. For reasons of tax avoidance (discussed a little later) Don and Shirley would not have the car in either of their names, so they had fabricated an answer to the inevitable question, "Why are you selling?" If the previous owner was male, they could say, "We are selling the car for our grandson, who joined the Air Force. Those dealers who advertise 'cash for your car' wanted to buy it for nothing, so we are helping out our grandson, who is now at training camp." Or he had taken a job out of the country, or they were selling it for Don's brother who had been placed in a rest home, or whatever. If the previous owner was female, they used variations on the same themes.

Don always set the price of the car at least $100 higher than the price he ultimately wanted. This allowed for horse trading. Don also set the price at about the average for the model, or higher, by checking used car dealers' ads in the newspapers. Don learned that if his price was obviously low, people would think he didn't have any confidence in the car, and he would get fewer bidders than if he started with a price that was a little high and horse-traded down.

Besides, once in a while he got a buyer who thought horse-trading was immoral, thereby giving Don an extra $50 or $100 profit. Don set a floor under his price so that the buyer would start the bidding at a price that guaranteed him a profit. This floor also guaranteed that he wouldn't be giving test drives to people who lacked the money Don needed for his profit.

Now we come to the real underground part of Don and Shirley's little business — avoiding taxes. The main way Don and Shirley avoided taxes was by remaining invisible to the taxing agencies. If they don't know you exist, they can't tax you. Of course, Don and Shirley had no licenses, since getting a license is asking to be taxed. They posed as private parties, not dealers, in all transactions, and therefore remained invisible, underground entrepreneurs. This allowed Don and Shirley to avoid license fees, inventory taxes, business activity taxes, sales taxes, etc., just by simply never telling the tax parasites they were doing business.

It was important that their names not appear in records of ownership, which were processed through the state, and might therefore bring them to some bureaucrat's attention. They did as follows:

When buying a car, they paid cash, got a receipt, a bill of sale, the properly signed title, and the registration. The key to the transaction was the bill of sale. In speculating, Don and Shirley did not want to have to pay registration expenses on each car they traded, and they wanted to keep their names off all documents which the government received so they wouldn't have to buy a dealer's license. Don and Shirley wanted it to appear that the car was transferred directly from the previous owner to their customer.

- Method 1: They could forge the previous owner's name onto a bill of sale to be used in the sale of the car to their customer.
- Method 2: They could have the previous owner sign a bill of sale which had blank spaces for price, date, and name of purchaser.
- Method 3: They could make a Xerox copy of the complete bill of sale with the information pertaining to the sale to their customer on strips of paper pasted over the original information. (They could erase shadow lines off a Xerox copy, or paint around the edges of the original paste-up with "White-Out," available from office supply stores, before Xeroxing.)
- Method 4: They could get a four-leaf carbon speed letter form from their local office supply

store, locate the places where the undesirable information would appear, and cut holes in the second carbon at the appropriate spots. They completed the original bill of sale on the first sheet — even the most exacting seller would sign without detecting that the third copy would be used to avoid registration expenses.

- Method 5: They could simply tell their customer that he didn't need a bill of sale because, while they would give him a receipt, the government had its own form (the title in title states) which he should sign to state on what amount he would have to pay sales tax. Alternately, they could say that their bill of sale wasn't valid because the only really valid bill of sale was one where he swore before a notary public what price he paid for the car for which he had the signed registration or the signed title.

The best was Method 2. If the seller asked them why they wanted blank information on the bill of sale, Don and Shirley provided a cover story. They explained that while information describing the car such as the VIN number, must be on the bill of sale, they haven't decided for insurance purposes if the car should be registered in one of their names. Eventually, it might be in the name of their nephew (or niece, or son-in-law, or whatever). While it wouldn't really hurt anything to fill in the date, Don and Shirley always insisted that the price be left blank so they could save some money on sales tax by filling in a lower sales price later. Most people would understand and not object. If Don and Shirley got a particularly suspicious seller, they could always use one of the other methods outlined above.

BILL OF SALE

Date_____

I, (previous owner's name), hereby sell my 1976 Pinto, color beige, VIN # 12345678 for $ cash, to

Signed (previous owner)
Address

Witnessed
Address

This was the format for a bill of sale that could be used to transfer the car directly from the previous owner to Don and Shirley's customer, without them

Deep Inside the Underground Economy
How Millions of Americans Are Practicing Free Enterprise in An Unfree Society

114

incurring registration expenses. If the transfer of registration was across state lines, or if the title or registration was missing, Don and Shirley got it witnessed by a friend; otherwise, most states didn't require a witness. If the previous owner insisted on specifying more than the date and car description (even after the arguments Don and Shirley used about why they wanted the price and purchaser's name left blank), Don and Shirley just let him complete the information, because they could always use one of the other methods above.

In selling the car, Don and Shirley remembered the ruses they developed to keep from appearing as dealers in explaining why they were selling a car not registered to them. In selling the car, they accepted only cash, cashier's check, certified check, money order, or bank draft. These were all financial instruments which could be easily converted into cash without leaving embarrassing, telltale stains in bank records.

Don took the money and handed the buyer the bill of sale (which he had rigged to transfer ownership directly from the previous owner to the new owner, as described above) the signed title and the registration.

If the buyer wanted Don or Shirley to accompany him to get the title transferred, or if he wanted a bill of sale stating that they are the agents for the previous owner, Don offered him a receipt and said, "Don't be absurd. Can't you see that the title has been signed over by the previous owner? If you want to deduct applicable car expenses from your income tax, I will give you a receipt, but there is nothing else needed to transfer ownership."

Here are a couple of handy little-known facts that Don and Shirley always kept in mind:

1. They didn't really even need a title or registration to transfer ownership because these papers might have been lost or the car might have been freshly manufactured from parts. Each state had its own routines, but they all reduced to swearing under oath before a notary that you are the owner. The state then issued a temporary registration and checked to be sure the car wasn't stolen. Since Don and Shirley were not dealing in stolen cars, they never had a problem with transferring ownership.

2. The only purpose of the bill of sale was to give the state a price on which to charge excise or sales tax. (A car need not be sold in order to transfer ownership. Cars are frequently transferred from mother to son, brother to brother, or whatever looks plausible without the payment of money, and therefore, with the smallest possible payment of sales tax.)

What Don and Shirley were doing was illegal, and they could even have gone to prison in the unlikely event they were caught. The authorities would call Don and Shirley "cheaters" and "criminals." They would say Don and Shirley were "not paying their fair share." What do you think of these retirees who never wanted anything more than to be productive and self-reliant people? Who would have been better off if they lived in poverty, on welfare, Social Security, and food stamps?

Don and Shirley thought and talked it over, and they decided that the chance to be self-reliant was worth the risk of apprehension. When it comes to the underground economy, we must each make our own choices.

Note: Due to changes in laws regarding the sale of used cars, and due to inflation, there is hardly anywhere Don and Shirley's business would work today, but their story is an excellent example of the kind of thinking necessary to succeed as a guerrilla capitalist.

Notes

1. Jordan L. Cooper, *How to Make Cash Money Selling at Swap Meets, Flea Markets, Etc.,* Loompanics Unlimited, Port Townsend, WA, 1988, p. 4.
2. *Ibid.,* p. 136.
3. *Ibid.,* pp. 135-36.
4. Al Sacharov, *Offbeat Careers: The Directory of Unusual Work,* Ten Speed Press, Berkeley, CA, 1988, pp. 34-35.
5. Jordan L. Cooper, *Shadow Merchants,* Loompanics Unlimited, Port Townsend, WA, 1993, p. 31.
6. *Ibid.,* pp. 87-92.
7. Stuart Henry, *The Hidden Economy: The Context and Control of Borderline Crime,* Loompanics Unlimited, Port Townsend, WA, 1980, pp. 22-23.
8. Jean Sherman, "Moonlighting Revisited," *Cosmopolitan* 208, no. 5, May 1990, p. 266.
9. Related to the author by a successful panhandler in return for a meal.
10. Gale Miller, *Odd Jobs,* Prentice-Hall, Englewood Cliffs, NJ, 1978, p. 123.
11. *Ibid.,* p. 150.
12. *Ibid.,* p. 131.
13. *Ibid.,* p. 156.

14. *Ibid.*
15. *Ibid.,* p. 40.
16. Lauren Chambliss, "Cheating Hearts: The IRS Is Zeroing in on the Taxpayers Who Tend to Fudge the Most on Their Returns," *FW* 159, no. 11, 29 May 1990, p. 60.

Chapter Eight
Contract Labor

Contract labor provides opportunities for reducing the tax bite, or eliminating it altogether. This is why it's worth looking at contract labor closely, as contract labor offers many permutations, and smart operators can reduce their taxes by contracting out openly, or eliminate them by working underground.

There's not much difference between a wage-earning employee and a contract employee with regard to the nature of the work, but there's a big difference between the ways they're paid. A wage earner is a legal employee working for an hourly or weekly wage and is subject to withholding on his paycheck. The contract employee does approximately the same work, but is paid by the "job," and gets to keep it all. Of course, he must pay his taxes, but the legal responsibility is his, not his employer's.

Let's take a close look at exactly what a contract employee is, both the practical definitions and the IRS's. The contract employee is a temporary worker, not committed to the job or the company. He accrues no seniority, gets no fringe benefits, and his employment lasts only for the life of the "contract," which is often verbal. In short, he's nominally a temporary employee, although in practice his term of employment may be longer than some "permanent" employees, who may be laid off when the workload slows down. He collects his full contracted fee without any withholding. The word "fee" is very important. He charges a fee because he's self-employed. He bills the company, and is not on the regular payroll.

The IRS doesn't like contract labor, because it offers opportunities for unreported income. IRS personnel much prefer it when your employer amputates part of your salary before you even see your paycheck. To minimize the number of people working as independent contractors, the IRS has set up rules regarding who can be classified in this bracket, and imposes penalties upon any employer who, by accident or on purpose, wrongly classifies an employee as an independent contractor.[1]

This can cut both ways. You can get stung if you mistakenly hire someone to help you in your business as an independent contractor. This is why it's important to know the rules that distinguish the two. These cover several areas.

Control

Who decides how the contractor or employee will do his job? Who sets the hours he works? If you contract only for services, but leave it to the contractor how he goes about his work, you're in the clear.

Tools and Equipment

Who owns the tools and equipment the contractor uses? If he does, this is an indication that he's legitimately independent. However, if he works using the equipment and/or tools you furnish, he's an employee. One trucking company that hired drivers as independent contractors to drive its trucks lost out because the IRS ruled that drivers were company employees.[2]

Facilities

Where does the contractor work: at his shop or office or yours? The answer can cut both ways. An accountant might work in your office while doing your books. A window washer must work at your facility, obviously, to wash your windows. On the other hand, a proofreader could easily take the work home with him.

Exclusivity

Does your contractor work only for you, or is he free to work for others? Does he in fact have other accounts? If he's exclusively your hireling, this tends to make him your employee.

Deep Inside the Underground Economy
How Millions of Americans Are Practicing Free Enterprise in An Unfree Society

118

Training

Who trains the employee or contractor? If you do, this tends to make them your employees.[3]

Hiring and Firing

Can you summarily fire the contractor without incurring liability for breach of contract? Employees can be fired or laid off; contractors generally cannot, except for breach of contract or at the end of the contract.

Some of the occupations in which it's possible to work on contract are:

Accountant	Janitor
Appraiser	Machinist
Beautician	Nurse
Broker	Photographer
Copywriter	Printer
Dog Trainer	Rental Agent
Editor	Salesperson
Exterminator	Typesetter
Gardener	Window Washer
Instructor	Writer

The advantages of being a contractor are immediate and significant. One of the most important is that the paycheck you get is intact.

This does not absolve you from the obligation to pay taxes, however. You have to keep your own books, and send in a quarterly estimated tax payment. However, while you're earning, you deposit your checks in your business account and collect the interest on the money. The IRS, even if it gives you a refund at the end of the year, does not pay you interest on the money it held. This can make a significant difference. The government invests the money it collects until it needs it, but it doesn't give you even a share of the interest of dividends earned on the money it refunds you. By even a mundane investment, such as in a bank account that pays 1.5 percent, you'll collect interest on it, which is better than nothing, even if that interest is taxable.

The benefits to the employer are also immediate and significant. He doesn't have to keep a payroll record, calculate your withholding, and issue you a check each week. In fact, he may ask you to bill him once a month, to save him time in writing checks. It also absolves him from paying matching Social Security tax on your labor. You're no longer covered by worker's compensation or unemployment insurance, which means he saves there, too. If he has a pension plan for his employees, he'll drop you from it. The

deal is attractive to him. He withholds roughly three dollars from the pay of a ten-dollar an hour employee, and has to pay yet more himself, depending on the fringe benefits.

Since he doesn't have to pay the additional expenses on your work, you can ask him to pay you more. It'll be a net gain for both of you. He'll also find it attractive that he's not committed to paying for forty hours a week. He'll simply call you as he needs you. This can be good or bad for you, depending on how you handle it.

If you're working for minimum wage, or slightly above it, you'll lose if you become a contract employee. If you're a skilled tradesman, you'll definitely gain.

As a self-employed person, you can deduct your mileage to and from work. This adds up to a lot at the end of the year. Even in a city where it doesn't pay to drive, you can deduct your commuting costs if you take public transportation. As a self-employed person, the trip to the bank to deposit your check will be deductible, as will any trip connected with your business.

You can deduct eating out, unlike an employee. If you incur any legal fees as a contractor, they're also deductible. Any business license you need also comes off your taxes. Generally, you can deduct more for tools, machinery, postage, and telephone than you could if you were an employee. Furthermore, if you take work home with you, and use one room of your home exclusively for that, you can deduct your rent or mortgage and utilities in proportion to what you use.

You'll have to provide your own health insurance. Various insurance plans to which you may subscribe become deductible. In short, you have available to you far more deductions than you would as an employee.

Not only will you have to manage your money very well, but your time. You may not have the security of forty hours work per week from an account, and in fact it's better if you don't. Working full time for one company makes you seem like an employee to the IRS, and it may disallow your status.

If you have several accounts:

- It establishes you as a truly self-employed person, which is very important if you're ever audited.
- It gives you more security. The worst possible case is to have all of your eggs in one basket, depending on one job.

Many people think that a "steady job" means security, but in fact many jobs are not "steady" at all. Even the largest companies have layoffs, with thousands of employees suddenly out in the cold. Even civil service jobs aren't necessarily secure; New York City laid off thousands during its fiscal crisis. Recently several cities have had to cut budgets because of decreased revenue. Having income from more than one source means that if one dries up, you haven't lost all your income and you can use the free time to seek more accounts.

You have to cope with being out in the cold. You won't have employee benefits, but it's not as bad as it seems at first. You can provide medical insurance for yourself and still come out ahead. You ought to be aware, though, that individual medical insurance costs more than does a group plan of the sort employers have. As for unemployment, the payments are so low that even a part-time job pays more. In fact, you can get along better by working some small contracts than if you were on unemployment.

This brings us to managing your time. What do you do during your off hours? If you don't need any more money, you can rest. You can also use the time to sell yourself, seeking new accounts. The problem with accounts is that they don't necessarily last. Companies go out of business, relocate, and have slow periods, and these affect contract employees as well as regular ones. It's a mistake to assume that your main account will be with you forever. You're even better off without a main account, but a slew of small ones. That way, no account can hold you in bondage.

As an example, Joe had set up his own graphic arts shop, and his main account was a large department store nearby. This account gave him eighty percent of his business, and he knew he couldn't survive without it; his other accounts were too small to pay even his overhead. The problem was that the head of the advertising department knew it too, and had the personality of a tyrant. This executive habitually cracked the whip, and made unreasonable demands, knowing Joe could not refuse. Joe tried halfheartedly to get other accounts, but was not able to build up his other business enough to enable him to get out from under. His was a "captive shop."

Possibly the greatest benefit of being self-employed is psychological. You do your work, whatever it may be, without having someone over you. While it's true that you have to be responsive to your accounts' needs and keep them happy, you can deal with them on more equal terms than you were able to as an employee and subordinate. Simply, you get more respect.

In dealing with your accounts, you'll find they won't show you the resentful attitude many of them have for their regular employees. They'll see you as a fellow business owner, one who is on the same side of the fence as they are, instead of an opponent in the labor/management struggle.

The question of loyalty also comes in. As an employee, your boss may resent your working part-time for another company, especially if the other is a competitor. He'll label it a "conflict of interest" if he wishes, and can hassle you for it. Some companies oblige new employees, as a condition of employment, to sign forms that they will not work for any competitor for as long as they work for that company.

Some employers are very possessive about their workers, forgetting that they don't own them, but merely rent their time. As an independent contractor, you'll be free of this hassle, and will be able to contract with a number of other companies. Moreover, the owners won't expect that sort of blind loyalty from you as a rule, and if one does make such an unreasonable demand on you, you'll be able to abandon the account.

While it's true that there are unreasonable and abusive people in every line of work, and that you'll find some of your customers to be that way, you're not in the terribly vulnerable position you'd be if you were bound to them for forty hours a week. You'll even be able to pick and choose your customers after a while, dropping the troublesome ones and staying with those who treat you well.

Even the problem personalities found in many workplaces won't seem as bad. You'll be able to console yourself with the knowledge that you have to see them only for a few hours per week, and pity their employees who are trapped and can't leave when one job is finished.

Incorporation

To incorporate or not? There are different opinions, and the proper course depends on your level of income. While it's true that incorporation definitely sets you up as an independent contractor with the IRS, it's also costly. There are legal kits to permit you to incorporate for fifty dollars, but in a matter such as this, it's best to be cautious.

Deep Inside the Underground Economy
How Millions of Americans Are Practicing Free Enterprise in An Unfree Society

120

Generally, unless you earn fifty thousand dollars a year or more, it doesn't pay to incorporate. It seems prestigious, but the benefits are small. There are some tax advantages, such as paying the corporate tax rate instead of the individual tax rate of the sole proprietorship, but the cost of incorporation is an "overhead" that will eat up your tax savings below a certain income level. The best way to decide this is to ask your accountant, who is familiar with the laws in your state and knows your situation.

Beating the System

One problem that arises with any sort of salary is the paper trail through the worker's Social Security number. We've seen how some avoid this by giving the employer a false Social Security number, and how they can prolong the process before they move on to avoid an IRS investigation. Contracting offers another method of "beating the system."

Johnny hated the Internal Revenue Service and took every opportunity he could to beat the system. Johnny was the owner of a small firm, and one of the devices he used to beat the system was to employ contract labor. Typically he'd hire his friends, and arrange an unusual system of payment with them.

He knew that, at the time, the Internal Revenue Code required him to send in a Form 1099 on each contractor to whom he paid more than six hundred dollars each year. Therefore, he listed them under assumed names, and falsified Social Security numbers. On his books no contractor received over four hundred and fifty dollars, low enough to avoid arousing suspicion in case of an audit. When the inevitable inquiry regarding the Social Security number arrived, Johnny could reply that he was unable to clarify the matter, as the contractors had moved on without leaving a forwarding address.

He found that this system worked well, even in the eventuality of the rules being changed and his having to send in a Form 1099 on each one regardless of the amount. This also had the side effect of degrading the IRS's performance, because they'd be kept busy chasing down nonexistent people to collect taxes from them, a task that would overload even the most sophisticated computer. Johnny worked this system year after year, keeping the same faces in his shop, but on the books he had a column of names representing short-term contractors who left every couple of weeks.

A Widespread Practice

How common is this? How many people evade paying taxes this way? The fact is that nobody knows, although it's possible to make an estimate by indirect means. The estimate, by whatever methods, is bound to be inaccurate because the government's figures don't cover the whole realm of working for a living. For example, adding up the people employed and declaring taxes and Social Security payments can show the number doing this, and subtracting this figure from the available work force can give a very rough figure. One problem with this method is that many people, contractors, are not listed in the official figures used in calculating the employment rate.

This is because of bureaucratic methods used to compile these figures. The official, documented wage earners are the basis for further calculations. This number does not include the already self-employed professionals and contractors. When an employee becomes unemployed, and applies for unemployment "benefits," he goes on another list, and remains there until he either finds employment or the state's benefit period expires. He may be working "on the side," as many do while collecting unemployment, but this is undeclared work, and it doesn't appear on any list.

> **Discouraged workers disappear from the official totals used in calculating the labor force and the unemployment rate. The information is available, but the government doesn't bother to pick it up.**

A peculiar thing happens when the benefit period expires and the unemployed person can no longer collect: the government loses interest in him. As it no longer collects taxes from him, or pays him subsistence, he doesn't matter anymore and becomes a statistical nonperson. The compilers make the assumption that he's not working because he doesn't want to work, and delete him from their statistics. Bureaucrats have a neat term for these people: discouraged workers. Strange, but true. They disappear from the official totals used in calculating the labor force and the unemployment rate. The information is available, but the government doesn't bother to pick it up.

Only the Internal Revenue Service remains interested, in one narrowly defined way. Its agents will "flag" anyone who fails to file a return that year. This, by itself, isn't significant. People fail to file for all sorts of legitimate reasons. They die. They move abroad. They become injured or ill and no longer able to work. They retire. Failure to file does not mean that there will immediately be an intensive search for the nonfiler, although the IRS does try to maintain an image of terrifying efficiency and dogged, relentless pursuit of tax delinquents.

How Tommy Beat the System

Tommy lost his job in a mass layoff when his employer's lush government contract came to an end. There would be a six-month gap between Tommy's termination and his rehiring when a new contract came through, and Tommy's first stop after getting his pink slip was at the unemployment office, where he registered for benefits.

A condition of registering for unemployment benefits is to register with the state employment service, and to be willing and able to take employment in one's job category. Tommy knew that this was only a formality, as three thousand other machinists had been laid off on the same day and dumped into the labor pool. The staffers at the state employment service also knew this, and realized that the local economy would not be able to absorb three thousand machinists. In fact, all of the state personnel involved knew that the laid-off employees would be taking part-time and underground jobs while waiting for their company to hire them back. The state benefits were simply not enough to feed a family, make house and car payments, and meet the other expenses of daily living.

> **It's a characteristic of government employees that they follow the rules only enough to "cover their asses."**

It's a characteristic of government employees that they follow the rules only enough to "cover their asses." They go through the formalities, in this case asking Tommy, "Are you looking for work?" and noting his answer in their records, only to avoid an accusation that they're neglecting their jobs. They follow the prescribed form, even if they know that it's utter nonsense. That's the way the system is, and there are not many zealots.

Tommy, sharper than most, had a friend who owned a fast food stand and needed some temporary help. He went to work, although his hourly wage was not even in the same bracket as what he'd been earn-

ing. Added to the unemployment check, though, it enabled him to keep his head above water until he was able to find something better.

Tommy's father-in-law was the owner of a tool-and-die company, and wanted to hire him as a salesman, not only because he had the technical knowledge, but because Tommy had a likeable personality and had worked at several machine shops in the area. These were all actual or potential customers. Tommy accepted the "old man's" offer, and they came to an agreement. Tommy would not be listed as an employee. He'd work on a commission basis, and his father-in-law would make out the checks in different names each time, because Tommy had lined up a clever method of cashing them.

Tommy's neighbor owned a gas station, and was able to cash the checks for him, even under assumed names. As Tommy gave him all of his gasoline and repair business, and was able to bring the company car to him for service, this proved a mutually profitable arrangement. One important point is that they were good friends. Tommy felt able to confide in his neighbor without fear that he might turn him in out of spite or jealousy, as some tax informers do.

Tommy quit his fast-food job and was an immediate success in his new field. His commissions averaged slightly more than he'd been earning as a machinist and the work was much easier. He collected commissions while continuing to collect unemployment, knowing that this was a violation. He also knew that the bureaucrats understood that remaining unemployed for a protracted period was not unusual in these circumstances, and they didn't aggressively follow up each case to ensure that the people were looking for work.

> **He knew that not filing a return for that year would provoke an inquiry, because the IRS would be curious about how he was able to pay his bills and support his family with no income.**

Once the unemployment benefit period ended, Tommy had to make an arrangement for continuing his profile with the IRS. He knew that not filing a return for that year would provoke an inquiry, because the IRS would be curious about how he was able to pay his bills and support his family with no income. Tommy knew that he'd have to emerge above ground, at least partly, to avoid becoming the subject

Deep Inside the Underground Economy
How Millions of Americans Are Practicing Free Enterprise in An Unfree Society

122

of an investigation. This was another important point. Tommy was not greedy. He knew the limits.

His father-in-law took him on officially as a salesman, and paid him a "draw," an advance against commissions. This gave him an official income to show to the IRS, keeping them happy, and offered an opportunity for extra tax-free income. Tommy was a very successful salesman, and improved as time went on and he became more familiar with his accounts. His father-in-law agreed that he'd arrange the books so that Tommy's commissions, on paper, would approximately balance his draw, set at an amount that would be credible to the IRS. The excess he paid by checks made out to other names, as before, enabling Tommy to cash them anonymously and get the best of both worlds.

Why Tommy Succeeded While Others Have Failed

"Beating the system" involves some discretion and a sense of proportion. It's more difficult to get away with concealing income for an unreasonably long time.

We see from Tommy's example that "beating the system" involves some discretion and a sense of proportion. It's more difficult to get away with concealing income for an unreasonably long time, especially if it is necessary to remain in the same location. Transients can and do conceal their incomes, and remain virtually untraceable, but a family man with a permanent address must be careful.

We also see the need for help from trustworthy associates. It's possible to go it alone, but it's much easier to have help. Involving others can be risky, but the key to reducing the risk is to make them parties to the enterprise. Tommy's neighbor, if ever the truth came out, would have a hard time explaining why he cashed checks from nonexistent persons. Likewise, Tommy's father-in-law had to do some creative accounting with his books, and disclosures would have exposed him, too. In this case, every person involved had an interest in keeping it quiet.

Transients

There are several million migrant workers and other transients in this country. Nobody knows how many, because they don't stay in one place long enough for the census to catch up with them.

Typically, these people are true "journeymen," day laborers without long-term contracts who get paid by the day, every day, unless there's a more permanent arrangement. Payment is necessarily in cash or barter. Sometimes a hobo will trade a day's work for three meals and a bed. In other instances, there's a little money for him in the deal.

Migrant farm workers travel from state to state with their families, showing up to work at harvest time, then moving on to the next opportunity. These people are true nomads, with no fixed addresses and sometimes not even birth certificates. The government knows that they exist, but can't identify them individually. They don't have bank accounts, because their pay is too low to go beyond buying the immediate necessities. For this and other reasons payment is almost always in cash, and this makes it untraceable.

There are several reasons why many transients often don't pay income taxes.

1. With cash payment, transactions are hard to trace, and there's not even an endorsed check to tie the laborer to the payment.

2. There's no check on true identity. The farm operator or his foreman doesn't care about the laborer's background. Transient laborers are hired and fired on the spot, and the employer's consideration is whether the laborer does his job.

3. Farm transients, as contract laborers, "take the money and run." They're here today and gone tomorrow.

4. Sometimes the government assists them in running. Many migrant workers are also immigrant workers, and the Immigration and Naturalization Service and its police force, the U.S. Border Patrol, conduct periodic sweeps to find and deport illegal immigrants. The Border Patrol officers round them up, load them on a bus, and conduct them over the border, out of reach of the IRS. This, incidentally, is an excellent example of how different government agencies sometimes work at cross-purposes.

The Border Patrol officers round them up, load them on a bus, and conduct them over the border, out of reach of the IRS.

5. Finally, the amount of money involved, although it comes to many millions of dollars, is not very

much when spread over millions of migrant workers. Internal Revenue Service agents work on a quota system. The most commonly accepted figure is that the Service considers an agent productive if he can recover one hundred dollars in taxes for each hour he spends working. Whatever the actual quota, it's obvious that recovering taxes from a person who is hard to trace and can yield only a few dollars if caught is not a productive activity. This also explains why the IRS hits hardest at the segment of the population that typically is the most law-abiding and responsible, the wage-slaves with a permanent address. They're the most vulnerable.

Let's look at a few more examples of people who worked at contract labor, including some that took on temporary cash jobs.

Andy was between jobs, temporarily out of work while waiting for another job in his field to open up. He knew he'd be back to work in a couple weeks, and also knew the state unemployment office, with its complicated rules and massive bureaucracy, would oblige him to spend several hours of his time traveling to their office, filling out forms, reporting for interviews, and generally wasting his time. He also knew that, with the mandatory one-week waiting period, he'd hardly collect anything for his efforts. Consequently, he didn't bother applying for unemployment benefits.

Instead, he went to an employment agency that specialized in temporary low-grade help, and got a one-day job as a deliveryman that very morning. He found that he had to pay the ten percent fee, in advance, but that the employer paid him for eight hours' work even though he worked only six because of traveling time. The next morning, he went back to the same employment agency and got a one-day job for a different company. The next morning, he got a day's work delivering for a third company. To his surprise, all paid him in cash, not checks. The pay was minimum wage, but eight hours' pay and no taxes meant that in reality he earned more than minimum.

The drawback was that up-front, ten-percent agency fee. It was like a tax, but still lower than the federal government's rate. The work was not too unpleasant, and as a temporary employee he simply did his job and went home at the end of the day with no hassle and no worries about company politics. Within a couple of weeks, the job he'd been awaiting opened up for him. He felt as if he'd been on vacation for

several weeks, although he'd earned money almost every day. There were no kickbacks, since what he'd earned from each company was far less than the minimum amount requiring the employer to send the IRS a Form 1099 on his earnings.

Temporary employees are privileged, as we've seen. In some instances, they earn more than permanent staff.

Mickey was an electronics engineer, "job-shopping." This means that he worked for a temporary agency, not the company. His terms of employment never lasted more than four months, but his hourly wage was higher than that of the permanent engineers. As a temporary, he was on hourly, not salary, and got paid for overtime, too. The regular staff did not. This was not underground work at all, as he had to pay taxes on his income. But after several years and experience at many different companies, he put the word out that he was available as a freelancer. That meant he'd work temporarily, but charge a lower rate than the agency would charge the company, as the agency had to mark up his pay to make a profit. He asked for payment in cash and a few employers agreed. When he got checks, he laundered them. In effect, he set himself up in competition with the agency that provided him with temporary jobs, secure in the knowledge that he had enough private accounts not to be hurt if they found out and stopped dealing with him.

This is very much like contract labor, with all the opportunities for earning more money than working at a conventional job and of keeping more of it. In some fields, it's lucrative. Some of the fields in which it's worthwhile are nursing, engineering, construction, casual labor, and general office work. One field in which it doesn't work as well is teaching. While there are many substitute teachers filling in for special classes or when regular teachers call in sick, schools are highly structured and very prissy about cooperating with an undergrounder and paying cash. It's necessary to have a way of laundering all the income, which might not be possible with schools.

Those who can best get away with temporary work are those with other ostensible means of support, such as housewives.

Those who can best get away with temporary work are those with other ostensible means of support, such as housewives. With the husband as the declared

Deep Inside the Underground Economy
How Millions of Americans Are Practicing Free Enterprise in An Unfree Society

124

wage earner, the housewife can sell her time and skills without causing a ripple and attracting investigation. There are many housewives who gave up lucrative careers upon marriage, and who are still registered nurses and licensed teachers.

Arlene was a registered nurse, married to an insurance agent. She was listed with an agency that provided temporary medical staff. Her two children were old enough to be "latchkey children" on the days when she got calls. When she filled in at hospitals, she declared her income. Some days, however, she filled in at doctors' private offices, and sometimes the doctor, himself hiding part of his income, would sympathetically pay her cash. She also developed a clientele among a few doctors who were pleased with her work and would call her at home when they needed her, instead of going through the agency. This enabled her to avoid the paper trail that would betray her if ever there were an audit and investigation.

Iva was also a registered nurse, specializing in special duty nursing. Married to a millionaire, she wanted to earn her own money, since this provided more freedom for her. Originally she worked through an agency that provided temporary nursing help, but after making some contacts she went out on her own. Iva landed a job caring for a pre-teen girl who was paralyzed and needed twenty-four-hour care. She was able to negotiate with the parents, who were glad to pay her in cash, for a salary less than what agencies in her area charged. This enabled her to earn 100-percent-tax-free income, and the arrangement worked well for both her and her clients.

From the foregoing, we can build up a picture of how the system works, and how to take advantage of loopholes and weak points. For most, this will mean being very discreet and clever, accepting the limitations of a fixed address and depending on finesse, rather than being nomadic, to beat the system.

The final word about temporary work is that it can be very pleasant indeed. If you're a temporary, you're not involved in office or shop politics. The other employees don't worry about your angling for their jobs, or for a promotion. When you go home, you can relax. Even a high-pressure environment is not as bad as it is for the people who have to look forward to it for many more months or years. If you find a workplace you don't like for any reason, you can simply refuse to go back; there are always other openings available.

Form 1099

If you perform work for private individuals, such as plumbing or delivering a baby, no law requires them to report the payment to you as a separate form.

This well-known IRS form is the means by which businesses report miscellaneous income, such as contract labor, to the IRS. In theory, whenever you perform contract labor for a company, the amount is reported to the IRS. In practice, you can get away with a lot, for two reasons: The system itself is imperfect, and if you perform work for private individuals, such as plumbing or delivering a baby, no law requires them to report the payment to you as a separate form. Individuals may deduct some expenses on their tax returns, but this doesn't involve generating a separate piece of paper to feed the income reporting system.

Even today, not all businesses send out Form 1099s or their equivalents. There are too many violators for the IRS to hammer, and this provides an escape hatch for hiding income, because if someone who pays you a fee fails to send the proper paperwork to the IRS, the fee doesn't exist. However, don't depend on this; it's becoming less and less feasible each year.

A practical problem is determining which of your business accounts filed Form 1099 with the IRS and which didn't. If you don't receive your copy, it doesn't necessarily mean that the account didn't file one. Your copy may simply have gotten lost in the mail. Conversely, your copy might have gotten to you safely, but the IRS copy might have been misplaced by the post office. If you understate commercial account income, you run a risk.

Businesses often file Form 1099 with the IRS because they're very visible and vulnerable to audit. As we've seen, if you're in a business such as lawn maintenance or TV repair, and dealing with private citizens, it's certain that none of your accounts will file the telltale paperwork. Some small businesses, according to one authority, refuse checks or credit cards because they don't want paper trails following their incomes.[4] In today's environment, this is a poor practice to follow, because dealing in cash screams "tax evader" or "drug dealer." It's a red flag that merely draws attention to you.

This is why the IRS pays very close attention to self-employed people such as doctors, lawyers, and plumbers. Many deal in cash and their income is hard to pin down. This picture is changing, though, as more of these professionals and tradesmen become tangled in paperwork. Doctors, for example, no longer receive most of their payments in cash. Today they file tons of forms with health insurance companies, and get paid by check. This documents practically all of their income, as well as adding to their office expenses.

The rule of thumb is that the income you list on your return must equal or exceed the total of your Form 1099s.

The rule of thumb is that the income you list on your return must equal or exceed the total of your Form 1099s. If your income comes from businesses in the form of interest income, royalties, and other documented sources, you'd better not have any unlisted 1099s floating around. On the other hand, if part of your total comes from documented income and part from cash payments, obviously the total income you list had better exceed the amount on the Form 1099s.

How much it exceeds the Form 1099 total is up to you. You might decide to list almost none of your cash income, but you're taking a chance if your lifestyle exceeds the income you report.

Moonlighting

"Moonlighting" is a word used to describe either an above ground second or part-time job, or one that is "off the books." We've already studied several examples of these. Many people, especially today, need a second job to make ends meet, and some find it expedient to make an arrangement to avoid paying income taxes on their second jobs.

In many instances, this isn't possible. "Butch," the owner of a print shop, said "I just won't do it. If someone works for me, I won't do anything illegal to help him avoid paying taxes. It's not worth it to me if I get caught." Terry, another employer, answered: "I can do it, but it means I have to pay him cash out of my own pocket. I have to pay the taxes myself, but I'd do it if I needed someone badly enough."

The difficulty lies in the records employers are required to maintain, and the cut of the pie the IRS expects. To save the employee's having to pay income taxes, the payment must be in cash. Paying by check, on a contract labor basis, avoids withholding taxes but the employee must still report it as income and

pay taxes on it. As banks routinely microfilm all checks, the IRS can find the extra income if it investigates.

With all that, your chances of moonlighting off the books are still good, as many employers routinely pay their workers this way. One of the biggest categories is that which employs illegal immigrants. Such labor is typically very inexpensive, and employers take the risk of discovery and regularly pay in cash.

There are several incentives, not all of them financial, for an employer to pay his hired help in cash.

1. The employer must keep records of payments and of various withholdings on every employee legally employed. This can be a chore, especially if there is high turnover. Paying hired help off the books simplifies the employer's record keeping.

2. The employer legally must pay more than wages for all on-the-books employees. He must pay for workmen's compensation insurance, Social Security, and unemployment insurance. This increases his labor costs for his "visible" employees.

3. Usually, off-the-books employees don't receive the fringe benefits that regular employees do. Depending on the company and its benefits, hiring underground workers can save quite a lot in the costs of benefits.

4. Because of their underground nature, moonlighting workers are never unionized and earn less than their unionized counterparts. Many employers do not like unions, or even the prospect of a union recruiting their employees, and hiring undergrounders avoids this risk.

5. Many moonlighters demand less pay than their legal counterparts. Often they'll work extra hours without expecting time-and-a-half. This saves employers a significant amount of money. Illegal immigrant labor is a classic example.

So far, we've considered only moonlighters working for a company. There are many more working for themselves, such as the plumber who does extra work on weekends. These moonlighters, although working at their trades, deal with individuals, and often get paid in cash. At times they must accept checks, but that still leaves cash payments to pocket unreported.

There are some problems with moonlighting, entirely apart from the IRS's expectation that you'll hand part of your income over to the government. Your full-time employer may take exception to your performing work for anyone else, under certain conditions. One individual, in an article laying out policy for air conditioning contractors, defines "moonlight-

Deep Inside the Underground Economy
How Millions of Americans Are Practicing Free Enterprise in An Unfree Society

126

ing" as performing the same kind of work after-hours, and urges contractors to adopt a policy against this practice.[5]

Employers resent their employees using company tools and equipment for outside work, especially if they enter into competition with their own employers. The article suggests that moonlighting is a "disservice to the consumer," while noting that the moonlighter who offers to return after-hours "can do it cheaper that way."

The suggested policy is far-reaching, prohibiting all after-hours work, and even advising the contractor's suppliers not to sell parts to the contractor's employees unless they present a company purchase order. The contractor strong-arms the supplier by telling him that "failure to adhere to this policy could have a damaging effect on the business relationship."[6]

This is why if you try to moonlight by using your regular job skills after-hours, you may incur the wrath of your employer, especially if you're pirating some of his customers. If you use your employer's truck, tools, or other equipment, you're definitely risking your job if he finds out, because to him, you're running the risk of liability in dealing with his customers. If they're not satisfied with the work you performed, they can sue him because you used company equipment.

Other employers prohibit any outside work that may create a conflict of interest. Yet others expect their employees to put in so much overtime that holding an outside job is impossible.

There are some exceptions. One small print shop operator knew that his pressman, Joe, occasionally came in after hours to run jobs for a few of his own customers. The boss tolerated this, partly because Joe was an excellent employee who gave him 100 percent during working hours, and because there was so much work to go around that Joe's running a few private jobs didn't hurt his business at all.

Apart from part-time employment that conflicts with your employer's needs or policies, there are many possibilities you can exploit. Continuing a trend that began during the 1980s, moonlighting was an economic necessity for more people in the 1990s. By 1990, according to official U.S. government figures, more than 7.2 million American workers held two or more jobs to make ends meet.[7]

Jesse, an unemployed auto mechanic, owned a house with a large shed and did repair work on friends' and neighbors' vehicles to feed his small family. Many customers paid in cash and he devised a clever way of disguising payments by check. He had his wife cash them, or use them for payment at the grocery store. In Jesse's small town, everyone knew everybody else, and there was no problem when Jesse's wife gave the grocer a third-party check to pay her bill.

There are some dangers in moonlighting.

Mark, a technical equipment repairman, did not moonlight in his trade because he knew that his employer would consider him a competitor, and would probably accuse him of stealing his accounts. This could have gotten him fired, and Mark bided his time, building up contacts and gaining the friendship of his clients. Finally, he made the break cleanly, quitting his job and setting up his own business. As his own boss, he was now able to do a certain proportion of his business off the books.

James, in a related field, has a legitimate, above ground job in the same line as his regular job, but his employer knows of it and does not mind because James works for a competitor instead of being a competitor himself. The part-time job is for a company in another part of town, with a largely different clientele. Although none of James' work is underground, his example is worth noting because it shows that it's possible to moonlight openly if the conditions are right.

If the moonlighter operates a totally separate business, conventional advertising is dangerous because government agents read ads too.

Advertising can be tricky for the moonlighter. If the moonlighter operates a totally separate business, conventional advertising is dangerous because government agents read ads too. If the moonlighting is part of his regular operations, advertising is safe, because the moonlighter is running an above ground business and only skimming a fraction of his income.

One final point relates to the moonlighter: Friends and acquaintances will happily provide work for the moonlighter, expecting and getting a lower charge. Above ground or underground, the moonlighter, because he has little or no overhead, can charge less and still earn good money. This is worth looking at in detail because, despite tighter restrictions and enforcement, the underground economy is prospering. Businesses who hire underground labor find ways to pay for it without much risk of detection, depending on the exact method they use.

Some pay their workers out of their own pockets, paying the income taxes themselves. They calculate that because the moonlighter works for less, and there are no other expenses connected with his employment, it's cheaper this way.

Some business owners use creative methods of accounting, burying the illegal labor costs with other expenses. The president of one electronics company went so far as to hire prostitutes to entertain his clients, burying their fees under "sales expense."

Another way to bury the cost of underground labor is petty cash. False "mileage" reimbursements and various cash register receipts can cover the amount of cash for some types of underground labor.

The employer operating a cash business can skim part of the receipts to pay for moonlight help. This is the safest method, because it creates no paper trail, unlike faked petty cash vouchers, etc.

There is no way to estimate reliably how many people moonlight illicitly. The opportunities are so numerous, the chance of detection is so small, and the prospect of tax-free income so appealing, that we can only say "many."

Case History: Bob, the Underground Diamond Dealer

Bob, thirty-three-years-old, was an assembly-line worker at an American automobile plant in Flint, Michigan. When he got his job, he began to earn more money than he knew what to do with. At least, it seemed that way at first. He got married and began enjoying the high life. He bought a snowmobile and spent many winter weekends in northern Michigan. He and his wife took vacations in the Bahamas. Before long, he made a down payment on an expensive new car. With overtime, he was earning enough money to pay the rent, pay off the car, keep his wife happy, and still have enough left over for season tickets to the minor league hockey team's home games. Life was rosy for Bob.

After Bob had been on the job for five years, the union went on strike. At first Bob didn't worry. While he had no savings, he expected to receive strike pay. His wife, Mary, found a job as a cocktail waitress. While this job paid less than a quarter of what Bob had been earning assembling automobiles, they expected to make ends meet with this and the strike pay by cutting back on expenditures. In any

event, they lived in a union town, and expected that their landlord wouldn't evict them for being behind on the rent and the finance company wouldn't miss a few payments. Bob expected to be back at work soon, raking in the big bucks as in the past.

As the strike dragged on, Bob fell further behind in his payments, but so did his colleagues from the assembly line. However, they felt that the strike would be over soon, so there was no reason to worry.

One morning he awakened to find his car gone. It had been repossessed. Bob looked at himself and realized that he had damn little to show for his five years of loyal devotion to his company. He was deeply in debt; his only income was his wife's earnings and his paltry strike pay. His wife didn't complain but he knew she resented the abuse heaped on her by some drunken customers.

On the picket line one day, Bob ran into Joe. Joe worked on the same assembly line as Bob, but he seemed different from the other pickets somehow. While the others discussed their financial worries, Joe was silent. While the others talked about the local hockey team, the Flint Generals, and about how they had sold their season tickets, Joe spoke about going to the Detroit Red Wings home games, leading Bob to wonder how Joe was able to afford the expense. Even before the strike, season tickets to the Detroit Red Wings had been beyond Bob's budget.

Bob had first met Joe back when he had told his buddies he was getting married. One friend had suggested that he buy his engagement ring from Joe. "You can save lots of money," he told Bob, "and Joe is an honest guy." Bob met Joe at work one day and asked about a diamond ring. "Sure," Joe said, "I can fix you up." Joe showed Bob a catalog of diamond engagement rings and explained that he could sell Bob any of the rings in the catalog for less than fifty percent of what a jeweler would charge. Bob was suspicious, wondering if there were something illegal about Joe's offer. He didn't want to buy a stolen ring. But Joe explained that he was able to undercut retail jewelers' prices by keeping his overhead low — "No fancy showroom, no fancy advertising." He offered Bob a guarantee: If Bob would pick a ring he liked, Joe would deliver it to him in three weeks. If Bob took the ring to a local jeweler for an appraisal and the jeweler did not value the ring for at least twice Joe's price, Joe would give Bob a full refund.

Bob selected a ring and Joe quoted a price of $500. A couple of weeks later, Joe delivered the ring. It was brand new and in a plush-lined gift box, just like the

Deep Inside the Underground Economy
How Millions of Americans Are Practicing Free Enterprise in An Unfree Society

128

ones Bob had seen at a jeweler's store. Bob was still dubious as he paid Joe in cash ("I gotta have cash — it keeps the overhead down," Joe said). But Bob's worries ended after he took the ring to a jeweler in a shopping mall. The jeweler examined the ring under his microscope, measured it with strange-looking instruments, and gave Bob a written appraisal stating the ring was worth $1,200. The appraisal had cost Bob $60, but he was happy knowing he had gotten a good deal.

Bob now wondered if there was a connection between Joe's apparent prosperity and his part-time diamond dealing. He asked Joe about the diamond business, but Joe just hemmed and hawed and changed the subject.

The strike ended and Bob was able to pay his back rent and bought a used car, while his wife quit her waitress job. But Bob, remembering well what had happened, vowed to be more careful with his spending and to try to reduce his dependency on his assembly-line paycheck. Never again would anyone come in the night and repossess his car. Never again would his wife have to take abuse from any drunk with the price of a beer.

A couple of years later, Joe took early retirement. Bob saw an advertisement for a garage sale at Joe's and went there to look for bargains. The best bargain, however, was what Joe told him:

"A couple of years ago, you asked me if my diamond business was making me any money. I didn't want to answer then, because I didn't want you to know just how much money I made in my little part-time business, and I still won't tell you exactly. Hell, I don't even know how much I made, but I made plenty. I'm retiring and moving to Florida where I won't suffer through the freezing Michigan winters anymore, and I don't see how I could be hurt by competition now. If you're interested in making money by dealing in diamonds, I'll even help you get started."

Bob was very interested. He asked: "How much money will I need? Doesn't it take years of study to learn about diamonds?"

"You can answer those questions for yourself," Joe answered, "By coming with me on a diamond-buying trip next Tuesday."

"Now hold on, Joe," Bob said. "I can't get enough time off for a trip to the diamond centers like Antwerp, and I sure as hell can't afford the trip."

"I buy diamonds right here in Flint," Joe responded. He agreed to pick up Bob at 10 A.M. on Tuesday.

They spent Tuesday driving around Flint, stopping at an odd variety of places: pawnshops, mostly, but also coin dealers, flea markets, and secondhand shops. At each, Joe would ask the owner if he had any diamonds for sale. In most cases, the owner would show Joe a few items, mostly used engagement rings. Joe examined them with a duplex magnifier, pulled another strange looking instrument from a leather case, and used it to measure the stone. In most cases, he'd offer the dealer a cash price for the rings. The dealers sometimes haggled a bit, but before Bob and Joe left the shop the dealer almost always accepted Joe's offer.

By the end of the day Joe had spent almost $2,000, all in cash taken from a roll wrapped in a rubber band he carried in his pocket. "It was a good day," Joe told Bob. "The diamonds I bought today have a conservative wholesale value of about $3,000, but by the time I sell them, I'll have done far better than that."

Bob was intrigued, and when Joe offered to train him in the business, Bob quickly accepted. Joe told Bob he'd charge him $1,500 for his training, but Bob could pay him from his profits once he got his business going, and did not have to pay unless he felt he'd gotten his money's worth. "One more thing," said Joe. "I'm leaving for Florida in four weeks, so we'll have to begin right away."

"That's okay," Bob responded. "I'll call in sick if I have to. But what will it cost besides your fee? I may not have enough cash."

"I started out with less than $500 in cash. Of course, that was a few years ago. Right now, I'd say you'd have to have $1,000 or so. You'll also need a few tools: a loupe, diamond tweezers, a carbide scribe, a set of diamond gauges, and a diamond wallet. I think you should buy the best, but the best doesn't cost too much. I think you could get by for less than $100. You need a few hundred dollars for inventory, but more would be better."

"I've got about $5,000 in savings," Bob responded. "When can I start?"

You'll need some knowledge, not just knowledge about diamonds, but also about people and how to deal with them.

"There are five things you need to make money in this business," Joe told him. "The basic tool kit —

you've already seen most of my diamond tools. Good places to buy diamonds. You've already seen where I buy my diamonds, and if you make the rounds with me for the next couple of weeks, I think you'll be able to take over most of my sources. You also should develop new sources of your own. You need a good place to sell your stones. You already have that: You can sell them at work. You'll need cash, like I said before. Finally, you'll need some knowledge, not just knowledge about diamonds, but also about people and how to deal with them."

Bob called home and told his wife not to hold dinner; he would be late. Joe began training Bob that same night. Joe took him to a room in his basement where he did his diamond work. First, they put the rings they had bought into Joe's ultrasonic cleaner. "You don't really need this jeweler's model," Joe said over the faint whirring sound the cleaner made. "I used ammonia and an old toothbrush for years. Then I bought a cheap ultrasonic cleaner designed for cleaning false teeth. I got this one a couple of years ago from a jeweler going out of business."

After cleaning the rings, Joe examined them to see if any were in nice enough shape to sell as is. None were. "That's usually the case. If the ring is nice enough to resell, the pawnbroker will usually sell it himself. Besides, just about all the rings I get from my dealers are engagement rings. No one wants to buy a used engagement ring, anyway. But once in a while I'll get a nice cocktail ring or pendant or something."

There are really just four factors in evaluating a diamond: its clarity, its color, its carat weight, and its cut.

Next Joe showed Bob how he carefully removed the stones from their mountings. Then Joe showed Bob how to grade the diamonds. "There are really just four factors in evaluating a diamond: its clarity, its color, its carat weight, and its cut." For the next two hours Joe examined stones through his magnifying loupe and described them to Bob. He pointed out the black carbon in one stone, and the white "feather" in another. He noted that one stone had a pronounced greenish color, and others had a yellowish hue. They looked at diamonds of various cuts. Joe pointed out that, even among brilliant cut stones (the most popular cut), the actual shape varied, and that the variations make a major difference in the brilliance of the diamond. Then Joe showed Bob how he determined

the carat weight of a stone. "The only really accurate way is to weigh the stone, but usually a diamond will be offered to you already set in a ring or other mounting, and you'll have to offer a price based on examining it without removing it." First, Joe showed Bob how to estimate the weight with a small aluminum gauge, punched with holes of various sizes. By holding the gauge over a diamond, Bob could quickly estimate the weights of mounted stones.

By the time Bob went home that evening he had practiced evaluating over fifty diamonds from Joe's inventory. He examined them closely, and told Joe what he thought about the color, clarity, cut, and weight of each diamond. He was surprised when Joe told him he was already pretty accurate. "Learning how to examine the diamond is probably the easiest part of learning to deal diamonds," Joe said, "but a lot of people think it's the hardest. The idea of examining a diamond and placing a value on it is simply scary to most people. Don't worry about it and you'll do okay. Anytime you think it's hard, remember that I learned it myself with nobody to teach me, and I'm no Albert Einstein."

Bob was really excited when he went home that night. Mary didn't like the idea at all, especially when Bob told her that he was going to have to use some of their savings to get started, but Bob's enthusiasm discouraged her from objecting too strenuously. "I can always go back to waitressing," she thought.

Bob put in his shifts at the plant during the next few days and went over to Joe's every evening to study his rocks. He examined hundreds of diamonds, looking at them through his own loupe and measuring them with his gauge. He learned to use a Jo-Di gauge, the strange contraption he had seen Joe use when buying diamonds from pawnbrokers. He learned to test a diamond for hardness with a carbide scribe. Joe also showed him how to check for flaws hidden beneath the prongs of the setting.

Most of all, he listened as Joe related anecdotes about various deals he had made, and stressed the importance of developing good contacts with pawnbrokers and other small businesses. Joe explained the techniques that enabled him to quickly convince pawnbrokers he was an expert, and how by earning the confidence of pawnbrokers he was able to obtain good buys. He told him how he helped supply pawnbrokers who needed diamonds for retail sales, even though it sometimes meant selling a stone for less than its wholesale value. "These guys are your bread and butter," he told Bob. "You gotta keep them

Deep Inside the Underground Economy
How Millions of Americans Are Practicing Free Enterprise in An Unfree Society

130

and butter," he told Bob. "You gotta keep them happy."

Joe put Bob to work selling diamonds that night. He gave Bob two men's diamond rings and told him to wear them to work. He told Bob what he wanted for them, and Bob did wear them to work, but all they got him were some strange looks from his friends. The next night Bob told Joe that he did not much like wearing a diamond ring in hopes of selling it. "I feel uncomfortable wearing that ring," he said. "Besides, when I bought my engagement ring from you for Mary, I didn't buy a ring you had all made up. Your jeweler made mine. Isn't that a better way to sell diamond rings?"

"It all depends," said Joe. "If a guy is buying an engagement ring, chances are he doesn't want a used ring. You know, women are pretty silly that way. They want their ring to be new, and to last forever, just like their marriage. But with men's rings, it's different. Thank God men are not so sentimental: they would just as well wear a used ring if the price is right. The same usually holds for women's rings they wear for ornamentation."

"But most of the diamonds I sell are in 'custom made' rings. It's really the simplest thing in the world to do. I have a catalog of rings, and when a customer picks a style he likes, I order a copy of the ring made from a special kind of wax. I give the wax copy and enough scrap gold to make the ring to a guy who makes jewelry as a hobby. He charges me about $15 per ring to manufacture it. The wax copy costs a couple of dollars too, but that, plus the cost of the gold, is all it costs me. Then I select the right diamond and set it in the ring. After I pay for the gold, the wax copy, the manufacturing, and I install a diamond I bought from a pawnbroker, my cost is less than half what the jeweler in the mall pays for an identical ring. That's how I sell so cheaply, and that's also how I get a reputation for doing custom work."

"But you have to wear diamonds for two reasons. First, that's the best way to sell used merchandise. More importantly, it's the best form of advertising I can do. Whenever anyone says anything about a diamond I'm wearing, I explain that I'm a dealer in diamonds. Naturally, if the person ever wants to buy a diamond, they come to me. Or if they want to sell a diamond, they come to me."

Two days later Bob sold one of the rings Joe had given him to another employee. It was a big man's pinky ring with a large diamond, which Bob sold for $1,000. Bob realized the diamond was good-sized

(about ¾ carat) but of poor quality (it had two carbon spots, was poorly cut, and yellowish in color) but it was the sort of ring the jewelry store in the mall would sell for $2,500. He gave the buyer the same guarantee that Joe had given him on his engagement ring. The very next day, the buyer told him it had cost him $100 to have it appraised, but the jeweler had valued it at $2,700. Joe had made $100 on the deal. "The easiest hundred I ever made," he told Mary.

Over dinner next evening, Mary asked Bob if she could sell some diamonds for him. He brought her back a cocktail ring with a half-carat stone and nine small stones. Joe wanted $850 for it, he told her. A week later, she sold it to a member of her bowling team. She made $250 on the deal, and her attitude towards Bob's ambitions as a diamond dealer began to change.

By the end of the second week, Bob was very tired from all the work he'd done studying diamonds. He had learned how to grade and size diamonds, and had learned what different grades and sizes of diamonds are worth. He also had learned how to sell them, but still was worried about buying diamonds. "It's easy enough for you to buy from your dealers; they already know you and have confidence in you, but I am an unknown quantity," he said to Joe.

"I agree it'll take time for you to be confident with dealers," Joe advised. "And until you're confident yourself, it'll be hard to gain their confidence." Joe suggested that Bob take a few days off from work for one final lesson in buying from dealers.

The following Tuesday, Joe picked up Bob to "run the trap line" of dealers. Just as they arrived at their first stop, a seedy coin shop, Joe said, "You go in and see what you can do. Tell Jim that I am sick. He's seen you with me a couple of times; he ought to respond okay to you. Just remember how I act with them."

Bob went in before he had time to worry. He exchanged pleasantries with the dealer and told him that Joe was sick and had sent him. Bob had his little kit of diamond tools with him, and he studied the two engagement rings the dealer offered, while chatting amiably. Both rings were so filthy with grease and grime that Bob could not evaluate them very well. The first ring had a quarter-carat stone, which Bob figured was worth about $125. He offered $150 because he was concerned that Jim would reject his offer. Jim accepted, and Bob turned to the other stone, which was about a half carat. Bob figured it was easily worth $350, and offered Jim $300, which Jim accepted. Bob pulled out his roll of money, and peeled off four $100 bills and a fifty for Jim. He put the rings in his diamond wallet and rejoined Jim in the car. There he reviewed the deal with Joe. "You did okay," Joe said, "but you really could have bought that quarter carat for less."

By the end of the day Bob had visited seven of Joe's regulars, and all but one had sold him a few stones. All appeared happy to see him. They returned to Joe's home and cleaned the day's purchases. They removed all but one diamond from their mountings, and graded and sized each stone. Joe complimented Bob on his purchases and suggested that Bob call in sick again the following day.

Next morning Joe picked up Bob as usual, drove onto the expressway, and out of town. "We're going to try something different today," he announced. "We're going over to Grand Rapids and see what we can buy there."

Upon arriving in Grand Rapids Joe stopped at a pay phone. He returned in a few minutes with several pages from the Yellow Pages. "I cut out the pages for coin dealers, antique dealers, second-hand shops, and pawnbrokers. We're going to call on as many of them as we can."

As he stopped the car at the first shop, a slightly grungy pawnshop in a nasty part of town, he announced: "Bob, now you're on your own. I'll go along as your silent assistant and you make the deal." Bob hadn't expected this, but Joe hadn't yet led him wrong. They entered the shop and in twenty minutes they'd finished. Bob had purchased only one diamond, but it was a good one, more than a full carat. By day's end, they'd visited only six shops, but Bob had purchased diamonds at four of them. "Not bad for a beginner," Joe joked.

As they drove back to Flint that evening Joe spoke about his diamond business. "It was a good hobby," Joe said. At least it had started as a hobby, but over the years it had reached the point where he was earning more money dealing in diamonds than at the plant. He had kept his job on the line for two reasons, he said. He had many genuine friends there, whose company he enjoyed and who were good customers for his diamond business. The full-time job also helped explain his income. "I've never paid any taxes on my diamond business," he said. "That's why I do business in cash only. The pawnbrokers are glad to accept cash; I think most of them don't pay taxes on what they sell to me, either, and my retail customers

save so much money that they don't mind the inconvenience."

As they approached the city Joe made a surprising announcement: "I've really taught you all I can. The rest will come with experience. It'll take time, but I'm sure you'll do well at this thing. Remember, you'll be learning more about diamonds and people as long as you deal."

Joe was leaving for Tampa that weekend, he said. Bob could pay him his $1,500 fee whenever he felt he could. Meanwhile, Bob was on his own.

Six months later Joe received a small package with Bob's return address. Inside he found twenty $100 bills, along with a note thanking him for his help and explaining that the extra $500 was in gratitude for Joe's guidance.

Bob now has been dealing in diamonds for years. When hard times hit the auto industry in 1980, most of Bob's fellow employees panicked, but Bob didn't worry. His part-time diamond business was earning him more money than his paycheck. This time, he didn't worry about having anything repossessed, and in fact, had no money worries at all. By this time, he'd built up enough seniority to avoid layoffs. However, he was happy to be independent of his job, his union, and the company.

Mary had become interested in the diamond business as well, and took a course in jewelry casting at a local community college. This enabled her to take over casting settings for diamonds, and she appreciates the extra income and independence this has brought.

Joe has settled into life in a suburb of Tampa. At first he'd thought he'd sell his diamonds through classified ads, but before long he'd opened a small office and was selling diamonds about twenty hours per week. He still deals in cash, but now he pays "some" taxes. With the further shrinking of the American automobile industry, the company town of Flint has suffered economic loss. General Motors exported its plants to Mexico and other countries that offered cheap labor. However, Bob has not been hit as hard as his fellow employees who depended on General Motors for their entire income.

Entrepreneurs everywhere succeeded because they developed specialized knowledge.

Why have Joe and Bob been able to earn good money by dealing in diamonds? Like entrepreneurs

Deep Inside the Underground Economy
How Millions of Americans Are Practicing Free Enterprise in An Unfree Society

132

everywhere, they succeeded because they developed specialized knowledge. Through study and years of trial and error, Joe learned how to tell a genuine diamond from a fake, how to evaluate diamonds, how to buy diamonds from dealers and the public, and how to market them. Bob had it easier; he learned from Joe.

Specialized knowledge is a scarce commodity; it's greater than the knowledge possessed by the people Joe and Bob deal with. Because their knowledge enables them to evaluate diamonds more accurately than the pawnbrokers who are their major sources, they're able to pay those dealers high enough prices to satisfy them. Their knowledge of marketing enables them to resell the diamonds at higher prices still, and thereby earn a good profit.

This disparity in knowledge is the key to earning a profit in many businesses. Just as Joe and Bob's superior knowledge enables them to deal profitably in diamonds, superior knowledge of specialized areas enables other people to profit from dealing in old cars, rare coins, oriental rugs, or antiques.

Diamonds, however, are a special case. The diamond industry has long attempted to give diamonds an aura of mystery, and indeed the industry has conspired to keep knowledge of diamonds from the general public. Even most jewelers have little expertise or usable knowledge about diamonds.

There exist excellent sources of information for the prospective diamond dealer.

The Gemological Institute of America (GIA) offers newsletters, courses, and other information about diamonds and other gems. This nonprofit organization has educated people in the gem business since it was founded in Los Angeles in 1931. The current Chairman of GIA's Board of Governors, Richard T. Liddicoat, created and introduced the International Diamond Grading System in 1953. GIA has campuses in Los Angeles and New York, and a Web site for further information.

Gemological Institute of America (GIA)
World Headquarters
The Robert Mouawad Campus
5345 Armada Drive
Carlsbad, CA 92008
Phone: (800) 421-7250 or (760) 603-4000
Web site: www.gia.org/about/index.cfm

There are several books on diamonds on Amazon.com. The one most highly recommended by readers is *How to Buy a Diamond: Insider Secrets to Getting Your Money's Worth*, by Fred Cuellar, third

edition, November 2000, paperback, $14.95. One of the insider secrets he offers is never to buy a diamond that's in a setting, because the setting can conceal defects.

Networking to Promote Yourself

Interpersonal relations are more important than ever today for several reasons, as we'll see. Making friends and acquaintances can be mutually beneficial, which is why you should strive to get to know as many people as possible on the job, as well as in your personal relations. Meeting people with mutual needs can help you develop meaningful relationships. This is why you should never miss an opportunity to meet new people, especially in your line, or lines, of work.

There are few workplace situations worse than being "out of the loop." Even if you hear bad news, it's better to know about it before it strikes you than to be taken by surprise.

Networking Up

Networking begins with your boss. He is the one who has the power of economic life and death over you, and developing a relationship with him keeps communication open. This is especially important because there are few workplace situations worse than being "out of the loop." Even if you hear bad news, it's better to know about it before it strikes you than to be taken by surprise.

Granted, getting along with some supervisors and employers is trying. It's worth your best shot, though, even if your boss is a hopeless dork, because he is a good source of information that you can exploit.

One obvious area of useful information is how he treats his customers. Some business owners are slovenly, uncaring, and display bad attitudes towards their customers.[8] You may even hear grumbling from some customers, and this should be music to your ears. Your employer's unhappy customers are ripe for the picking if you decide to go into competition with him.

Fellow Employees

Fellow employees, of course, are important. You work with them at least forty hours per week, and developing a network of people who can help you will make your work easier, or help you earn extra money.

Rick worked as a photographer in one of the most noted art museums in the country. He was also a barber, and earned extra and untraceable cash doing haircuts for fellow employees. This was a perfect sideline, because he wasn't competing with his employer.

Karl, a low level K-Mart employee, resented both the low pay and the mass layoffs the day after Christmas. He began taking small items, smuggling them out when leaving work. He began giving his friends large discounts on tapes, cameras, batteries, and other hard goods. His fellow employees didn't rat on him to management, and one even went into business for himself, walking off with a huge amount of material. Before Karl quit, he noticed that even the security guards were walking off with merchandise.[9]

Paul, a clerk in another department store notorious for underpaying the hired help, networked with fellow employees to obtain huge discounts. His friend in the hunting department rang up a twelve-dollar sale for a shotgun that sold for $80 at the time. Other employees contributed to the free-for-all by tagging perfectly good merchandise for the damaged goods markdown table. They also noticed that store security was so lax that they were able to drive their vehicles up to the loading dock and take what they wished.[10]

A group of friends networked to obtain free food from a small neighborhood cafe that had a reputation for poor working conditions. Employees would neglect to collect payment for most of the food their friends ordered. When Joey, the waiter, got fired, another of his neighborhood chums took his job and continued the practice. The owner remained unaware of the networking that helped feed this "extended community."[11]

Another point about getting to know fellow employees is that you have a golden opportunity to assess their job skills, honesty, and general work attitudes. This can be very important if you later decide to start your own business. You'll have a cadre of potential hired help from former fellow employees.

Outside Networking

Now let's consider people outside the company. These may be clients, competitors' employees, suppliers, and assorted business contacts. Never neglect any of them.

When dealing with people, never underrate the value of a smile and a sympathetic attitude. Nobody, absolutely nobody, is too low to be worth knowing.

This includes the waiter and the bartender where fellow employees eat and socialize. A waiter who likes you may pass along a tidbit he overheard that can affect you.

Networking is crucial in underground dealings. If you're diverting supplies from your employer, you must find people to buy them. If you're searching for cut-rate goods, you need to make contact with a supplier or middleman. Networking can become very extensive and complex, and "people skills" are an important part of the guerrilla economy.[12]

Networking Checklist

Study this checklist as a reminder of how to cover your bases. Photocopy and use it as a worksheet, bringing it up to date as necessary.

Employer:
☐ Does he tell you the bad news, as well as the good news?
☐ During disagreements with your supervisor, do you keep your temper under control?

Fellow employees:
☐ Are you plugged in to the office and departmental grapevine?
☐ How many of your fellow employees can you trust:
☐ To keep any confidence you tell them?
☐ To punch your time card for you if you leave early?
☐ To help you scam the company?

Outside contacts:
☐ Do you attend union meetings, where you can informally meet people in other departments?
☐ Do you attend trade shows to meet your opposite numbers in other companies?
☐ Do you know your competitors' sales representatives and do you listen carefully when they speak?
☐ Do you know your company's suppliers?
☐ Do you know your company's clients?
☐ At trade shows, do you pick up samples of vendors' sales literature?
☐ Do your employer's customers complain about the way he treats them?
☐ How many of these dissatisfied customers do you think you could pick up for yourself?

Deep Inside the Underground Economy
How Millions of Americans Are Practicing Free Enterprise in An Unfree Society

134

Exploiting Relationships

One of the best strategies you can follow is to exploit your company's resources for your own benefit, and this can happen even with your supervisor's blessing. An example is if your company maintains a reference library, and you can use it to help complete a college credit. If you explain your need and ask your supervisor for permission, it's very likely that he'll give it, saving you perhaps hours of travel. He may even feel flattered to be in a position to help you.

It's a good idea, on general principle, to be well known. The principle of networking can work for you, as it has for many others. Many people have found new employment through networking. If you're dissatisfied with your job, answering want ads may produce results, or you may answer an ad placed by a personal friend of your boss, with possibly serious consequences. Networking allows you to troll and evaluate the job market informally, without making what appears to be a commitment.

One of your company's clients may need part-time help, and may ask you if you can spend a few hours working for him. The advantage is obvious. Part-time jobs can work into full-time careers, and this is the safe way to go about it.

One of your employer's competitors may know of you by reputation and ask if you'd be interested in coming to work for him. If you've done your homework and picked up his sales literature, you'll be able to show him what you already know about his company and be able to discuss intelligently where you might fit into his operation.

Networking and the interpersonal skills it develops are integral parts of many guerrilla capitalist operations. Fortunately, networking is a no risk, rewarding effort you can begin today.

Notes

1. "Watch Out for IRS Crackdown on Independent Contractors," *Profit-Building Strategies for Business Owners* 20, no. 6, June 1990, p. 3.
2. *Ibid.*, p. 3.
3. Stuart Duhl, "After You Hire a la Carte," *Nation's Business* 78, no. 6, June 1990, p. 32.
4. Jordan L. Cooper, *How to Make Cash Money Selling at Swap Meets, Flea Markets, Etc.,* Loompanics Unlimited, Port Townsend, WA, 1988, p. 134.
5. James P. Norris, "Why You Need a Policy against Moonlighting," *Air Conditioning, Heating, and Refrigeration News* 181, no. 14, 3 December 1990, p. 24.
6. *Ibid.*
7. John F. Stinson, Jr., "Multiple Jobholding Up Sharply in the 1980s," *Monthly Labor Review* 113, no. 7 (July 1990), p. 3. Official figures are based on the Bureau of Labor Statistics Current Population Survey, and are only as accurate as the people answering the questions. It's a safe assumption that official figures do not include much of the underground economy.
8. Jordan L. Cooper, *Shadow Merchants,* Loompanics Unlimited, Port Townsend, WA, 1993, pp. 67-70.
9. Martin Sprouse, ed., *Sabotage in the American Workplace,* Pressure Drop Press, San Francisco, CA, 1992, pp. 102-103.
10. *Ibid.*, pp. 102-104.
11. *Ibid.*, p. 123.
12. Stuart Henry, *The Hidden Economy: The Context and Control of Borderline Crime,* Loompanics Unlimited, Port Townsend, WA, 1980, pp. 17-41.

Chapter Nine
Smaller is Better

It's been a truism, in this country and others, that the future belongs to the large corporations, and that there is no room for the small business owner, who will be ruthlessly squeezed out by relentless competition from the conglomerates. Fortunately for those of us who like independence, the picture is not as bleak as this oversimplified view. In reality, many large corporations, although they have the capital for the large investments needed in heavy industry, don't have the flexibility to meet the changing needs of the market. Actually, despite the heavy load of propaganda, the big conglomerates don't hold all the cards.

Another problem large companies face is that they're attractive targets for lawsuits because they have lots of money to make the suit profitable for high-powered lawyers.

Big companies run into trouble and fail; a recent example is Enron, whose failure took down the large accounting firm of Arthur Anderson with it. Another problem large companies face is that they're attractive targets for lawsuits because they have lots of money to make the suit profitable for high-powered lawyers. Various busybody groups, such as environmental organizations, repeatedly sue large companies, such as strip miners, both to hamper their operations and to obtain large settlements. The small operator, especially the one who operates underground and maintains a low profile, does not face these hazards because he's out of sight and does not have enough money to make a lawsuit profitable.

Another reason the small operator prospers is simply because people want more than the big companies can provide, and the people who run the large corporations, feeling smug and secure, are not responsive.

An excellent example is the American automobile industry. The executives in Detroit convinced themselves they could dictate, by relentless advertising, the automotive needs of the American people, and compel them to buy their overly large, poorly made gas guzzlers. For decades they had squeezed small manufacturers out of business until the market became dominated by the "Big Three."

Since WWII, this has changed, slowly at first, then more quickly. Foreign cars have made a significant advance in the American market. The people, whom the Detroit executives viewed as mindless sheep responding to their advertisements, have chosen foreign cars in larger numbers, and we saw the partial collapse of the American automobile industry.

Auto manufacturers have also been harassed by government regulations dictating safety standards and fuel economy. Private groups and individuals have sued auto manufacturers because of safety defects, real and imaginary. With their deep pockets, automobile manufacturers have proven to be attractive targets for lawyers.

The telephone company, with its arrogant attitude and monopolistic pricing, has had serious competition from independents on what traditionally has been its home ground, long-distance lines and the manufacture of telephone equipment.

The auto industry is not the only example. The telephone company, with its arrogant attitude and monopolistic pricing, has had serious competition from independents on what traditionally has been its home ground, long-distance lines and the manufacture of telephone equipment. The independent telephone manufacturers, both domestic and foreign,

Deep Inside the Underground Economy
How Millions of Americans Are Practicing Free Enterprise in An Unfree Society

136

have to stand or fall on the merits of their products, not because they're the only game in town.

Small printing businesses have proliferated, with quick-print shops, both independent and franchised, springing up in every neighborhood. A customer who wants some business cards or some stationery is not going to want to send away to a large, mail-order outfit for them, because this usually means waiting several weeks, and he'd like them sooner. Although the small printer can't provide as low a price as the large company, he can provide better service.

Customers run into a couple of other problems with large companies. A mail-order discount printer has shipping costs, which will often eat up any savings in price he can offer. The problem of correcting errors also crops up. A small printer, if there's an error in his work, can quickly run the job again. The customer who orders by mail, on the other hand, often must wait to have the error corrected, and the time is as long as it was for the original order, because the large company, with a backlog of work, makes the customers wait in line.

A similar situation has sprung up in the computer industry. Computer buyers ordering machines from mass merchandisers have found that, although they pay lower prices, they do not get service when something goes wrong. Customers have to telephone service departments whose lines are almost always busy, and wait on "hold" until the next customer service person becomes available. If they have to ship the computer back for repair, they are denied its use until the repair department is able to get around to servicing their machines. The small neighborhood computer dealer, on the other hand, is always available to help them with their problems.

Returning to the auto industry, we see that, although the manufacturers have set up nationwide organizations for sales and service, small, independent concerns actually do the majority of maintenance and repair work on cars.

An automobile dealership is an excellent example of what can go wrong with growth. A small dealership, in which the owner is both salesman and service manager, is the ideal, even though he may not handle the volume to offer the best prices. Most of us who have bought cars have had the same experiences.

We go into the showroom of "Honest John's," and we run into a friendly, smiling salesman who does everything he can to make us happy and willing to buy a car. He promises the moon, the sun, and the stars, and tells us that his service department is sec-

ond to none. Some dealerships even have round-the-clock sales, in which the sales office is open late, to accommodate the schedules of working people. Even the most conservative dealers have sales offices that keep longer than usual hours.

When we return for service, it's a different picture. The repair department keeps only normal business hours, and we have to meet their schedules or go without service. We have to wait in line at the service desk instead of getting personal attention of the sort we got in the sales department. The service manager makes it clear, by an attitude that borders on discourtesy, that he'll get to us when he feels like it, not at our convenience. The message is clear: We've bought the car and now we're stuck with it.

If we go back to the salesman, expecting him to intervene to help with a special problem, we find that he's washed his hands of the affair once he's sold the car. It's not his department now, and he's uninterested in helping.

This is the key to personal service: The person who makes the promises has to be the one to fulfill them.

This is the key to personal service: The person who makes the promises has to be the one to fulfill them. If not, the company is departmentalized and the salesman can promise excellent service, knowing he can say what he likes, because he's not the one who will have to do the work.

In a small company, where the two functions are not separated, we can expect, and often get, better care. We don't have to go through a chain of bureaucracy to meet with the boss. In a large company, the owner is usually isolated from his customers by a gauntlet of receptionists, managers, and unmarked doors.

In dealing with a small company, it's possible to talk with the boss, and to resolve the problem quickly, without a chain of memos traveling up the line and the inevitable delays that this brings.

This is why there's a growing place for the small business that takes care of its customers. While the economics of mass production usually results in a lower price for many manufactured goods, there's more to a business transaction than price alone. People expect more, and they often will favor the small business that can provide more. This portends well for you, if you're thinking of going into business for yourself. You can provide personalized service, and in fact have little to fear from the large companies, who can't compete with you.

Smaller is better. One serious problem large companies face is that they develop bureaucracies in the same way, and of the same size, as do our various levels of government. This leads to inflexibility. Despite certain economies in large-scale manufacture, there's a point of diminishing returns. Flexibility of response is in many instances as important as price.

This is why many small manufacturing and service companies are emerging. They provide what the big ones cannot. This is true of both the overt economy and its underground counterpart.

The small entrepreneur holds most of the cards in this case. He does not have the high overhead that the large companies sustain. To the extent that he operates underground, he also does not pay the tax burden, and therefore has a competitive edge.

Case History: Tom, the Underground Trucker

Tom is twenty-seven years old and single. He earns a nice living with his pickup truck and van. What is unusual about Tom's business is that it is all done underground. None of the income from his business ever gets reported. Tom is a real go-getter, a good guerrilla capitalist. He earns fifty dollars an hour or even more by working hard and being on the ball. He is always looking for work to do and money to be made. Tom runs a small classified ad under "Services" in the Sunday paper.

> MOVING, HAULING. Pickup truck and van available for heavy appliances, house moving, brush piles, junk, whatever your hauling needs. Call Tom 123-4567.

He puts similarly worded ads on the bulletin boards at supermarkets, laundromats, and colleges. This is all the advertising he does, although Tom will also approach real estate agents, building contractors, co-op managers, apartment managers, etc., and leave a small card with his name, phone number, and "HAULING" on it.

This tiny bit of advertising brings Tom all the work he can handle, because Tom keeps his eyes open for other work, and for "junk" items he can salvage and sell. Let's follow Tom through a typical week and watch this guerrilla capitalist in action.

Monday

Tom is up at 7 A.M., fixes himself a quick breakfast, and then is off to work. He is meeting a college student at 8 A.M. and helping him move across town. The student and a couple of his buddies are helping, so Tom doesn't need to hire anyone for this job. He is just charging by the hour for the truck and himself. It looks like rain today, so Tom takes the van instead of the pickup. The job is done by noon, and Tom charges eighty dollars, which he collects in cash. Also, the student has left behind a box of books and an old sofa. Tom charges an extra twenty dollars to haul these "to the dump." Checking over the items carefully, Tom decides the sofa is too far gone to rescue, and he actually does haul that to the dump. But the box of books he saves to drop off at a used bookstore for cash. Tom often picks up some nice stuff for free when he helps people move, and often gets paid extra for taking "to the dump" valuable items which he later sells.

Tom grabs a quick lunch, then goes to his next job hauling away leaves and brush from a man's property. Tom uses his pickup for this, since it won't matter if this stuff gets wet. The job takes two loads, and after the second load is ready to haul away, Tom talks with the man, and makes a deal to do some interior painting on the next rainy day. By keeping his eyes open for extra work like this, Tom earns a lot of extra money. Once he did some hauling for a guy and wound up painting the entire exterior of the man's house, as well as some additional yard work. The man pays him cash for the hauling, thirty dollars per load for two loads.

By the time Tom gets to the dump, it is 2:30 P.M., and time for one more job. This time it is a contractor who needs a building site cleaned up. Three pickup loads at thirty dollars per load. On this one, Tom doesn't need to pay any dump fees, since he knows a property owner who needs fill. Tom is done by 5 P.M., and the contractor pays him with a check.

When he works for contractors, apartment managers, etc., they usually pay him with a check, since they need to have a record of the expense for their own tax records.

Deep Inside the Underground Economy
How Millions of Americans Are Practicing Free Enterprise in An Unfree Society

138

Tom has found that most individuals he hauls for will pay him in cash, but when he works for contractors, apartment managers, etc., they usually pay him with a check, since they need to have a record of the expense for their own tax records. Tom prefers untraceable cash, of course, but he knows how to handle checks to keep this income hidden. Tom pockets the check and heads home. Less his gas, dump fees, and related expenses, Tom has cleared over $225 today — all of it untaxed.

Tom checks his answering machine, as he does every night, and returns the calls. He lines up three jobs for Thursday and two for Friday.

Tuesday

Tom has two jobs scheduled for today, both local moves, one at 8 A.M., and one at 10:30 A.M. The first move takes a little longer than planned, and Tom is late starting his second job. He decides to skip lunch to get the work done quicker. He is finished by 1:30 P.M. A bonus for Tom on the second job is that the family had held a garage sale to get rid of unwanted items before they moved, and there was still quite a bit of stuff left over. Since they didn't want it anymore, they paid Tom to haul it away. Tom looks the stuff over and hauls about half of it to the dump. The rest he keeps in his garage until he can get around to selling it.

Subtracting out his expenses, Tom has made only about $100 today but he was done by 1:30 in the afternoon. He spends the rest of the day doing some maintenance on his pickup and van. Tom keeps his vehicles shipshape, since they are his livelihood. He checks his answering machine and schedules some jobs for next week, and one for the next weekend.

Wednesday

It is raining today, so Tom calls and reschedules the one job he had today for Friday. He goes out to the place he worked on Monday and does the painting he had arranged. On the way, he stops off at the bank of the contractor he hauled for Monday, and cashes the contractor's check. The bank charges him a four dollar fee for cashing a check without having an account there himself but Tom realizes this is just an expense of keeping underground. By having no bank accounts himself, and cashing all the checks he receives at the banks they are drawn on, Tom keeps his income well hidden.

Tom makes it a point to know the "right" people — secondhand dealers, flea market dealers, pawn shop owners, etc.

He finishes the painting by 2:30 P.M., gets paid in cash, and spends the rest of the afternoon going through the past two or three weeks' worth of accumulated "junk" he has salvaged from hauling jobs. It is a pretty typical assortment, nothing really valuable, but most of it saleable to the right people. Tom makes it a point to know the "right" people — secondhand dealers, flea market dealers, pawn shop owners, etc., so he can easily dispose of the old postcards, books, clothing, furniture, etc., for cash. He makes some calls and gets the stuff ready to move out on the weekend.

He checks his answering machine, returns his calls, and schedules some more jobs for next week.

Thursday

Tom is up early, as usual. He has three jobs today, two moves in the morning, and brush hauling in the afternoon. The moves are easy: one family, and a college student, and Tom acquires a couple more boxes of old postcards and books. By 1:30 P.M. he has finished both jobs, had lunch and is at the old farm to do the brush hauling. There is quite a lot of brush to be hauled, and it takes Tom until past six o'clock to carry it all to his friend's landfill. While loading up the brush, Tom notices an old half-fallen-down barn on the property. Tom makes a deal with the owner to tear down the barn. He will be paid in cash, plus he gets to salvage whatever material he can. Tom knows there is a good market for old barn boards in the city — people like to make picture frames out of them, and even panel entire rooms of their houses or businesses.

Tom will have to hire a helper (for cash, naturally) to help him with the barn. He arranges with the owner to do the job in a week or two. Tom figures he can clear at least $400 from salvaging the stuff from the barn, a job that will take him about a day.

Tom often comes across deals like this — one man's junk is another man's treasure. People often don't even know what they have. The best deal Tom ever came upon was a job he took cleaning out an old factory so it could be remodeled. The new owners considered everything in the building to be junk, and most of it was. But Tom found two spools of platinum wire, which he was able to sell for $2,500 —

pretty good, when you consider that he was being paid to haul it away! Tom knows he won't find platinum wire every day, but on every job, he keeps his eyes open for "junk" he can sell.

Friday

Tom has three jobs to do today: the two he had originally scheduled, and the rescheduled job from Wednesday. All three jobs are routine moves, so Tom is done for the day at three o'clock. He spends the rest of the day loading his van with the salvage he has accumulated, which he will take around to second-hand stores, etc., tomorrow. He also takes care of his answering machine, and schedules a couple more jobs for next week. Then he calls some used-wood dealers to get prices on wood from the barn he will be tearing down. Tom describes exactly the wood he will have, and pretends that he is looking to buy, in order to get the current retail prices. When Tom advertises his barn wood, he will charge slightly less than the used-wood dealers' prices.

Saturday

Today, Tom takes his salvage stuff on his rounds. Clothing he drops off at a used clothing store, old postcards and other "antique" type items he sells to antique dealers, phonograph records go to a used record store, books to used book stores, furniture to second-hand stores, etc. Tom has about a third of the stuff left over, and this he will haul to the dump next week with one of his other hauling jobs. Altogether, he clears over $100 for the "junk."

He is done by the middle of the afternoon, and takes the rest of the day, and Sunday, off. This week, after expenses, Tom has cleared well over $700, and he pays taxes on none of it. He averages about the same, week in and week out.

Tom prefers to appear as an ordinary wage-earner who has all his income taxes withheld.

Tom works a little scam to take care of his income tax. He wants to report enough income so that his visible lifestyle is accounted for, but he knows that if he starts putting his trucking business on his income tax returns, he will be calling attention to the fact that he is self-employed in a cash business. Tom prefers to appear as an ordinary wage-earner who has all his income taxes withheld.

Tom has a cousin in business, and has made an arrangement to give himself a visible means of support. The cousin pays Tom a "salary" for a nonexistent job. Tom picks up his paycheck every week and deposits it in his bank account (this is the only thing he uses his bank account for). Then he withdraws cash from the bank, and kicks it back to his cousin. At the end of the year, his cousin sends Tom a W-2, just like all his employees. So Tom's cousin gets a tax deduction for Tom's "salary" without having to pay anything, and Tom gets a W-2 showing enough income to account for his visible lifestyle, with all taxes withheld. Some years, he even gets a refund.

Tom's cousin's business also has gas and auto expenses, so Tom sells his cousin all his own gas, oil, and repair invoices for half-price — in cash. This way, Tom gets reimbursed for some of his expenses, and his cousin gets more "deductions."

He has no sign on his truck to indicate that he is doing commercial hauling, and has never bought any kind of license.

Tom started his trucking business part-time while in college and made the arrangement with his cousin after he had been full-time for two years. He has no sign on his truck to indicate that he is doing commercial hauling, and has never bought any kind of license. Tom figures if he is ever "caught" hauling a load, he can always say he is "just helping a friend move."

Tom is an honest man. He works hard for his money, and all his customers are well satisfied. Tom figures he pays enough in indirect taxes (sales tax, gas tax, liquor tax, excise tax, inflation, etc.) to support more than his fair share of bureaucrats. He doesn't feel a bit guilty about not reporting his income. He's the one who hustled to earn it, and he is the one who should get to keep it,[1] is the way Tom the underground trucker looks at it.

Flea Markets, Conventions, Shows, and Fairs

Good places to see the underground economy in action are various flea markets, shows, and conventions that take place around many cities on weekends. There are dozens of unlicensed or minimally licensed entrepreneurs buying and selling for untraceable cash.

Deep Inside the Underground Economy
How Millions of Americans Are Practicing Free Enterprise in An Unfree Society

140

There are many types of shows to attend, but the basic procedure is the same. You rent a table or booth, set up your wares, and sell to customers attending the show.

Flea Markets and Swap Meets

These can be pretty informal affairs, although some of the bigger flea markets are quite well organized by now. You can find just about anything at a flea market — knick-knacks, antiques, toys, second-hand goods, you name it. Flea markets can be either indoors or outdoors.[2] Attend a few and you'll begin to get an idea of the prospects.

Craft Shows and Art Fairs

Similar to flea markets, except the items for sale are restricted to "arts and crafts" items. This means almost anything you can make. If you have a woodworking or metal casting hobby, you're all set to turn this into a part-time business. Some arts-and-crafts fairs are big business. The annual bead show in Tucson, Arizona, attracts between 50,000 and 100,000 people during its three-week run. The Tucson show is actually thirty-four different shows with between 10 and 15,000 vendors at three different locations. The bead show in Santa Fe, New Mexico, is smaller but still attracts thousands during its run. It lasts five to six days, and has vendors in three different locations.

Some vendors don't fill out a receipt for every sale and they pocket the cash to avoid paying a commission to the promoter, and avoid paperwork that can nail down the amount they must pay in taxes.

Bead vendors work in different ways, depending on the show promoter. Some promoters charge a flat rate, usually more than $1,000, for a table. Others charge a nominal fee, under $100, for a table, but the vendors must give them ten percent of their sales. This leads to fudging by some vendors. Theoretically they're supposed to fill out a three-part receipt for each sale, one copy for the customer, one for themselves, and one to the promoter. Some vendors don't fill out a receipt for every sale, because many customers don't ask for a receipt, and they pocket the cash to avoid paying a commission to the promoter, and avoid paperwork that can nail down the amount they must pay in taxes.

If you're into arts and crafts, you can try making an underground business out of your avocation. If your items catch on you can make this a full-time occupation.[3]

Sarah makes silver belt buckles and small jewelry items. She started four years ago as a hobby, and when her friends admired her work, she decided to try selling them at a craft show. Sarah rented a table and, to her surprise, her jewelry sold like hotcakes. Eventually, she was able to pursue this line of work full-time. Now she works most of the year making her jewelry items, and does most of her selling around Christmas at the big craft shows she's learned are the most lucrative. She has a sales tax license because many of the craft shows and fairs will not rent her a table without one, but she reports fewer than half her sales.

Gun Shows

A gun show is just what it sounds like — a show where people buy and sell firearms. Gun shows range in size from small ones with a dozen dealers to large ones with hundreds of tables. Gun buffs love these shows because they can see a greater variety of merchandise than their local sporting goods stores and gun shops can offer. Often, because there are many dealers competing, you can find lower prices at gun shows than at stores. Plus, there is always the "just plain fun" of looking at all the guns, running into old friends, and making new ones. A significant fact is that you don't have to be a federally licensed firearms dealer, or even sell guns, to set up at gun shows.[4]

Accessories such as riflescopes, slings, magazines, and reloading equipment go very well, as does survival gear and army supplies. These are not firearms, and you don't have to have a license from the Bureau of Alcohol, Tobacco, and Firearms (BATF) to sell them.

Since most of his weekend sales were in cash, there was no way the auditor could prove he earned more than he'd declared.

Fred runs a survival store, selling dehydrated and canned food for long-term storage, camping and emergency gear, books, and related survival items. He runs a nice business and earns enough to get by. What makes a big difference for Fred is his weekend business in the underground economy. Without that extra and untaxed income, Fred would barely eke out a living. With it, he's "comfortable." Most weekends he loads up his van with material which experience has taught him moves well at gun shows, and he drives to a nearby gun show to set up a table. Fred deducts all his car expenses, meals, and table rent, but reports only one-third of his sales. Once he was audited by a sales tax examiner, but Fred just looked the auditor in the eye and told him he seldom did much business at the weekend shows, but felt he had to continue for "promotion." Since most of his weekend sales were in cash, there was no way the auditor could prove he earned more than he'd declared.

Gun shows are somewhat different from other sorts of shows, so let's study them in detail. Many of the people selling firearms are federally licensed dealers, their style cramped by federal regulations regarding record keeping. There must be federal paperwork filed for every firearm sold, so even if the purchaser pays cash, a paper trail exists. However, many gun shows allow nondealers to display as well. Nondealers can be hobbyists trying to dispose of guns in their collection, or actually underground dealers who sell as a business. Being an underground gun dealer is becoming increasingly difficult because of BATF surveillance of gun shows.

The happy hunting ground for guerrilla capitalists is selling other items, which may or may not be gun-related. At one gun show in Mesa, Arizona, one dealer in miscellaneous items even sold condoms! They were camouflage color, and the sign above the bin said: "Don't let them see you come!" In any event, BATF agents are not interested in dealers who are outside their jurisdiction.

Sports optics, such as binoculars, telescopes, night vision scopes, riflescopes, and range finders are hot sellers and require no federal license. Neither do hunting clothing, including camouflage suits, boots, hunting vests, and rainwear. At most gun shows, there are dealers specializing in knives, gun cases, holsters, ammunition belts, gun cleaning equipment, books, war surplus memorabilia, and other related items. There are even dealers selling Nazi insignia, flags, and uniforms to the collector crowd.

A gun show can also be a good place to pick up items cheaply for later resale.

A gun show can also be a good place to pick up items cheaply for later resale. There are a couple of rules of thumb that apply. One is to go early, and immediately proceed to tables farthest from the en-

trance, because generally dealers near the doors post higher prices. The rationale is that customers see them first, before they've had an opportunity to compare prices. By contrast, dealers near the back tend to have lower prices, because customers have seen their competitors' tables first. Another tactic for obtaining reduced prices is to attend during the last hours of the last day of the show. There will often be dealers who haven't taken in enough money to pay for their tables and expenses, and desperation drives them to lower their prices. This is the best time for bargain hunters.

Dealers near the back tend to have lower prices, because customers have seen their competitors' tables first.

Other Shows, Conventions, Fairs, etc.

There are many other types of shows, conventions, etc., where a guerrilla capitalist can set up and make cash sales. If you have a hobby, you must know of something like this in your field of interest. Coin shows, stamp shows, knife shows, science fiction conventions,[5] computer fairs — the list goes on and on.

The most attractive aspect of these shows is that you don't have to sell items pertaining to what the show covers — you could set up a food concession, or something similar, which would bring in extra cash at any show or convention. Wherever cash changes hands, you'll find the underground economy. Flea markets and similar shows are good places for the underground entrepreneur.

Garage and Yard Sales

Garage and yard sales are ways of getting rid of old and unwanted items cluttering your home, and of earning extra money. They are more common in some parts of the country than others. Traditionally, a yard sale is a way of getting back some money on unwanted goods. Some people call them "moving sales," which means they are offering for sale items that are not worth transporting to their new home. In principle, they offer these items, usually used, at prices that make them bargains for anyone who needs them.

Because most such transactions are in cash, and the people do not record the sales or pay taxes on them, yard sales are a strong part of the underground economy, although most are conducted by amateurs, not professional guerrilla capitalists. For the guerrilla

Deep Inside the Underground Economy
How Millions of Americans Are Practicing Free Enterprise in An Unfree Society

142

capitalist who has a system, these can be important moneymaking ventures.

Because most such transactions are in cash, and the people do not record the sales or pay taxes on them, yard sales are a strong part of the underground economy.

As a profit-making activity, yard sales are distinguished by one outstanding fact: The return per time invested can be very low. This isn't necessarily a disadvantage, because many people go to yard sales as a hobby and don't consider their time wasted if they don't always pick up a bargain or make a profit.

If you're interested in yard sales as a profitable venture, your best approach is to consider them as a moneymaking hobby. Having fun while earning a few bucks is definitely worthwhile, although obviously not for everyone.

If you want to hold a yard sale just to get rid of unwanted items, your approach can be very simple. You place a classified ad, erect signs, mark your prices (prices are generally between five and thirty percent of what you paid for the item), display your goods, and wait for buyers. At the end of the day, you donate what's left over to Goodwill or the Salvation Army.

If you're seeking to become a guerrilla capitalist, on the other hand, the procedure becomes more complicated, although it can be a lot of fun if buying and selling interest you. It's more work, but doesn't seem like work because your time is your own and you operate according to the schedule that suits you.

Your starting point is to go to garage sales in your area. You'll learn a lot from observing how others conduct their yard sales.

Yard sales are among the few remaining "free market" ventures, in which trade is unrestricted by taxes, price controls, subsidies, and other forms of government interference.

It's important to learn the prevailing prices for various items in your area. Yard sales are among the few remaining "free market" ventures, in which trade is unrestricted by taxes, price controls, subsidies, and other forms of government interference. They're also uninfluenced by other factors such as monopolies and price-fixing that affect other businesses. Therefore, you must know your market in order to make your prices competitive and not price yourself out of the market. Remember that many people who go to garage sales make the rounds and know the prices your competitors are charging.

By attending others' sales, you'll learn the general layout and modus operandi of a garage sale. While books are available on the subject,[6] you need to observe first-hand to learn the fine points. Going to yard sales will also quickly teach you what the books cannot tell you: prevailing prices in your area, what goods sell quickly, and how much haggling and price negotiation you can expect. Local conditions are all-important, and no book can tell you what they are where you live.

Observing bargaining tactics is valuable because one day you'll be on the other side of the table and you'll want to be prepared if a potential customer tries to beat you down on price.

Scouting for bargains is an obvious purpose. As you're going to look for profits, you'll have to buy merchandise at prices lower than average, enabling you to resell it at a profit.

Making Money and Maximizing Your Sales

The key to running yard sales as profit-making ventures is to sell your goods at enough profit to make it worthwhile, and to sell enough of them. You'll have to deal in two dimensions: price and volume. Let's examine the principles involved:

Buy low and sell high.

Look for volume-producing items.

Fast turnover of items always in demand will generate profits for you because it's better to sell a large quantity of low-priced goods than one or two high-priced, slow-moving items. If you expect to sell only two items a day, and you sell only one, your volume drops by fifty percent. If you sell dozens or hundreds, missing a few sales won't make that much of a difference.

A lot of this depends on your neighborhood. In a community composed mainly of young families, baby items will be more in demand than among retirees. Paperback books generally sell well everywhere. Learn what sells quickly and concentrate on these items.

Price to Sell Volume

This is a vital point often overlooked by those running garage sales and it cuts heavily into their sales when they neglect it.

You can, for example, price paperback books at fifty cents each, or you can post a sign reading:

Books — 50 cents each or five for $2.00

This encourages people to buy quantities instead of individual units to take advantage of the volume discount. It also tends to avoid price haggling because it offers a lower price for volume purchases.

Many people will walk away if they don't see a posted price. Failure to post prices will lose sales for you.

It's important to post prices conspicuously to encourage sales and avoid wasting your time answering questions. Also, many people will walk away if they don't see a posted price. Failure to post prices will lose sales for you.

Include Ringers

A "ringer" is an item you're trying to sell for much more than you paid for it. These are items you would not normally sell. Your regular items will pull in customers who will then get a chance to see your ringer. The logic behind this is direct. You're going to hold a sale anyway. You'll be paying for an ad, you'll be putting up signs, etc., so including a few extra items won't cost you much.

A decorative item such as a wall plaque, an art object, an antique, or a collector's item, is not subject to a standard price and many people don't know what the items sell for anyway.

Scrutinize your possessions with a critical eye and ask yourself if you'd want to sell them if the price were right. Put whatever you decide to sell as a ringer on display, and make sure the price IS right. This way, you have a chance of selling a high-priced, high-profit item during your selling day. Understanding what determines the price someone might pay will enable you to make a good selection and fix a very profitable price. Generally, standard items can't command a high price. A standard item is one generally available in the shops in your area. You can't price a calculator or a TV at more than local stores

charge, and most likely you won't be able to sell it for more than a fraction of the store price, anyway. However, a decorative item such as a wall plaque, an art object, an antique, or a collector's item, is not subject to a standard price and many people don't know what the items sell for anyway. Apart from a few sophisticated collectors, people buy these items on impulse and desire. Price is secondary.

It's literally true that one person's gold is another's garbage in this field. A non-functioning grandfather clock with its guts rusted out is very valuable to someone who thinks of it as an "antique," while a TV set with a blown picture tube is just scrap. You may have a box of junk in your garage filled with old bottle caps or baseball cards, or other items that have no intrinsic value. If you lay these out at high prices, sooner or later someone will buy them.

One mistake to avoid is buying these from another person in the hope of reselling them, unless you can obtain them at a scrap price. The odds are that the seller is already taking his profit and you'll have a hard time getting more than what you paid, if you can sell them at all. Here are some other mistakes to avoid.

Failure to advertise in the classified ads. These, despite the fine print and the competition from others also advertising garage sales, have a lot of pulling power. More people will see them than will see any signs you may put up. Simply list your sale giving the hours and the address. That's all you really need, and you can save money by avoiding listing all of your goods.

Listing what you have to sell is counterproductive. Garage sales are often impulse buys, and giving away the information in advance will only keep away potential customers if they decide that they don't want what you have to sell. In any event, you often add last-minute items, which will render any listing obsolete.

Listing any guns you have to sell is dangerous. While it's legal to sell guns in the states which don't have strict firearms laws, publicizing this risks attracting one or more agents of the Bureau of Alcohol, Tobacco and Firearms. They prowl gun shows and try to trap the unwary. They also read the classified ads to discover who has guns for sale. There is a kink in the law that makes it illegal to sell a gun to someone who is not a resident of the same state. Often, private sellers ignore this, although licensed dealers have to follow the law exactly and ask for ID. BATF agents have posed as customers trying to buy fire-

Deep Inside the Underground Economy
How Millions of Americans Are Practicing Free Enterprise in An Unfree Society

144

arms, and if they were able to buy a gun, they arrested the seller for a violation. The agent making the buy is from out-of-state, and thus has prima facie evidence of the "crime."

It you have guns to sell, put them out on the tables, and have their prices clearly marked. Don't ask for ID, because some of the potential buyers will not want to show it. They're not necessarily criminals, but simply gun hobbyists who fear eventual confiscation laws, and want firearms that don't have paper trails leading to them.

Gun hobbyists, especially if they're survivalists, are sometimes willing to pay more for a gun that is untraceable.

This suggests something about pricing these weapons. Gun hobbyists, especially if they're survivalists, are sometimes willing to pay more for a gun that is untraceable. They know that buying from a licensed dealer obliges them to fill out a BATF questionnaire and to present ID, which federal agents can use to trace them. They prowl the garage sales with a pocketful of cash, seeking a suitable firearm. The part about cash is necessary for them and interesting to you. A check leaves a paper trail, and they know that many people will ask for ID before accepting a check, thus the cash.

Failure to make readable signs is a mistake. Many people place signs, despite having advertised in the newspaper, because they seek impulse buyers who are casually driving by. The signs also confirm that there is a sale, and many classified ad readers will look for them. Another reason is that many addresses are not on main streets, and the signs can give directions to the sales. These can simply be arrows.

Many people holding garage sales print their signs on shopping bags, or brown cardboard, which makes them hard to read. Some write too small, trying to crowd as much information as they can onto the sign. They don't stop to realize that most people who read them are motorists, who have to watch the road and can't scrutinize the signs closely. The signs must give the vital information in one glance: "GARAGE SALE" and the address. That's it.

Failure to have the prices marked on each item will lose sales. Some sellers, imagining themselves to be clever negotiators, don't mark their prices. Others are just lazy. This may work in an Arab market, but it just doesn't go in America. Americans are used to having prices clearly marked and not having prices

visible will simply turn off a number of potential buyers.

Not marking prices brings another problem. You'll be wasting a lot of time answering people who just want to know the prices. This takes you away from the business of closing sales and collecting money. Having a long line will deter people from asking, or buying, and if you have to give verbal prices to a line of people, you'll turn away potential buyers.

We must note here that price marking is controversial. There are some people who think that not marking prices is the way to separate the buyers from the lookers. This is nonsense. It doesn't hurt you if people look. They still may buy, especially if the prices are attractive. Marking the prices is a service to those who are too shy to ask.

Failure to understand the value of the items for sale can lower profits. Some people have items, such as old sewing machines and other antiques that have been gathering dust for years. They put them up for sale, not realizing that these items can command far higher prices than they ask. There are many antique dealers and collectors who prowl garage sales like a pack of hungry wolves, seeking to buy antiques cheaply from people who don't realize their value. They'll snap up any bargain, and some even have the nerve to try to negotiate the already low price further down. That's why, if you have any such potential antiques, it's good to know what they're worth. You don't have to be an expert. The way to find out is to go to an antique shop and try to find a similar item, and note the price. If you can't find it, ask the shopkeeper.

One way to ask is to say that you're looking for such an item to complete your collection, and then ask him how much he'd charge you if he had one. You can then calculate that his buying price would be between twenty and fifty percent of his asking price.

Deal in Cash

This is obvious if you've gotten this far in this book. However, there are a couple of subtleties involved as well. What if someone wants to pay you by check?

Not all checks are good, and a particular check is no better than the person who writes it. If someone offers you a check, you can simply tell him: "Look, I'm just having a yard sale to get rid of some stuff I don't need. I'm not a business. I don't want to get involved asking you for your driver's license and all that. Can't you just go to the bank and get the cash if you really want the item?"

This is an honest tactful way of refusing a check, and the sincere buyer should not take offense. You can offer to take a deposit, and hold the item for him as an accommodation until he returns with the cash. This may not be until a day or two later, since the best time to hold a garage sale is on weekends, when banks are closed. However, increasingly bank branches in supermarkets are open on weekends, and the proliferation of automatic teller machines (ATMs) means many people can obtain cash quickly.

It's obvious that garage and yard sales and the like are good ways of generating untraceable cash, and many guerrilla capitalists take advantage of this. You can too.

Home Businesses

This is a very old idea and the basis of "cottage industries." Today it has a new meaning because of some provisions of the Internal Revenue Code. A home office can bring you further deductions, and if you operate your business totally underground, the home is the logical place for it.

If you've decided to reduce your tax bite by legal means, opening up a business in your home is one way of increasing your deductions. Another way is to bring work home with you.

If you've decided to reduce your tax bite by legal means, opening up a business in your home is one way of increasing your deductions. Another way is to bring work home with you, if your job allows this. Each has its advantages and disadvantages. Bringing work home is common, and it's foolproof. It depends on your occupation, of course. Some are just not adaptable. Others are.

Sam, a psychiatrist, had it made. He worked at a psychiatric hospital during the day, and he had converted his garage to an office to see patients there during the evenings. This meant that both his and his wife's Cadillacs had to stand in the driveway, but Sam didn't mind, as most private patients paid in cash. The extra untaxed income allowed him to buy another Cadillac for his daughter.

Ken, a commercial artist, brought work home with him from the agency where he worked. A corner of his bedroom was set up as a studio, complete with

drawing board and art supplies. He has had to clean up his act in recent years, because the IRS, aware of this dodge, stipulated that to qualify as a deduction, the entire room must be devoted to this task and not used for anything else.

There are many types of businesses you can operate at home. The variety is so vast that we can examine only a few here, and suggest sources for further information. You can use your job skills at home, as we have seen in other chapters. A bookkeeper can do the record keeping for small businesses in his or her spare time at home, for example. A computer programmer can write programs at home.

Roughly the same principles apply to the home business as to a freestanding one. It must make a profit, at least to endure the long run. It must build up a clientele if it depends on repeat business and not one-shots.

Clientele is very important. One-shots, such as selling vacuum cleaners door-to-door and keeping one room at home for inventory, are very volatile and unstable. Anyone selling vacuum cleaners needs to hustle for each sale, week after week, and work hard to see fresh people each day to find possible buyers. Repeat business enables slowing down on selling effort and redirecting the time to producing and servicing, which are usually more profitable.

A new business can attract deadbeats who can't get credit anywhere else in town and swarm around a new business like killer sharks.

One word of warning regarding clients: Depending on the type of business and the locale, a new business can attract deadbeats who can't get credit anywhere else in town and swarm around a new business like killer sharks, hoping the new proprietor won't be in business for long.

The same basic rule regarding taxes applies to the home business as to the hobby turned into a business. The IRS will scrutinize it very carefully, and it must show a profit over a period, or the IRS will disallow it. Generally, if it goes for three years without showing a profit, the IRS will clamp down hard.

With these basics laid out, we can turn to the characteristics a home business should have to serve as a tax shelter.

- It should be work you do at home. Although you may work out of your home, if your actual work

Deep Inside the Underground Economy
How Millions of Americans Are Practicing Free Enterprise in An Unfree Society

146

is off the premises, whatever fee you charge, you'll have to pay part of it in taxes.[7]

- Heavy manufacturing is out, as is anything requiring elaborate, expensive, or noisy special equipment. There are zoning laws, and it's pointless to try to evade one set of laws while laying yourself open to others.
- "Make-money-at-home" schemes are really that, just systems for the advertiser to make money off you. Start your own business, not a branch of someone else's.
- Generally, anything that is intellectual and creative will serve as a home business. It may require some equipment, such as a camera, but it's not heavy equipment and doesn't make noise enough to be conspicuous.

Many people have second or even third skills. Jack, a bookkeeper for a grocery chain, learned gunsmithing in the army, and repairs guns in his home workshop as a sideline.

Since computers are not only the coming thing, but have already arrived in many fields, let's look at these prospects first. The field is wide open, and getting wider. If you're into this, you can earn money in many ways, such as writing articles about computers, repairing them, developing and selling both software and hardware, consulting, and teaching, to cover some of the possibilities.

Phil works out of his home as a computer consultant. After retiring from a large computer manufacturer, he got the word out among friends and acquaintances that he would set up their computers, repair them, and even sell them new computers, as his contacts enabled him to buy computers and components at a discount. Phil makes house calls, which many computer dealers and repair technicians do not, and this makes his services valuable to his customers because they don't face the hassles of disconnecting their computers and driving them to a shop for repairs and upgrades.

There are many gun owners in this country, and some of them earn money on the sale and trade of guns. We've already looked at gun shows, but haven't covered gun dealing from home.

Selling guns out of your home isn't as easy as it was years ago. The reason is that the Bureau of Alcohol, Tobacco, and Firearms (BATF) has tightened its regulations, supported by federal laws such as "Brady II." Many federally licensed "kitchen table" dealers found their licenses yanked during the Clinton administration, which was resolutely antigun. That left those dealing without a license, and these people found the going tougher.

The BATF considers anyone who sells more than a handful of guns a year to be a "dealer," and it's illegal to be a dealer without a license. If you plan to deal in guns without a license or a shop, you have to be more careful than before. Advertising guns for sale in the classified ads is risky if you advertise more than one or two a year, because BATF agents regularly scan these ads to spot those dealing from home. Therefore, your advertising, like advertising for many underground businesses, will have to be by word of mouth.

Letting a stranger into your home can be risky under other circumstances, but when advertising guns for sale, it's a serious risk.

Some criminals also scan gun ads to find out who has guns, and pretend to be potential customers when answering the ads. The dealer who lets one of these into his home risks being ripped off, as some have discovered. Letting a stranger into your home can be risky under other circumstances, but when advertising guns for sale, it's a serious risk. By contrast, word of mouth is safer. The reason is that anyone whom you let into your home has been recommended by a friend or acquaintance, and this means that you already know something about him.

Model-making for architects is one craft that pays well if you develop the right contacts.[8] Model-making skills are not exotic talents, just careful work and craftsmanship, and it is a good choice for a home business.

Art of any sort is a natural for working at home. A commercial artist can freelance for advertising agencies. It seems easier than it really is, though. There's a special hazard connected to working for or with ad agencies, which the books don't tell you. Advertising people are flaky. You may get an assignment from one and find that when it's almost finished, it has to be changed so extensively that you have to start over. Short and unreasonable deadlines are another problem. People in the "ad biz" are supreme egotists and think that anything is possible if they command it. You will find yourself working late into the night to meet a deadline if you lay yourself open to this. Finally, and perhaps decisively, ad agencies are typically deadbeats. The best of them pay very slowly, and you'll be carrying them for a long time (ninety days is a good average) before you see your money.

Fine art is another field. Lisa was a painter who created paintings in her spare time, and consigned them to art galleries for sale. In her area, many part-time artists created paintings, sculptures, and sand painting for retail. Her earnings from selling paintings made up a significant part of the household income, and allowed her and her husband to enjoy some luxuries they would otherwise have been denied.

Having only one or two accounts makes you a "captive shop." It's almost like having a regular job.

Freelancing of any sort[9] that you can do at home is worthwhile, if you have the skill. Many people feel very insecure with this prospect, preferring to have one or two solid accounts, but this is a trap. Having only one or two accounts makes you a "captive shop." It's almost like having a regular job. It seems secure, but actually you have all your eggs in one or two baskets. If you lose the account, for whatever reason, you're in trouble.

Captive shops suffer from another problem that comes with this. The big account knows his power, knows the captive shop needs him more than he needs it, and often makes unreasonable demands, sometimes being crude enough to use the fear technique: "If you can't do it, I'll find someone who will."

Spreading the business around provides insulation from these problems. It multiplies the chances of running into bad clients, and slow payers, but these undesirable features tend to average out. It makes it much easier to drop a truly bad account.

Light mechanical work is another possibility. Watch repair, appliance repair,[10] and other light repair work which you can do at home without disturbing the neighbors are suited to this purpose.

Crafts of any sort are risky. These include jewelry, glass blowing, and candle holders. Such crafts are drugs on the market, and unless you already have a market lined up, stay away from them. You'll eat your heart out trying to sell your works. The advantage is that you don't need much capital investment to start, and if you find it doesn't work for you, you can quit without incurring a heavy financial loss.

Luck helps in getting started, but in the long run your ability, or lack of it, will be decisive.

Writing freelance is fairly secure, if you have the ability and are able to start at it part-time, working up your clientele. Luck helps in getting started, but in the long run your ability, or lack of it, will be decisive.

Naturally, dealing in cash is better than accepting checks, because it doesn't leave a paper trail. Checks are advisable only if you can cash them without leaving an obvious trail, and this doesn't mean at your friendly local bank where the teller will write your account number on the check. If you have a grocer who trusts you enough to accept a third-party check, this is the way to go.

For those interested in gambling, holding card parties in the home is a profitable sideline. *How to Hustle Home Poker*, by John Fox, Ph.D., GBC Press, 1981, is an operational and technical manual for those who want to run a home poker game for profit.

Another good book on milking home poker games is Frank R. Wallace's *Poker: A Guaranteed Income for Life Using the Advanced Concepts of Poker*, from Warner Books. Literally millions of dollars in untraceable cash changes hands each year over home poker tables, and it is not difficult for a skilled player to do very well for himself.

Literally millions of dollars in untraceable cash changes hands each year over home poker tables, and it is not difficult for a skilled player to do very well for himself.

Many people play a musical instrument. Giving lessons at home is a way to make that skill pay. It is especially worthwhile if your main occupation is not connected with music, since your sideline will be less visible to the IRS. Raoul, a skilled machinist, spent many evenings playing with a small local band, providing music for weddings and other social functions. Raoul got paid in cash, which made concealing the extra income easy for him.

Fewer people today have sewing skills than before. For those who do, dressmaking and clothing repair at home can be a source of extra income.

Most people have stereo tape systems; many have home video recorders and CD burners on their computers. The lucky person who has two machines and

Deep Inside the Underground Economy
How Millions of Americans Are Practicing Free Enterprise in An Unfree Society

148

knows how to use them can earn money by copying videotapes or CDs for friends and acquaintances. Duplicating tapes and music CDs is not much work, just a matter of inserting the cassettes or discs and pushing the buttons. It is technically in violation of the copyright laws, but this is not a serious hazard unless you advertise. Recording companies have investigators who chase down ads to determine the origins of their materials.

This sampling of methods of earning money at home is obviously not a complete list. It is not even a layout of the categories. It should serve to stimulate your imagination and help you find a sideline that will earn you some extra, untraceable income.

Some goods or services are available, but at prices which most people consider excessive. That may mean an opportunity for you.

Another method of stimulating your imagination is to open the Yellow Pages and start with "A," working your way through the book. See Appendix One for some ideas you can glean from the Yellow Pages. As you scan each business category, ask yourself if you could earn money doing that at home. Also ask yourself if there are any goods or services not being provided, creating a gap which you could fill. Possibly some goods or services are available, but at prices which most people consider excessive. That may mean an opportunity for you. Your skill is what will sell, but your best asset is your imagination.

Working at home is worth the effort if you're lucky enough and you approach it in the right way. Once you decide that tax relief is possible by changing your occupation or lifestyle, you can work out your step-by-step plan. You'll either phase yourself into it, or jump in with both feet, depending on your occupation, skill, responsibilities, and most importantly, your personality.

Case History:
Tim, The Underground Printer

Tim runs a small print shop in his garage. His equipment consists of an A.B. Dick 360, a Multilith 1250, a homemade plate burner, and a homemade padding press. The printing presses are obsolete, and he was able to buy them for almost nothing from a print shop going out of business. Although he lives in a residential neighborhood, Tim operates his business in his home, because his operation has a couple of features that enable him to get away with it.

First, since he is operating totally underground, he has never applied for a business license, and thus never gave the city a head start in running him down. He knew full well that people often reveal themselves unnecessarily when dealing with government agencies, and give up their right against self-incrimination.

The second reason he remains invisible is that he picks up and delivers the work and does not have customers parking in front of his house every day.

The second reason he remains invisible is that he picks up and delivers the work and does not have customers parking in front of his house every day. Excessive traffic is one reason there are zoning restrictions, and Tim does not alert his neighbors and give them cause for complaint.

Tim operates what is known as a "trade shop," soliciting overflow business from other printers who are happy to have him do work for them at a substantial discount. Without any walk-in trade, he is able to keep his low profile. He is also able to launder the checks his customers give him by passing them on to his suppliers in exchange for paper and ink.

Small printing presses are not as noisy as large newspaper web presses, which sound like subway trains. Keeping the garage door closed suppresses enough of the sound so that it doesn't disturb the neighbors, most of whom work and are not home during the day.

He does not have paper company trucks delivering to his door, either. He picks up all of his orders, and brings them home in his van.

Tim started out as a paper salesman, and therefore knew all the print shops in the large city in which he lived. He knew the mortality rate among small printers was high, and he was able to close in and buy equipment at very low prices when one failed. This gave him an edge over other people starting in the business, who had to pay dealer prices, even for second-hand equipment.

As a salesman, he was able to ferret out the printers who would give him their overflow work, and line them up as accounts. He was also able to procure paper from the company for which he worked, at a substantial discount. This gave him another edge over his competition.

Tim worked seven days a week, five of them for his company and weekends for his underground print shop. As a salesman, his time was his own, and he did not have to put in forty hours a week making the rounds. With a voice pager, he was able to check if there were any calls for him or any problems, and spend many hours at home taking care of his business.

Slowly, the business built up enough to enable him to quit his sales job and work full-time at his printing shop. He'd left on good terms, and was able to continue to buy his paper at a discount, especially as he saved the paper company the cost of delivery by picking up his orders in his van.

For several years, Tim ran his operation while keeping his regular job as cover, to explain his means of livelihood to the IRS. When he quit and went full time, he simply stopped filing tax returns, and even went on unemployment for six months. When the unemployment payments stopped, he continued as before, but planned to move out of state before the IRS caught up to him.

He had originally come from another state, and still had contacts there. This enabled him to start up again in another location, leaving no forwarding address, and going completely underground.

He accomplished this by renting a garage from a friend and living in an apartment with his family. With a going business, he was able to rent premises, keeping the payments underground, in cash, so that his friend and collaborator did not declare his rental income on his taxes.

With a false Social Security number and other supporting ID, he was able to open up a bank account to deposit his checks.

A friend of his was manager of the local branch of the paper company for which he'd worked, and the cozy arrangement which let him buy paper at a discount and launder his checks continued. It also helped for Tim to offer his customers discounts for cash. Later, with a false Social Security number and other supporting ID, he was able to open up a bank account to deposit his checks, and was able to stop offering discounts for cash.

Tim's success story is valuable, not because you necessarily can follow in his footsteps, but because it

shows a few important lessons in how to start an underground business.

We've already noted the high failure rate among small print shops in Tim's city. Some started by investing money in franchise operations, not knowing anything about the business. The franchise companies are all too happy to take people's money and run them through a one-week crash course in how to operate a small printing press. They're not taking any risks. On the other hand, they're profiting by selling these small investors equipment and supplies at a hefty markup. That's how they make their money.

Many who started small print shops invested their life savings in their equipment, and had no operating capital to keep them going during the lean initial period. Not knowing where to find the business, they started cold and scratched for work, while their equipment was standing idle.

Tim, by contrast, knew how to operate the equipment, having worked as a pressman before becoming a paper salesman. He also knew the contacts, which was all-important in his line of work.

He knew every print shop owner, knew who their customers were, knew what they charged for their work, and even knew their employees.

Tim kept his finger on the pulse of the printing industry in his locale, and his job enabled him to do this full-time. He knew every print shop owner, knew who their customers were, knew what they charged for their work, and even knew their employees. This was because Tim, like most salesmen, was out for Number One, but kept a friendly, cheerful "front" when he contacted his customers. He also kept his eyes and ears open, and took notes in a small book when he left each customer.

While he never asked his customers what they charged for their work, he often saw their price sheets, and sometimes was able to take a copy with him, on the pretext that he'd pass it on to someone who was interested in having some printing done.

He eased into his business, first working part-time, and only when the business grew did he go full-time.

He was able to watch the struggling businesses, and jump in with cash when they were failing and about to liquidate their assets. When a franchise fails,

Deep Inside the Underground Economy
How Millions of Americans Are Practicing Free Enterprise in An Unfree Society

150

the owner is stuck with the equipment. Thus, he was able to build up his capital equipment while still holding on to his regular job, and at the same time build up a list of potential clients. This was the key to starting a business that required substantial capital. He eased into his business, first working part-time, and only when the business grew did he go full-time.

He was able to obtain everything at a discount. Not only was he able to get his supplies at cost, but he also bought odd lots from other printers. Printing is very wasteful of paper, and often printers over-buy, then store the excess. There were always odd lots of paper around his accounts' shops, which he was able to pick up for almost nothing. He saved them and offered them to customers who wanted their printing done on fancy grades of paper, at a huge profit to himself.

He kept his overhead very low. Unlike print shop operators who rent commercial property and then have to pay a high rent each month, Tim ran his business at home.

This shows how to do it: Learn the business, have contacts, go slowly and carefully, avoid crippling investments, keep a low profile, have customers lined up before starting, and keep control of every phase of the operation, for maximum profit. This ensures a healthy cash flow because capital and operating expenses are so low.

If you're not in the printing trades, forget this line of work. However, be aware that you can adapt Tim's methods to other fields. The principles are the same. Only the details differ.

Making Money From Your Hobby

There are basically two ways to make money from a hobby — using it as a peg from which to hang additional deductions, and as a totally clandestine means of earning money. Both are in wide use, and each has its virtues and drawbacks.

The first way is sometimes overdone by people who think the IRS is stupid or naive. Calling a hobby a business and taking large deductions will work only for a time. The Internal Revenue Code covers exactly what is allowed in deducting hobbies, and lays down some strict limitations.[11] Generally, a person who raises horses or collects stamps cannot call his hobby a business unless he earns money at it. Declaring a loss for several years running, while claiming deductions, is an old trick and the IRS has seen it many times before.

There is only one way to succeed at deducting your hobby — you must show a profit, and pay taxes on it.

There is only one way to succeed at deducting your hobby — you must show a profit, and pay taxes on it. It only pays if you are already spending a lot of money on your hobby, not if you have to lay out more money to earn those deductions.

Damon is a gun hobbyist, spending at least a thousand dollars a year on his guns and ammunition. He reasoned that if he took up writing about guns, he would be able to deduct the money he was already spending on his hobby. He did, and has succeeded in selling several gun-related articles a year to magazines, and even having some gun-related books published. The deductions he gets as a result eat up most of the income, but leave him with enough so he is able to show a slight profit each year, making his deductions completely legitimate and above board. Although Damon is not, strictly speaking, a guerrilla capitalist, because he declares his writing income, he's learned how to beat the system.

The second way of earning money from your hobby is to be completely underground. It is like moonlighting, except in this case you are not using your job-related skills, but your hobby. The electronic hobbyist who repairs appliances on the side, for cash or barter, while working as a full-time bookkeeper, is an example.

It is like moonlighting, except in this case you are not using your job-related skills, but your hobby.

Once you decide to turn your hobby into a business, you can proceed slowly and cautiously. There is no need to hurry, because you're already earning a living. You can take your time and do it right.

In starting up a business, there is usually a capital investment to make. With a hobby, you already have all or most of the tools and supplies you'll need, and this gives you a flying start. It also helps you beat the competition.

It gives you flexibility. You don't have to meet a payroll or cover overhead, and therefore can earn money without being forced to have a certain volume of business each month. You can choose the amount of time you want to devote to it, not being confined to a certain schedule.

A fringe benefit of earning money from your hobby, or any underground activity, is the security that comes from having more than one source of income. We've seen this in the case of Bob, the underground diamond dealer, and others we've discussed. Most Americans have been indoctrinated to believe that security comes from having a steady job, with a paycheck coming in each week. This is as secure as walking on quicksand, since all your eggs are in one basket, and your economic future can be threatened if you lose that job. Most Americans are aware that perfectly competent workers are laid off every year, through no fault of their own, and that a layoff can hit almost anyone. A company may have to cut back because of a recession or it may decide to stop producing an unprofitable product, or to buy its subcomponents instead of making them in house. In each case, employees find themselves out on the street, facing a bleak economic future.

Businesses know the value of diversification, and you should also be aware that having two or more sources of income gives you additional security, since it is unlikely that all of them will fail you at once.

There are two basic types of hobbies — making products and using skills — and they often overlap.

Almost any hobby can be turned into a moneymaking venture under the right circumstances. There are two basic types of hobbies — making products and using skills — and they often overlap.

Connie has a skill, painting, which is her hobby. She uses it to turn out products — paintings — that she is able to sell for cash. Her father-in-law's business is wholesaling imported picture frames to department stores, and is able to sell her paintings along with the frames. This gives her a connection that most people don't have. As a housewife, she is able to enjoy her hobby and earn untaxed income by painting in her spare time.

Debbie also has a skill, making small statues of dragons and other animals that in the past, she sold to friends and fellow employees. She recently lost her job and is struggling to make her hobby pay to support herself and her small child.

Red plays the accordion. He works as a printer during the day, but evenings and weekends he plays his instrument for money. His clientele is of two types: the one-shots who hires him to play at weddings, and

his regular accounts, including a social club which books him many Friday and Saturday nights.

Diane is a housewife who likes to write poetry. She has a part-time job teaching literature at a local community college, which earns her some declared income. Like many poets, she went through a long and frustrating period during which she sent her poetry to magazines and accumulated reams of rejection notices. One day she decided to take a risk and had a book of her poetry privately printed. She makes the rounds of the bookstores in her area, selling her books out of the trunk of her car. She sets up a table at art shows and sometimes sells over a hundred volumes in one day. She reports none of this money.

John, a karate hobbyist, works as a mechanic during the day. On weekends, he holds classes in self-defense, which affords him tax-free income.

Cyril is a stamp collector. He specializes in early American issues, mostly mint, but will not pass up a nicely centered and lightly cancelled used item. He subscribes to stamp magazines, belongs to the local stamp club, and gets the various catalogs, such as Scott's, as they come out in order to monitor prices. He also closely tracks auction results. His knowledge of prices is of great help to him in speculating. When he attends a stamp show, he is easily able to spot undervalued items, and picks them up at bargain prices.

Two days a week, Cyril runs the stamp counter at a local coin shop. He pays the coin dealer $150 a month for his counter. When he is not there, he leaves stamps on display for the coin dealer to sell, and they split the profit from these sales. The coin dealer is happy to have a stamp expert in his shop, since people who stop by to look at stamps often become customers for coins. His deal with Cyril allows him to keep all the money from the sale of stamp supplies. This arrangement gives Cyril a place of business with small overhead and few expenses. All his sales are in cash, and he pays the coin dealer his rent in cash. Cyril has been doing this for six years now, and has never been hassled.

Loretta likes to bake. Her specialty is fruitcakes laced with brandy and rum, which she sells at a modest profit to her friends and neighbors. Each Easter and Christmas, she clears several hundred dollars selling her fruitcakes, which are of much better quality than supermarket or commercial bakery products. Her clients buy her fruitcakes not only for themselves, but as gifts for others. Her main problem is keeping up with the demand, and each season she

Deep Inside the Underground Economy
How Millions of Americans Are Practicing Free Enterprise in An Unfree Society

152

drafts her husband to help her in the kitchen. Her income is tax-free, of course.

These examples give you an idea of the possibilities for underground entrepreneurship in hobbies. It is a field in which individual initiative counts for more than in many other moneymaking ventures. A hobby-business can be as simple or as complicated as you wish to make it. If you decide to use it as a peg for extra deductions, you'll have to get involved in record keeping to satisfy the demands of the IRS. If you keep your hobby's earnings completely underground, you can save yourself trouble.

Notes

1. If you would like to learn more about the opportunities available in trucking and hauling, underground or otherwise, a good book is by Don Lilly, *How to Earn $15 to $50 an Hour and More With a Pick-Up Truck, or Van.* Darian Books, 1999.

2. Valerie Bohigian, *Successful Flea-Market Selling,* TAB Books, 1981. See also, Cree McCree, *Flea Market America,* John Muir Publications, NY, 1983; and Robert G. Miner, *Flea Market Handbook,* Main Street Books, Mechanicsburg, PA, 1981.

3. Steve and Cindy Long, *Success Is Not Working for the Pharaoh,* Idahome Publications, 1983.

4. Thomas Thielen, *The Complete Guide to Gun Shows,* Loompanics Unlimited, Port Townsend, WA, 1983. This title is out of print.

5. Erwin S. Strauss, *The Complete Guide to Science Fiction Conventions,* Loompanics Unlimited, Port Townsend, WA, 1983. This title is out of print.

6. Ryan Petty, *How to Make Money with Your Garage Sale,* St. Martin's Press, NY, 1981. This is a good basic book on how to conduct a garage or yard sale, and covers everything you need to know. Many of the points the author covers are elementary but you'll be surprised, as you make the rounds of yard sales in your locale, how many people overlook them. This book is out of print, but has limited availability on Amazon.com. Also worth reading is *Don't Throw It Out.*

7. George and Sandra Delany, *The #1 Home Business Book*, Liberty Publishing, Cockeysville, MD, 1982, p. 67.

8. *Ibid.,* p. 64.

9. *Ibid.,* pp. 67, 68, 79, and 81 for a start.

10. *Ibid.,* p. 127.

11. The Internal Revenue Code, section 183, deals with "Activities Not for Profit" and explains — once you get through the opaque language — how the IRS treats those who deduct their hobbies.

Chapter Ten
Other Ways to Hide Income

We've seen several ways of obtaining untraceable income. There are also ways of diverting part of your income if you're operating an above ground business, so that it doesn't register as income on your books. With these methods, discretion and good judgment are very important, to avoid lopsided income tax returns.

If we believe the prophets of modern technology, cash is, or will be, on the way out. VISA International would like to see everyone using its plastic and has devised a new type of card to replace cash completely. This high-tech device, called an "electronic purse," contains a microchip like the one in prepaid telephone cards, "loaded" with a preset sum, and the user would spend it in whatever amounts he wished at terminals in stores, gas stations, telephones, parking meters, and other outlets. One consortium of manufacturers is trying to develop the hardware to make this practical, because while card technology already exists, low-cost terminals do not. At the moment and for the foreseeable future, the all-purpose cards seems to be just science fiction.[1]

Cash vs. Plastic

At least two decades ago, the idea of a "cashless society" was originally promoted by credit card companies.

At least two decades ago, the idea of a "cashless society" was originally promoted by credit card companies for obvious reasons, and quietly applauded by the IRS. While VISA and MasterCard would love to see us buying our newspapers with their plastic, it didn't happen and it may never happen. On the contrary, one type of plastic that's become very popular is the Automated Teller Machine card, which enables people to obtain cash at their convenience, even at night and on week-ends.

night and on week-ends. The fact remains that cash is the most convenient way to pay for many transactions.

The increased use of credit cards for purchases, even incidental ones, makes it more difficult for the business owner to skim part of his receipts.

Credit cards require that the merchant have the correct account and the electronic hardware that goes with it. Today most merchants accept credit cards, and it's even possible to buy motor fuel and "pay at the pump." Supermarkets have electronic pay points, and some people pay for their groceries with plastic. The increased use of credit cards for purchases, even incidental ones, makes it more difficult for the business owner to skim part of his receipts. Even some flea market vendors today have credit card machines. As anyone who writes checks knows, merchants today require at least one form of picture I.D., and sometimes two to verify the writer's identity. On top of that, both checks and credit cards expose their users to various frauds that can be quite costly to the victims. With cash, the most you can lose is what you carry in your pocket.

There's another danger to credit cards. They enable the government to track you when you travel. If you pay for your hotel by credit card, an electronic record instantly appears. Even during the day, if you buy gasoline at a pump that accepts credit cards, and most do, you leave an electronic trail behind you.

Although the idea of a cashless society still appears to be a dream, the IRS fervently hopes for it to come about, because cash transactions are hard to trace and hard to control. Still, many self-employed people deal partly or wholly in cash, and IRS agents concentrate their efforts on these potential violators. Others who handle a lot of cash are waiters and waitresses, who

Deep Inside the Underground Economy
How Millions of Americans Are Practicing Free Enterprise in An Unfree Society

154

pocket tips. However, the IRS has laid out draconian rules to plug this potential leak, and waiting on tables today is less fun than ever.

Drug money is the largest contributor to money-laundering operations, and serves as an excuse to pass laws allowing the IRS to monitor financial transactions more closely.

It would be an error to think that the IRS operates in a vacuum, because at times, despite sporadic rivalries, separate government agencies help each other. One example of U.S. enforcement agencies working hand-in-hand is the partnership between the Drug Enforcement Administration and the IRS. Drug money is the largest contributor to money-laundering operations, and serves as an excuse to pass laws allowing the IRS to monitor financial transactions more closely.

Despite a law requiring banks and businesses to report all cash transactions larger than $10,000, drug traffickers still outwit the authorities. One countermeasure was to hire part-time launderers, such as college students and senior citizens, to buy cashier's checks in amounts just under the magic number of $10,000.[2]

The IRS responded predictably. It requested, and got passed, a new law requiring reporting of all cash transactions just under $10,000, on the ground that such amounts were selected only to evade the previous reporting requirement. Now it's also illegal to circumvent the $10,000 transaction law by making groups of smaller deposits.

The events of September 11 have provided a new reason for tracking money. Interrupting the financing of terrorist networks has also provided a convenient excuse to step up surveillance of all Americans, including financial surveillance.

Professional, high-volume money-launderers are running rings around American customs and tax authorities.

Still, the IRS, DEA, and other government police forces are largely spinning their wheels, because their authority stops at the U.S. border. Professional, high-volume money-launderers are running rings around American customs and tax authorities because money-laundering is an international enterprise. As we'll see, it's state-supported by small countries that profit from the traffic in laundered money.

How the Pros Do It

One American, seeking a way to conceal the origins of a six-figure "windfall," enlisted the help of a French bank with an office in the Netherlands Antilles. The scheme involved a front corporation in Rotterdam, controlled by an Antilles trust company to disguise its ownership. This type of convoluted transaction isn't unique, nor is it confined to drug traffickers and wholesalers. Many screen actors and business executives launder their incomes to avoid or reduce the tax bite.[3]

One IRS estimate, covering only legitimate business earnings, is that as much as fifty billion dollars annually is diverted into laundered accounts to evade taxes.

We're talking about billions of dollars here, enough incentive for American authorities to embark upon an all-out effort to trace "dirty" money.[4] One IRS estimate, covering only legitimate business earnings, is that as much as fifty billion dollars annually is diverted into laundered accounts to evade taxes.[5]

Even within our borders, money launderers take simple precautions to remain one step ahead of the authorities. Buying convenience stores and restaurants as fronts for money laundering is now a big-time operation. You might have noticed a large retail outlet near where you live that remains in business year after year, although few customers appear to patronize it. It doesn't have to be a restaurant, fast-food outlet, or convenience store; in fact, it's better if it isn't. IRS and DEA agents aren't total fools, and sooner or later it sinks into their perceptions that certain economic activities fit a common money-laundering "profile."

Breaking that profile then becomes the money launderer's high priority, and he branches out into hardware stores, surplus stores, and other types of businesses that deal mainly in cash. Practical psychology also enters into the picture. The money-launderer knows that the IRS will make an effort to detect underreported income, but will almost always accept at face value overreported income. The IRS won't send out investigators to check whether or not a certain business had only $100,000 of business last year, while reporting $10 million.

Electronic fund transferring, with its tremendous volume, works to the advantage of the money launderer. Granted that EFT produces an electronic trail, in tangible form this trail is only an electronic whisper inside a computer. To become meaningful information for an investigator, it has to be translated and evaluated by a human intelligence analyst. Government agents can't track every transaction, instead focusing only on those that have attracted their attention for other reasons.

Electronic fund transferring, with its tremendous volume, works to the advantage of the money launderer.

Some foreign countries earn a large part of their incomes as safe havens for tainted money. Switzerland has been a repository for secret accounts since the 1930s, because of its impenetrable bank secrecy laws. Many of these accounts financed espionage operations, while others comprised getaway money for Europeans with good reasons to flee their countries. Some accounts financed the escapes and relocations of high German officials after the war, while others were old Gestapo accounts lost when the people who started them died. Switzerland gains because it takes over abandoned accounts.

It's now harder to obtain an impenetrably secret account in Switzerland, and Swiss law enables disclosure of account information.

Diplomatic pressure from the United States, based on strong evidence that Swiss bank secrecy laws were being exploited by criminals, resulted in changes in Swiss banking laws. It's now harder to obtain an impenetrably secret account in Switzerland, and Swiss law enables disclosure of account information in certain cases where the deposits are tainted money. As a practical matter, this hasn't choked off secret accounts. Other countries have picked up the slack.

During the 1980s, bank deposits in Luxembourg more than doubled as the word got around that this country was a safe haven for funds people wanted to keep hidden. The Isle of Man, off the English coast, is another safe haven for laundering and stashing money. Money laundering isn't necessarily illegal, and it doesn't necessarily involve cash transactions.

Many multinational corporations employ a practice known as "reinvoicing." The parent company sets up a dummy company in a country with a low tax rate. The dummy company buys materials and resells them to the parent company at a high markup. This dodge, perfectly legal, keeps most of the profits offshore in a country where they remain intact.

Diverting Income

Cash income is very easy to earn and hide by simply not listing the transaction. If you're a plumber who is paid in cash, you can omit that transaction. You can even encourage cash payments by offering a discount for cash.

Lawyers, doctors, accountants, plumbers, and other self-employed persons, professionals, or tradesmen, sometimes ask their nonbusiness clients to make their checks out to them personally, instead of to their companies. They then simply cash the checks at their banks. They avoid depositing them to break the paper trail.[6] Another way is "skimming," a widespread technique worth a detailed look.

Skimming

Skimming is diverting some of your company's resources to personal use. Commonplace examples are making personal phone calls on your business phone and using a company vehicle for personal use. Butchers take home steaks and other cuts of meat to feed their families, grocery store owners stock their pantries from their inventories, and of course, appliance dealers take home everything from a "Walkman" for their kids to washing machines for their spouses. Other examples are liquor dealers stocking their home bars from inventory, automobile dealers letting their families drive "executive cars," and using the company postage meter for personal mail. The jeweler picks items from his inventory as gifts for family and friends. All of these are widespread, but unimaginative, ways of skimming, and a lot of people are successful with these methods.

The practical limitation in skimming for personal use is consumption.

In this section we'll consider some advanced methods, all of which are easy and even more profitable. The practical limitation in skimming for personal use is consumption. You can only get away with so much because you can only use so much, no

Deep Inside the Underground Economy
How Millions of Americans Are Practicing Free Enterprise in An Unfree Society

156

matter how large your company may be. Advanced techniques are limited only by the size of your business, which must have enough volume to hide the amount you skim.

Advanced skimming consists of operating part of your business underground, and the simplest and best method is to sell inventory under the table, for cash or barter.

As a liquor store proprietor, you sell stock to your neighbor at slightly more than wholesale, listing the missing inventory on your books as "breakage," or "shrinkage." If you operate a supermarket, you sell food at a deep discount to family and selected friends, writing the missing items off as "shrinkage." If an IRS auditor questions you regarding your figures, you can very reasonably and credibly explain that shoplifting is a major problem.

Trade-outs are barter deals between businesses, for business purposes, such as to save on outgoing cash flow.

At this point, let's note a subtle difference between "trade-outs" and "skimming." Trade-outs are barter deals between businesses, for business purposes, such as to save on outgoing cash flow. Skimming deals are strictly for personal use.

Your neighbor owns a travel agency and you own the local Honda dealership. He books a trip to Europe for you and your spouse, and you let him drive an executive car for a year or two. Each of you is skimming, swinging a barter deal for personal use on each side.

You're a plumber and your neighbor needs a new hot water heater. When he comments to you that advertised store prices appear high, you mention that you can get him one for less than he'd pay in any store. He accepts your offer, paying you in cash. He's gotten a good deal on his hot water heater and you have untraceable cash in your pocket.

Another way of skimming, whether you own the business or not, is to overestimate the amount of materials needed for a job.

Another way of skimming, whether you own the business or not, is to overestimate the amount of materials needed for a job. A construction foreman can order extra lumber, or apply only one coat of paint instead of two, selling the surplus underground.[7]

A burglary or robbery has its silver lining for the skimmer. A business owner over-states the amount stolen, both to collect extra from the insurance company, and to cover the merchandise or cash he's skimmed from his business.[8]

Check Deposit Slips

An age-old method that still works is to take part of a deposited check in cash by filling in the appropriate line on your deposit slip. That way, you can receive a check for $400 worth of plumbing work, get a cash return of $100, and enter it on your books as $300, supported by your deposit ticket.

Note that this only works with accounts that do not turn in Form 1099s to the IRS. If you try this with commercial accounts, you'll end up with a discrepancy between reported income on your books and the total the government gets from its Form 1099s.

A quick and expedient way of making use of a check without leaving an obvious paper trail is to cash it instead of depositing it in your account.

A quick and expedient way of making use of a check without leaving an obvious paper trail is to cash it instead of depositing it in your account. While this still will appear in the account of the person who gives you the check, it's not in your account. When cashing a check at a bank, you usually have to have an account there, with enough on deposit to cover the check's value. The teller will write your account number on the check, but it won't appear in the permanent record of your account. You can make the trail harder to follow by cashing the check against a personal account at another bank. An investigator would have to track all accounts of all of your business contacts to follow up adequately on this type of transaction.

A better way is using it to pay for some goods and services you buy. This type of transaction works only with a vendor who knows you well and is willing to accept your third-party checks.

Yet another way is to maintain a small personal account under a false name at another bank. Keep the account balance small (less than $1,000) so that the interest isn't enough to attract the attention of an IRS investigator.

Banks are concerned about patterns of activity that indicate check kiting and other frauds against them.

Setting up such an account is easy, because many banks still do not ask for positive I. D. from new customers. You just have to provide a Social Security number — not your own, of course. Maintaining it is even easier, because banks and IRS investigators are attracted by account activity, not dormancy. The only caution you must observe is to show activity in the account, as many states have laws providing for state takeover of accounts that have been inactive for a certain time. Banks are concerned about patterns of activity that indicate check kiting and other frauds against them.

What if, after several years, a government investigator follows up on the phantom identity and Social Security number and interviews you regarding this technical violation of the law? He's got you dead to rights, so don't even bother trying to deny it. Do not, however, admit that it's part of a money-laundering scheme. Instead, use the tried-and-true technique of the "story within a story." Your prepared cover story contains something derogatory about yourself to make it more credible.

One thing to tell the investigator is that you're on the verge of divorce and are trying to hide some of your assets from your wife. Another variation is to "admit" that you have a mistress who provides more satisfying sex than your wife. Only the most fanatical and single-minded investigator will pursue such a case to its limit. However, use a little common sense; don't try this story on a female investigator.

A persistent investigator might want to check out your story anyway, and demand the name of your mistress. You can forestall this if you use your imagination. Tell the investigator you've got a "gay" lover. If the investigator demands his name, tell him that you'd rather go to jail than reveal his name because your lover is a schoolteacher or a clergyman, and that if his sexual propensity got out, it would destroy his career.

Do not try to pay all your bills in cash to avoid having a credit card or checking account. That sort of behavior stands out like a red flag today.

Do not try to pay all your bills in cash to avoid having a credit card or checking account. That sort of behavior stands out like a red flag today.

Other Sources of Untraceable Income

There are still ways of obtaining untraceable income, and as our technological society becomes more complex, more ways will appear. One method takes advantage of twentieth century mass-marketing techniques.

Rebates
Many manufactured items today come with rebate coupons, which you send to the manufacturer to obtain a partial refund of purchase price, or rebate. Some are worthwhile, but others are stupid. For example, if you use a 37¢ stamp to send in a coupon that gets you 25¢ back on a tube of toothpaste, you're the loser. On the other hand, a big-ticket item, such as a computer, which you can legitimately deduct if it's a business expense, often has a big rebate coupon attached to it. You save the receipt for your tax return, send in the rebate coupon, and when the check arrives, cash it. That's right, cash it. Do not deposit it or it will leave a paper trail.

One problem with rebate coupons is that many specify that you must send in the original receipt with them, to prevent dishonest customers from making multiple copies of their receipts, sending them in with separate rebate coupons, and getting multiple rebates for one purchase. The solution is simple: make a copy of the receipt for the IRS and send the original with the rebate coupon. The IRS accepts photocopies unless there are too many.

Petty Cash Revenue Enhancement
Petty cash offers many opportunities for extra income to the alert enterpriser. Big business constantly fudges expense accounts — big-time. Examples are the corporate jet used to take Mr. Bigshot's family on vacation, and the posh private resort used for business "conferences" and "seminars." A small business owner can get his share, as well. Here are some ways to obtain personal profit from petty cash if you operate an above ground small business.

If you use your personal vehicle on company business, compensate yourself at a reasonable rate for the miles you accrue.

Deep Inside the Underground Economy
How Millions of Americans Are Practicing Free Enterprise in An Unfree Society

158

If you use your personal vehicle on company business, compensate yourself at a reasonable rate for the miles you accrue. For the 2001 tax year, the IRS allowed thirty-four cents per mile. If you inflate the miles driven, you collect extra bucks from the petty cash account. You're the boss, who's to question you?

A group of jurors completing claim forms for travel expenses spent some time discussing how to inflate various items, such as car mileage reimbursement, loss of regular income, etc. An irony of this is that they had just finished serving on a case where the amount stolen by a teenager was much less than the average fudged expense by each juror.[9]

If you buy a piece of hardware for personal use, you can cover the price from petty cash if it's an item that can be plausibly used in your business, especially if you cover your tracks. If you want a new 27-inch TV, for example, you buy one, pay for it from petty cash, and bring your old TV to your workplace for the reception room or employee lunchroom. In the remote event an IRS auditor later asks you why the receipt is for a 27-inch TV but the one in your lobby is only a 19-incher, you can always say the big screen was stolen. Don't worry too much if you don't have a police report to justify this. Many people do not report crimes to police because they feel the cops won't do anything, anyway.

There are also stupid ways to hide income. Some seem to imply that IRS agents are deaf, dumb, and blind. One is trying to hide contract labor income under the category "Other Income," to avoid paying Social Security taxes.[10] This is an old trick, and IRS agents know it.

Barter

Barter is a basic element of the underground economy that has probably existed for about as long as the human race. Money is a recent invention. Trading goods for other goods or for services was the basis of trade for the thousands of years that preceded the invention of money. In turn, buying for cash existed long before checking accounts and credit cards.

Today barter is illegal unless reported to the IRS for the "fair market value" of the transaction.

This is the original method of economic transaction, and not surprisingly, today barter is illegal unless reported to the IRS for the "fair market value"

of the transaction. Barter existed long before money, long before recorded history, and before the advent of government-minted currency, during the time when open-air markets were the normal methods of conducting business in ancient civilizations.[11]

Some suggestions have been made for using labor credits as a money substitute, but a quick look will show why this would not work. If people exchanged certificates, each representing an hour of work, inequities would soon appear.

A doctor or skilled craftsman would argue that his time is worth more than an unskilled worker, and it would be necessary to assign values to each hour of labor, according to its nature. This would create a paperwork system much like money, and we would be back at our starting point.

Trading goods for other goods or services is simple, direct, and satisfying. It is also too inefficient to use as a basis for an industrialized economy. Barter requires that the one who needs something and has something to trade for it meet with another person who needs what the first party has to trade and is willing to exchange something that the first party wants.

Today, with inflation and deficit spending, paper currency is debased and even coins are usually not made of precious metal.

Money works as a lubricant in transactions; it is a medium of exchange. For centuries, the money system worked well, because it consisted of coins of precious metal, or certificates representing a quantity of precious metal. Today, with inflation and deficit spending, paper currency is debased and even coins are usually not made of precious metal. Add to this the substitution of checks, credit cards and revolving accounts for real money, and a partial return to the barter system is inevitable.

The IRS does not like barter for the same reason that it does not like cash transactions: neither leaves a paper trail that can be traced and taxed. In fact, one of the first questions that an IRS examiner will ask in an audit is: "Are you a member of a barter exchange?"

Today barter still exists and is a legitimate method of conducting business. However, governments have decided that barter, if not declared illegal, must be strictly supervised and legislated to keep earned income from leaking through the cracks in the bureaucratic fence.

Given today's tax structure, barter is mainly useful as a means of avoiding taxes.

Given today's tax structure, barter is mainly useful as a means of avoiding taxes. The IRS's question regarding barter exchanges reveals this. It is necessary to understand exactly how the IRS views barter, and how it enforces its views, to be able to make the best use of barter.

The IRS doesn't tax gifts or small favors. What interests the IRS is goods or services provided that are a person's regular line of work. A plumber who moonlights or does plumbing work in exchange for goods, will have to be careful not to let the IRS know of this unless he is willing to pay taxes on it. A dentist who extracts a tooth from a mechanic in return for a tune-up is liable to a tax bite if the IRS finds out. A person who lends his lawnmower to a neighbor in exchange for the loan of a spray gun is in another category, since these loans are personal favors and not taxable.

The key phrase is: If the IRS finds out. With no money changing hands and no paperwork trail, it is hard for the IRS to find out.

Barter is not just a device used by unskilled or illiterate individuals who have little to trade. It is often used by high-income people with profitable skills to avoid paying more than what they feel is their fair share of taxes. Doctors, lawyers, and other professionals use barter.

Ross, a computer specialist and woodworking hobbyist, earns an income far above average, and consequently pays more than the average amount in taxes. He systematically uses barter, exchanging his skills and products for goods and services. His wife's last baby was delivered by a midwife who took a playhouse for her daughters in exchange. Since Ross is a skilled woodworker, the playhouse, measuring eight feet square, was a work of art.

Ross also refinished an antique table in exchange for a painting by an acquaintance who is an artist. The artist is currently doing another painting for Ross, who is making a teacart for him.

Ross acquired an air compressor and spray gun, for which he traded a handmade trestle table and benches. Ross's family doctor provides medical services at no charge while Ross reciprocates by making him a magazine rack and other office furniture.

In his line of work, Ross has "bought time" on computers in exchange for designing programs for their owners. His family barters actively, too. His oldest daughter trades babysitting for concert tickets.

We see from this quick sketch of Ross's bartering that it takes in the spectrum from an exchange of personal favors which is not normally taxable, to outright trade of professional services, which is. In this one instance we can see the many reasons why the IRS is so concerned about bartering. Not only is it hard to trace, and thereby hard to tax, but in many instances it falls into a legal gray area. Where there is an unmistakable trade of professional services, there is no question. However, in the case of the family doctor, the doctor is trading his services, while Ross is giving him wood furniture, and woodworking is Ross's hobby, not his trade. Linda, Ross's daughter, is a minor. While theoretically income from babysitting is taxable, it is hard to imagine even the IRS auditing a minor.

Bartering takes in the spectrum from an exchange of personal favors which is not normally taxable, to outright trade of professional services, which is.

The major problem in barter is meeting people who want to trade with you and have something you want. You might be tempted to join a barter club, as many have recently. This will expose you to a risk, unless you are prepared to pay taxes on your trades. Barter exchanges, by their very nature, have to keep records.

The major problem in barter is meeting people who want to trade with you and have something you want.

Even today, the IRS could be building up a suspect list of barter exchange members. One way is by suborning an employee of an exchange who is having tax troubles. In return for a list of members, the IRS could barter away his tax liability. Another way is to place an undercover agent as an employee of a barter exchange, to observe and report. Having your name on a membership list could cause you problems, because the IRS might interpret your membership as prima facie evidence of intent to evade taxes.

If you want to be a successful guerrilla capitalist, stay away from barter exchanges.

Right now there is no law requiring barter exchanges to send periodic reports to the IRS, but this

Deep Inside the Underground Economy
How Millions of Americans Are Practicing Free Enterprise in An Unfree Society

160

could change suddenly. Even now, in individual cases, the IRS can subpoena their records, and one proprietor of such an exchange warns that this could happen. This means that if you want to be a successful guerrilla capitalist, stay away from barter exchanges.

You may place a newspaper ad describing what you have for barter, because the IRS just doesn't have the manpower to scrutinize newspaper ads for what might be illicit trading and following up on these leads. The same is true for cards left in laundromats and on supermarket bulletin boards.

More Examples

As an auto mechanic, you work out a deal with a computer technician who needs his automatic transmission overhauled. In return for your work, he installs a new hard drive in your computer.

Individuals who join barter exchanges can deal this way, but they pay taxes on their deals. A honeymooning couple bartered for a Vermont vacation, but had to pay $45 for taxes. The problem for the guerrilla capitalist is that barter exchange firms report slavishly to the IRS. Anyone dealing with one of these exchanges can expect the IRS to have his name, address, taxpayer ID or Social Security number, and the dollar value of each item bartered.[12]

The *USA Today* article cited above doesn't state how many barter deals are off the books, discreetly staying away from that hot-potato topic. However, common experience shows that a lot of off-the-books barter takes place. This, too, is part of the underground economy.

Trade-outs: Business Bartering

Many companies engage in barter, although another term for it is "trade-out."

While barter of personal items and services is common among individuals and not taxable anyway, such barter among business owners often takes place "off the books." Many companies engage in barter, although another term for it is "trade-out." Barter items include travel, hotel costs, car rentals, advertising, medical services, and company gifts. One surgeon traded out his services, performing an eye operation for barter.[13]

Other examples abound:

A hotel chain, for example, will trade out accommodations in return for advertising. In such cases, the nature and amount of the trade-out has to show on the tax return, and is treated as income according to its "fair market value," which means value as if it had been sold. Large companies, because of their intricacies and detailed bookkeeping, cannot easily hide trade-outs, and usually pay taxes on them. Still, they find trade-outs profitable, because they can enter them at a discounted value. Discounts are common in many businesses, and in this application are useful as tax-saving measures.

Vince, a photographer, took photographs for a restaurant owner. Informally, without stipulating that this was payment, the restaurant owner invited him to a choice meal. He also gave him some steaks to take home with him. Later, during an assignment in a motel, Vince provided some extra prints for the manager. The manager invited Vince and his wife to spend a night in the motel's new waterbed suite. Neither of these two, nor many similar transactions, ever found their way onto Vince's tax return.

Survival Bartering

In reality, "survival" simply means coping with many threats.

We've seen how barter is useful for evading taxes. There is also another use for barter: survival. This is a little-understood and emotional topic, often sensationalized for the sake of selling books and magazines. In reality, "survival" simply means coping with many threats. Some are threats to your life, such as riots, terrorism, and nuclear war. Other more common threats are threats to your lifestyle, such as taxes, inflation, and gas shortages. Trading goods and services instead of paying cash is one way of coping.

What do you have to trade? People need both products and services.

To prepare for bartering, assess your skills and possessions. What do you have to trade? People need both products and services. Your products and skills can be either something you do to earn a living, or as a hobby or second trade.

Some products you could use for barter are:
☐ Foods grown in your back yard
☐ Things you can make, such as furniture or sculptures.

Some services you can use for barter are:
☐ Babysitting, which does not require great skill
☐ Plumbing and electrical contracting

☐ Midwifery
☐ Tutoring
☐ Medical care
☐ Accounting or bookkeeping
☐ Manual labor of various sorts, such as helping with a harvest in return for food.

The central problem with bartering is that the two parties must meet face-to-face and have items that each wants. One way to compensate for this inefficiency is a barter exchange, which exposes the participants to the risks of dealing with the IRS. However, there is another way. In ancient societies, people soon found items that were useful as media of exchange, such as salt. The old expression, "not worth his salt," came from this practice.

A medium of exchange works like money. It is a commodity everyone can use, is durable, and is commonly accepted as having value. Call it barter currency.

Barter currency is different from fiat currency, or money, in at least one significant way: it has value by itself, unlike money. You can't eat money. You can't build a house with it. You can paper your walls with Federal Reserve notes, and you can use coins for slingshot ammunition, neither of which is very practical. Barter currency has immediate and practical value. Salt, one of the oldest, is obviously and commonly useful. In our industrialized society, other items have value as barter currency, such as .22 ammunition and fuel.

Fiat currency, or money, has value because the government says it does. Money used to be backed by commodities of commonly accepted value, but no longer. Now it is just the product of a printing press, and this debased currency is directly linked to inflation.

Thus, you can work barter two ways: by a direct swap of your skill or product for something you need, or by exchanging it for something you can use as "trade goods" later — barter currency.

Thus, you can work barter two ways: by a direct swap of your skill or product for something you need, or by exchanging it for something you can use as "trade goods" later — barter currency.

You can get a head start in barter currency by buying some for cash now, while it is still commonly available at a low price. Buying commodities is one way of making your savings inflation-proof and pre-

paring for possible shortages or even a breakdown of the economy.

Some items are better than others as choices for barter currency, for various reasons. Above all, barter currency must store well, which limits the possibilities. Secondly, it must be commonly accepted.

Canned and Dried Foods

These are obvious, since people always need to eat. The limitation is that foods do not keep as well as some other, more durable items.

Alcoholic Beverages

These have always been in demand, and probably always will be. They keep well, as a rule, although some not as well as others.

Silver Coins

Although you definitely can't eat silver, a lot of people will accept coins made of this metal as having real value. This is a critical point. Real value partly depends on the opinions and perceptions of the person making the judgment, and a commodity that is accepted by a great many people is useful, even though the person using it may not have any need for it himself. The next item is an excellent example of this principle.

Cigarettes

We know that smoking is harmful, and many people do not smoke because their religion forbids it. Yet since the twentieth century, cigarettes have been widely used as barter currency and are worth stockpiling for this reason.

If you're thinking of stockpiling ammunition, it is worthwhile to run a test to find out which brands store best.

Ammunition

This is a gun-oriented society, but apart from that, hunting with firearms is one common way of getting food. The most widely used caliber of gun is the .22 Long Rifle, which, despite the name, is used in both rifles and pistols. .22LR ammo is compact, not very expensive, and keeps well. It is important to note that some brands keep better than others, and if you're thinking of stockpiling ammunition, it is worthwhile to run a test to find out which brands store best. Take a box of each brand you want to test, open it, and leave it outside in your yard or on the roof for a few weeks, where it will be exposed to the elements. Then test-fire it. You will see there will be more mis-

Deep Inside the Underground Economy
How Millions of Americans Are Practicing Free Enterprise in An Unfree Society

162

fires with some brands than with others, and this will give you an idea of what brands store best in your locale. One test conducted a few years ago found that ten out of ten CCI Stingers immersed for a week in a glass of water fired, and that other brands did not do as well.

Primers

Many gun hobbyists reload their shells, and a fresh primer is essential for each reloaded cartridge. While it is possible to improvise the manufacture of gunpowder, primers are much more difficult to make. Right now they are cheap, compact, and easy to store. In some locales, where there are a lot of ammunition reloaders, primers will be an excellent medium of exchange.

This is a very incomplete list, and you might find many other items worth stockpiling as barter currency, such as fuel, motor oil, batteries, and even medicines. The choice is up to you, and one important factor is whether or not you are in a position to buy some of these items cheaply. If, for example, you have a friend who owns a gun store, you may be able to persuade him to sell you cartridges and primers wholesale. If you're a pharmacist, you can stockpile medicines. If you work in a food business, you may be able to get various food products at a good price, stretching your limited dollars further.

To start out in barter, it is important to develop a barter mentality.

To start out in barter, it is important to develop a barter mentality. While it is difficult to walk into a store and offer barter instead of cash, in some instances you can work out trades with friends and neighbors. If some of them own small businesses, you may be able to work trades for items they make or handle.

Right now, while the currency is still relatively stable, you can build up a list of traders. You can help spread the practice by encouraging others to barter instead of paying cash.

If you live in a rural area, you're probably already bartering, since barter is an established practice among farmers. In a city, it is not as common, and you may be tempted to join a barter exchange. Don't do it, for the reasons you already know.

Barter is one key to survival. It will help you in the short run to survive the ravages of taxation, and in the long run you'll have a means to cope if the economy crashes, whether it is a sudden crash or a long downward slide, as we are seeing now.

Notes

1. Albert Crenshaw, "We're Still Seeking the Way to Create a Cashless World," *Washington Post*, reprinted in *Albuquerque Journal*, 11 April 1994, Business Outlook section, p. 5.
2. Pico Iyer, et al, "Fighting the Cocaine Wars," *Time* (25 February 1985).
3. Jonathan Beaty and Richard Hornick, "A Torrent of Dirty Dollars," *Time* (18 December 1989), p. 50.
4. This is also enough money to provide for generous bribes to officials at all levels. How much illegal money goes for bribes is impossible to determine, because obviously leaders of drug importing rings don't publish stockholders' reports. One of the unknown aspects of the "war on drugs" is how much of its lack of success is the result of corrupting officials at the highest levels, including police agency heads, prosecutors, and legislators.
5. "A Torrent of Dirty Dollars," p. 50.
6. Lauren Chambliss, "Cheating Hearts: The IRS Is Zeroing in on the Taxpayers Who Tend to Fudge the Most on Their Returns," *FW* 159, no. 11 (29 May 1990), p. 60.
7. Stuart Henry, *The Hidden Economy: The Context and Control of Borderline Crime,* Loompanics Unlimited, Port Townsend, WA, 1980, p. 32.
8. *Ibid.*, p. 51.
9. *Ibid.*, p. vii.
10. Paul N. Strassels, "The IRS Digs into Pockets of Noncompliance," *Nation's Business* 78 (Jan. 1990), p. 67.
11. Jordan L. Cooper, *How to Make Cash Money Selling at Swap Meets, Flea Markets, Etc.* Loompanics Unlimited, Port Townsend, WA, 1988, p. 3.
12. Denise Kalette, "Firms Use Barter to Avoid Cash Crunch; System Offers Creative Twist," *USA Today*, 18 October 1990, Money section, p. 12B.
13. Denise Kalette, "Bartering Services, Products at Your Firm," *USA Today*, 18 October 1990, Money section, p. 12B.

Part Three
Underground Lifestyles

We've seen enough of the lifestyles of the rich and famous, who attract media attention to inflate their egos. The smart underground worker does just the opposite, shunning publicity and trying very hard to blend in with the other "nobodies" in his area.

It's not enough to earn and dispose of income secretly during our modern age of universal surveillance. Your general lifestyle must be such that you don't wave a red flag in the faces of those whose job it is to snoop on you. Several people, such as Charles Keating and Leona Helmsley, became so conspicuous in their efforts to amass mega-bucks that they ended up in prison after conviction for economic crimes. Avoiding such a fate is partly a matter of keeping a low profile, and partly knowing how to break paper and electronic trails. It's also wise to be discreet and avoid making public statements such as "Only little people pay taxes."

The next few chapters examine how to keep a low profile, and how to keep from making waves that can betray your secret lifestyle. They present advanced methods of operating an underground business, as well as ways of putting part of your business underground if you operate an above ground business. They also look at techniques of more underground workers to demonstrate other possibilities.

Chapter Eleven
Maintaining Privacy

Beating the system means not outright confrontation, but finessing your way around the rules and regulations.

"You can't fight the system" is a widely quoted saying. It is mostly true. You can't fight it because most people don't fight it, won't fight it, and in fact will be against you if you try. The key is not to fight it, but to fool it. Beating the system means not outright confrontation, but finessing your way around the rules and regulations.

Fighting the system is what people in the above ground tax protest movement do when they file "Fifth Amendment" tax returns and other tactics. They generally lose, and even when they do not, they must waste enormous amounts of time and energy in court.

Others suggest different ways of fighting the system and maintaining privacy, such as filling out checks with a nonreproducing-blue pen to prevent their being microfilmed.[1] This isn't really very useful, because if you do it, you are drawing attention to yourself and your activities, and suggesting that you have something to hide.

Another suggestion is to not have a bank account, because the government intimidates bankers into revealing your confidential financial details. But it is very difficult to run a business of any size without some sort of bank account. A checking account is the minimum that will suffice. Many suppliers expect to be paid with a company check, and will question any customer who doesn't have one. A business that requires credit will have to prove credit references and other information that will have to be verified by a bank.

There are other impractical suggestions for maintaining privacy, such as using "dead drops," avoiding the use of the mail, and even writing messages under the stamp on the envelope. These are techniques more suitable to a spy than a guerrilla capitalist, and generally involve so much inconvenience that it's cheaper and easier to pay the taxes.

We even see some impossible advice, such as the suggestion that one must never let customs officials stamp his passport, because it makes a record of his travels. The writer making this suggestion does not explain precisely how to prevent a customs or immigration officer from stamping your passport if he wishes.

To maintain privacy in the underground economy, there must be outward compliance with the law, especially in showing a legal means of support.

To maintain privacy in the underground economy, there must be outward compliance with the law, especially in showing a legal means of support.

Privacy at Risk

The threat to your privacy is greater today than ever before. Both government agencies and private businesses are collecting vast amounts of data about you, and keeping it in their computers. While private corporations, such as credit reporting bureaus and "data brokers," have no enforcement powers, they sell information to government agencies and other police forces. The threat to your privacy, and that of everyone who lives in an industrialized country, is real and growing.[2]

Safeguarding your privacy is harder than ever today. It requires subtle tactics, not a head in the sand approach.

Deep Inside the Underground Economy
How Millions of Americans Are Practicing Free Enterprise in An Unfree Society

166

Tactics to Protect Privacy

What, then, can we do? The answer revolves around tactics, not principles. Some tactics to create financial privacy are using cash as much as possible, avoiding leaving a paperwork trail of your activities, using money orders purchased under false names to make untraceable payments, and keeping some hidden money in travelers' checks, cash, or precious metals.

The smart operator will set up a conventional business, comply with the law, and use it for a cover for his underground activities.

Each of these tactics has its advantages and disadvantages. For example, paying for everything with cash would work for a very small business or one that is labor-intensive, that uses man-hours rather than materials, but not for even a medium-sized business. The smart operator will set up a conventional business, comply with the law, and use it for a cover for his underground activities, which might include skimming. The moonlighter will hold a cover job, real in both form and substance, to show that he has a legitimate income, and keep his sideline hidden.

Similarly, precious metals are fine for investment or long-term storage, but it is impractical to use them for everyday transactions. You can't buy a loaf of bread with a Krugerrand or silver bar.

So we see that maintaining privacy is not a matter of having a hostile, closed-in attitude, but one of outer conformity. Blending in with the crowd is the best way to do it.

It is impractical, if not impossible, to lead a totally underground existence. It is impossible to avoid revealing some personal details to friends, neighbors, and fellow employees. For most who have held jobs, there is already much information on file, accessible to the government or private agencies, such as credit bureaus. We can't eliminate this, but we can minimize its impact.

To understand this, we have to get into a little information theory. Those of us concerned with the information about us on file realize that we are not the only ones who have paperwork trails, because the government keeps files on everyone, and this is where the basic principle of privacy lies.

Communications theory tells us that a vital part of distinguishing a meaningful message is the "signal to noise ratio." This means there must be something outstanding about a message in order for the receiver to separate the message from the background static. For example, imagine a gun owner and hobbyist who is fearful of gun control efforts. He is worried about joining the National Rifle Association, fearing that if he does, his name will go on a list that will provide government investigators leads if the day for gun confiscation ever comes.

What this guy doesn't realize is that, with over four million members, the NRA membership list is an unwieldy document, and that investigators would also be working from lists of subscribers to the many gun publications in this country, gun registration records, hunting license applications, and a large number of other lists. He also fails to realize that many people on these lists are not even gun owners, but simply like to read about them. Government confiscation squads would have to plow through each name on the list and conduct an extensive investigation of each person to ferret out gun owners. With current personnel levels, this would take decades.

This shows us that if we are simply names on a very long list, it is not particularly dangerous for us.

This is where signal-to-noise ratio comes in. A person listed on the NRA membership rolls doesn't stand out from the rest unless he does something else significant, such as getting an arrest record for a violent crime. An NRA member who also files "Fifth Amendment" tax returns, is a member of a "subversive" organization such as the Posse Comitatus, has been arrested for a violent crime, and has a long record of nonpayment of taxes will make waves, and cross-checking, easily done with computers, will "flag" him.

The flag is the critical element in attracting the attention of an investigator. This is what makes an individual stand out from the crowd.

Another example is the intelligence reports predicting a terrorist attack before September 11. There were many rumors, indications, and other bits of information, but none were specific enough to allow the government to pinpoint the attack.

Also, many people are concerned that their telephones may be tapped, since there are many outrageous examples of both legal and illegal tapping by government and other agents. In reality, tapping a phone takes both equipment and manpower, and it is impossible to tap every phone in the country. Those likely to have their phones tapped are already subjects of investigations, or have stood out in other ways. This is true even though federal authorities recently received enhanced wiretapping authority as an aftermath of September 11.

Even if it were possible to tap every phone in the country, someone would have to listen to each conversation, screening it for details significant to an investigation.

Even if it were possible to tap every phone in the country, someone would have to listen to each conversation, screening it for details significant to an investigation. For years there have been rumors of computers that can be programmed to recognize certain words, and proposals to use these to screen every telephone call in the country. Voice recognition software is a fact. With the electronic switching system (ESS), this is actually becoming possible, and one suggested application is to search through the nation's telephone conversations for significant words, such as "bombs," "explosives," or "fuze," in an effort to detect terrorist activities. The computer would flag conversations in which these words occurred, for further investigation by a human policeman.

Trying to detect hidden economy activity by using such a computer would be impossible. It would mean flagging on the basis of some very commonly used words, such as "cash," etc., and would generate so many flagged conversations that there could never be enough investigators to follow up on even a small proportion of them.

We see that any activity that is both legal and ordinary, i.e., one that many other people share, is not particularly dangerous. There is no need to hide the details of everyday life. In fact, any successful effort to hide them will make one stand out from the crowd, which is the opposite of the desired results. Someone without a visible past attracts attention. An employment application, for example, listing no previous work experience and no Social Security number will cause raised eyebrows.

Let us examine two hypothetical individuals to illustrate what works and what doesn't work in keeping privacy and avoiding unwanted attention, and keeping a low profile. Let us assume there are two individuals, both of whom are gun hobbyists and both of whom are concerned about government firearm confiscation. One is successful in covering a trail, and one isn't.

Mr. A has purchased several guns, some from licensed dealers, and some from private parties with no paperwork. He plans, if ever there is a confiscation, to give up only the registered guns and hide the "clean" ones. He is a member of the National Rifle Association, and subscribes to half a dozen gun magazines. He has purchased ammunition for each of his guns in retail stores, signing for it each time. The record shows the caliber of the ammunition as well as the quantity. He has ordered reloading equipment from various manufacturers, paying by check and having it shipped to his home. He has been arrested for carrying a concealed weapon, which is only a misdemeanor in his state, was convicted, and paid a $100 fine. He is a member of a couple of extreme political organizations and once was arrested at a demonstration that became violent. He was acquitted for lack of evidence, but the arrest is still in police records. He is also a hunter, has purchased numerous hunting licenses, and once was fined for hunting without a license. His friends, neighbors, fellow employees, and acquaintances know of his guns and his political convictions, since he forcefully lectures anyone who will listen on what he thinks is wrong with the country, and what should be done about it.

Mr. B, by contrast, is far more discreet. He, too, owns many guns, and is a member of the NRA. He has purchased all his guns from private citizens, paying cash and not leaving his name. He never buys ammunition himself, instead asking a shooting buddy to "pick some up" for him when his buddy is shopping. He owns reloading equipment, all bought over the counter for cash. Since there are no current controls on reloading equipment, he was not required to sign for it or give his name. He casts his own bullets, and obtains other ammo components through the purchases of friends. He doesn't hunt. He is not a member of any extreme political organization, although he is a registered Republican. He doesn't attend political demonstrations and has never been arrested on weapons-related charges. Both at home and at work, he is discreet about his political convictions, preferring to let others do the talking, while he listens quietly. To those who know him, he is a typical middle-class American, a steady worker, family oriented, and a homeowner. Although his neighbors know he owns a couple of guns, nobody suspects that he has fifteen of them and over thirty thousand rounds of ammunition, with some buried in isolated spots.

Deep Inside the Underground Economy
How Millions of Americans Are Practicing Free Enterprise in An Unfree Society

168

Maintaining privacy involves discretion, not absolute secrecy. It requires good judgment, not a paranoid attitude.

Which of these people has the better chance of surviving an investigation? More to the point, which one has the better chance of avoiding an investigation?

Maintaining privacy involves discretion, not absolute secrecy. It requires good judgment, not a paranoid attitude. It doesn't matter what level of society you occupy, as long as you know how to be discreet and avoid attention. A good example of how not to do it is the case of Howard Hughes. Hughes tried very hard to keep a solid wall of secrecy around himself and his activities, but his extreme behavior only succeeded in getting him several decades of headlines. Many other wealthy people, who knew enough not to be so obvious about their secretiveness, managed to avoid publicity and attention much better than Mr. Hughes.

You can see from this discussion that keeping your privacy means keeping a discreetly low profile, not building a very visible wall of secrecy around yourself. Blend in, don't stand out, and people just won't notice you.

The Hard-Core Underground Life

Pedro is an illegal immigrant. Although he lacks formal education, his native intelligence is high, and he uses it to earn more money in his adopted country than he did in his native Mexico. His life is almost totally underground, with the help of some friends and relatives.

When he arrived, he "borrowed" his cousin's Social Security card and used the number to file a spurious W-4 with his employer, the owner of a body shop. Pedro claimed a wife and seven children, when in fact he was unmarried, in order to reduce his withholding to zero. He earned much more money at this than he would have in agriculture as a migrant worker, which is the way many illegal immigrants earn their livings.

He didn't like the idea of agricultural work, because he knew through the grapevine that the employers took advantage of the workers' plight and paid them substandard wages. There was also the ever-present danger of a raid by the U.S. Border Patrol and agents of its parent agency, the Immigration and Naturalization Service. He'd even heard that

some employers, at the end of the season, would "tip off" the agents themselves, and have the workers rounded up before payday. This was their way of economizing on payroll.

One day, after working at the body shop for a year, his employer told him that there was a mix-up with his income tax, and that the Internal Revenue Service had asked for a clarification. Pedro had been well briefed by his cousin and asked what the problem might be. The employer told him the IRS had no record of him with that Social Security number, and had asked for a correction. Pedro replied that he didn't have his Social Security card with him, but that he'd check when he got home.

The next day, after consulting with his cousin, he gave the boss a "correct" number, knowing this would keep the bureaucrats going around for a few more months. Before the IRS got back to him, he quit and went to work for another shop, using a totally new identity.

Americans who haven't traveled abroad don't appreciate how truly free and loosely organized life in the United States is.

Americans who haven't traveled abroad don't appreciate how truly free and loosely organized life in the United States is. Even the democratic Western European countries have much more official control over the lives of their citizens than the American government does. To an American, the requirement of registering every change of address with the local police station seems oppressive, but the Swiss live with it, as do the French. National identity cards, as in France, Germany, and other countries, are unknown here, although the September 11 terrorist attack has brought renewed demands from law enforcement authorities and legislators that the United States adopt such a system. We travel to Canada and Mexico without passports. Even with all the bureaucratic paperwork imposed by the various levels of government here, we are still more "free" than the citizens in most other countries.

Evasion of identity is easy here. There is no law requiring us to be fingerprinted at birth. We have no single document following us around through our lives, although this may change soon. A birth certificate is a just a piece of paper, without a photograph or any other conclusively identifying data, and access to another's birth certificate is quite easy for anyone who wants to build a false identity.

Perhaps some Americans were surprised to see how easy it is to assume the identity of another person in order to get a false passport, as laid out in the novel, *The Day of the Jackal*.[3] The events take place in Europe, but the methods are even easier to apply here, where there is less bureaucratic control.

Very few, if any, employers ever ask to see a Social Security card. Few ask for proof of identity.

Regarding working in the underground, the case of Pedro shows how easy it is to work at above ground jobs without paying taxes. Very few, if any, employers ever ask to see a Social Security card. Few ask for proof of identity. Some, if the requirements of the job so dictate, may ask to see a driver's or a chauffeur's license, or other certificate of skill. Although every job application has space for the applicant to list his education, almost nobody asks to see a diploma. In fact, there have been many instances of people listing false credentials in their application papers, even in such supposedly closely guarded fields as medicine, education, and even the National Security Agency.

The long career of Aldrich Ames, who worked for the Central Intelligence Agency while selling its secrets to the Russians, shows how easy it is to carry on a clandestine life under the noses of the authorities. It took years before the FBI and CIA task force identified him, and then only because he'd set a pattern that they could trace back to him. If he'd been hired under a false identity, and had simply done his job, he probably would have retired undetected.

Assuming a new identity is easy, under one condition: It must be someone unknown to the person you're trying to fool. This would not apply, for example, to taking over a man's identity to try to fool his wife.[4] Employment situations, though, are different. Typically, many job applicants are strangers to the employer, and claiming a name not one's own doesn't present a major problem. We live in a paper society. Getting a spurious birth certificate or Social Security card is almost routine.[5]

Generally, low-grade jobs are the easiest to get without ID or references.

There are limitations to the kind of jobs one can get using a false identity. Generally, low-grade jobs

are the easiest to get without ID or references. Those that require technical skill usually demand references. This is a critical point, because references are almost impossible to falsify effectively. While it's true that almost anyone can have a fake letterhead printed, and type his own letter of reference, employers who require references will often telephone the alleged former employer. Today it's becoming increasingly common for employers to carry out background checks on applicants, and indeed there is a cottage industry of security specialists who perform these services for employers to detect fakes. In many instances, an applicant will claim job experience in another company in the same locale, and this means that the two employers know each other. A former employee from the claimed company may be working in the same shop.

Word-of-mouth job referrals are what we call "the hidden job market," and entry into this market is practically impossible for the falsifier. The only workable way for him to get a job is by "walk-in," taking his place in line with many other anonymous applicants.

Another limitation is that jobs that require any sort of security checks are out. Not only the government, but certain private companies require applicants to fill out comprehensive security questionnaires, and sometimes even to submit a set of fingerprints. The questionnaires cover many details of the applicant's life, such as requiring him to list each school attended, and each job he's had. Some require him to list the last five or ten addresses at which he's lived.

Prospective employers in this category defeat the impersonator by running field checks to verify information. An investigator will visit or telephone some or all of the references listed to verify that the applicant actually was there. He may ask other questions pertaining to work habits, personality, and disqualifying characteristics, such as alcoholism, a criminal record, etc. This field check quickly discloses the applicant who has picked up the birth certificate of another who died in childhood.

If you want to earn tax-free income at an above ground job, the first step is to take a job under a false name and Social Security number.

If you want to earn tax-free income at an above ground job, the first step is to take a job under a false name and Social Security number. Claim enough de-

Deep Inside the Underground Economy
How Millions of Americans Are Practicing Free Enterprise in An Unfree Society

170

pendents to cancel out your withholding. Be prepared for an inquiry from your employer or the IRS when the Social Security number doesn't check out. If you've claimed a number that you simply made up, the computer will disclose that the number either hasn't been assigned yet, or belongs to someone else. This won't happen for many months. This does not automatically result in IRS Special agents coming with an arrest warrant. Mistakes in numbers are everyday happenings, and the first step will be to ask for a correction.

This is the first warning. You'll have many weeks or months before anything serious happens. Use this time to get another identity, another job, and disappear.

Filling in a tax return form when it becomes due is a waste of time. If you have had no withholding, you can't get any refund. In any event, you're not going to be there when the IRS audits your return, if it does.

The underground life will determine your lifestyle. You'll find it much easier to rent an apartment than to buy a house.

The underground life will determine your lifestyle. You'll find it much easier to rent an apartment than to buy a house. You'll need mobility, and moving into and out of a furnished apartment is quicker and easier than getting rid of a house and all the furniture. A large apartment house, furthermore, provides more privacy than living in a one-family dwelling. Many apartment houses are filled with transients, and there isn't the danger of everybody knowing everyone else's business.

Friends can be a problem. You will probably find the need to make a new set of friends about once a year. If you're very successful in your underground lifestyle, investigators will eventually start looking for you. Although you can easily cover your obvious tracks by moving and leaving no forwarding address, one well-known way of tracing a wanted person is through his friends. If you keep in touch with them, they may unwittingly betray you.

A special interest, such as chess, can betray you if you regularly attend meetings of a chess club and participate in tournaments.

Starting a new identity about once a year requires a total break. Not only does it mean a change of address and giving up old friends, but also means giving up small details, such as magazine subscriptions and associations. These often link one identity to the next. Sending in a change of address card to a magazine provides an investigator with a link, in your handwriting, to your new location. If you're a member of a lodge or other association, this will link you. A special interest, such as chess, can betray you if you regularly attend meetings of a chess club and participate in tournaments.

Finally, we have to look at your emotional stamina. Is the underground life, with its rootless existence, really for you? Americans are mobile people, moving from one end of the country to the other more than any people in history, but usually they keep in contact with their friends and relatives, and seek to settle down when they arrive. The underground life is truly a nomadic existence, and although it seems attractive at first, it can become tiring as the years go by. It requires a total commitment to the demands of the lifestyle, and constant attention to details to avoid exposure.

In one sense, it's very much like being an enemy agent in your own country. It means living a "cover," always watchful, and simply doesn't permit the activities that many people enjoy, such as settling down, getting married, and raising a family. Not everyone can handle this.

You're the only one who can tell if this lifestyle is for you. Ask yourself if you want to live under the conditions laid out here. If your situation is like Pedro, you might find it easy to adapt. You might find the prospect unattractive, and might prefer to live an above ground life, with only a part of your activities hidden from the light of day.

More Underground Workers

Ron is a police sergeant, the commander of his department's SWAT Team. Like other members of the team, and the force in general, Ron is very frugal and keeps his eyes open for easy ways to pick up extra money. He picks up the empty cartridges after each session of firing range practice for sale to reloaders, or in barter. Recently he traded 7,500-fired .223 cases to a gun dealer for a new .308 caliber rifle. None of this ever gets reported on Ron's tax returns.

Daryl lives in Arizona, and his four-wheeler is well equipped with a winch, several five-gallon cans of gasoline, containers of water, rope, shovels, a comprehensive tool kit, and a first aid kit. On weekends he goes out tooling around in the desert, just driving around, exploring, camping, shooting, and generally having fun. Sometimes he takes a girlfriend or buddy along with him. Often he runs across people who are stranded for lack of gas, oil, or water, or are stuck in the sand and can't get out. Daryl is glad to help them out, and can usually pay for his weekend, or more, by towing and selling gas, oil, and water. Daryl has a very helpful attitude and people show their appreciation in a monetary way because what they pay him is much less than the cost of a tow truck. He doesn't report any of the money he makes this way.

Sandy buys and restores antique cameras and sells them to collectors. A camera collector herself, she knows what to look for when she visits garage sales, second-hand stores and antique shops. Sometimes Sandy will place a small ad in her local shopping guide, and will put 3 x 5 cards on local bulletin boards. In this way, she is sometimes able to purchase old cameras that people have had tucked away in their attics for years, often needing only cleaning and not repairs. Sandy also buys old cameras that do not work, because she knows she can get them cheaply. If she can't fix them, they will be useful for parts, since new parts for these old cameras are not being made anymore. Before she was married, her camera collecting was strictly a hobby for Sandy, but with one child in the family and another on the way, she has turned her hobby into a modestly profitable business. Sandy sells most of her restored cameras for cash at flea markets, so keeping the income off the books is no problem for her. She has built up a list of collectors and their specialties, and can often get sales just by making a phone call.

Bonnie was an office worker all her life and retired from the civil service after heading the payroll section of her agency. She knows her way around bookkeeping and after retiring, she put her skills to work in an underground part-time business. Through a neighbor, she met Danny, who was struggling to set up a landscaping business. He was good at his work, but not enthusiastic about all the paperwork that even a small business requires. Bonnie began handling Danny's paperwork, collecting his invoices, paying his bills, making out his payroll, and acting as an answering service for his calls when he was out on a job. She allowed him to use her home as the mailing address for his business, which was a convenience for her, since then Danny's bills and checks came right into her mailbox. Danny pays her a modest monthly salary for these services, and pays her in cash. He does not take a deduction on his income tax for her salary, but does "adjust" his books in other ways to absorb the expense. Bonnie has no other clients and isn't looking for any. Danny's work keeps her exactly as busy as she wants to be, and the money is a nice supplement to her pension. She has never reported any of the money from her little sideline.

Jesse is a mechanic for a Nissan dealership, but also does weekend work for private customers. He works both in his backyard and at customers' homes, and has no trouble keeping busy. His regular boss does not object, because he sells and services only Nissans, and Jesse confines his moonlighting to other makes. With new car prices sky high and not about to come down, Americans are keeping their old cars longer, which creates an increasing market for skilled repairs. Jesse advertises by word-of-mouth, and can easily undercut the prices of the above ground repair shops which have to have licenses and pay taxes, as well as obey zoning and other restrictive ordinances. Jesse had most of his own tools when he started his little sideline, and buys additional ones with the income from his business. Most of his customers pay in cash, so hiding the income is no problem. When he gets a check, Jesse simply signs it over to an auto supply store for parts and supplies. Jesse has been doing this for years and sometimes his weekend income exceeds what he makes on his regular job.

Carmen runs a modest off-the-books business in her low-income neighborhood, writing letters for people who cannot read or write very well. The only equipment she needs is a typewriter, and all her advertising is done on community bulletin boards. Her ad, on a 3 x 5 card, reads:

> LETTERS WRITTEN. DO YOU NEED TO SEND A LETTER TO A FRIEND, OR FAMILY MEMBER? DO YOU NEED TO SEND A LETTER TO THE GOVERNMENT, OR TO A COMPANY? LET ME HELP YOU WRITE IT. YOU GET A NEATLY TYPED LETTER, SAYING EXACTLY WHAT YOU WANT TO SAY, AT LOW COST.

Her price and telephone number are also listed on the card. Since her fee is so small, all her clients pay her in cash. She has never reported any of this income.

Judy has an expensive electric typewriter and uses it to earn extra money, tax-free. Married to a deputy sheriff, with two children, she finds it hard to balance the household budget on her husband's salary alone.

Deep Inside the Underground Economy
How Millions of Americans Are Practicing Free Enterprise in An Unfree Society

172

They live in a college town, where many students need someone to type their handwritten manuscripts, since instructors now require all term papers to be typewritten. Judy advertises by placing 3 x 5 cards on campus bulletin boards, and this brings her all the business she can handle. She works out of her home, which is near the campus, so the students deliver their papers to her, and come back to pick them up. This enables Judy to take care of her household and she doesn't have to leave the children alone. With no overhead, she can afford to charge less than commercial typing services. The students always pay her in cash. If one of them tries to give her a check, she just tells them, "Look, I have kids to take care of, and don't have time to run to the bank. Can't you cash your own check at the bank and just bring me the money?" This has worked every time so far, leaving no paperwork trail to incriminate her.

Janet runs a telephone answering service out of her apartment. She doesn't patch into her clients' phones, just has them list her number on their business cards and invoices for their customers to call when they get no answer at the regular numbers. Her clients are mainly one-man business owners, such as electricians and plumbers, who are often out on business and unable to answer their phones. Janet has four phones in her apartment, in four different names. She doesn't want the telephone company to know she is running a commercial service, both to save money and to avoid the awkward questions that can produce. She doesn't want to be listed in the yellow pages, which would be a sure tip-off to prowling government tax agents. Janet has one helper, a friend on Aid to Families with Dependent Children (AFDC), who comes in four hours a day so Janet can have some time off for shopping, etc. Janet is on AFDC herself and doesn't want any on-the-books earnings, so she just doesn't report any of her income. When she is paid by check, as she usually is, she just simply deposits the checks in her personal account. She hasn't been caught yet, and does not expect to be. That extra income means a lot to her and her four-year-old daughter.

Bill works as a maintenance man for his city government. After hours and on weekends, he runs his own small air conditioning business, off the books, using the city's tools. His supervisor doesn't know about Bill's little sideline, and it isn't hard for Bill to keep it to himself. When his customers pay him in cash, he simply pockets it. When he receives checks, he endorses them over to his supplier, with whom he has done business for many years and who is quite willing to help out a client.

The supplier suspects exactly what is going on, but is willing to accept third-party checks from Bill because he knows Bill will make good on any that bounce. He also knows that Bill would take his business to another supplier if he weren't willing to do this little favor for Bill. Bill advertises only by word-of-mouth, and services a small handful of office and apartment buildings. Like most moonlighters, he gets and keeps clients because he charges less than his above ground competitors. He keeps his client list small enough so that he can do all the work himself, and thus avoids the paperwork, hassles, and expenses of hiring employees.

Rudy runs an after-hours club. While the laws in his city are strict governing the operation of bars open to the public, private clubs can do as they please. Rudy does not allow the general public in. Anyone seeking admission must join the club by paying a nominal fee, and get a membership card. The card entitles the bearer to service at the bar and to bring as many guests as he wishes. Rudy rented an old building on a side street. He runs the club on weekends only, and doesn't need a liquor license since it is a private club. It's a cash business, and Rudy doesn't bother to report any of the income. He has some experience bartending, as does his wife, who helps him in the club. Rudy's club is a very low-profile operation, and his only advertising is word-of-mouth. He has run his after-hours club for three years, and the income is now equal to what he makes on his regular job.

Pat is a confirmed gun hobbyist, and so are most of his friends. Many of them cast their own bullets, and complain about the high price of bullet lubricant. Pat mixes his own in gallon batches and makes money on the side by selling or bartering bullet lube with his re-loading friends. Bullet lube is not covered by any firearms laws, so Pat is in the clear there. His friends pay him with cash or barter, so he doesn't report any of this income. Some of his friends are doing similar things, and none of them ever expects to be caught.

Maria is an underground cleaning lady in New York City. She has a list of clients, acquired over the years by word-of-mouth, and spends her workdays scurrying from one apartment to another, taking the subway or bus, or walking if the distance permits it. She tries to arrange her schedule so she services clients close to each other on the same days, thus saving time as well as subway and bus fares. Her clients usually leave her fee on the table, and tell Maria to help herself to the leftovers in the refrigerator for lunch. Maria's clients are affluent business couples, so she eats well, and often is able to take some of the leftovers home with her in her shopping bag for supper. Another fringe benefit Maria gets is when her clients discard clothing, which has gone out of style. Maria's clients like her and usually offer her first choice before donating the clothing to the Salvation Army. All her clients pay her in cash and do not withhold any taxes. Maria does not report any of her income.

Frank is a police officer with a friend who runs a private security agency. At times, an out-of-town client wants an armed bodyguard, and if his friend hasn't got anyone available, he turns the business over to Frank. As a police officer, Frank can carry a concealed firearm legally, and this seems to be the main qualification to the client. His clients pay by check, and Frank deposits them in his personal account. He doesn't declare this extra income on his tax return. Although this creates a paper trail, Frank knows that tax collectors can't monitor all bank accounts in existence, and to date he's managed to keep his extra income concealed.

Tommy works as a printer and is exceptionally good at his trade. A printing equipment service technician suggested to him that he pick up extra money by working as a consultant, pointing out that many print shops had problems with their equipment, techniques, and hired help, and expert advice could save an owner much more than the fee he'd pay for it. Tommy's first client had a technical problem that neither he nor his employees could master. Tommy solved the problem for him, spending several hours at the client's facility, and charging him three times his normal hourly rate. This client paid Tommy by check, but referred him to others, who were willing to go along with Tommy's proposal of a discount in return for cash. One client, sympathetic to Tommy's goal, paid him by check to provide a deduction for his own tax return, but cashed the check for Tommy, to break the paper trail.

David always had a green thumb, even as a child. He spent fifteen frustrating years working at dull, unrewarding jobs before he started his own landscaping service, accepting commercial clients but concentrating on homeowners, who more often pay in cash. He declares less income than he actually makes, and is careful to keep his deductions down to fit the profile of his type of business, even throwing away legiti-

mate receipts to avoid giving the impression of ordering too many supplies for the declared volume of business.

Ed, a technical writer for a major electronics company, owns a word processor, which he uses for his above groundwork and for writing novels, his real love. He recently sold his first novel, but despite his heavy schedule finds time to write resumes for people in his plant who need them for job-seeking. As there's a high turnover, he has a constant source of clients. His word processor enables him to use a timesaving method to turn out resumes for his clients. He has several standard forms (called "matrixes") recorded on a disk, each with the framework for words and blank spaces for names, dates, and other particular information. When he gets a job he brings the most suitable one up on his screen and fills in the blanks. This takes very little time, compared to typing it from scratch, and within a few minutes he has a high-grade printout. He has a top quality laser printer that makes originals suitable for offset reproduction at a quick-print shop. He offers his clients a choice of services, from just making up a resume to a complete package. He is friendly with a quick-printer near his home, and if the client buys the whole package he'll have the quick-printer turn out the number of copies ordered, which he sells to the client at a markup.

Samantha is a very mature fourteen-year-old and has a reputation for reliability among her neighbors, who have known her since her family moved in ten years ago. She baby-sits almost every night of the week, collecting in cash. At a client's house, she's careful not to abuse her trust, and does not invite boyfriends over or tie up the telephone. After putting her charges to bed, she does her homework, and the sight of her poring over her studies when the parents come home enhances her image. She has no trouble staying "booked," and stashes most of her income in her parents' savings account, rather than opening one of her own. Her father, a lawyer, advised her to use this method to keep her income untraceable, and willingly pays the tax on the interest her savings earn.

John is a backyard mechanic, not employed in the field, but very handy with small tools and skilled enough to do his own automotive repairs and maintenance. In fact, his hobby is cars, and he earns extra money by buying broken-down old clunkers and restoring them to almost-new condition. This takes many hours, but this is his hobby, so he doesn't mind. Every year or two, he finishes a restoration and sells it for several thousand dollars. This gives him some

Deep Inside the Underground Economy
How Millions of Americans Are Practicing Free Enterprise in An Unfree Society

174

extra tax-free income. Although his buyers always pay by check, and he cannot launder such large checks, he feels safe in depositing the checks in his personal account. This is because he holds a regular job as an aircraft assembler, and his station in life and the tax picture the IRS has of him, are so conventional they don't attract attention. He has never been audited.

Amy is a good-looking co-ed who earns money by selling sandwiches to office workers. With her mini-skirt, attractive smile, and a basket full of assorted sandwiches, she makes the rounds in an office building just before lunchtime every day, selling her homemade sandwiches to those who are too busy or too lazy to leave their desks. She does well for several reasons. She has an attractive body and personality. She offers good food, always fresh and attractively prepared, and her portions are generous. She has the connivance of both company executives and the management of the building. They let her make her rounds, without even asking for a percentage of her sales, because she is a student working her way through college. She is able to earn a good rate of profit because the building she works is in mid-town Manhattan, where there is a huge lunchtime crowd, and the restaurants have long waiting lines, as do many sandwich shops. They charge what the traffic will bear. Amy is able to charge the same price, but offers sandwiches that are as good or better, and the convenience of delivery right to the customer's desk. She is always slightly overstocked, and what she doesn't sell she offers to building maintenance men and others as she leaves, building good will at no additional cost.

Dick works as an airport security police officer, and on his days off he installs burglar alarms. He's a partner in a security business, covering alarms, armored automobiles, special weapons, and other defensive paraphernalia, and thus can't run his sideline completely underground. However, he services both businesses and private homes, which gives him the opportunity of offering the private homeowner a discount for cash. This lets him "skim" a lot of money on his own accounts, with his partner's knowledge and consent. Another sideline he runs is pure installation. He lets the customer choose and buy the alarm system he wants, through his firm or another, and Dick does the installation. This way, there's no record of his buying any components, and he gets away cleanly if the customer pays cash. This is an important point, as an IRS audit can reveal the purchase his

company made, and the auditor can infer the number of installations from the number of components.

As a boy, Frank learned the shoe repair business, working in his father's shop. He decided not to enter the field, instead working as a telephone installer. This brings him into contact with many people, especially fellow employees who need repairs on their expensive work boots. He does this as a sideline, charging about one-third the price that a shoe repair shop does, and has enough cash customers to fill many of his off-duty hours.

Bud used to be an upholsterer until he became an electronics technician for a large manufacturing company. He still operates a private practice, during the evenings and on weekends. He earns more per hour, and gets to keep it all. His medical plan, retirement, etc., are all paid for by his regular employer, which enables him to enjoy the best of both worlds.

All of these people understand the need for discretion and moderation in their underground lives. This is why they've been successful.

What You Can Learn From Spies and Criminals

Because underground workers violate the law, the government calls them "criminals." This means that because of the need for them to conceal their activities and avoid apprehension and prosecution, it is necessary for them to understand some of the techniques of real criminals.

The real clandestine operators, spies and criminals, have developed their "tradecraft" over centuries, and are more adept at covering their tracks than are people who lead a normal life. We will examine how spies and criminals work, and which of their techniques are adaptable to the underground worker.

The word "underground" is apt. One of the first uses of the term was the Underground Railroad that was operated by abolitionists before and during the War Between the States, to help escaping slaves from the South reach safety in the North. It had to be kept secret because if they were discovered, the slaves would be returned to their plantations and the operators of the railroad prosecuted.

During World War II, the French "Maquis" were often called the "French Underground" because of the clandestine nature of their activities. This is a good example of a project that was illegal (the occupation forces made the laws, remember) and yet that many citizens felt was not "criminal," because the invaders were unwelcome and did not have the whole-hearted support of the community, despite the large number of collaborators. Among the operations of the French Underground was a system to help the aircrews of shot-down Allied planes escape from the Germans. These networks operated very much like the Underground Railroad in America a century earlier.

Many of the tools and techniques of spies and criminals are not adaptable to the underground worker. For example, a tax evader should not use weapons. A confrontation and shootout with authorities puts him into the category of the common criminal, and hurts his cause. Normally, the underground worker's activities are only the concern of the IRS and the real police don't become involved, but an armed confrontation changes that situation in the government's favor.

Many of the tools and techniques of spies and criminals are not adaptable to the underground worker.

Similarly, some of the other paraphernalia of espionage and crime aren't very useful to people in the underground economy. The underground worker doesn't need clandestine radios and suicide pills. The problems which the underground worker faces in common with the spy or criminal are the ones which interest us, as are the measures which he can adapt to cope with these problems. Consider them one by one.

Cover

A spy or criminal needs a cover — he must pass as just another undistinguished member of the population. For a spy, the problem is at once simpler and more severe. It is simpler because his agency can easily obtain good forged ID documents, and also more severe because if the authorities break his cover, he could face a firing squad, instead of a fine or short prison term as does the tax evader.

The underground worker lives his real life while working underground, and must keep the two halves separated to some extent.

The underground worker lives his real life while working underground, and must keep the two halves separated to some extent. His purpose is to avoid dis-

covery for a very long time and thus his cover is somewhat simpler, but must be more durable.

The spy has to fabricate an entirely new identity in order to inject himself into the other society. His manufactured background may not pass a close inspection. Forging papers is simple compared to "backstopping" a cover. For example, if a spy claims to live in a certain town, his cover will fall apart if an investigation reveals that no one in that town has ever heard of him, or if the spy doesn't know the layout of the town. By contrast, the underground worker has an easy task, since he is already a bona fide resident. His cover is his real identity, and a "real job" provides an explanation of his means of support. Keeping a low profile is the key to the matter.

Some undergrounders need deeper cover, such as illegal immigrants who seek jobs in this country. For them, the problem of obtaining ID is simple, compared to that of the spy in an occupied country. Typically, occupation forces require that every adult carry what has come to be called an "SUI," a Single Universal Identifier. This is usually a card listing the name, address, occupation, physical description, and special status, and carrying a photograph and a fingerprint.

There does not exist, and never has existed, any comparable document in this country. What we use for ID is usually a driver's license, a bankcard, a draft card, or employee or student ID cards. Some of these are easy to forge or obtain clandestinely.

We should note, however, that there have been proposals for an American SUI since the terrorist attacks of September 11, 2001. This may make it more difficult for the underground worker if the SUI becomes required for opening a bank account or making purchases.

There is still a good deal of respect for privacy in this country, and this aids the underground worker, as it does the criminal. Even today, it's quite possible to rent an apartment in a city and never meet one's neighbors. Keeping to oneself is not cause for suspicion or alarm. Criminals take advantage of this when they go into a "hideout" (or in espionage circles, a "safe house") until the "heat" is off.

Backstopping — A Vital Point

The Federal Witness Protection Program, administered by the U.S. Marshals' Office, disguises and relocates people who testify against members of organized crime, to protect them from retaliation by the

Deep Inside the Underground Economy
How Millions of Americans Are Practicing Free Enterprise in An Unfree Society

176

"mob." Contrary to the image of underground life presented in fiction, this doesn't involve plastic surgery, but rather a complete changing of identity, and building up a new, and totally false, background for the witness and for his family.

It helps to have the cooperation of the registrar of births when creating a new birth certificate, to insert the proper documents into the files.

The change of identity is total; it involves stopping membership in any clubs or associations, magazine subscriptions, and anything else which might permit tracing the witness. That's the negative part of it, and the positive aspect is building up a new identity, which we'll examine closely.

It's a great help to be with a government agency when you do this, because you can get the cooperation of many other government agencies and bureaus at various levels in building up the cover. First, there's a need for birth certificates. These can be obtained by taking over the identities of real people who died at an early age, or created from scratch. It helps to have the cooperation of the registrar of births when creating a new birth certificate, to insert the proper documents into the files. Birth certificates are available to the public, and it doesn't take much effort to inquire to verify one.

Next comes the school record. The U.S. Marshals' Office has obtained the cooperation of several schools in backstopping these. There's a college in the Midwest, for example, which will insert false records to support a diploma issued by the Marshals' Office to a relocated witness.

This is necessary to support the witness's lifestyle as well as to prevent tracing by a vengeful "mob." The witness will have to apply for a job in his new locale, and all employers today require some statement of background and work experience. Almost all require filling out an application form, listing education and work experience. A minority of them, usually larger companies that have personnel departments, will do a routine background check on everyone considered for a job, simply to verify the information listed.

Generally the lowest-level jobs don't require much. An employer seeking field labor or a dishwasher won't ask for much, but these are not the kinds of jobs that relocated witnesses usually want. Any employment that pays a worthwhile salary will require a fairly comprehensive background and listing of qualifications and experience, and this is the hard part.

This background check can be superficial or very comprehensive. It might simply involve a telephone call to the last listed employer to verify that the person actually worked there. It might mean verifying everything on the applicant's paperwork by telephone calls or letters to the schools he claims he attended.

It's necessary not only to backstop school records, but to make arrangements with private companies so that they'll confirm inquiries regarding claimed employment.

This shows how complex the backstopping can become. It's necessary not only to backstop school records, but to make arrangements with private companies so that they'll confirm inquiries regarding claimed employment.

With all this, it's impossible to backstop a witness enough to allow him to take several categories of jobs. Anything requiring a security clearance, for example, is out. Typically, a security clearance requires listing not only every school attended, but every job and every address. Any gap of a few weeks or more will be cause for an additional investigation. Routinely, government investigators, and members of the intelligence offices of the armed forces will verify every detail listed. This investigation, while very routine, is also very thorough. Investigators will interview former employers, former teachers, and former neighbors to verify that the person actually attended or lived there, and will ask for character references.

Even jobs that don't require security clearances can involve investigations. Some companies employ private investigation agencies, for example, to verify that their applicants are who they claim to be and don't have criminal records that might cause a problem. Any job that involves dealing with money obviously will require a background check. Private investigators are not as thorough, nor usually as competent, as government investigators, because they don't have the huge budgets and resources that many government departments enjoy. Despite this limitation, they can still uncover a background that hasn't been backstopped, simply by a few phone calls or letters.

Another category of users of forgeries is espionage agencies. Sending an agent into a foreign, and perhaps hostile, country requires a lot of effort, and often the best effort is not quite adequate. Totalitarian powers usually require an identity document, carried at all times by all adult citizens. Forging one of these is the easiest part. Backstopping it is almost impossible. A routine identity check in the street can lead to discovery if the police check with the central registry to verify that such a document was actually issued.

Espionage agencies often sidestep outright forgery by having their agents assume the identities of real people who have real and documented histories.

This is why espionage agencies often sidestep outright forgery by having their agents assume the identities of real people who have real and documented histories. The KGB sent several agents into the United States by having them assume the identities of real Americans, in one case a man who'd become a Roman Catholic priest. In Great Britain, a Soviet agent assumed the identity of a Canadian citizen, Gordon Lonsdale, and ran a spy ring for several years before being arrested. He was disclosed through the indiscretions of one of his subordinates in the ring, not because of a fault in his cover. His cover held up perfectly until after his arrest, when a comprehensive background check revealed that he wasn't who he claimed.

During World War II, many espionage agents infiltrated their target countries disguised as citizens of neutral powers. This was easier to arrange, because the security police of the belligerents did not have the same free access to the records of neutrals as they did to those on their own territories.

Sometimes a lack of backstopping will reveal the forgery during an investigation, even though the forgery may be perfect.

It was relatively easy to set up a dummy company, a "front," on neutral ground, to support penetrators. With a real passport from the neutral power, the agent would enter the target country quite openly, presenting his credentials at the border checkpoint and pretending to be a traveling business owner. Often this cover was quite elaborate, and the dummy company was not simply a rented office and a telephone, but actually did business as claimed. It's relatively easy to set up a cover company when you have the financial support of a government espionage agency, and the primary mission is to gather information, not to make a profit.

All of this is relevant to people who try to forge documents to support an effort to evade taxes. Sometimes a lack of backstopping will reveal the forgery during an investigation, even though the forgery may be perfect.

Need to Know

Both spies and criminals have good reason to keep their secrets private, and to restrict access to special information only to those who have a "need to know." It is obvious that the more people who know a secret, the greater the chance that someone will reveal the secret to the wrong person.

This applies to anything involving security, but most conspicuously to criminals. The police don't publicize it, but most of their criminal investigations center around informers. TV cop shows emphasize physical evidence and the role of the laboratory technician in building a chain of evidence, but in reality, the informer dominates. The lab technician who retrieves a hair sample from a crime scene must have a suspect against whom to match it, and this information more often than not comes from an informer.

Don't tell anyone who has no "need to know" how much you made last year, and in particular tell no one (except maybe a partner) anything about your underground activities.

Criminals are reluctant to reveal how many of them have been caught because they foolishly bragged about their crimes. The perpetrators of the Hollywood Video murders in Albuquerque talked too much, and to the wrong people. One of these turned them in for the reward money. You can see from this that it is a good idea to resist the temptation to talk about your financial affairs. Don't tell anyone who has no "need to know" how much you made last year, and in particular tell no one (except maybe a partner) anything about your underground activities.

Some of your activities will be hard to hide totally. If you moonlight at a second job and are paid "under the table," neighbors will know you are away from home more than regular hours, but they don't need to know how much you earn or get paid. If you moonlight at home, earning extra money from your hobby, there is no need to tell anyone that your ac-

Deep Inside the Underground Economy
How Millions of Americans Are Practicing Free Enterprise in An Unfree Society

178

tivities are anything but a hobby. Bragging can be hazardous to your lifestyle!

Actually, information about what you earn and where you earn it can be quite easy to safeguard. Strangely enough, in America many people are more willing to talk about their sex lives than their financial affairs. This attitude helps to protect you. Always remember that you do not have to reveal anything at all about your finances to anyone who is not an official investigator. Insofar as nosy neighbors and fellow workers are concerned, just tell them, "None of your business." This might seem hard to do, but telling the person who asks an indiscreet question that it's none of his business will be more embarrassing to him than to you.

Your Rights

If you run afoul of the IRS, the auditor may question you, but he's not going to beat information out of you.

Spies, when caught, basically have no rights, although criminals in the United States and most Western countries have certain rights. The American criminal is informed of his rights upon arrest by the police officer who reads the "Miranda Card" to him. Basically, the criminal has the right to remain silent and to legal defense. If you run afoul of the IRS, the auditor may question you, but he's not going to beat information out of you. The basic principle, therefore, for both the classic criminal and the underground worker, is not to reveal information unnecessarily. Many people, both criminals and those with tax problems, do not understand exactly what this means and how to avoid the dangers.

The first rule is: Don't volunteer information. If a police officer or tax examiner asks for a piece of information, you may be obliged to give it to him — an example is a driver's license when you are stopped for a traffic violation. Another example is IRS Form 1040, which the IRS requires from taxpayers each year. But beyond this, it is unwise to give anything away unless the authorities specifically ask for it. Remember that they can't coerce you with violence.

The investigator has to prove that you are a lawbreaker. You do not have to prove your innocence.

The second rule is: Don't show hostility. The best way to handle an investigation, tax or criminal, is to play it cool. The investigator has to prove that you are a lawbreaker. You do not have to prove your innocence. Let him do the work. Let him ask the questions, while you answer them as briefly as possible. Remember, you want to play the part of the innocent citizen, willing to cooperate but eager to get it over with and go on your way. Protesting your innocence too much, or showing hostility, will suggest to the investigator that you have something to hide.

Even if you're caught not declaring income, or claiming a false deduction, you should remain cool. Admit only what is on paper, what can be documented, and don't volunteer anything else. Claim it was a mistake. It is up to the examiner to prove fraud — it's not up to you to confess it.

Bringing a lawyer or accountant to a tax audit can be unwise in some circumstances.

A third rule is: Don't overreact. For example, bringing a lawyer or accountant to a tax audit can be unwise in some circumstances. While you do have the right to have your accountant, tax advisor, or lawyer present, it can create suspicion if you are claiming to be simply an ordinary Joe with a simple tax return. Corporations always send a lawyer or accountant to a tax audit because their returns are so complicated that they need a specialist. A taxpayer who claims to be merely an employee, with nothing special about his return, cannot claim this, and the presence of an attorney at the first meeting will only attract attention.

If a violation is detected, you can plead ignorance of the law, and this will often pass.

An exception is if you had a tax accountant do your return for you. Then it's wise to have him present, and the tax examiner will not be suspicious. If you do this, say as little yourself as possible during the meeting. Let your tax accountant handle it. Resist the temptation to show off your knowledge of the tax laws, because this can work against you if the examiner discovers a violation. If a violation is detected, you can plead ignorance of the law, and this will often pass, because the IRS Code is so complicated that no one person can understand it all.

Let us assume, for example, that you have deducted your mileage driving to and from work, and claim your wages as an employee to be your sole income, keeping your off-the-books activities out of sight. The examiner will explain that the mileage deduction is not allowed as a business expense for an employee, only for the business owner. Then you can say with an embarrassed smile, "Gee, I didn't know." He will disallow the deduction, assess you the extra tax, and that is that. But if you have been showing him that you are familiar with the various provisions of the tax code, it will be obvious that you knowingly tried to claim an illegal deduction, and that can mean big trouble.

Laundering Money

Fiat currency — good old cold cash — is the basis of the most espionage, crime, and underground transactions.

One of the least-told aspects of espionage agencies is their effort to procure the currencies of the countries upon which they spy. A spy parachuting into Germany or German-occupied territory could hardly expect to get along with a supply of British pounds or American dollars. He had to have German marks or some of the local occupation currency. Throughout WWII there was a considerable effort by the Allies to establish dummy companies in neutral countries still trading with Germany in order to obtain supplies of Reichsmarks. Counterfeiting was another way to provide agents with the currency of the enemy, but this was not widespread.

Criminals need to dispose of the fruits of their crimes. There is an elaborate network of fences to buy hard goods from criminals at a substantial discount and to dispose of them in untraceable ways. Fences also launder currency for criminals who steal it.

For example, bank robbers can hardly expect to demand and receive pre-1964 silver coins. They have to take what they can get — currency. Banks pose an extra hazard for them with "FBI Packages" of money with the serial numbers recorded. Similarly, a kidnapper can expect that part or all of the ransom he gets will have recorded serial numbers.

If the criminal is affluent enough, he can flee to foreign shores where he can dispose of the money with relatively little risk or loss. The small criminal must either take his chances that spending the bills will leave a paper trail that points to him, or else get rid of the money through a fence.

Spending the money himself is possible only if he is highly mobile and willing to lead a nomadic existence. If he stays in one place long enough for the bills to be banked and noticed, the authorities would be able to track him down eventually. If he fences the hot money, he must take a loss. The fence will pay only a fraction of face value.

The underground worker faces a slightly simpler problem. He does not collect marked or recorded money — he only has to make use of his cash without changing his lifestyle so much that he attracts the attention of the IRS. One way is to cache it. Taking a vacation under an assumed name is another way, as long as he doesn't use credit cards or checks, which leave paper trails. Reinvesting in his underground business is another, as is improving his home. As long as he is not throwing so much money around that people start wondering where he gets it all, he will be OK.

Caches

The underground worker can also use a cache, but he has more latitude.

Both spies and criminals have needs for caches. They need to hide the tools of their trades and the products of their activities. The underground worker can also use a cache, but he has more latitude.

A son or daughter, if old enough to understand the need, can use their Social Security card to establish a bank account.

He can use a simple cache, buried underground or concealed somewhere else. Another way to cache money is to rent a safe deposit box under an assumed name, and pay cash for the rental fee. Some underground workers will open a bank account under their wife's maiden name, although this offers only medium security. Here, a lot depends on whether or not the husband and wife file joint returns, which link their Social Security numbers together in the IRS files. A son or daughter, if old enough to understand the need, can use their Social Security card to establish a bank account.

Deep Inside the Underground Economy
How Millions of Americans Are Practicing Free Enterprise in An Unfree Society

180

Drops

For a live drop, a simple post office box will usually suffice, although a mail forwarding service is safer.

There are two types of drops: "live" drops, and "dead" drops. The first is a contact with whom the spy or criminal leaves something valuable. A dead drop is simply a temporary hiding place, such as a gap in a stone wall or a hole in a tree, inside which the person leaves something for another to pick up. For example, a spy might leave a canister of microfilm in a dead drop for later pick up by a confederate, or a kidnapper might stipulate that the victim's relatives leave the money in a remote place where the kidnapper can pick it up later, after surveying the area for surveillance. The drop, live or dead, is a way to break one's trail.

The underground worker will not need a dead drop for his purposes. For a live drop, a simple post office box will usually suffice, although a mail forwarding service is safer.

Criminal Investigation Techniques

As an underground worker, you may be vulnerable to two things: tax collection and prosecution. You must be aware that the government is very serious about collecting taxes, and often takes extreme steps to collect.

The big problem is for the person who doesn't know that he's being investigated, and who unwittingly helps the government by unwise or indiscreet actions.

Collecting and prosecution are complex, but compared with the steps the government takes to discover tax evaders, very simple. The overriding fact is that the person who gets a tax bill or indictment from the government can hire expert talent in the form of a tax or defense lawyer. A specialist who knows all the ins and outs can help tremendously, and many people do conduct successful defenses with their aid. The big problem is for the person who doesn't know that he's being investigated, and who unwittingly helps the government by unwise or indiscreet actions.

"The police" is a convenient term that we'll use to apply to various levels of government and their law enforcement arms in this discussion. Whatever the purpose of a law enforcement agency, many of the investigative tools and techniques are the same. They don't all use them equally, for some are appropriate to certain situations and not to others. We'll briefly sketch criminal investigation techniques so you can understand them and make an informed judgment as to whether you're vulnerable to them. This will expose some of the otherwise hidden dangers inherent in what you may be doing.

First, don't become paranoid. Don't expect that "Big Brother" is watching you all the time. He simply doesn't have the manpower or the resources to watch everyone every moment. The main value of the information here is to alert you to not only the technical means of privacy invasion, but the forms of behavior that arouse police interest, though they're not illegal themselves.

The police often use both legal and illegal methods, sometimes in very imaginative ways.

The police often use both legal and illegal methods, sometimes in very imaginative ways. Although they won't use every method on you, these techniques are available to them, and you may wind up in their files by accident, if they're investigating someone with whom you came into contact.

Some of the techniques and equipment are classified, like some of the computer equipment used by various branches of the government, and much of the rest, like investigative techniques used by police agencies, are not general information. Still, enough information has come out over the years to sketch possible lines of investigation. Let's build up a picture of what's available to the police and how they use it.

Electronic Surveillance

This is commonly known as "bugging," and is a technique useful for intensive investigations. It requires a certain amount of manpower and a court order to gain access legally to premises in order to install hidden cameras, microphones, and transmitters.

"Bugging" is an old technique, dating from around the turn of the twentieth century, and police have used it, sometimes indiscriminately, with and without court orders. This is a very sore point, and there have been Congressional investigations regarding illegal audio and video surveillance, both by local agencies and federal ones, including the FBI and the Internal Revenue Service.

Today, video cameras are as small as sugar cubes, and microphones can be smaller than rice grains.

Today, video cameras are as small as sugar cubes, and microphones can be smaller than rice grains. This makes them easy to install. A favorite method of introducing an electronic bugging device, audio or video, is to put it into an object, such as a desk set or an electric clock, that can be sent as a gift. This obviates the need for entering the premises.

There are many methods of electronic surveillance[6] and they don't all apply to you. If police interest in you is such that they actually bug you, it's time to look for a lawyer.

Black Bag Jobs

This refers to surreptitious entry to install an electronic surveillance device or permit a physical search for evidence. Again, it can happen with or without a court order.

The problem of illegal entries by police has been with us for decades. Even the most respected agencies, such as the FBI, do it.[7] It's not enough to install alarms and high-security locks for protection. Police agencies employ experts at forced entry, and they're knowledgeable enough to defeat almost any security system.[8] Even private investigators and amateurs have available information regarding the opening of locks.[9]

Formerly, tools for such entries were available only to locksmiths and police, but sources are now open to private investigators and, in fact, anyone else who has the modest amount of money required.[10]

Bank Records and Transactions

Most bank records are computerized, but it's important to deal with them separately, because they pose special dangers. A cancelled check for a safe-deposit box rental, a Post Office box, a mail drop payment, or a private vault can provide an investigator with a valuable lead.

If high school students can penetrate sophisticated computers and gain access to their information, it's not too hard to

imagine that the police employ experts to tap into computers when they can't get a court order for the information they want.

Computer Search

There are computerized files on almost everyone and everything, and they're becoming more comprehensive every day. There is a federal privacy law, and a number of local ones, but in fact they don't stop the determined investigator. If high school students can penetrate sophisticated computers and gain access to their information, it's not too hard to imagine that the police employ experts to tap into computers when they can't get a court order for the information they want.

A short list of some of the records available in computer memories includes: airlines (airlines use computers, too — keep this in mind when planning a trip), car rental records, criminal records, tax files, bank records — including your savings and checking accounts, Social Security accounts, automobile registrations, driver's license records, and passports. Obviously, this list only gives a sampling, but it does provide the dimensions of the problem. Unless you were born and raised in the backwoods, with no birth certificate, never attended school, never were hospitalized, never were in the armed services, never had a driver's license or owned a car, never filed a tax return, never took a commercial flight, never took out a loan or had a bank account, and generally lived out of contact with civilization, you're in a computer somewhere.[11]

Informers

Informers, or "snitches," are a traditional investigative tool. Many private individuals have knowledge that interests the police, and drawing it out of them can be rewarding.

Mail Cover

Because of a tradition of cooperation between police agencies, postal inspectors provide information to other agencies at all levels.

This little-known tool of the Postal Inspection Service is available to all police agencies. The law states clearly that first-class mail may not be opened except

Deep Inside the Underground Economy
How Millions of Americans Are Practicing Free Enterprise in An Unfree Society

182

with a court order, but there's nothing to prevent the postal inspectors from recording the return addresses of a target's mail, or to record the addresses on outgoing mail.

Because of a tradition of cooperation between police agencies, postal inspectors provide information to other agencies at all levels. Here's a list of possibilities:

☐ Mail covers of sexually oriented publications to provide a suspect list for investigation of sex crimes.

☐ Covers of subscribers to paramilitary publications to develop a list of potential illegal firearms owners or militia members.

☐ Subscribers to gun magazines.

☐ Persons who order gun-related supplies by mail.

☐ Lists of subscribers to certain extreme political organizations and publications. This includes persons who are members of tax protest organizations. It's not too much to expect the IRS to have a special interest in such persons.

This is not to say that surreptitious opening of mail never happens without a court order. It does show, however, that it's not necessary to open an envelope to obtain damaging information about a person under investigation, or to develop a list of suspects.

Telephone Taps

Properly, this belongs under electronic and audio surveillance, but it's a special case, and deserves a special section. The old days, when a police agent had to gain access to his target's telephone or wire to install a tap, are gone. With the introduction of the electronic switching system (ESS), it's possible to tap into any phone line from a central location. It's also possible to trace a call in seconds, something which formerly took several minutes at least.

Federal government agencies, such as the National Security Agency (NSA), have computers which they use in computer-espionage work, which are capable of monitoring many telephone calls at once, scanning them and recognizing specific words programmed into them. This speeds up telephone line monitoring, and enhances detection of conversations about certain subjects that might interest investigators. That the government monitors telephone conversations is an open secret, and not only in this country.

The introduction of cellular telephones has made electronic eavesdropping on calls easier.

The introduction of cellular telephones has made electronic eavesdropping on calls easier. The NSA was able to pick out of the air the cellular conversations between members of the September 11, 2001 airline attack perpetrators, and even listen in to some of Osama bin Laden's calls. Many people discuss private topics on their cellular telephones, unaware that they're broadcasting to the world.

Putting It All Together

Let's take a hypothetical case, that of Mr. X, to see how he may be vulnerable to investigation. We'll assume that the police make use of computers to tie information together and narrow the range of investigation to suspects who offer maximum chances to them.

A mail cover of a political organization shows that Mr. X regularly receives literature from them. A computerized crosscheck shows that he subscribes to several gun magazines. Another crosscheck shows that he has ordered reloading tools, perfectly legally, by mail from several suppliers. His checking account (all checks are now microfilmed by law) shows that he makes regular contributions to an organization that promotes tax avoidance and evasion. He also has written checks to a private mail drop, a private storage vault, and to suppliers of plumbing equipment, in amounts that suggest he may be running a business on the side and salting away the profits without paying taxes on them. An investigator drives down his street to look at his house, and a comparison with his tax records suggests that his house is out of proportion to his income. Checking airline records, suggested by his credit card records, shows that he's taken several vacations that cost a good part of his declared income, so much that he's almost certainly a tax evader.

The picture that emerges is that of a politically extreme person, certainly armed and possibly dangerous. Even the most unimaginative investigator can see that there is justification for a careful audit of his tax return by the Internal Revenue Service, and the possibility of a criminal prosecution.

Computer checks by the police aim not so much at finding individual names and actions, but at finding people who fit a "profile," a pattern of behavior which suggests they're serious violators.

This hypothetical case shows some of the dangers of carelessness in the underground economy. We have to see the picture in perspective, though. There are many people who subscribe to various magazines or are members of political organizations of all complexions. Most of them are not tax evaders, at least not conspicuously. This means there's latitude for a few mistakes. Computer checks by the police aim not so much at finding individual names and actions, but at finding people who fit a "profile," a pattern of behavior which suggests they're serious violators.

This means that a "hit" in one area is not as significant as fitting a pattern with hits in several areas, as we've seen in the case of Mr. X.

Entering the underground economy means more than just not declaring income. It also means being watchful, and not giving clues to the activity.

Notes

1. *Personal Privacy* (n.p., n.d.), p. 12. The markings made by a nonreproducing blue pen cannot be photographed or photocopied.
2. Tony Lesce, *The Privacy Poachers,* Loompanics Unlimited, Port Townsend, WA, 1992.
3. Frederick Forsyth, *The Day of the Jackal,* Viking Press, NY, 1971, pp. 71-104. In these pages, Forsyth uses his fictional character to demonstrate how easy it is to procure several different identities by different methods. One is by assuming the identity of a person his own age who died as a child, getting a copy of the birth certificate and using that to obtain a passport. Another is by stealing the passports of men who resemble him closely enough to permit his disguising himself as them. A third method is to forge the documents outright. Not only is *Jackal* an exciting novel, it is realistic.
4. John Sample, *Methods of Disguise,* 2d ed., Loompanics Unlimited, Port Townsend, WA, 1993. As explained in this book, trying to fool close friends and associates is almost impossible. Disguise has its limitations, even with extreme methods such as plastic surgery. Assuming the identity of a person whom your contacts have never met, on the other hand, is ridiculously easy.
5. Barry Reid, *The Paper Trip*, Vols. 1 and 2, Eden Press, Fountain Valley, CA, 1971 and 1978. See also *New ID in America,* Paladin Press, Boulder, CO, 1983. These books give de-tailed instructions on getting fake ID, not only detailing the methods step by step, but even providing the address of the public records office for every state, and artwork for forgeries. With these volumes, it's possible to put together almost any sort of ID needed.

These books not only give information on how to procure new and serious ID, but much background material on how to use it, and what pitfalls to avoid. Anyone contemplating getting false ID should read this to get a well-rounded picture of what he faces.

Also see *Who Are You?*, Scott French, Intelligence Here Inc., www.intelligencehere.com. This recent book, dating from 2000, provides a comprehensive guide to manufacturing or stealing I.D. It covers credit cards, stealing identity, passports, obtaining copies of real documents, using a home computer, and other topics.

6. *How to Avoid Electronic Eavesdropping and Privacy Invasion,* Investigator's Information Service, Los Angeles, CA, 1976. The semi-technical discussion of audio surveillance, including phone tapping, is oriented towards the person who wants to protect himself against it, and lists many techniques and devices useful for countering such intrusion.
7. Fred J. Cook, *The FBI Nobody Knows,* Macmillan & Co., NY, 1964, pp. 28-31.
8. Scott French, *The Big Brother Game,* Lyle Stuart, Secaucus, NJ, 1975, pp. 110-41.
9. *Locks, Picks, and Clicks,* Diamondback Books, Phoenix, AZ, 1975. This book, although dealing methods dating from the 1940s, is still valuable because many locks from that era are still in use. This is just one of the many books available on the subject.
10. Items which can be purchased include a master lockpicking kit in a small case, and "Slim Jims," tools for opening car doors without keys. Many companies selling these devices advertise in paramilitary magazines and gun magazines.
11. *The Big Brother Game,* pp. 163-83.

Chapter Twelve
Spending Unreported Income

For most of us, what to do with our income is not a severe problem — we spend it as soon as we get it just to make ends meet. However, some guerrilla capitalists, while not getting filthy rich overnight, will have enough of a surplus to inspire them to seek ways of using the extra income that will not bring them to the attention of the IRS.

We have seen that the key to staying out of the clutches of the IRS is to keep a low profile. Keeping your purchases inconspicuous and not leaving a paper trail is vital to this end. Charging an expensive vacation to Bermuda on your credit card is a very good way to leave a paper trail that will be difficult to explain away if you are ever audited.

If you decide to buy consumer goods, such as furniture or a stereo system, buy for cash and don't keep the receipts.

If you decide to buy consumer goods, such as furniture or a stereo system, buy for cash and don't keep the receipts. That way you can always claim you bought the articles cheaply at a garage sale or a second-hand store.

Buy Major Items from Private Individuals

If you walk into a car dealership with a brown paper bag or a satchel full of currency, you'll attract immediate attention.

One way of keeping your enhanced lifestyle from the notice of tax authorities is to avoid leaving a trail of high-dollar purchases. Paying by check for a high-priced car leaves a paper trail obvious to any auditor checking over your finances. Paying by cash can make things even worse.

If you walk into a car dealership with a brown paper bag or a satchel full of currency, you'll attract immediate attention because almost nobody pays cash for a car. The other side of this is that you'll be part of a report to the Internal Revenue Service, because of a decade-old law that all cash transactions over ten thousand dollars must be reported to the IRS. Today, only the least expensive models cost less than ten grand, and paying cash creates an avoidable paper trail.

The private individual advertising a clean car for sale, on the other hand, won't look askance at you if you show up with a suitcase full of cash. He might be nervous about accepting a check from a stranger, but cash is cash.

The same applies when buying any big-ticket items. Obtaining them from private sources is less noticeable than buying from a dealer.

Saving Assets

Some people, not having enough immediate needs to absorb the extra income, will want to find some way of saving it. We already know that putting it into a bank is the kiss of death, because of the paperwork involved. Banks are required to make reports on accounts, and this could tip off the IRS. But what about safe deposit boxes?

Is it safe to keep that extra cash in a safe deposit box in a bank? No it isn't. In fact, this is one of the most dangerous mistakes you can make.

If a tax auditor knows you have a safe deposit box, he can guess at what you have in there, without having to look himself, and without you even knowing you are under investigation!

Deep Inside the Underground Economy
How Millions of Americans Are Practicing Free Enterprise in An Unfree Society

186

The reason for this is that if a tax auditor knows you have a safe deposit box, he can guess at what you have in there, without having to look himself, and without you even knowing you are under investigation! While an IRS auditor would need a subpoena to actually get into your safe deposit box, he needs no subpoena to look at the records of when you got into the box. Tax investigators are trained to reconstruct your financial history from just such scraps of information as this. For example, if an auditor learns that you visit your safe deposit box every Monday, he would suspect that you were doing something to generate income on the weekends, which means he is tipped off to the fact that you are avoiding taxes.[1] The wise guerrilla capitalist will avoid not only bank accounts, but safe deposit boxes in banks as well.

In any event, saving cash, in most forms, means watching your precious savings shrink from inflation. For the hardcore guerrilla capitalist, real goods are the only things that are inflation-proof.

Buying and stockpiling items that you know you'll be using sooner or later is a splendid way of both disposing of your extra income and of beating inflation.

Buying and stockpiling items that you know you'll be using sooner or later is a splendid way of both disposing of your extra income and of beating inflation.[2] It is important enough to rate mention in a "mainstream" book on investing.[3] We can categorize this as "survival stockpiling." It is a cushion against hard times, loss of income, collapse of the economy, and all of the other threats to your lifestyle that are happening now and may happen in the future.

Home Improvements

Many communities use aerial photography to spot additions to buildings made without permits.

Putting money into fixing up one's own home is a good way to spend/invest unreported money. Many guerrilla capitalists remodel their homes with things like nice cedar paneling they have bought for cash at lumberyards in neighboring towns. The wise undergrounder avoids building permits. However, be aware that today, many communities use aerial photography to spot additions to buildings made without permits.

If you're going to make improvements to your home, make them inside where they can't be seen by an "eye in the sky." A new stereo system, whirlpool tub, or a new kitchen are safe prospects.

Unreported money can also be reinvested in the underground business, itself. Acquiring better tools and equipment, and stockpiling supplies can soak up some of that untaxed income.

Investments

Most forms of investment are traceable, which puts you in the uncomfortable position of having to explain where you got the money to invest.

Some may be interested in investments. The problem here is that most forms of investment are traceable, which puts you in the uncomfortable position of having to explain where you got the money to invest. Many investments generate further income in ways that can be traced. This can be very awkward because an IRS auditor may wonder where you obtained the money to generate your returns. This is why you have to think several steps ahead to beat the system.

Another more serious drawback, even for the above ground investor, is that most of the conventional forms of investment are volatile and uncertain. The stock market is the most conspicuous example. Every year we see a flood of books on the stock market come out, each with its "system" of beating the market and getting rich quickly. The obvious question that comes up is: "Why is the author not taking his own advice and getting rich by playing the market, instead of wasting his time writing a book and telling everyone his secrets?"

The hard, brutal fact is that getting rich in the market is mainly a matter of luck, and there is no reliable way of predicting the future in stocks.[4] Any person who invests in stocks, bonds, or futures is gambling, and stands to lose his investment. Stocks of reputable companies, such as General Electric, may be safe, but you might also buy into another Enron. Futures are crap shoots. You can lose almost everything overnight.

Another hard fact about playing the market is that you have to work through a broker, who collects his commission on every transaction.

Another hard fact about playing the market is that you have to work through a broker, who collects his commission on every transaction. His cut, taken off the top, eats into any profit you might make, and you have to pay his commission even if you take a loss. Some popular discount brokers, such as Charles Schwab, charge small commissions, but you still have to pay, win or lose.

Some of the more prudent investors choose to place their funds in investments that are untraceable, durable, and easy to store secretly. One excellent example is silver coins, which have steadily increased in value since the government stopped minting them. Despite large fluctuations in the market value of silver in the last decades, coins have retained their value, and today no silver coin is worth less than its face value.

Silver coins are easy to buy without paperwork. Although some brokers handle them, it's also possible to buy silver coins from private individuals and in coin shops for cash.

Coins do not deteriorate with age, and are liquid, which means they are easily spent, at any time, anywhere. By contrast, ingots of precious metal are not as liquid. You can't buy a tank of gasoline with a bar of silver, gold, or platinum. To get your profit, you have to sell it through a broker most of the time, and that exposes you at least to a capital gains tax, if not further investigation by the IRS.

There are many ways to construct hiding places in your home, both to evade search by the IRS or, more likely, as protection against burglary.

This brings us to what you do with the investments you are holding. One easy answer is to bury them or hide them in some other way. There are many ways to construct hiding places in your home, both to evade search by the IRS or, more likely, as protection against burglary.[5]

Open stockpiling is another answer. Many families normally keep a supply of canned food on hand, and many people who own cars keep spare parts, such as points, plugs and tires. This is so common that it attracts little attention from either neighbors or the IRS, and is a good way to lay something aside for the future.

Some people feel that underground income is "mad money" to be used for purposes that would otherwise be impractical. Expensive hobbies are one way to spend hidden income, as long as the hobby is not conspicuous. If your hobby is cars, having a Rolls-Royce parked in your driveway will make you stand out, may inspire a jealous neighbor to report you to the IRS, and may be a sign to criminals that you are worth kidnapping or robbing.

Some people like the nightlife, and these people know that it's easy to spend several hundred dollars in an evening. This is an untraceable way of spending untraceable income. Another way is gambling, for those who enjoy it as recreation. A trip to Las Vegas or Atlantic City is easy to disguise if you tell your neighbors that you're going to visit your Aunt Minnie in Podunk, and pay for everything in cash. Today, with tribal casinos in many states, it may not be necessary to take a trip out of state to gamble. However, don't make the mistake of thinking that gambling is a way of building up your hidden assets. Casinos take their percentage off the top, and in the long run you lose.

Travel is yet another way to spend hidden income on yourself as long as you don't visit any country that requires a passport.

Travel is yet another way to spend hidden income on yourself as long as you don't visit any country that requires a passport, which would betray your trips. We are fortunate to live in the United States, with its large area, and to have neighboring countries which do not require passports to visit. If you want to keep the scale and expense of your travel hidden, don't send back picture postcards from Maine or Vancouver, as the case may be.

Most forms of entertainment, while they may seem unduly self-indulgent to some, are ways of spending hidden income in an inconspicuous way, and this appeals to some people who like to live the high life.

Eating out is another practical way to spend money without leaving a trail, and it is a good way if you enjoy eating but hate to cook or brownbag. "Brownbagging" your lunch is an excellent way to save money, and the reverse is also true. While you can spend as little as five or six dollars a week by having granola bars for lunch, if you like elegant dining, you

Deep Inside the Underground Economy
How Millions of Americans Are Practicing Free Enterprise in An Unfree Society

188

can easily spend fifty. Taking the wife out to dinner several times a week can get rid of between sixty or more dollars a throw, and if you remember to pay cash and not run your mouth off to friends, it is truly untraceable.

Most forms of entertainment, while they may seem unduly self-indulgent to some, are ways of spending hidden income in an inconspicuous way, and this appeals to some people who like to live the high life.

Whatever your lifestyle, whether you choose to invest for the future or spend it now, there are ways to dispose of your bonus income without attracting attention to yourself. The basic rule is to keep a low profile. Just use good common sense. Don't go driving around in a Jaguar wearing $600 suits when you are reporting $6,500 a year on your income tax return. Treating your new wealth wisely is as important as earning it.

More Mileage From Your Money

Even the least experienced income earner knows that obtaining income is only half the battle. Getting something in return, and making the most use of the few dollars available, is the other half. Unfortunately, most of the attention is focused on earning, not smart spending, which leaves the householder in a bind.

There are social and cultural barriers, too. One of the most persistent is "keeping up with the Joneses," which moves people to spend conspicuously to keep a certain status among their peers. The extreme of this is "All flash and no cash," the spectacle of the high roller without a cent to his name and deeply in debt.

One unfortunate fact about getting an increase in earnings is that spending seems to rise to absorb it.

One unfortunate fact about getting an increase in earnings is that spending seems to rise to absorb it. It's bad enough that a raise often leads to "promotion" into a higher tax bracket. This means that the higher earner faces a disincentive. Additionally, inflation seems to absorb the rest, but perversely many people want to have something to show for their enhanced economic status, and buy more.

This is one cultural barrier to getting the most from your money. An economic barrier is credit buying, with its many disadvantages. Credit, an unofficial form of taxation, has serious effects. It's true that "a

penny saved is more than a penny earned."[6] We often see people unwisely taking out unneeded loans and paying dearly for them. We'll discuss this extensively later, but for the moment, let's look at a couple of problems credit buying brings with it.

One enticement that banks and other lenders use is the offer to accept a savings account as collateral for a loan. This means that the borrower earns maybe two percent interest but has to pay as much as twenty percent, depending on the sort of loan he gets. This is stupid.

Another is buying a house or car on "time" while having the cash to buy it outright. Some people eye the deduction allowed for interest payments, but forget that a deduction is not a refund, and to get the deduction one has to pay the interest first.

There is truly no more frontier, no more free and undeveloped land where someone may settle down.

There are limits to what we can save on spending. During the 1960s, many hippies tried to drop out of "the system" and retreated to rural areas to live off the land.[7] This was practical a century ago, but it's just about impossible today. We can take it as an axiom that it's impossible to live without some money today. There are two reasons for this. First, there is truly no more frontier, no more free and undeveloped land where someone may settle down. All land in this country is either privately owned, or in the hands of the local, state, or federal government.

Second, the "system" is all-pervasive, and is set up to prevent anyone from "dropping out." Even land is taxed today, and anyone who buys a piece of property must come up with tax money each year. Failure to pay the tax results in confiscation, and the land is sold to pay back taxes. This requires some income, which makes the landowner subject to other taxes as well. The people who run the system fear noncompliance most of all, and they have set it up to make it impossible to live without some sort of participation. Taxation hits both income and spending, and even simple ownership, as with land and motor vehicles. Still, there are some advantages to the rural life, and some ways to make it work. More about this later.

We can't drop out totally, but we can reduce our dependence on the system drastically, depending on how well we apply ourselves. An example is the person who grows his own vegetables. Growing one's own food can save in several ways, in the costs of labor, profit, distribution, and taxation.

Making spending more efficient isn't penny-pinching. It's getting more from what you spend. The first step is budgeting. This enables you to know what you spent last year, and what you anticipate spending this year. It gives you a handle on the problem. The second step is "zero-base budgeting," going over each item to see if it's truly justifiable before spending the money. This isn't as hard as it seems, as most of these decisions make themselves. However, there's a need for flexibility and creativity, because often there are unexpected options that enable big cuts in the budget.

In budgeting, you must distinguish between needs and wants. People often burden themselves with wants so that they have a hard time taking care of the needs.

In budgeting, you must distinguish between needs and wants. People often burden themselves with wants so that they have a hard time taking care of the needs. It's necessary to make a meticulous analysis of needs, and examine ways of obtaining them more cheaply.

The unwritten rule that we must always take a job that pays more than the previous one, gives more status, is "secure" because it's "permanent," and is within our line of work is an intangible but real barrier to living free.

Another barrier to enjoying a debt-free lifestyle is cultural. The Protestant work ethic, while it has its positive side, also carries with it some attitudes that are counter-productive and even economically dangerous. The unwritten rule that we must always take a job that pays more than the previous one, gives more status, is "secure" because it's "permanent," and is within our line of work is an intangible but real barrier to living free. This restricts and contradicts a quality that seems to be built into most human personalities, flexibility. This also restricts freedom of choice when there's good economic logic. It makes good sense, for example, to take a lower-paying job if the commuting savings outweigh the cut in pay, but many people can't bring themselves to do it.

There are economic barriers, too, restricting job choices. The larger companies have systems of deferred rewards to keep their employees chained to their jobs. A pension plan is one example. Today, more than ever, a pension plan is a fraud for most employees. They get nothing until they retire, or at least, become "vested." Layoffs and other means of inducing turnover are ways to get rid of employees who are coming close to collecting the promised rewards.

Economic status is important in America, and buying secondhand is a confession of poverty.

Another cultural barrier is the prejudice against buying second-hand goods. Economic status is important in America, and buying secondhand is a confession of poverty, something which some people fear more than being naked. Actually, many Americans are resigned to buying secondhand cars, but not many to buying second-hand clothing.

Buying secondhand can be a splendid way to get value by spending less. Realistically, buying new has two great disadvantages. First, the price is often based on production and distribution costs and profit margins, not real market value. Second, anything you buy new becomes secondhand quickly. This is most evident when buying a car, and it's been true for decades that when you buy a new car and drive it around the block, it immediately loses one-third of its value. Actually, what it loses is one-third of its market price in inflated dollars. It will still get you there and back as well as a car with no miles on it.

It's often possible to get great savings on secondhand clothing. An asking price of one-tenth of the new, store-bought price is typical. Garage sales are good sources of secondhand clothing, and it's often possible to find items in excellent condition.

Flea markets and secondhand stores are also good sources, perhaps even better, because they save the buyer a lot of running around.[8] This is a real saving. Going to a Goodwill store, where you can find exactly what you need in several categories in one trip, is a better deal than the hit-or-miss of driving around to a hundred garage sales. You pay more, but save a lot of time, gasoline, and wear-and-tear on your car.

Barter is yet another well-known technique, one that requires no further explanation here because we've dealt with it in an earlier chapter. It's a grow-

Deep Inside the Underground Economy
How Millions of Americans Are Practicing Free Enterprise in An Unfree Society

190

ing practice in this country, as a part of "guerrilla economics."[9]

What people throw away is surprising.[10] What's equally surprising is the value of items to be found at "dumps." Often, people receive gifts they don't want or simply get tired of something they bought and throw it away.[11]

We see, therefore, that it's possible to get a lot more mileage from money than most of us do. Savings on expenditures are not only real savings, but are not taxable. Furthermore, some people do so well at this that they can commit the sacrilege of taking a lower-paying, or part-time job, which cuts the tax bite.

There's no way to measure the value of free time, or relief from the pressure of a job.

This last part is the real benefit of smart economics. While we can devote many pages to specific techniques of earning tax-free income, and analyze patterns of spending, there's no way to measure the value of free time, or relief from the pressure of a job.

Many people suffer from their jobs. Overwork is a real cause of illness, and stress from work causes heart attacks, high blood pressure, and other disorders. This is not counting illnesses and deaths from radioactivity, asbestos, and other industrial hazards.

The boredom of spending five days a week in the same place, doing the same work with the same people, takes its toll.

Many people, although not afflicted by physical illness, suffer psychologically from work. This is so common that we don't often notice it, and take it for granted. The boredom of spending five days a week in the same place, doing the same work with the same people, takes its toll. The harmful effects of abuse suffered on the job are intangible, but real.

Anyone who has worked for a living knows, either from his own experience or that of fellow employees or friends, that the psychological hazards are more severe than the physical ones. Eating your heart out for a raise, the strain of office and shop politics, the endless waiting for a promotion, are just a few of the common stresses. The day-to-day hassle of being an employee, the petty aggravations, all take their toll. This is one reason why "happy hours" and "liquid lunches" are so popular.

Psychologists are part of the establishment, and they focus on blaming the individual, not the system, for mental problems that lead to alcohol abuse and other chemical abuses. They rarely admit that the pressures of the job can and do unhinge their patients. This leads to increased pressure on the people who are suffering the most, as they are coerced into reexamining their pasts to uncover the cause and roots of their "problems."

There are simpler solutions. Reduce the pressure. Reduce the dependency on wage earning. Seek the job satisfaction that self-employment affords. Find the freedom that comes with being your own boss. Often, a change of scene will abolish the symptoms. Taking up the rural life, although it has its problems, is one way to do this.[12]

There is no total or ideal solution, only a number of partial ones. Earning extra income is one way to cope. Reducing expenses is another way. If you're lucky or skillful enough to make the two meet, so that you can work less because you can get along on your lower income, the whole will be greater than the sum of its parts.

Avoiding the Credit Trap

Living a good lifestyle means getting the most for your money. However, you can work very hard earning untraceable income and get very little for it if you don't spend wisely. This is true of both above ground workers and undergrounders.

Ronald earned a living wage as a city employee. He also moonlighted at various jobs at various times, working weekends at pest exterminating and other pursuits, all of which he arranged through his many friends who took steps to keep him "off the books." His yearly income was substantial, but although unmarried, he was always caught short, always in debt, and always seemed to need more money.

Inflation eats up the value of your cash supply, and each year brings with it a reduction in your purchasing power. Plastic is far worse.

The reason for his chronic financial bind was simple: he was addicted to buying on credit. His wallet was filled with plastic, not paper. We already know the value of paper money is shaky. Inflation eats up the value of your cash supply, and each year brings with it a reduction in your purchasing power. Plastic is far worse.

With credit cards and revolving charge accounts, you pay dearly for the privilege of spending your money. It's surprising how many people complain about the copious way the government spends money it doesn't have, and yet in their personal lives adhere to the same practices.

Ronald is a good example. Let's look at only one card in his wallet, a bank credit card. He used the revolving feature to the limit. He charged purchases to the end of his line of credit, which for this card was seven thousand dollars. Each month, he paid enough to reduce his balance so that he could buy more, bringing it up to the limit again. He didn't realize that, in effect, he was paying interest on seven thousand dollars all year long, reducing his buying power by that amount.

This is serious; the figures add up. Bankcard interest rates are high, usually around eighteen percent, as of this writing. Eighteen percent of seven thousand dollars is $1,260. Ronald had this amount amputated from his spending power with this one card alone!

It's practical to carry a credit card or two for emergencies. You might need a tank of gasoline and not have enough cash. You might have a tire blow out, or have to stay overnight at a motel because the road home is flooded out. You might also see something that's such a good buy you can't pass it up. All of these are sensible reasons for using credit cards.

If you've made credit buying your lifestyle, you're voluntarily submitting to private taxation that reduces your buying power.

On the other hand, if you've made credit buying your lifestyle, you're voluntarily submitting to private taxation that reduces your buying power both in the short and long runs. The worst credit situation (for you, not the bank or finance company) is the revolving account that's stretched to the limit.

Another example is Tommy, an impulse buyer. Each week, he'd see something advertised, decide he "needed" it, and put it on his card. Unfortunately, his wife was that way, too. Both of them worked, Tommy for a newspaper and she for the telephone company, and their combined incomes were more than adequate. They had no children, and should have been able to get along very well on their earnings, despite the federal income tax. Actually, they were al-

most always "strapped." Because of the incessant hemorrhage in their financial situation, Tommy drove a beat-up old car that he felt he should have scrapped long ago, but he couldn't afford to buy a new one. They lived in a ramshackle house in a declining neighborhood, because the mortgage payment was low and they felt that they couldn't afford to move to a more expensive house.

Tommy and his wife are typical Americans. They are trapped by the system, but only because they let themselves be enslaved.

Are you this way? Be honest. Do you think you'd like to break out of this trap, if you're in it? Do you want that badly enough to take a couple of unpleasant steps to do so?

Make it a rule, one you won't break, that you won't buy anything more on credit unless you know that you can pay off the entire balance.

If you want to reduce your credit dependency, start by cutting down on your credit purchases. Make it a rule, one you won't break, that you won't buy anything more on credit unless you know that you can pay off the entire balance, when the bill comes.

There will be occasional emergencies. That's all right. Put the absolutely necessary purchase on your card, but reduce the rest of your spending to make up for it.

The result will be that you won't, if you're stretched to the limit, be putting anything on your plastic account until it's all paid off. You really shouldn't need to. If you've been spending to the limit, you probably have many of the goodies that money can buy, anyway, such as a couple of color TVs, a stereo, a videotape machine, a few guns, perhaps a pool table, etc. You can entertain yourself with these items while you're passing up those glittering new toys you see advertised.

Ask yourself before you lay out a dime: "Is this purchase really necessary?" You might find that it's not.

Consider every expense. Do you buy your lunch each day? Why? Because you've always done it? Do you have to keep doing it? Would you consider "brown-bagging" until you get your finances in better shape?

Deep Inside the Underground Economy
How Millions of Americans Are Practicing Free Enterprise in An Unfree Society

192

Don't suddenly go on a saving binge and buy only hamburger if you're used to eating steaks and chops.

How much gas do you buy for your car? Is each trip necessary? Would better planning save you some mileage? Are you able to combine several shopping trips into one? Do you drive to a shopping center on a Saturday afternoon to window-shop, to kill time? Don't do it. Stay at home and entertain yourself there.

Of course, you have to buy food. You might be able to save a little on that as long as you don't go overboard and attempt the impossible. Don't suddenly go on a saving binge and buy only hamburger if you're used to eating steaks and chops. You might, however, be able to cut down on the number of times a week you eat Porterhouse. If you eat out a lot, that's a definite area to save money. A dinner out costs far more than it costs to prepare at home. In fact, you can often have steak at home for what it costs to eat a hamburger and fries out.

Cutting down on your eating is a psychological strain. Cutting down on waste can be satisfying. Are you one of those people who leaves a lot on his plate, or who prepares big portions and has a lot of leftovers? Some people who generate leftovers don't like to eat them. They leave them in the refrigerator until they throw them out. In that case, it's economical to prepare smaller amounts and cut the waste.

What it all boils down to is: Can you reduce an extravagant lifestyle to get more real value from the money you spend? If you can, you secure an advantage for yourself.

Now we come to the payoff. What have you sacrificed for, anyway? You're avoiding spending twenty percent of your money after taxes for interest. What will you now do with it?

You might put it in the bank, although today's low interest rates aren't encouraging. The payoff is that, if you now want a high-dollar item, you can take the money out of your savings account and pay cash, avoiding the interest charges, and thereby have more disposable income.

"Wait a minute, now," you say, "What's this about a bank account, if bank accounts leave a paper trail that the IRS can follow to trace your income?"

Let's consider that question carefully. A bank account can be very useful if you're not in the underground economy, but earning a wage from a regular job. Even if you are working a sideline, if what you put in the bank is reasonable, it won't attract atten-

tion. You'll have to pay tax on the interest you earn, but that won't be very much.

What if you just don't like banks, or if you don't want to pay the IRS a cent more than you absolutely have to? There are a couple of answers to this.

1. Put the money in a cache in your back yard. It won't earn any interest, but it will form a core of untraceable savings.
2. Buy silver (pre-1964) coins, still legal tender, but not liable to destruction by inflation like paper money. This can be very important if you're a survivalist. Silver coins are definitely good investments if you're economically oriented and are concerned with the effects of inflation.
3. Invest your liberated money in something that will help you earn more in the underground economy. If you're a plumber, for example, you might want an extra set of tools to take with you when you moonlight. Pay cash, of course.

Arranging your personal finances to make the most of your income is just good sense. We have good reason to berate the government for spending money it doesn't have, thereby creating inflation and increasing the national debt. But what we can control is what we do ourselves. The government can only tax us; it can't force us to spend what we have left after taxes. That's up to us. That's where we make it or break it.

Low-Profile Recreation

What good is money if you can't spend it? Obviously, earning income is only the first step. Spending it without posing a danger to yourself with an opulent lifestyle is the second part.

Low-Profile Travel

One way of benefiting from your extra income is travel. There are right ways and wrong ways to travel, though, because an important concern is avoiding a paper or electronic trail. Flying to a foreign country on a booked tour that includes hotel reservations and car rentals leaves a trail a yard wide, because of passport stamps and the paperwork associated with booking commercial flights, renting cars, and paying hotel bills.

If you want to visit a foreign country without leaving a trail, your choices are Canada and Mexico; you don't need a passport to cross their borders.

If you want to visit a foreign country without leaving a trail, your choices are Canada and Mexico; you don't need a passport to cross their borders. If you choose to fly, begin your trip from another city, to avoid leaving an easily tracked trail. However, be aware of one problem with flying across borders. You have to do it under your own name because customs officers will at least check your I.D. at your destination.

It's practically impossible to rent a car without a credit card, and this leaves an electronic trail. Taxis are much safer.

Within the United States, you can no longer book a passage under any name you wish. Paying in cash for an airline ticket used to be low-profile, but today it puts you in a "profile" that airline security personnel use to point out suspected hijackers. This suggests a way to visit Canada and Mexico conveniently without attracting unwanted attention. If your choice is Mexico, fly to El Paso, Texas, or San Diego, California, both of which are next to the Mexican border. Rent a car, or walk across. Keep in mind, though, that it's practically impossible to rent a car without a credit card, and that this leaves an electronic trail. Taxis are much safer.

One method for low-profile travel recreation is travel in an RV, because there are no checkpoints to track private vehicular travel in this country. State police regularly check out commercial vehicles to ensure that operators are complying with laws regarding hours driven per day and the vehicle's mechanical condition, but they pretty much leave RVs alone unless they observe them in violation of traffic laws.

One popular method of obtaining free parking for an RV is "boondocking," parking in commercial lots. Boondocking in supermarket lots during daytime works well for the RV driver who wants to take a short nap, and store personnel will assume he's a customer. In fact, if you do boondock, a supermarket lot provides the opportunity to reprovision, as well. A commercial strip center, after hours, almost guarantees hassle-free parking when it's deserted and stores are closed.

Motels and hotels also provide parking for guests, some of whom arrive in motor homes. Parking overnight is hassle-free in most cases, because the night shift has enough to do without patrolling the parking lot to match vehicle plates against guest registrations.

Police interference is very unlikely, for several reasons. Police officers have more serious crimes in their purview than boondocking, and usually respond only if there's a complaint by the property owner. Routine checks of license plates for stolen vehicles don't include RVs, because they're so rarely stolen. Finally, police patrols are thin during the late night and early morning shift, so the cops are rarely around to wonder about an RV parked in a department store or hotel lot.

Low-Profile Hunting and Fishing

Today you're required to obtain a hunting, fishing, or boating license almost everywhere you go. There are some exceptions, however, and if any of these apply in your state, take advantage of them.

Hunting licenses aren't usually required for shooting nuisances and predators, such as groundhogs and coyotes.

One exception is that not all boats require registration. Some states allow exceptions for boats under a certain length. Another is that hunting licenses aren't usually required for shooting nuisances and predators, such as groundhogs and coyotes.

If you know the area where you plan to hunt or fish very well, you can become familiar with game officers' patrol patterns. This allows you to be where they're not. However, even if you're out of their patrol areas, there are some cardinal mistakes to avoid.

First, don't use any sort of radio for communication, because many hunters and fishermen do and police listen to CB channels. If you babble with your buddy over the radio while hunting or fishing, you're advertising your presence. Another major error is to hunt by jacklighting, or spotlighting. Game officers fly night patrols, and you have to see it to believe how far a spotlight can be seen from the air at night. If a flying game warden sees your light, he'll vector in ground units for the apprehension.

Overall, there are many ways to spend money to enjoy your leisure time. Avoid the traps, and you'll be safe while having a good time.

Notes

1. *How to Determine Undisclosed Financial Interests,* Loompanics Unlimited, Port Townsend,

Deep Inside the Underground Economy
How Millions of Americans Are Practicing Free Enterprise in An Unfree Society

194

WA, 1984. The author was a criminal investigator for the IRS for twenty-four years, and in this book he reveals how the IRS determines unreported income, undisclosed financial interests, etc. Written for government investigators, this is a manual on how to catch people for income tax evasion, and should be read carefully by every guerilla capitalist.

2. John A. Pugsley, *The Alpha Strategy,* Stratford Press, Los Angeles, CA, 1981. Pages 147-210 lay out a strategy of investment that is applicable to anyone who has even a slight interest in safe ways of providing for the future.

3. Douglas Casey, *Strategic Investing,* Simon and Schuster, NY, 1982. Pages 177-188 deal with stockpiling or hoarding and offer good advice on what to stockpile and how to do it.

4. *The Alpha Strategy*, pp. 100-130 explain in detail the problems associated with playing the market and why predicting the future prices of stocks is such a risky undertaking.

5. Michael Connor, *How to Hide Anything,* Paladin Press, Boulder, CO, 1984. An excellent book on constructing secret hiding places inside and outside of the home. See also, eddie the wire, *How to Bury Your Goods,* Loompanics Unlimited, Port Townsend, WA, 1981.

6. Charles Long, *How to Survive without a Salary,* Sterling Publishing, NY, 1981, pp. 11-12.

7. *Ibid.*, p. 13.

8. *Ibid.,* pp. 134-37.

9. *Ibid.*, p. 167.

10. A "sanitation worker" told of the many usable items he found in making the rounds collecting garbage. He was not too proud to take the more valuable ones home to his family, saving the surplus to renovate and sell to friends and neighbors. These items included appliances such as toasters and TVs, toys, clothing, and even canned food.

11. In the experience of the author, going out to the desert each week has produced:
A five-dollar bill, probably lost
Countless coins, also lost
A jar of caviar
A new air conditioner
Thousands of pounds of aluminum cans, for recycling
At least twenty thousand fired cartridge cases, for reloading
Several boxes of unfired ammunition
Assorted lumber, for the fireplace or for casual construction
Assorted hardware, including nails, screws, washers, locks, etc.
Packs of cigarettes. This is a bad habit. Why pay to give yourself cancer? Pick them up free
Assorted medical supplies
A pocketknife in good condition
Spray cans of paint
This is only a partial list, from memory. In reality, there was a lot more out there, ignored because it was unneeded.

12. John L. Parker, *Living off the Country,* Bookworm Publishing, Ontario, CA, 1978. This is a comprehensive, no-nonsense book about the thrills and the problems that accompany a rural lifestyle. It suggests many ways of earning money from rural occupations, most of them centered around livestock and agriculture.

The advantages of rural life are many. On a farm, you save money by growing your food, instead of buying. You also have housing, and save on utilities.

With the rising cost of energy, saving on electricity becomes more important. In the city, you depend on it for transportation, even to run the elevator in your apartment building. You literally can't do without it, as using a fire for heating is forbidden in cities with pollution-control laws.

Water, basic to life, costs in the city. Having your own well can make you dependent of the water company.

Clothing, important for many who work in the city, is less of a problem on a farm, where jeans and boots are more useful than a three-piece suit.

Even basic sanitation is simpler and cheaper. A septic tank or outhouse eliminates the need to pay a plumber forty or more dollars an hour.

Finally, there is the air. The government hasn't yet put a tax on it, but in the city breathing is hazardous to your health.

Further Reading

There is not much in print on the underground economy as such — you have to know what to look for and read between the lines. The following works are good sources of information, and although some are rather old, they're not obsolete. You may have to find some titles in used bookstores, since some of them are out of print. You might be able to buy out-of-print books via Amazon.com or check with alibris.com (1250 45th Street, Suite 100, Emeryville, CA 94608). Other excellent sources for hard-to-find books are:

www.bookfinder.com
www.bestbookbuys.com
www.bookhunterpress.com
www.booksalefinder.com
www.addall.com
www.abebooks.com

You may also find some in your local library or through interlibrary loans.

Government Publications

Estimates of Income Unreported on Individual Income Tax Returns, IRS Publication 1104-(9-79). This is a description of how the Internal Revenue Service tried to estimate the size of the underground economy, and the guesswork and contradictions that went into their estimate. For those who still have some faith in the wisdom and power of the government, who feel that it may make some mistakes occasionally but essentially is running its affairs in the right way, this book will be an eye opener. Read it carefully and critically, keeping in mind the amount of time and effort by thousands of people that went into collecting the information summarized in this report, and note the unsoundness of the conclusions. This volume does not deal in abstractions, but in dollars, which should be easy to count. Despite this, the report fails to pre-

sent firm conclusions on the amount of tax evasion in this country.

Hearings before the Joint Economic Committee, Congress of the United States, 96th Congress, 1st sess., November 15, 1979, U.S. Government Printing Office, Washington, DC. This transcript is valuable because the committee called upon "experts" from inside and outside the government, and the transcript presents a picture of the experts running around in circles, contradicting each other. There are many people who have uneasy feelings about how the government runs its business, and this report will give them a lot of food for thought.

The Underground Economy

Beating the System: The Underground Economy, by Carl P. Simon and Ann D. Witte, Auburn House, Boston, 1982. This book covers mainly activities that are criminal in themselves, such as cigarette bootlegging, loan sharking, and the like.

The Black Market: A Study of White Collar Crime, by Marshall B. Clinard, Loompanics Unlimited, Port Townsend, WA, 1980. Originally published in 1952, this is a study of the price controls and rationing system in the U.S.A. in WWII, and goes into considerable detail as to exactly how the controls were evaded by the population.

Black Markets Around the World, by Burgess Laughlin, Loompanics Unlimited, Port Townsend, WA, 1981. Articles on various illegal markets around the world, from the labor market in the Netherlands, to apartments in Sweden, to illegal vegetables in Canada.

The Hidden Economy: The Content and Control of Borderline Crime, by Stuart Henry, Loompanics Unlimited, Port Townsend, WA, 1980. This is a

Deep Inside the Underground Economy
How Millions of Americans Are Practicing Free Enterprise in An Unfree Society

196

book about on-the-job pilferage, written from the British perspective, by a resident of a country where crime is supposed to be very low compared with "gangster America." The population Henry studies and describes consists of "ordinary people in legitimate jobs," very much like their American counterparts, and this book is worth studying for its applicability to this side of the Atlantic.

Job Opportunities in the Black Market, by Burgess Laughlin, Loompanics Unlimited, Port Townsend, WA, 1981. This book is an underground classic. It is an in-depth study of the illegal, but victimless economy in the United States. The single best book on illegal economic activities ever written.

Laissez Faire Books, 7123 Interstate 30, Suite 42, Little Rock, AR 72209. A good source of books on free market economics — comprehensive selection and good service.
Phone: (800) 326-0996
Fax: (501) 975-3651
Web site: http://www.laissezfairebooks.com/

National Taxpayers Union, 325 Pennsylvania Ave., S.E., Washington, DC 20003. An excellent source of facts, figures, and information on overtaxing and overspending by the U.S. Government.

The Organization of Illegal Markets: An Economic Analysis, by Peter Reuter, Loompanics Unlimited, Port Townsend, WA, 1986. Scholarly analysis of illegal businesses and how they are organized.

The Subterranean Economy, by Dan Bawly, McGraw-Hill, 1982. This is the best "mainstream" book on the underground economy, not only in the United States, but in other countries as well. The author states flat out that inept government, inflation, and taxation are what creates underground economies. Really worth reading.

The Underground Economy in the United States and Abroad, edited by Vito Tanzi, Lexington Books, 1982. Very dry and scholarly, but covers a lot of ground.

Starting New Businesses and Moonlighting

Armchair Millionaire, by Fred Hal Vice, Paladin Press, PO Box 1307, Boulder, CO 80306, 1981. A decent book on starting your own business.

Cash From Square Foot Gardening, by Mel Bartholomew, Storey Publishing, Pownal, VT, 1985. An excellent book on gardening as a part-time business, with emphasis on how to get paid in cash.

The Complete Book of International Smuggling, by M.C. Finn,. Paladin Press, Boulder, CO, 1983. Not all smuggling involves high-risk items like guns or dope. A decent living can be made bringing in low-risk items. This book covers the big time smuggling scene.

Duty Free: Smuggling Made Easy, by Michael Connor, Paladin Press, Boulder, CO, 1983. A how-to-do-it handbook on smuggling whatever you want through Customs.

555 Ways To Earn Extra Money, by Jay Conrad Levinson, Holt, Rinehart, and Winston, NY, 1991. Many ideas for earning extra money.

Government By Emergency, by Gary North, American Bureau of Economic Research. This book contains the essay "Inflation and the Return of the Craftsman," one of the most intelligent pieces we have seen on choosing a career in inflation-ridden times.

How I Found Freedom in an Unfree World, by Harry Brown, Avon Books, NY, 1973. The author, who a few years before had published *How You Can Profit From the Coming Devaluation*, an accurately prophetic book about the economic events of the Nixon years. In this newer book he explains his philosophy of freedom. He points out that today's government does not exist because of the enthusiastic support of the governed, but by their tacit and resigned acceptance. Part I of his book explains why many people are not free, because they accept the traps that have been laid for them, unable to fight back against emotional and intellectual blackmail that the manipulators practice upon them.

The rest of his book deals with how to attain freedom from the traps, and how to lead an independent life by circumventing both the laws and social conventions. This is the single best "breaking free" book ever written. Full of practical advice on getting yourself free from government, jealousy, exploitation, the rat race, etc. I can't recommend this one highly enough.

How to Become a Modern Day Gold Prospector, American Association of Jewelry Brokers, 1984. Mistitled — this is not about prospecting out in the desert — it is about buying scrap gold and reselling it. Published as a companion to *Secrets of Diamond Dealing* (below). Very practical and useful.

How to Convert Your Favorite Hobby, Sport, Pastime or Idea to Cash, by Al Riolo, Business Development and Research Center. Good advice on making a business of your hobby.

How to Earn $15 to $50 an Hour & More with a Pick-Up Truck or Van, by Don Lilly, Darian Books, 1982. Very practical book on making money hauling.

How to Hustle Home Poker, by John Fox, GBC Press, Las Vegas, NV, 1981. An excellent manual on making money in home poker games.

How to Collect Unemployment Insurance (Even if You're Not Eligible), by H.R.D., Loompanics Unlimited, Port Townsend, WA, 1981. Many Guerrilla Capitalists collect unemployment while moonlighting off the books.

How to Make Money as a Process Server, by Ralph D. Thomas, Thomas Publications, Austin, TX, 1985. This explains a sideline business that you can operate on a cash basis.

How to Sell Your Homemade Creation, by Allan H. Smith, Success Publishing, Lake Park, FL, 1985. Selling home crafts in today's marketplace.

In Search of Gold, by Stephen M. Voynick, Paladin Press, 1982. This one is about finding gold outdoors, and covers every possible way and place. Panning, rock mining, treasure hunting, beachcombing, artifact excavating, and even graverobbing!

Increase Your Take-Home Pay Up To 40%, by Ted Nicholas, Enterprise Publishing, Inc., Wilmington, DE. Working as an independent contractor, written from the employee's viewpoint, rather than the employer's.

Make Money By Moonlighting: Own Your Own Low-Risk Business, by Jack Landers, Enterprise Publishing, Inc. 1982. Excellent book on starting up a part-time business.

Make Money in Diving, by Jon-Paul Giguere, Rave Publications, Milwaukee, WI, 1981. Many different ways of making money underwater.

Money Is My Friend, by Phil Laut, Trinity Publications, Hollywood, CA, 1979. Good book about mastering money, instead of money mastering you.

Money Making Secrets of the Millionaires, by Hal D. Seward, Parker Publishing Company, 1972. Chapter Two tells how some famous men "made it." However, you must be cautious about accepting all of the ideas laid out in this inspirational book. Don't believe that all you need are imagination and determination. While these are important, it's also necessary to back them up with technical know-how, and to have a certain amount of luck on your side. It's easy to cite selected examples for "success stories," and to ignore all the people with brilliant ideas who lost their shirts because they didn't do their homework or simply had bad luck.

Moonlighting: A Complete Guide to Over 200 Exciting Part-Time Jobs, by Peter Davidson, McGraw-Hill, 1983. Just what the title says.

The #1 Home Business Book, by George and Sandra Delany, Liberty Publishing Company, Cockeysville, MD, 1981. How to start a business in your home.

Offbeat Careers: The Directory of Unusual Work, by Al Sacharov, Ten Speed Press, Berkeley, CA, 1988.
This is a thorough listing of uncommon occupations, some of which are easily adaptable to earning underground dollars. Organized alphabetically, this volume lists and describes eighty-six occupations from acupuncturist to wine steward. Some, such as "kibbutznik," are mainly for persons of the Jewish faith who can feel comfortable living in Israel and paying Israel's confiscatory taxes. Others, such as chimney sweep, are naturals for the subterranean entrepreneur. In fact, most of these occupations can be salaried or freelance. It's all what you make of them.

On Your Own, by Kathy Matthews, Random House, NY, 1977. Alternatives to a 9-to-5 job.

Over 325 Ways to Make Money While Living In The Country, by Bill Camp. BC Studios, Huntington Beach, CA, 1985. Rural money making.

Poker: A Guaranteed Income for Life Using the Advanced Concepts of Poker, by Frank R. Wallace,

Deep Inside the Underground Economy
How Millions of Americans Are Practicing Free Enterprise in An Unfree Society

198

The definitive book on making money in home poker games. Very ruthless and practical.

Sabotage in the American Workplace, edited by Martin Sprouse. Pressure Drop Press, San Francisco, CA, 1992. This is a gold mine of personal accounts of harried, dissatisfied employees who have struck back at their tormentors by botching up the work flow or by exploiting their jobs for extra income, often at the expense of the boss. Covering a wide variety of occupations, legal and illegal, this book is practically a how-to manual for the employee who resents having his face stomped repeatedly by a tyrannical or exploitative boss. This book is a good object lesson in how not to treat employees, above ground or underground.

Secrets of Diamond Dealing. Vanguard International, Bullard, TX, 1982. The definitive manual on speculating in diamonds. Expensive, but worth every penny.

The Seven Laws of Money, by Michael Phillips, Random House, NY, 1974. An excellent book on money and your relationship to it and its relationship to you.

Sewing For Profits, by Judith and Allan Smith, Success Advertising and Publishing, Lake Park, FL, 1985. How to start a home sewing business.

Shortcuts to a Fortune in Appliance Repair, by Frank M. Cassaday, Cassaday Enterprises, 1981. An excellent manual on starting an appliance repair business. Good opportunity!

Sneak It Through: Smuggling Made Easier, by Michael Connor, Paladin Press, Boulder, CO, 1984. More on smuggling techniques by the author of *Duty Free*.

Temporary Employment: The Flexible Alternative, by Demaris C. Smith, Betterway Publications, White Hall, VA, 1985. All about temporary employment, from both employee and employer points of view.

Treasure Hunting: A Modern Search for Adventure, by H. Glenn Carson, Carson Enterprises Ltd., Boulder, CO, 1973. How to find all sorts of lost stuff, both with and without a metal detector.

Underground Car Dealer, by Maxwell DeSoto, Underground Reports, 1983. Blueprint for an underground used car business.

Flea Markets, Conventions, Garage and Yard Sales

The Complete Guide to Gun Shows, by Thomas W. Thielen, Loompanics Unlimited, Port Townsend, WA, 1980. Just what the title says — contains a wealth of information on buying and selling at gun shows, and even how to put on your own gun show.

The Complete Guide to Science Fiction Conventions, by Erwin S. Strauss, Loompanics Unlimited, Port Townsend, WA. 1983. Good book on how SF cons are run, including dealer rooms.

Don't Throw It Out — Sell It, by Joe Sutherland Gould, Prentice-Hall, Englewood Cliffs, NJ, 1983. Good book on selling used goods through garage sales, flea markets, second-hand stores, etc.

Farmers Markets of America: A Renaissance, by Robert Sommer, Capra Press, Santa Barbara, CA. Farmers markets, roadside stands, etc.

Flea Market Handbook, by Robert G. Miner, Main Street Books, Mechanicsburg, PA, 1981. Excellent book on selling at flea markets. Full of practical advice.

How to Make Cash Money Selling at Swap Meets, Flea Markets, Etc., by Jordan L. Cooper, Loompanics Unlimited, Port Townsend, WA, 1988. Written by an author who has been a successful flea market operator for a decade as well as an astute observer of the commerce around him, this book is a nuts and bolts text on how to sell profitably at flea markets. It is very readable, written in Cooper's conversational style, and it's no exaggeration to say that if something about flea markets isn't in Cooper's book, it's not worth knowing.

How to Make More Money with Your Garage Sale, by Ryan Petty, St. Martin's Press, 1981. Good advice on getting the most out of garage and yard sales.

Shadow Merchants, Jordan L. Cooper, Loompanics, Unlimited, Port Townsend, WA, 1993. Written by the same business owner who wrote *How to Make Cash Money Selling at Swap Meets, Flea Markets, Etc.*, *Shadow Merchants* is a how-to book for the wage slave sick and tired of the demands of the workplace. It's a realistic guide to starting a low-capital, low-overhead business, written by someone who's been there, and is still there and thriving.

This book covers starting up, location, diversification, sales skills, and hiring help. It discusses the complexities of various types of shadow businesses, and even how to survive during the off-season. Totally realistic, it points out the dangers of letting success go to your head and locating in the high-rent district. All told, this book is a must for the prospective undergrounder.

Success Is Not Working for the Pharaoh: An Introduction to High Yield Cottage Industry, by Steve and Cindy Long, Idahome Publications, Sandpoint, ID. An excellent book on running a craft business, and how to set up and sell at shows, etc. Written by a couple who actually earned their livings this way, it is full of valuable tips and information.

Successful Flea Market Selling, by Valerie Bohigian, TAB Books, 1981. Worthwhile book on flea markets and how to sell at them.

Barter

The Barter Book, by Dyanne Asimow Simon. Doubleday, 1979. This is the single finest book on barter ever written. The author is very sympathetic with the tax evasion aspects of barter.

The Barter Way to Beat Inflation, by George W. Burtt, Everest House, 1980. Covers the possibilities of barter, but with way too much emphasis on barter clubs and exchanges.

Fundamentals of Successful Bartering, by Ron Levy, Koala Press, Santa Barbara, CA 1982. Good tips on haggling, but the author recommends barter exchanges.

How to Get on the Barter Bandwagon, by Mark F. Fournier, Phoenix Books, Phoenix, AZ, 1980. Beginner's book on barter.

Let's Try Barter, by Charles Morrow Wilson, Devin-Adair Co., Old Greenwich, CT, 1976. Probably the best book on barter, next to *The Barter Book*.

Survival Bartering, by Duncan Long, Loompanics Unlimited, 1981. Treats barter in an "after the crash" situation.

The IRS, Taxes, and Fiddling the Books

How to Determine Undisclosed Financial Interests. Loompanics Unlimited, 1984. A manual for tax agents on how to snoop into your financial records and uncover unreported income. Very comprehensive and thorough. Also very scary. Must reading for all guerrilla capitalists.

Clarkson's No Checks, by Robert B. Clarkson, Constitutionalist Press, Greenville, SC, 1982. Booklet by a tax protestor on how to avoid checks, how to use non-reproducing blue pens to evade bank microfilming of checks, etc.

The Great Income Tax Hoax, by Irwin Schiff, Freedom Books, Hamden, CT, 1984. Points out, among other things, that the 16th Amendment (Income Tax Amendment) was never properly ratified by the states, and that the income tax is null and void.

Hit Back at the I.R.S., by Ragnar the Avenger, The Technology Group, Pasadena, CA, 1986. Hardcore guerrilla war against the IRS, includes how to get the home addresses of IRS agents.

How to Cheat on Your Taxes, by "X," C.P.A., 1040 Press, 1983. Exactly what the title says — a book that has been needed for years. Very well done, and should be read by all guerrilla capitalists.

How to Obtain a Fair Trial, by Eugene Wilson, J.C. Printing Co., College Park, GA, 1983. Covers how to handle yourself if the IRS brings criminal charges against you. Written by a lawyer.

Illegal Tax Protester Information Book. Secret report for IRS agents, which is actually a "hit list" prepared by the IRS's Criminal Investigation Office of Intelligence. The IRS ordered all copies of the report destroyed.

In This Corner, the IRS, by J.R. Price, Dell Publishing, 1981. Includes a good section on how the IRS discovers unreported income.

Internal Revenue Service Strategic Plan. IRS Document 6941 (5-84). The official IRS plan to ferret out Guerrilla Capitalists.

IRS In Action, by Santo M. Presti, Bristol Publishing Co., Fairport, NY, 1983. Good book about how the IRS operates, written by a former treasury agent.

Deep Inside the Underground Economy
How Millions of Americans Are Practicing Free Enterprise in An Unfree Society

200

The Mirage, by Zay N. Smith and Pamela Zekman, Random House, 1979. One of the most interesting books ever written. A team of investigative reporters opened a bar in Chicago and recorded all the corruption, bribes, shakedowns, and tax evasion schemes they encountered. Fascinating reading!

Screw The IRS, A Card Game, Century Game Co., St. Louis, MO, 1984. A fun game for the whole family. This company also sells "Screw The IRS" coffee mugs, buttons, and stickers.

Taxpayer's Survival Manual, by Howard Fishkin, Book Promotions Unlimited, Flushing, MI. Interesting book on dealing with the IRS, written by a professional tax preparer.

To Harass Our People: The IRS and Government Abuse of Power, by George Hansen, Washington, DC, Positive Publications, 1984. Good expose of fascist IRS methods, written by an ex-Congressman who was the target of IRS harassment.

Twelve Deadly Negatrends, by Dr. Gary North, American Bureau of Economic Research, Fort Worth, TX, 1985. North is one of the better conservative and hard-money writers.

When You Owe the IRS, by Jack Warren Wade, Jr., Macmillan, 1983. What to do when the IRS comes after your goods.

"Write-Off Tax Tips H&R Block Won't Give You," by Joan Flynn, *High Times*, April, 1980. Article on tax evasion, with particular attention to concealing assets, keeping a low profile, and laundering money. Written especially for dope dealers, but useful for any guerrilla capitalist.

Dodging Big Brother

The Code Book: All About Unbreakable Codes and How to Use Them, by Michael F. Marotta, Loompanics Unlimited, 1983. How to conceal information: a second set of books, directions to buried goods, whatever secrets you want to keep.

How to Get ID in Canada and Other Countries, by Ronald George Eriksen 2, Loompanics Unlimited, 1984. Step-by-step instructions for obtaining alternative ID in Canada and other foreign countries.

Liar's Manual, by Roland Baker, Nelson-Hall, Chicago, IL, 1983. A how-to-do-it manual on telling lies. Might be useful to underground workers.

"Media Research Reports," available from EPIA Society, San Bernardino, CA. Many fascinating reports encouraging citizens to resist government licensing of all sorts, including business licenses, marriage licenses, drivers' licenses, and birth certificates.

Methods of Disguise, Second Edition, by John Sample, Loompanics Unlimited, Port Townsend, WA, 1993. Everything you ever wanted to know about changing your appearance.

The Paper Trip I, The Paper Trip II, and *The Paper Trip III*, by Barry Reid, Eden Press, PO Box 8410, Fountain Valley, CA 92708. The classic and original books on getting alternative identification papers.

Privacy: How to Get It; How to Enjoy It, by Bill Kaysing. Eden Press, 1977. A fine book on how to live your life in privacy from Big Brother.

Privacy Journal, PO Box 15300, Washington, DC 20003. Monthly newsletter on all aspects of privacy invasion, corporate as well as government.

The Privacy Poachers, by Tony Lesce, Loompanics Unlimited, Port Townsend, WA, 1992. This book explains how both the government and private industry work day and night to collect information about you, and what they do with it. It's a good idea to know your enemy, and this book is a good place to begin if you want to keep both the government and private snoopers from finding out things about you that you'd prefer to keep to yourself.

Related Topics

The Alpha Strategy, by John A. Pugsley, Stratford Press, 1981. An excellent book on investing in real goods, instead of paper stocks, etc. Good advice on stockpiling and hoarding. Must reading for all guerrilla capitalists.

Alternative Americas, by Mildred J. Loomis, Universe Books, NY, 1982. A classic book on political decentralization.

The Best Investment: Land in a Loving Community, by David W. Felder, Wellington Press, Tallahassee, FL, 1982. Advocates moving to a rural community as a good investment.

The Big Book of Secret Hiding Places, by Jack Luger, Loompanics Unlimited, Port Townsend, WA, 1987. This book is an encyclopedia of methods of concealing things inside and outside your premises. If you want to hide a stash, or cash, this book will tell you many ways of doing it.

Crisis Preparedness Handbook, by Jack A. Spigarelli, Resource Publications, Provo, UT, 2002. A comprehensive guide to home storage of food and emergency supplies. What to store and how to do it.

Cut Your Electric Bills In Half, by Ralph J. Herbert, Rodale Press, Emmaus, PA, 1986. A penny saved is more than a penny earned.

Ecotopian Encyclopedia, by Ernest Callenbach, And/Or Press, Berkeley, CA, 1981. Full of ideas on how to save money.

Getting a Roof Over Your Head, compiled by the Garden Way Editors, Garden Way Publishing, Charlotte, VT, 1983. Affordable housing alternatives.

Gene Logsdon's Money-Saving Secrets: A Treasure of Salvaging, Bargaining, Recycling & Scavenging Techniques, by Gene Logsdon, Rodale Press, Emmaus, PA, 1986. Good tips on saving money — remember, a penny saved is better than a penny earned.

Home Food Systems, edited by Roger B. Yepsen, Jr., Rodale Press, Emmaus, PA, 1981. How to produce, process, and preserve your own food.

How to Bury Your Goods, by eddie the wire, Loompanics Unlimited, Port Townsend, WA, 1981. The most comprehensive manual ever written on long-term underground storage. For hardcore individualists.

How to Launder Money, by John Gregg, Loompanics Unlimited, Port Townsend, WA, 1982. How the big boys do it. Using offshore corporations and tax havens, investing money without reporting it to the IRS, etc.

The Survival Retreat, by Ragnar Benson, Paladin Press, Boulder, CO, 1983. Very practical and down-to-earth book on putting together a safe place, well worth reading.

Survivalist's Medicine Chest, by Ragnar Benson, Paladin Press, Boulder, CO, 1982. How to stockpile medicines, with emphasis on buying them cheaply.

Appendix One
Underground Occupations

There is a variety of potential occupations that you can use to earn underground money. Most of these are "dual use" occupations, in the sense that you can work above ground, or totally underground. In Appendix Two, we'll examine some occupations that, while appearing attractive, are false starts, traps, and dead ends.

Earning Money in Alaska

For the young and adventurous person, Alaska seems to be the only frontier left in the country. There's an opportunity to earn big money, but in arduous and distasteful work such as fishing.

There are other industries, such as lumber and oil, but all are dominated by the weather. Basically, Alaska is for summer employment.

Even in fishing, the variety of jobs affords the willing worker choices in evading taxes. Some jobs are salaried, which means a big tax bite. Others are essentially contract labor, which gives the worker a very good opportunity to sign on under an assumed name and keep all that he makes.

Alaska will suit very few people, but it's worth a look, just for the sake of comparison.

Appliance Repairs

This can be a lucrative field, but it's not for everyone. Appliances can range from radios to air conditioners, and no repairman can be a specialist in all appliances.

Obtaining supplies can be a problem if you make it so. Some advisors suggest buying them on credit, which usually means an open thirty-day account. Applying for credit leaves you open to two problems: It establishes a paper trail and you forego the opportunity to pass on your checks, and may have to deposit them in your account. Paying cash is best. You may have to patronize a smaller supplier, with whom you have a personal relationship.

A point of concern might be that your supplier has knowledge, or at least a good guess, of what you're doing when you pay him with third-party checks. According to the principle of keeping guilty knowledge to yourself, you might feel that he's one person too many to be "in the know." While this is a risk, it's a tiny one. He depends on you for business, and stands to lose if he informs the IRS and puts you out of business. He may even be sneaking a few things by the government himself, which makes him your tacit ally.

You'll want to advertise mainly by word-of-mouth. Don't make the mistake of advertising in the Yellow Pages or classifieds. Never even have business cards, because this is overt evidence that you're operating a business, and can count against you if ever you have to face a tax collector. One way to do it without risk is to telephone businesses that might need your services.

Remember that you'll be able to attract clients because your overhead will enable you to under-price the established businesses. If you do good work, people will recommend you, and your clientele will grow.

Avoid stupidities such as getting a loan from the bank or the Small Business Administration (SBA) to help you get started. This creates a paper trail that will be fatal to your underground business. Avoid business licenses for the same reason.

Starting small, with tools you already own, you can reinvest your earnings in tools and supplies, and make your sideline grow. Be content to go slowly, in order to avoid the risks.

Arbitrage

Arbitrage means buying and selling the same items or commodities simultaneously, and earning money while doing it by taking advantage of different prices

Deep Inside the Underground Economy
How Millions of Americans Are Practicing Free Enterprise in An Unfree Society

204

in different markets. This is an ideal underground money-maker for someone in the right occupation.

In the legitimate economy, we find a broker buying, say, gold in one exchange and re-selling it in another where it pulls a slightly higher price. The advantage of arbitrage is that, with fast footwork, it requires no investment, as the arbitrageur pays his debt with what he collects. Arbitrage in stocks inevitably leaves a paper trail, and thus is not for the undergrounder.

However, the undergrounder can make use of another sort of arbitrage. Airline flight crews are perfect examples. If, for example, a pilot or stewardess knows that the London Exchange is paying a higher price for gold than the New York, and he or she is on that run, it's not hard to buy in New York and sell in London. It doesn't necessarily involve smuggling, which can lead to serious consequences, as there is usually an exemption allowed for a small amount of valuables, such as money, even if it's in gold coins.

In many countries, the legal currency exchange rate is quite different from the underground rate. Soviet Russia was an example of this, with the dollar/ruble rates differing as much as ten to one. Unfortunately the Soviet government took currency violations very seriously, and some Americans who were caught at it found that the Soviet police handed out harsh treatment to foreigners who played at this.

Dealing in currency is the safest way, in countries which don't have harsh policies or in which it's a matter of private market, rather than official, rates. Unless the arbitrageur gets greedy, and tries to smuggle more currency than legally allowed, there's no risk of hassle.

The return is slim, but it's extra income, earned while doing a job. It's a cash business, which makes it tax-free.

Commercial Artist

Many commercial artists, while working in the art department of a large corporation or advertising agency, will moonlight for their private accounts. Because commercial art does not need to be signed, it's difficult to establish that a particular artist did it, which helps to retain anonymity. This can avoid "conflict of interest" problems with the boss. This can be important, because commercial art and advertising people can be as possessive as editors and publishers, and considerably more irrational and jealous.

In some areas, artists are a dime a dozen, and the going is rough for a commercial artist starting out. He or she faces fierce competition in a buyer's market.

To succeed at after-hours commercial art, contacts are all-important. Advertising is a cutthroat business, and often taking an account from an employer is the only way to get it. The competition is often on price, because the freelancer can offer his services at a reduced rate.

Business cards are essential, not for advertising but as a convenience to the account. Word-of-mouth is the best, and often the sole way of letting your clients know that you're available. A freelancer can advertise in newspapers and trade publications, but not a moonlighter. Advertising is limited at best, because accounts assume that anyone who needs to advertise is "hungry," and can be exploited.

If you're thinking of this field, make sure that you have some talent and experience, but most of all, make sure that you know the local market. This can make you or break you.

Bodyguarding

One unusual method of earning extra money is working as a bodyguard. This occupation can work for you, but only in certain low-level situations. The reason that it can work is because it fills a gap between the high-priced executive protection services and the low-grade "rent-a-cop" shops.

There is a whole range of clients needing some sort of protection. Often, merchants in a shopping mall will band together to hire a "security guard," derisively called a "rent-a-cop." Occasionally, these are real cops, working privately on their days off, if their departments allow "moonlighting." If so, they don't come cheaply, usually charging at least what the department pays them per hour.

At the top end of the scale is executive protection, a very expensive service offered by specialized agencies often started by men retired from the U.S. Secret Service or some other government agency. These are usually extremely good, and extremely expensive private protection agents, and the services of one competent agent start at thirty thousand dollars a year and can easily be much higher. This is beyond the reach of most citizens, and these agencies' clientele is usually very wealthy people fearing kidnapping or terrorism, and major corporations assuring the safety of their top executives.

You can't compete with either of these types. The rent-a-cops usually work out of a private investigative agency, and are licensed in many states, which takes them right out of the underground. The high-grade executive protection agents have extensive backgrounds to bring to their jobs, and unless you're already involved in this sort of work as a police officer or government agent, you haven't much hope of even breaking into the field. There are two reasons for this: You haven't got the background or training required. The second, and more important, reason is that you're not "one of the boys." These people are very close and mutually protective, and even form associations of former agents. Some are members of the American Society for Industrial Security (ASIS). They hire their friends and colleagues with whom they've served for years in the same government agency. This is not only because of long-term friendship, but because they've worked with these people and have strong reasons to trust in their skills and reliability. They are reluctant to take a chance on an outsider, whom they would probably have to train.

The middle ground that you can exploit is part-time, informal bodyguard work, such as accompanying a merchant who takes his day's receipts to the bank to deposit, or the little old lady who wants someone to walk with her to the store to forestall muggers. These are basically low-risk assignments, and within your likely level of competence. Your main value will be deterrence, not fighting power, as muggers tend to seek the most vulnerable targets, and pass up the ones who seem to have some ability to defend themselves.

This still makes it difficult for you, because you have two obstacles to overcome: You will not be representing an above ground, well-known agency, and therefore will not have the prestige of a big name to help sell your services. This is why you won't find it very helpful to advertise; nobody will be impressed by you or your services. You simply will not be able to handle any high-risk assignments, which would pay well.

Bodyguarding, more often known as "executive protection" these days, is no longer a matter of having a hulking type whose knuckles drag on the floor accompanying the protectee wherever he goes. Brains and specialized knowledge count more than brawn. A good example of this is the Bobby Kennedy assassination in 1968. Roosevelt Grier, the football player, was serving as one of Senator Kennedy's bodyguards, since this was before the U.S. Secret Service had the task of protecting presidential candidates. His brawny build and great strength did not stop the as-

sassin, who was armed with only a .22 caliber revolver. He had the brawn, but not the specialized training to enable him to recognize potential threats and to avoid dangerous situations.

The main idea in protecting a client is avoidance, not confrontation. Your task will be to keep away from danger, not to fight it out while he stands and watches your heroism. If you get into a fight, with or without weapons, you've already failed at the more important half your job.

If you try to serve a high-risk client, you'll very frankly be out of your league. The high-risk client who fears terrorism or kidnapping, is likely to get the attention of some very tough and determined people, not just casual muggers. The terrorists who kidnapped Aldo Moro in Italy did not pussyfoot around. They stopped his car and waxed his five bodyguards.

Terrorists and kidnappers are likely to be professional criminals or ideological guerrillas, both of whom are not afraid to risk their lives and are likely to be heavily armed. If anything does come down, a six-week course from a karate school will not help you very much, nor will a quick course in armed defense from one of the many shooting schools springing up around the country. You'll simply be outnumbered, outclassed, outgunned, and surprised. The attackers wait for the right moment and place, and strike when they have most of the advantages. You have to be alert and ready every moment, which is really difficult.

This is why the basic principle is avoidance, presenting an elusive and moving target to evade the attack, not to meet it. This is a highly specialized skill, one that you can't learn in a course at your local karate school or community college. There are schools that teach this, but they are very expensive and you'll probably have to travel away from home to attend. The basic tuition is about five thousand dollars, and usually one course is not enough. In any event, this violates the principle of avoiding a heavy investment at the outset. You might sink many thousands of dollars into this project, and then find that you can't find enough clients to make it worthwhile.

This is why you have to work the middle ground, and pick up the crumbs that the bigger outfits don't bother to eat. You want to keep your venture underground, which means to collect in cash if possible, and since bodyguard work will not be a full-time occupation for you, you'll have to do it in your off-hours.

Deep Inside the Underground Economy
How Millions of Americans Are Practicing Free Enterprise in An Unfree Society

206

Advertising must be by word-of-mouth. For this, an imposing appearance is very helpful. The basis for your service is deterrence, so you'll be more impressive if you're big and muscular. If you look tough and formidable enough that petty criminals will be deterred from taking you on, and you can impress a potential client with your appearance, you'll have your start.

Regarding special fighting skills, armed or unarmed, your main job will be not to have to use them. To repeat the most important principle of bodyguarding; if you have to fight, you've failed at the more important half of your job.

Collecting for your services takes a little finesse, if you're to keep your effort underground. You can tell a little old lady that you don't have a bank account, and that it would be helpful if she paid you in cash. A merchant is another story. They prefer to pay by check, but if the merchant sells goods or services that you can use, try to arrange for a trade-out. A restaurant owner, for example, might be happy to pay you in meals, for yourself and/or a companion.

Car Moving

Anyone who lives in a city with alternate side parking knows the hassle of the "eight o'clock club," in which people who have to leave for work wait for others to take their cars so that they may move theirs on the side of the street allowed that day. This is endless irritation, occurring several days a week, and it causes many to be late for work.

If you have time free in the morning, one possibility is to offer a car-moving service to your neighbors. This will require you to get their spare keys, will require you to be diligent, and will take up some time. It's labor-intensive, needing no investment at all. Advertising is by word-of-mouth or cards.

Diligence is most important. Having a customer get a parking ticket because you did not move his car is bad news.

Cement Work for the Undergrounder

This is an easy trade, but one in which you must hustle. This doesn't imply dishonesty in any way; it just means that you have to pursue potential clients aggressively.

The basic mode of operation is to cold canvass. Walk down a block, looking for cracks and holes in driveways and sidewalks. This makes canvassing very quick, as you can judge potential customers as you walk along, without wasting any time.

One important point is "call-backs," a technique that professional door-to-door salesmen know well. The odds are that some of the prospects won't be home. Note the addresses and come back later. Call-backs are time-savers, even if you have to work some evening hours canvassing.

Unfortunately, this work is somewhat seasonal. In certain parts of the country it's impossible to pour concrete in the colder months. It's also dependent on the weather. Rain will wash you out. However, if you're doing this strictly as a sideline, and not committed to a fixed volume of business each week, the breaks from the work will be refreshing.

In this business, you go mainly for the small jobs, the quick patch jobs that don't require a lot of time or concrete, and for which you can collect in cash, on the spot. This saves untold hassle.

Coin-Operated Machines

We see a lot of these, selling anything from candy and cigarettes to admission to the subway. Some people scrounge an extra dollar or two by feeling the return chute of coin-operated machines they pass. Inevitably, some people forget to pick up their change from these chutes.

Another way to earn money directly is to hoard tokens. The New York City subway system, for example, uses tokens instead of U.S. coins in their machines. Every several years, the fares go up, and the riders have to pay more for the tokens. Buying extra tokens and hoarding them against the next fare increase is one method of investment that is undetectable, tax-free, and typically offers a good return. It's easy to predict when a fare increase will come. It's always several years after the previous one, and for several months beforehand, there are media accounts of discussions regarding the increasing costs of operating the system. The Chairman, or another official, will ask for permission to increase fares, and there will be committee hearings.

The alert rider who starts buying tokens some months before the increase sees the value of his investment go up from ten to twenty percent when the new increase comes. It's not hard to estimate the timing within a year, and often within a few months. Not many investments pay off at the rate of ten or twenty percent a year. The underground investor can buy the tokens for his own later use, or to sell to fellow employees at a profit. There is no law against this.

Collection Agency

This can be a bad business, but I include it to show a good example of what not to pursue. Starting up your own collection agency is an idea that you'll find in many "earn extra income" books.

Unless you're an "enforcer" for organized crime, you'll have to operate above ground. An extra hazard is that many federal regulations apply to collection agencies, among them those of the Federal Trade Commission, Federal Communications Commission, and the U.S. Postal Service. Some states require licensing, too.

Otherwise, the business isn't too bad. It's labor-intensive, which means almost pure profit, and you can operate it out of your home. The overhead, for lighting, stationery, and telephone, is slight.

The entanglement with paperwork, which can even include bonding, makes this out of the question for the person who wants to operate underground.

Companion

We often see classified ads for "professional companions" or a "live-in companion." Several different types of people advertise this way. Some are shut-ins, handicapped people who are lonely and disabled, who need someone to help them with household tasks, and also simply for company. In such cases, the companion provides what we can call low-grade nursing care at a cut-rate price.

Such people usually have a chronic, but not life-threatening disorder, one that doesn't require high-grade care, and they don't want, or can't afford, to pay a nurse. A hired companion can help with the routine tasks, such as administering pills, and helping the shut-in to bathe, and will also be willing to do things that an R.N. would not. Going on errands, such as shopping, are tasks which a nurse simply will not do, even though she's paid more than a professional companion.

Others are wealthy people who are not necessarily disabled, but want company, often on a trip abroad. The advantage to them is that, for a price, they get a companion who has a firmly fixed position, and will not pose a social problem. An escort or chaperone is one way of describing such a paid companion.

The rate of pay is not high, but it does usually include room and board if the requirement is for a live-in companion. In the case of a traveling companion, the pay includes certain fringe benefits, such as traveling expenses.

The disadvantages are that the hours are usually long, very long, and that the pay per hour is small. In addition, the person who hires a paid companion often has to do so because of a difficult and demanding personality.

If you're thinking of this sort of employment, you have to like people, and be genuinely sympathetic. Only with such traits will you be able to tolerate the needs of your clients.

Another important question is how will this job fit in with your lifestyle? If you're regularly employed, you won't be able to take care of a shut-in who needs 24-hour attention. Some, however, only need someone to look in on them for a few hours a day, to clean the house, cook a meal, do the shopping, and help them with tasks that they can't do for themselves.

A traveling companion, on the other hand, can fit it into his or her vacation. For the fortunate few who can find this sort of arrangement, it's a good way of getting an expenses-paid trip. The limitation, if you take this sort of employment, is that your time will center around your employer's needs and demands. You won't be able to go where you want to go, see the sights that you want to see. You might take the attitude of, "What the hell, it's free." On the other hand, you might feel unduly restricted. This is why it's important to discuss the conditions before you accept such an engagement.

You will find such work two ways: by word-of-mouth and by answering classified ads. You almost surely will need references, to present the image of an honest, dedicated, hard-working person. Landing the first job will be the hardest part, but after that you'll be able to use your first client as a reference if all goes well.

Evidence Collecting

This field, which seems attractive if you read the right book, has its problems. While it's a possibly lucrative occupation to collect evidence on behalf of a client, this falls right into the field of private investigating. Private investigators have to be licensed in most states, which pushes you right out into the open, spoiling any chances you might have had of keeping your work underground. With a state license, there is a paper trail that brings the tax collector right to your door, because tax collection bureaus scan lists of license holders to ensure that they're paying taxes.

Another problem is that you need the proper skills for this work. Accident investigation, for example, is a part of police work, and it's a specialized skill that

Deep Inside the Underground Economy
How Millions of Americans Are Practicing Free Enterprise in An Unfree Society

208

a newcomer can't master without specialized instruction and experience. In reality, many private investigators do accident investigations for lawyers and insurance agencies, and many private investigators are retired police officers who make use of their twenty or more years' experience to earn supplements to their pensions.

This is a field for you to avoid unless you have the background and can work for a buddy who runs an agency and is willing to pay you under the table.

Earning Finder's Fees

A finder, also known as a "bird dog," is a person who puts one party in contact with another. Some commonplace examples are the car owner who refers a friend to the agency where he bought his, or the person who recommends a certain repairman to a friend. These are casual examples, but there are more systematic ones, some of which are unethical or even illegal. One such is the common practice of "kicking back" or "fee-splitting" among doctors.

However, being a finder, a middleman of sorts, is a legitimate occupation in the business world. There's nothing dishonorable about helping one interested party to find another.

Sometimes finders go by the name of "brokers" when they restrict themselves to one line of work. Real estate agents are also finders, as are rental agents, employment agents (bad reputation there), and business agents.

A finder can be above ground or underground. The above ground finder has his own agency, a formal business, licensed and listed in the telephone directory. The underground finder works out of his hat, depending entirely on his system of contacts.

Among the properties, products, and commodities that pull finder's fees are: campers, motel franchises, redwood sawdust, tennis courts, antiques, towns, gravel, clay, carbon rights, leather, bricks, plastic scrap, mausoleums, and bicycles.

The key to being a freelance finder is that you must deal in a product or other substance in which there isn't an established trading place. Stocks are not good prospects, because there are many established brokers working out of closely-regulated stock exchanges. The regulars get there before you.

Finders and the people seeking them usually don't advertise. It's very much a word-of-mouth business. Often, it's a very opportunistic business. There is no network, and it depends highly upon personal contacts. The finder often happens upon a "deal" that can

earn him a fee if he puts the right two people in touch with each other.

By the business's very nature, the finder doesn't invest much, except time, some letters, or phone calls. Some finders are very formal, requiring a signed contract before making the contact. Others are free and easy, relying on a customer's word to assure payment.

There's a risk of getting burned, of course, and much depends on how well the finder knows the people with whom he's dealing.

The manner of payment can be a problem. If you have a signed agreement, drawn up by a lawyer and notarized, you're laying your arrangement out in the open. If you work underground, you can stipulate that the payment be in cash. Another way is by hard goods that you can sell. Yet another way is by trade-out, exchanging goods for services instead of cash. If you have a mind agile enough to let you work as a finder, you can also find the best untraceable way to collect.

Finding isn't for everyone. If you're gregarious, think quickly on your feet, have a nose for money or the opportunity to make money, perhaps it's for you. Oh, yes, you also need contacts.

Let Your Fingers Do the Walking

Brainstorming for ideas on how to make money is hard at first, for most people. That's why it's helpful to use some cues, the sort you find in the Yellow Pages. Look at a few categories and see if they tie in with some of the money-makers discussed in this volume, or even suggest something new:

Acupuncturists

Do you do this for a living? How about another healing skill? Do you know any folk medicine? Do you know any home remedies that you could manufacture and sell under the table?

Air Conditioning

What does this suggest? Repair? Maybe, if you have the skill, but what about preventive maintenance? Can you persuade a few people that, although you don't have the training to repair an air conditioner or evaporative cooler, you have enough skill to check it out, recharge it, and to do it at lower cost than the punitive prices that established above ground air conditioning people charge?

Animal Carcass Removal

This might be worth a phone call. Not because you want to get into the business, but because these companies use animal by-products. Is there much roadkill in your area? Would it pay to keep a couple of boxes and plastic bags in your trunk just in case? What do they pay? A phone call will get you an answer.

Apartments and Rooms

Right! If you have a room you'd like to rent, this can be profitable and tax free as well.

Blood Bank

Here's something you might consider if you're in very good health, and want to earn a few bucks every now and then. A phone call will tell you what they pay, and you can then decide if it's for you.

Building Contracting

Maybe you know one who needs casual labor, such as cleaning up a job site. This might not be the job for you, but for your teenager, if the boss pays cash.

Carpet Cleaning

These people have big commercial machines, but maybe you could still use the carpet cleaner that your wife got you to buy last year, and which sits in the closet most of the time. Ask your neighbors if they want you to clean their carpets, cut-rate. Another idea is that they might rent the machine from you, if you charge less than the supermarket down the road.

Catering

You don't run a restaurant, but didn't your neighbor complain to you last week about the high estimates he got when trying to find someone to cater a party? Can you do a good job for less?

Dealer in Used Books

Do you pick up scrap paper? Newspaper? Do you ever find any books in the pile? Maybe some people will buy them from you at more than scrap paper price. Ask and earn some extra bucks.

Dentists

Dentists use X-ray machines, and X-ray film has silver in it. A dental X-ray packet also has a lead foil backing. Is this scrap reclaimable? Does your dentist already sell it? If not, will he give or sell it to you? Where can you sell it? Look in the phone book under "scrap metal."

Editorial Services

Some small publishers can use part-time proofreaders. This is work you can do at home, and it offers two prospects:

If your client's willing to pay you cash, you can hide the income completely.

If he pays by check, you can still get some benefit, because if you can devote one room of your house or apartment completely to this, you can take an extra deduction. You can also deduct mileage and utilities. This isn't underground, but it's still better than being a wage slave.

Florists-Retail

Do you like gardening? Like raising flowers? Next time you're near a florist, take along a few of your flowers as samples. Ask if he'd like to buy from you. You can surely beat the commercial florists' prices, since you do it for a hobby. Ask for cash payment in return for low prices. It's all gravy.

Gift and Craft Shops

Do you make macramé, pottery, or anything else that people use as gifts? If it's your hobby, you might make it pay. Go to a local gift shop with some samples. Perhaps you can interest the owner in buying from you. Cash, of course.

Hobby Shop

Now here's a live one! Have a talk with the owner. Suggest to him that you might hold classes in one of the hobbies for his customers. It's not likely that he'd be interested in paying you for your instruction, but you might work out a deal, anyway. Suggest that, in return for you holding classes, for which he would not charge the students but which would help stimulate his business, you would be able to buy your hobby supplies from him at cost. This is an example of a trade-out, which is utterly safe because it's untraceable. It happens to be legal, too, because as a business owner, he can charge the prices he wishes.

Janitorial Service

There are many janitorial services listed, which shows that the business is there. One key to determining if there's room for you is if there's much new construction of industrial parks in your area. A new concern is a hot prospect, since you're less likely to find that they have a service and are satisfied with it.

Deep Inside the Underground Economy
How Millions of Americans Are Practicing Free Enterprise in An Unfree Society

210

Lawn Maintenance

Ditto. Check new housing developments. Some builders don't even landscape the buyer's lawn. They throw a bag of grass seeds at him and he's on his own. There's potential business among new house buyers who want more than just grass, and are willing to pay for bushes and flowers.

Maternity Assistance

This offers an unexpected opportunity. If you're a midwife or a childbirth instructor, don't think you can get referrals from doctors or hospitals. They don't like the competition, and won't give you the time of day. A maternity shop is a good place to post a flier advertising your services, however. An excellent approach is to give a freebie to the owner, if she's female and pregnant. Deliver her baby at home and she'll give you a personal recommendation. This can count a lot with her customers.

One possibility is to offer a free orientation course to all customers. This initial session will enable them to see what you have to offer, and you can sign up those who find your services attractive.

Paper Hangers

Can you do this? It's a useful adjunct to painting, and you can get the same sort of customers. This also suggests some ways to advertise; leaving a flier or a short stack of your cards in a wallpaper dealer's.

One incentive you can use with the dealer is to offer him a commission on any accounts you get through him, or offer to buy all of your supplies from him.

Reading Improvement Instruction

One listing here is for Evelyn Wood, a nationwide firm which teaches speed-reading. This suggests that there's room for you. You don't have to compete with Evelyn Wood, because there are many children who have trouble reading. Let's face it, the schools are lousy. If you can read well, and if you are patient and have a good manner with children, you may be able to seek out parents of children who are not reading well and offer your services coaching. This also applies to other types of tutoring.

Riding Academies

Can you ride a horse? Do you own a horse or two? If so, and if you have the time, you can give riding instruction, cut-rate. Don't try to leave your cards at stables or riding academies, though. Try sporting goods shops, outdoor shops, those specializing in western wear, and saddleries.

Sharpening Saws and Scissors

Can you do this and do you have the tools? If so, you surely have friends and neighbors who'll pay for your service. It won't make you rich, but you'll earn a few bucks, tax-free. Take it where you find it.

Veterinarians

No, you can't go into competition with them, but if you offer a pet grooming service, you can leave your cards at a vet's. Most likely, you have a pet of your own. Go to your vet and tell him that you're in business. To accommodate a customer, he'll let you leave a stack of your business cards on his counter.

Watering Service

Will your neighbors pay you to water their lawns? This is labor-intensive, since they provide the water. Many people forget, or are too involved with other things, to remember to water their lawns regularly. This is a project that you can undertake very economically. You don't have to stand by and watch the water flow. When you've got one hose deployed, walk down to your next account and set his up, then to the next, etc. By the time you've made your rounds, it's time to shut off the water at the first one.

The Big Picture

The U.S. Department of Labor has a huge volume listing all of the occupations with their code numbers. It has well over thirty thousand between the covers, yet it's almost useless for your purpose, because the people who compiled this volume simply don't understand all of the subspecialties in each broad category. In any event, the official names of these occupations are not very useful or thought stimulating.

The Yellow Pages are best, if you use them properly. One feature of the phone book that you should not overlook is the large number of display ads. The simple listing of names, addresses, and phone numbers doesn't tell you as much as the ads.

They list what services a company provides, and tell you a bit about the occupation. From this information, you can decide if there's a part of the job that you could do. You can also read and infer what they're missing or overlooking. Maybe there's a gap that you could fill. For example, a construction company produces a lot of scrap on each job. They have to haul it away and clean up after themselves. Can they use an independent hauler? If you have a pick-up truck, you might offer this service to a small contractor. Don't call the large ones. They have their own trucks and their own full-time hauling services.

Read every display ad carefully for these details. Think about what they offer, and what they don't provide. Don't be discouraged by the size of the phone book, or the huge amount of reading you might have to do. Start with the "A"s and go from there. The odds are that you won't get far down the alphabet before you find something worth pursuing.

Another value of the Yellow Pages is that the volume gives you specific information. No mere listing of occupations can tell you what companies supply what. No book on sideline jobs or underground money-making, even this one, can tell you what's available in your own neighborhood.

With the Yellow Pages, you can see immediately if anyone is covering a certain field, and make a judgment of how large and successful their operations are by the location and size of their business. This enables you to estimate the competition you'll face.

Scan the phone book, and scan it critically. Keep thinking, and you'll find several hot prospects for earning extra money!

Guides

Many people hunt and fish, and the more affluent ones can pay their way to remote areas. Out in the boonies, they're unfamiliar with the locale, and willingly pay guides. This can be a worthwhile underground occupation for someone who lives in the area. It's seasonal work, but very profitable.

The requirements are: first, the guide should live in the area and know the geography intimately. He should be a hunter or fisherman himself, and be able to recommend the best spots to his clients. Second, he must have a superior skill at hunting or fishing. Many of his clients will be tenderfoots, stumbling around for the one or two weeks they get out from behind their desks, and will need all the help they can get. In extreme instances, the guide may have to shoot game or catch a fish for them, so that they may bring a trophy home and claim that they caught it. The guide must be a practical psychologist: feeding the egos of his charges is one of his duties.

An unusual, but helpful background is to have been a member of a police force in a recreational area, such as the U.S. Park Police. They're experienced at keeping order among vacation crowds, and this skill can be very useful, as sometimes a guide's clients can become drunk and disorderly, and the guide must be able to keep control without antagonizing and losing his clients. Park police develop strong interpersonal skills as their stock-in-trade because they're dealing with citizens who are temporarily boisterous, not hardened criminals, and diplomacy is better than force in such cases. An additional advantage of this occupation is that recreational area police tend to be experienced outdoorsmen.

Advertising is by word-of-mouth, and direct solicitation. Frequenting areas where hunters and fishermen gather, such as a sporting goods store, can provide introductions to potential clients. A store owner who passes on recommendations can be very helpful.

Some guides advertise in sporting magazines, but these are usually owners of large concerns, with several employees, and they offer more comprehensive services, such as renting hunting, fishing, and camping gear. It's difficult to keep this sort of operation underground, especially if there are any ammunition sales, which pose the problem of a federal license.

The small operator, accepting the seasonal nature of the business, can earn extra money without risk. While it's hard to keep a secret in a rural area, where everyone knows everyone else's business, a guide who is well-liked has little to fear from informers.

House Sitting

This is a sporadic business, as house-sitting clients don't have schedules for your convenience. The only way to put it on a regular basis is not to do the work yourself, but open up an agency.

This puts you right out in the open, and you may have to get a license, generate a lot of paperwork, and bear all of the other undesirable paraphernalia of a regular business. The only way for you, as an undergrounder, to operate it is as a one-man show. Looking after peoples' houses while they're away can be profitable, although irregular. You can also tie it in with a pet-sitting service, and you can offer comprehensive care, according to the client's needs.

This can include, at an extra charge, plant watering, lawn mowing, repairs, and painting. You can do the work yourself, or subcontract it out if it's beyond you, as might be the case with some repairs. A good way of avoiding handling large sums of money, including checks, is to have the customer write out the checks to your subcontractors. Tell him that you'd prefer to do it this way so that there will be no question of overcharging him by marking up the amounts.

Deep Inside the Underground Economy
How Millions of Americans Are Practicing Free Enterprise in An Unfree Society

212

Advertising can be by display cards, but the most effective will be by word-of-mouth. Clients who give you the keys to their homes will want to be able to trust you, and a personal referral is far more convincing than an impersonal advertisement. Business cards are a must, because some of your referrals can come from business owners and shopkeepers who know you. Some of their customers will need house sitting, and having some of your cards to hand out will enable them to give you more referrals.

The arrangement can vary. Some people expect a live-in arrangement, which can be good for you if you're single and living with your parents or in a small apartment. It will let you enjoy larger living quarters for the term of the sitting. Most, however, will be satisfied with your coming to the house at least once a day, to pick up the mail, water the plants, feed the pets, and perform whatever other services they request. You can run several accounts like this simultaneously.

Interior Decorating

This is a lucrative full-time occupation, and is also a well-paying part-time one for certain individuals who have a flair for it. Some people develop an interest in interior decorating as a hobby, and a few of these decide to earn money from this pastime.

The main requirement is talent for this skill. Some community colleges have courses in interior decorating, and some high-prestige furniture stores offer classes at minimal cost as an accommodation to their clients, but without a knack for it the individual won't get much out of formal training.

Anyone who does this for a hobby has a head start in breaking into the field professionally. For the undergrounder, there are some special rules.

The first concerns method of payment. Many interior decorators obtain part of their incomes by ordering furniture and materials from regular suppliers. The suppliers in turn pay them commissions. This creates a paper trail. The undergrounder must work for a fee paid by the client, preferably in cash, and let the client order the items. The decorator can assist, by referring the client to outlets that will give the client a professional discount, and save the client money this way.

To do this, the decorator must know the sources of supply, and if possible, have a personal or professional relationship with them. Sending them clients will help establish this relationship.

It's also necessary to have fabric and carpet samples. These can be quite bulky and costly for the manufacturers to produce. Normally, they're for the trade only, and the trick is to get accepted enough by the suppliers so that they'll give samples.

Catalogs are easier to get; they're relatively cheap and normally for general distribution. The outcome is that it's necessary for the interior decorator to carry what amounts to a very large portfolio, to show the customer the many choices available.

Advertising by word-of-mouth works, but not cards on bulletin boards. Classified ads are inexpensive, but don't have much "pulling power."

Much depends on the locale. In some areas, people don't have the money for fancy decorating, while in others keeping up with the Joneses in interior decor is almost mandatory.

Coaching for Interviews

Many people approach employment interviews with well-justified apprehension. They're worried over the impression they'll make, and whether or not they'll get the job.

There are some very simple and very tangible reasons for this anxiety. The job applicant has more at stake than does the interviewer. For the interviewer, the person before him is only one of a number that he or she will see that day, and his job does not depend on the outcome of one interview.

The second reason is that the interviewer is a professional, and the applicant is not. The interviewer has been through it hundreds, or thousands of times, and is well rehearsed, asking basically the same questions day after day.

Another reason is that the interviewer is prepared and directs the interview. There aren't any surprises. The applicant does not know, except in a very general way, what questions the interviewer will ask, or how he'll ask them. The applicant, moreover, may have a blemish on his record, something which he feels will make an unfavorable impression if it comes out. Many people have been fired, for example, and this causes a lot of needless anxiety. It requires "explaining away." Others have prison records that mar the picture they wish to present of a capable or honest employee.

There are different personality types among interviewers, as there are among people in general. Some are direct, straightforward, no-nonsense types, asking about employment experience and training the applicant has had for the task. Others play games.

There's a need, often unfulfilled, for practical, no-nonsense coaching for job interviews. Many people, unless they're very experienced at job-seeking, don't have the practice in handling interviews that the pros do. The little information that is commonly available is usually limited to advice on how to dress, and to be on time for the interview. It completely neglects the important points, such as how to present the picture the applicant wants, and how to direct the interview subtly, without offending.

If you have enough experience at interviewing or being interviewed, and have had a chance to meet and analyze the different types of interviewers, you have a start at building up an informal business by coaching people to survive interviews. Part of your coaching will be to describe what employers seek in applicants, and how they frame their questions to elicit this information. Part of it also will be "role-playing," in which you and your pupil will enact interviews, to give him or her the practical experience at the task.

Exchanging roles is also valuable, to give your student the point of view from behind the desk.

Reducing anxiety level is an important part of your coaching. You do this by "desensitization," running your student through mock interviews in the secure practice setting until he or she understands that there is nothing to fear and calms down.

A part of coaching that absolutely nobody mentions is the valuable field experience that the student can get at no cost to him by going for fake interviews, applying for jobs which he does not intend to take, just to get the experience of surviving interviews.

At first, this might seem unethical, wasting an employer's valuable time with the applicant having no intention of accepting the job. Actually, it's no more unethical than an employer's expecting several applicants to come in for interviews, knowing that only one of them will get the job. In effect, the employer will have wasted the others' time, but nobody makes an issue of this.

Debriefing the student after the interview is important. Go over the interview with him, ask him where he felt that his strong points showed, and where he made his mistakes. Most of us learn from our mistakes, and it's far easier and more comfortable to learn when we don't have to pay the price for them.

Advertising can be by word-of-mouth, or classified ads. Another way is to put up notices on bulletin boards. Your printed advertisements will have to ex-plain exactly what your service provides, because interview coaching is not a common field, and most people don't know about it.

A Home Kitchen Business

This idea is attractive, but requires careful handling. Some people, starting small and literally at home in their kitchens, have been successful enough to expand into large businesses. Others did not try to grow too much, and kept their volume small enough to be manageable.

It's one thing to have a small business operating out of your kitchen and selling informally to friends and neighbors. It's another to distribute the food products over a wide area, selling through stores. At that point, some serious complications can creep in and imperil the underground nature of your operation.

Federal regulations also come into the picture, and you may have to guarantee freshness of your products and print "pull dates" on the labels, another problem.

The key is to start small and to stay small. Keep the profile of a small, home and neighborhood operation and you'll reduce the chances of getting into more than you can handle. Avoid brand names and labels. Avoid selling to retailers, to maintain your anonymity.

You give up something for the privilege of staying small. You may not be able to buy the ingredients from wholesalers, since the big distributors have the market locked up so that a private party can't buy from them in many areas. Without a "resale number," which means a tax-collecting license, they won't sell to you. Paying more for the ingredients at retail is not as bad as paying income tax on your earnings, however, and if you can be realistic and keep a sense of proportion you can have a modestly successful and officially hidden enterprise.

Language Tutoring

This falls into a special category because conventional tutoring is usually in an academic setting. Teaching a language is sometimes different, because it's for a different purpose.

There are basically two reasons for most people to learn a language:
1. Immigrants need to learn English to get along in their new country. Usually, but not always, they can enroll in night school for this. The exceptions are in small cities that do not have large immi-

Deep Inside the Underground Economy
How Millions of Americans Are Practicing Free Enterprise in An Unfree Society

214

grant populations. In such a case, a bright immigrant may want you to help him polish his skill, if he already has a rough knowledge of English.

2. The second reason is that some people want to learn a foreign language, either because they anticipate needing it in traveling abroad, or for snob appeal.

Language tutoring is not a steady occupation unless you work for a specialized language school, such as Berlitz, or a conventional school. For the undergrounder, any sort of school is out. Private lessons are the only way to go, because holding classes is too conspicuous.

The first need is a genuine skill in the language you intend to teach. Anyone who's taken a foreign language in school has probably noticed the low skill of the teachers. This is especially noticeable to a person who was raised in the language. For that matter, many Americans don't speak English properly. This includes some teachers. Many of us with a skill in a foreign language, because we have foreign-born parents, have noticed language teachers know the grammar and the literature, but can't easily carry on a conversation in the language they teach.

It's important to know your limitations. If you're not very good in English, you can help foreign-born people to improve their English, and carry on simple transactions, but no more. On the plus side, often this is all that they need. All they want is to be able to get along at work, and while shopping, not to learn the fine points of English.

The second need is getting clients. Word-of-mouth will do it if you work with many foreign-born people, or live in a neighborhood that's largely foreign-born. Card advertisements cost nothing, but advertise yourself as a tutor, or write that you give lessons. Don't suggest that you're running any sort of a school. This point's important because in many states schools have to be licensed, which takes you right out of the underground.

Locksmithing

With the high rate of property crime in this country, locksmithing is a growing industry. There's another reason to regard locksmithing as a secure and growing field — the economy. Right now, our economy is in trouble, whatever the crystal ball gazers might predict.

Locksmithing is an excellent trade to have during hard times. When the economy declines, crime goes up, and so does the need for extra security. This creates a demand for locksmiths, as well as other people working in the "security" industry. Given the extra hazard of terrorism, people have reason to be anxious. This makes locksmithing interesting for survivalists, since it's a practically inflation-proof trade and the demand is inverse to the state of the economy. One obvious point is that for the survivalist, locksmithing will be more useful in economic blowouts than in catastrophic situations such as nuclear war.

Some people, oddly enough, are self-trained because locksmithing is their hobby. They already have the needed tools, and indeed often earn extra cash by doing work for friends.

Following the principle of investing little at the outset, it's possible for you to dip your toe in by acquiring a few books and trying to learn locksmithing on a modest scale. Two sources for books on locksmithing are Prentice-Hall (Englewood Cliffs, NJ), one of the biggest publishers of "how-to" books in the country, and Paladin Press (Gunbarrel Technical Center, 7077 Winchester Circle, Boulder, CO 80301), which specializes in unusual books and has various books on locksmithing, lock picking, and related subjects.

The tools required are small hand tools, not expensive equipment. The investment, therefore, is small. There is a need for supplies and spare parts, which makes the locksmith dependent on regular suppliers. This cuts both ways, though, as the supplier is an aid to "laundering" checks, as mentioned many places in this book.

It's also necessary to keep a small stockpile on hand to meet day-to-day needs. Again, this is a small investment, and for the underground locksmith, possible to build up progressively as the business grows.

One problem is advertising. Many people feel that the person dealing with locks to their homes and businesses must not only be respectable, but utterly above reproach. Many above ground locksmiths advertise that they're bonded, an additional selling point. The underground locksmith, for obvious reasons, cannot be bonded, and his low-profile approach can deter many potential customers, who may view him as a fly-by-night if he doesn't have a shop and isn't listed in the Yellow Pages.

Mail Drops

Running a mail drop as a home business is one good way to earn extra cash in the underground economy. There's almost no investment. The labor is minimal, and because there's no time-pressure, you can run this business in your spare time.

A mail drop, also known as an "accommodation address," is a service to people who want to receive mail without revealing their addresses or even their identities. The classified pages of many magazines, especially the sexually-oriented ones, have ads for mail drops, which gives a good indication of why some want this service.

Another reason for a mail drop is to provide a break in the chain for people who practice fraud of any sort. Unfortunately, the need for a secret address among criminals is just as urgent as among people who just have secret sex lives.

Post Office regulations make it illegal to rent a Post Office box under an assumed name. There is no law regarding a mail drop, and your clients may use any name that suits them, even "Boxholder," as long as you protect yourself by collecting in advance. This point is essential, as some of the people who rent mail drops are unsavory types.

Advertising is by classified ads. To safeguard yourself, you ask for payment in cash or money order, in advance. You offer to remail whatever the client receives to his real address, to avoid having to "mind the store" while awaiting your clients' pick-ups. In exceptional cases, you can specify that the pick-up hours are those convenient to you.

In reality, operating a mail drop takes very little time. The Post Office does most of the work for you.

One point of concern for you is that, if someone uses the mail drop for anything illegal, it might make you an accessory. There's no need to worry if you can show that you don't know what the envelopes contain, and it's up to the prosecution to prove that you have knowledge of your clients' activities. A strong point in your favor is that it's a felony to open another's mail, and you will be able to claim truthfully that you forwarded the mail unopened. The prosecution has to prove otherwise.

One book that will tell you all you need to know about setting up a mail drop service is: *How to Use Mail Drops for Profit, Privacy, and Self-Protection*, Second Edition, by Jack Luger, Loompanics Unlimited, Port Townsend, WA, 1996.

Mail Order

Mail order is an iffy business. It requires an investment, both in stock and in advertising, but it's possible to start on a shoestring and keep it underground.

Jerry devised a plastic accessory for pistols, which he was able to have injection-molded very cheaply, and sell at a good profit by mail. He did this as a sideline, to supplement his job as a mail-carrier. With the profit he made from this, all undeclared, he opened up a gun store upon retirement from the Postal Service.

Rather than answering an ad promising him big profits in mail-order sales, he devised his own product. The stark fact is that enterprisers who answer such ads find that they are the customers, rather than the sellers, and that if the product sold well, the seller would be retailing it himself.

Jerry took a risk. He used his home address, which made his traffic traceable. He took the risk knowing that the odds of getting caught, as long as he was discreet in other ways, were minimal. He got away with it for years.

Finding a salable product is one hard step. Not everyone can do it, and it's wise not to accept someone else's retreads.

Advertising can be inexpensive, at first, until the volume justifies the expense. Classified ads run in almost any publication, even national magazines, and they aren't costly. Paying for them with a money order helps break the paper trail.

A mail drop is better than a post office box. Renting a post office box under an assumed name is illegal, but a mail drop operator doesn't care; he only wants the money. This helps keep a low profile and break the trail. In fact, a mail drop or an ad will attract no undue attention if it's under what seems to be a company name, such as "Synertronics."

Another is what to do with all the checks you get. "Laundering" them is possible, but can be unwieldy. If you have a source of supplies, you can pass them as third-party checks if you're friendly with the owner.

Despite its hit-and-miss nature, mail order can be a profitable sideline. Approaching it correctly will minimize the risks.

Martial Arts Instruction

Partly because of concern over the crime rate, and partly because they see martial arts as good sport, many people take up judo, karate, kung-fu, and others. There's a proliferation of store-front businesses set up as "schools" in every city and many towns.

There are also persons skilled in martial arts who offer instruction at rates lower than those charged by the schools. They can do this because they have no

Deep Inside the Underground Economy
How Millions of Americans Are Practicing Free Enterprise in An Unfree Society

216

overhead. They hold the sessions in their homes, or in open areas, such as parks.

Jim is a practitioner of an obscure Chinese form of karate. Each Saturday, he and his "class" gather on a field in a park downtown. At this time, people are either out shopping or still asleep, and the park isn't crowded. He holds two-hour-long sessions, with eight to twelve students attending. Of course, he collects in cash. He lives in a university town, and most of his clients are students who saw the cards he put up on the display boards spotted around the campus, or heard of him from friends.

This is an example of a low-key and successful effort at earning untraceable extra income by using a skill originally acquired for other purposes. It's labor-intensive, which means no supplies to buy, and is consequently pure profit.

There is a danger — liability. Even the most competent instructor can't supervise his students closely enough to avoid any chance of injury, and they sometimes happen. It's possible to forestall a lawsuit by having the students sign releases beforehand, but an angry injured party with a smart lawyer can work around any paperwork and carry a suit through. This doesn't mean that he'll win, but he can give the defendant a very bad time for the months or years it takes for the legalisms to run themselves out.

The most attractive aspect is the money, of course. With no overhead, it's possible to undercut the established schools by a wide margin. Even a ridiculously low rate of five dollars an hour will bring, with ten students, fifty an hour pure profit for the instructor. The cost of advertising is nil. Not declaring the income enables the undergrounder to keep it all.

Moving Company

An informal moving van service is possible even in the largest cities. One successful outfit operated in New York City, where the regulations on businesses are almost unbelievable. These people operated very much like gypsy cab operators, but with a slightly different twist. As students, they were able to appeal to other students, and to solicit their business. Their competitive position was based entirely on price, and they were able to charge about one-third of the commercial movers' rates and make a good profit. This was because they had no overhead, and operated smaller trucks.

Part of the overhead which they passed up was insurance, a must for a commercial mover. This limited their business slightly, in that they paid for any dam-age out of their own pockets, and had to pass up any delicate or especially valuable items. This wasn't much of a problem, because fellow students, their main sources of business, didn't have many valuable or delicate items.

Not having any sort of business license didn't bother them, and they mostly passed unmolested by police and public inspectors. The advantage of anonymity a huge city provides, added to the saturation of the public services, helped to ensure that they remained officially unseen, economizing on another set of overhead expenses.

It's not necessary to have a large moving van, with its high cost and running expenses. A large van simply helps in carrying several jobs at a time, but if you're willing to take them one by one, you can get by very well.

Charging low prices means that you're more likely to get paid in cash, which helps your low profile. You may need some hired help for the jobs. Hiring them on a contract basis is the best way to go, and this will enable you to pay them well and yet not be overwhelmed by employee expenses.

Painting

Debbie, the painter, learned her skill working in the maintenance department of a large hospital. She had a pick-up truck, and on her days off she worked at painting jobs for individuals to earn extra money. When she became a new mother, she used her painting skills to earn undeclared income for her new family.

This is a prospect for the truly small undergrounder. The investment is not very great, and indeed if you decide to go into it, you probably already have most of the hard equipment you'll need, such as brushes, rollers, and a ladder. You'll buy supplies, such as paints, brushes, and thinners, as you need them and for each job.

Needing fresh supplies for each job is an important plus factor for you. Not only does it minimize your investment, but patronizing one favorite supplier gives you an excellent opportunity to get rid of your checks. Because painting often runs into hundreds of dollars, you can expect to be paid by check for most of your jobs.

You don't really need a truck. A station wagon will do, or even a passenger car with a roof rack to hold a ladder.

The odds are that you already have the skills needed to be a house painter, as almost anyone has done some painting at some time in his or her life. What you probably lack is the array of professional short-cuts that help to make painting profitable for the pros. You can either pick these up as you go, or learn them through apprenticeship to a painter.

Advertising can be any or all of three ways:

1. Word-of-mouth.
2. Cards on display boards. In this regard, one experienced painter suggests claiming that you're a "student who needs work," because this will induce more people to hire you. Supposedly student labor comes cheaply, or at least many think so.
3. Canvassing, as you walk through a neighborhood and solicit business door-to-door. "Cold canvassing," as salesmen call it, is not as futile as it normally is because as you walk through a block, you can see which houses need painting. Any house with cracked and peeling paint can mean one of two things: It's due for a paint job, and there's a prospect for you; or the owner doesn't care, and you can't sell him.

Certain neighborhoods are run-down, with many shoddy-looking houses. These are poor prospects. Others are better looking, and you have a better than even chance.

As word-of-mouth and personal references are all-important, your main task will be to "crack" a block and hustle the first job. Once you've done that, and painted the exterior of a house, your workmanship is there for all to see. You can then canvass every other house on the block, using your first job as an advertisement, and solicit interior work, too.

There's a bad side to it, too. You should be aware that not all is rosy and lucrative in this business. Some people just don't want to pay, believe it or not. There are also disagreements as to exactly what the job is to involve. Be cautious. Be realistic, and you'll have an easier time of it, as well as fewer disappointments.

Pet Sitting

This is one of the most neglected fields in the country. Many people with pets can't or don't want to take them on vacation with them. Their choices are either to ask a friend or neighbor to watch their pets while they're way, or to board them with a kennel or vet.

Pet sitting requires no monetary investment, a little time, and a genuine love of animals. The best way to do it is to offer to look in on a client's pet once or twice a day as required, not to board the pet at your home. This is because boarding pets can be difficult. You'll have to set aside an area for them, buy cages, clean up after them, etc., and keeping a large number of animals in or around your home may attract undue attention. It may also be impossible if you're an apartment dweller and the landlord doesn't allow pets. Caring for the pet at the client's home is usually more acceptable than transporting it to your home.

Advertising is by word-of-mouth and by cards on display boards. Since you'll need access to the client's home, he'll be concerned about your reliability and honesty. This means that word-of-mouth will be more effective.

The client will surely want to meet with you to introduce you to his pet, explain its care and any special needs, and to hand over his keys. Any pet owner who cares for his animal will be watching very carefully the interaction between you and his pet. He'll want his pet to get good care, and won't want to leave it in the charge of someone who will be neglectful or who doesn't care for animals. This means that you must be a genuine animal lover, something almost impossible to fake. A pet owner will see through insincerity immediately, and the animal will be able to sense if you don't like or are afraid of it.

Payment can be by cash or check, and can be pure profit. Most likely, you won't have to buy food, because the pet owner will have laid in a stock of food, enough to last while he's away. If not, you can buy food, save the receipts, and expect reimbursement upon the client's return. You might, though, consider including food in your service.

Look the animal over very carefully each day, to observe any signs of illness. If there's a problem, the client will expect you to take the initiative and get veterinary care. It's a good idea to ask for the name of his veterinarian when taking the job, which will show that you're thinking of the animal's welfare. This may even avoid your having to lay out money if a visit to the vet becomes necessary, because you'll be able to tell the vet to charge the fee to your client.

Veterinarians, usually more ethical and caring about their patients' welfare than medical doctors, are not a problem. If the client doesn't have a regular vet, it's safe to pick one out of the phone book. However, the chances are that you have a pet of your own, and know a vet whom you trust.

Be prepared to spend some time with the pet each day, talking to and playing with it. The animal's emotional well being is important too, and many pets like

Deep Inside the Underground Economy
How Millions of Americans Are Practicing Free Enterprise in An Unfree Society

218

attention. This is part of handing the pet back to the owner in the same condition as you got it, and will enhance your reputation.

Opportunistic Photography

If photography is your job or hobby, or if you own a fairly good camera, you may want to try opportunistic photography. This means carrying a camera with you at all times and photographing accidents, fires, and other newsworthy events.

At best, this is an uncertain business, and definitely not worth any investment apart from a roll of film. Accidents and fires occur unpredictably, although there are some ways to increase the odds in your favor. If you get photographs of a major accident, you can sell them to a newspaper if you act quickly, and to an insurance company later on, which can earn you several hundreds of dollars. The major concerns for such an enterprise are these:

- Carry a camera at all times, because you never can tell when the opportunity will come. If this is inconvenient, forget it.
- Keep it loaded with a full (36-exposure if it's a 35 mm camera) roll of film. Avoid odd sizes. The best choices of film are Kodak Plus-X or Tri-X. The reason is that these are commonly available and in wide use, and that the newspaper darkroom technician will know how to process these films.
- If it's a digital camera, make sure your batteries are fully charged.
- Keep an ear out for sirens, and of course, watch for fires. Remember that the media are interested only in major occurrences, not fender-benders and dumpster fires. The philosophy of "body bag journalism" means that: "If it bleeds, it leads."
- When an accident occurs, get photographs of everything. The newspaper technician will develop it all, whether it's full or whether you've left twenty frames blank. The usual plan is to shoot several long shots, from at least four different angles, to show the accident scene and surroundings. Then close in, taking shots of each car, any victims, and close-ups of the sheet metal damage. You need close-ups for the news and longer shots for the insurance company or lawyer.
- The media are interested mainly in dramatic shots, although most of them don't want "blood and guts" photos. The insurance investigators are interested in static shots that show the positions of the cars, bodies, etc., right after the accident, before anyone moves the bodies or tows away the cars. These long shots, showing the cars in relation to surrounding buildings, curbs, traffic lanes, etc., are critical for legal settlements.

- As you're shooting, notice any other photographers on the scene. If you see the photographer from one newspaper, you'll know not to offer your pictures to that one.
- Before leaving the scene, look for the cop with the clipboard. He's the one doing the police report, a copy of which will go to the lawyer and the insurance investigator. Leave your card with the cop, and tell him that you have photographs of the scene. If the police later contact you and ask for a set of prints, let them have the shots, to foster a spirit of cooperation. It's helpful to be on good terms with the cops, since they can let you through the police line if they like you, which makes your task easier.
- Take the film down to your local newspaper right away. Ask to speak to the city editor, and tell him what you've got. If he's interested, he'll take the film from you and have his technician develop and print it. Make sure that you negotiate a price before you leave. He may hedge, saying that he can't offer you a price until he sees what you've got, a reasonable bargaining position, but stick around until he sees the photos, and get an agreement before leaving. If, for some reason, it's not acceptable to you, you can always take the film elsewhere.
- Even a television station may buy your black and white photos if they didn't have a camera crew covering the event.
- Having your own darkroom is helpful for selling prints to insurance companies or lawyers. If you don't have one, at least get a contact sheet made, to show what you have available. You can always sell the negatives, or have prints made once you've got an offer from the lawyer or investigator. Remember that it's best to sell prints, not negatives, because in a serious case that results in long and expensive litigation, you can sell the same photos to both sides. If you're using digital, the chances are you already have a computer for processing and printing your pictures.
- If you're doing well in this business, you may consider buying an inexpensive scanner to enable you to listen in to fire and police radio calls. This can be an advantage, although in reality you may

not be free to go to all of the calls you hear, because you're at work or have another obligation.

This opportunistic business, while it can be remunerative at times, is uncertain. You can't make a living at it, but it can earn you extra money to pay for a lot of goodies. The odds are that you won't earn enough to attract the attention of the IRS. The big disadvantage is that you'll almost invariably get paid by check, but you can always "launder" the checks.

Produce for Retail

In old neighborhoods in eastern cities, we used to see produce trucks and pushcarts selling on the streets. The economics of mass merchandising have pretty well knocked these small business owners out of the field. However, some people are still selling produce at retail and working out of their trucks.

One man, working in Chicago, went in his truck to pick up fresh produce each morning and sold it successfully out of his truck in neighborhoods that didn't have good supermarkets conveniently close by. It cost residents more in time and travel expenses to go to a less expensive source than to buy from him.

One woman ran an even lower-profile operation. She sold her garden vegetables to her friends and neighbors.

Running this sort of operation requires knowing the prices in a shifting, seasonal market. It also calls for a reliable vehicle. Advertising is nil, because you advertise from your truck. If you're successful, people will come out to buy when your familiar truck arrives on the block.

It's necessary to keep to a regular schedule to build the confidence of the customers. It's also vital to stock only high-quality produce. One customer dissatisfied with a purchase can bad-mouth you enough to hurt you. You'll offend fewer people with high prices than you will with low quality or wilted produce.

There isn't much profit in these operations, but it's possible to run them in a way that frees you from taxes. A modest side-line, bringing in enough money to supplement your regular income, may be all that you need. The overhead is small; gas and maintenance for the truck, and some paper bags. You will also need a portable scale to weigh the produce for your customers. Without a business license and other paperwork, you'll be free to earn more profit.

One variation still seen very often is the farmer who retails his watermelons or other produce from his truck at the side of the road. This is a weekend af-

fair, when there are many holiday-goers on the roads. Since this is a direct-to-consumer operation, the farmer can charge higher prices than he customarily gets from his wholesalers, and the customers pay less than they do in supermarkets. Usually the goods are fresher, too.

Rebates and Coupons

This is an extremely low-profile operation that can net you a few tax-free dollars each month with not much work. Manufacturers' rebates are part of their merchandizing operations, along with their coupon offers. The two tie in together because while you're looking for one, you can scan for the other.

It's important to be realistic about this. You won't earn much money, but it will be easy money. The pennies add up, though, and you'll find it worthwhile to keep in mind the old saying: "Don't work hard, work smart." See *The Mother Earth News Handbook of Home Business Ideas and Plans* (1976) for some good suggestions.

Stockpiling Precious Metal

Precious metals are easy to buy over-the-counter. Even a person who knows little about gold or silver can obtain gold or silver coins with little chance of being swindled if he's even moderately prudent.

Precious metals hold their value, in the sense that they don't deteriorate in storage. Twenty years is a short time. Many companies here today will not exist in twenty years! This long life is an advantage for someone who seeks an investment but doesn't follow the market. Investing in stocks requires a daily follow-up, as they are very volatile.

Another feature about precious metals is their stability and uniformity. There are standards for purity, and values are easy to calculate based on the form of the metal. Knowing the price of gold per ounce enables anyone to calculate the price various forms of gold. Some come in convenient forms, such as the South African Krugerrands, each weighing one troy ounce.

Unloading your investment is relatively hassle-free, especially if you hold it in the form of coins. These are ready-made increments that will pass anywhere in the country, and in many places outside the borders. Bullion is harder to unload, because unless it is accompanied by paperwork, which means that your possession of it is documented and registered, you'll have to have it assayed, which will cost several percent of its value.

Deep Inside the Underground Economy
How Millions of Americans Are Practicing Free Enterprise in An Unfree Society

220

The nuts and bolts of investing in gold or silver are relatively easy. Buy coins. There are several sources for these, the worst being small dealers, because they have already taken the maximum profit possible. Private individuals are the best, especially if you know them, because they're more likely to be open to negotiation. Buy small amounts from many different people to attract less attention. You'll also preserve your anonymity by paying cash, and this would be difficult if the amount were very large.

Another prospect to consider is government confiscation. In 1933, it became illegal for private citizens to own gold. It's not paranoid to suspect that if the government did it once, it might do it again. You then might be happy that your stockpile of precious metal was untraceable to you. You also have to consider that, as in 1933, coins might be exempt, which would leave you clear.

The best way to store precious metals, especially if you fear burglary or confiscation, is burial. The metals don't rust, and the possibility of tarnish is easy to overcome by wrapping in plastic.

Unfortunately, government agents have metal detectors, and if a radical confiscation law comes about, you might have cause to worry. Detection of buried metal can be impeded by littering the burial site with scrap metal, such as nuts and bolts and machine parts, and burying the precious metal deeper. An agent with a metal detector will become discouraged after getting several "hits," digging them up, and finding only scrap metal. With only a little luck, he'll stop before he gets to your cache.

Sperm Bank

The number of sperm banks in this country is tiny compared to blood banks, but if you're a male, and live near one, you can earn some extra money from occasional "contributions."

Donors must meet certain standards. They must be in good health, and must have good sperm motility. Good health means not having VD or an Rh factor. This is occasional work, but it's extra income for doing what most people do anyway. Getting paid for it is icing on the cake.

Stringer

This applies only to people who already are in the fields of radio or writing, not those wanting to enter those fields. There are many "writers' schools" and "broadcasting schools" that earn money by providing questionable instruction to anyone who can afford their fees. Most who take these courses are doomed to disappointment, because the operators of these schools are simply not honest with their students. Typically, they have the candidate take an "aptitude test," and no matter how badly he does, they tell him that he's got "potential" and that their courses will enable him to fulfill this potential.

If you're not already working in the field, or have no experience, don't bother with any of this.

The "stringer" is a moonlighter, working part-time or full-time. He's not on the staff, but gets paid by the job, or piece. If this is your choice, keep in mind that your work has to compete with that of people who are on the staff, which may not be as hard as it seems.

The rationale behind employing stringers is that it's uneconomical to have reporters in every location. A part-timer, if he's on the spot and gets an exclusive story, can compete with the pros, even though his reporting may not be as polished as that of the regulars. Both radio stations and the print media also need "fillers," which the stringer can provide.

If you're working full-time as a radio reporter, your boss may or may not permit you to supply material to other stations. He'll see them as competition, and if you work for another station, this will be a form of disloyalty. However, if you make contacts with stations out of your area, he may not mind.

Radio reporting is a high-profile occupation. Your voice goes out to anyone who can hear. This makes it impossible to hide from your boss or from the IRS. IRS agents listen to the radio too, and one of them may be working on your file next year. No matter how well you can launder your checks (and they all pay by check), you'll be up against it if ever you're audited. Indeed, one very valuable suggestion is to put aside some of the stringer income to pay taxes.

Writing

This is not the place to tell you how to write for profit, because this would require a book. I recommend James Wilson's *Freelance Writer's Handbook* (Loompanics Unlimited, 2001). If you haven't written professionally, but feel that you have a "feel" for words, you can dip your toe into the water with very little effort and investment. If you already own a typewriter or computer, or can borrow one, the cost of materials and postage will be your only "investment." If not, ask yourself if you want to make a capital investment without having tried your skill.

How lucrative can writing be? Very much so, with the skill, the right contacts, and luck. Almost every aspect of it is in your favor, if you earn money at it.

The greatest advantage of writing is that it's low-profile work. Your name does not have to go on the piece. Many authors use pen-names, and here's why:
1. To avoid taxes, obviously.
2. To avoid complications from their employers or publishers. Some magazine editors or publishers have unfair policies, in that they require an author to sign a contract that stipulates that he will not write for anyone else. Some contracts are less restrictive, in the sense that they require an author only not to write a similar work for anyone else. The reason for this is that the editor or publisher does not want the author helping his competitors, or writing a piece that may hurt the sales of material he publishes. Nevertheless, many publishers do have several competing authors in their "stables," and seem to feel that this is standard operating procedure.

Yet other editors have an unwritten policy of "Anyone who writes for another publication will never write for me." A pen-name is the author's only protection.

If the writer has a distinctive style, this may betray him. A publisher who scrutinizes the competition's output may recognize it, and confront the author with it. This is not as serious a problem as it might seem at first, because an author can, if he's competent, change his style when writing for other publishers.

Payment is always by check, posing a slight problem. You can launder checks, but only if you're truly a part-timer, and the payments from any one source are small. The IRS requires a payer to file a Form 1099 for all payees earning more than $1000 per year. Most play it safely and file a 1099 for all, regardless of the amount. Getting around this requires a little more work. The procedure is roughly as follows.

Use an assumed name in all dealings. Work out of a mail drop, and remember that renting a post office box under an assumed name is illegal. You can, of course, receive mail under another name at a box rented in your true one, but this attracts attention, and you may have the postal inspectors on your back, scrutinizing your affairs to determine if you're doing something illegal. In any event, they may notify the IRS.

With the assumed name goes a false Social Security number, since many publishers require this information before they'll cut a check. This ruse will work for about one year, because at the end of the year the publisher turns in his Form 1099s, and this may lead to awkward questions. The practical result is that the author must use many names, which complicates his problem. Many publishers will be wary of accepting work from unknown authors, and the underground striver will have to "break in" with each new name.

Toys

There is a market for wooden toys. These are usually handmade, which gives them additional value. We need to clarify the meaning of "handmade," though.

It means turned out by an individual, in a "cottage industry" setting, not mass-produced in a large factory. The factory product might even be better, but today there's a reaction against the many stamped-out and injection-molded plastic products, and many people will value a "hand-made" item more.

As a sideline, this can be very worthwhile, especially since the schedule required fits right in with the jobholder's. People attend fairs and craft shows on their days off, obviously, and these usually fall on weekends and holidays.

Wake-Up Service

There are many telephone-based services, from telephone sex to Dial-a-Prayer. The ones of interest to you are those you can operate from your home, and remain unnoticed by the tax people. One such is a phone wake-up call service, and people around the country have started this shoestring operation.

Some people try waking their clients up with fancy sound effects, which can be a useful gimmick, but another idea is the call-back. A very good selling point is to tell your customers that you'll call them back fifteen minutes after the wake-up call, to make sure that they're up and haven't rolled over and dozed off again.

Will this work in your area? Do your fellow-employees complain of not being able to wake up, or of sleeping through the alarm? Another way to find out is through a classified ad. If you get a few bites, you're on your way. The investment for you is really nothing. You almost surely have a phone already, and the only additional charges on your bill will be for calls to your accounts.

How big can this business get? Obviously, not so big that you spend all morning making calls, and

Deep Inside the Underground Economy
How Millions of Americans Are Practicing Free Enterprise in An Unfree Society

222

don't have time to get ready for work. If it is successful, you can enlist your wife or children to make calls. If this takes off enough, you'll find that an investment in a second phone line is worthwhile.

Window Washing

This is a good street trade that you can build into a more regular business. It requires minimal investment, and there are many potential customers out there. Window washing requires very little skill, and is easy to learn. It doesn't pay very well, but the tax-free part is the best advantage.

Advertising is by word-of-mouth, display boards, and cold canvassing. Classified ads don't seem to work as well. An advantage of this trade is the repeat business from satisfied customers, something not possible in many other fields. In this regard, it definitely pays to have business cards printed.

Appendix Two
False Starts and Dead Ends

If you're reading this book, then the chances are that you've read others on how to make money. Some of them are realistic, while others are simply mad fantasies. Some promise immense profits to the person who buys and reads the book. A few go so far as to promise that the reader will immediately become fabulously rich without doing any work. The advertisements don't discuss the chances of success and failure. They don't tell you that certain special conditions make their advice impractical for most people.

It's easy to write a come-on. Imagine an ad that says:

"SURE-FIRE WAY TO INSTANT MILLIONS."

It can be perfectly truthful, but of no help to anyone, because the response, when a sucker sends in his money, is: "Be born rich." That's true, but as practical advice it's about as useful as a condom with ventilation holes.

One question to ask yourself, when you see a book advertised promising you instant wealth in a foolproof way, is: "If this method's so good, what's this guy doing writing a book about it?" In other words: "Why is he wasting his time at the relatively unremunerative craft of writing when he could be out making millions with his sure-fire method?"

Another question: "How many other people have read this book?" Do you really think he's offering the method to you and you alone? What will be the effect of hundreds or even thousands of competitors in the field? Will there be anything left for you?

Also, how many people do you know who have gotten rich from reading a book? I mean people you actually know: friends, neighbors, people with whom you work. How did they do it? Will they tell you their "secret"? Did they get it out of a book?

Real life is different.

Many books will claim to have "systems" that will enable you to get great wealth immediately and without risk. Unfortunately, that's just not true. Business is risky. Small business is very risky. Most small businesses fold within five years.

One very realistic book is *Make Money By Moonlighting*, by Jack Lander. This 307-page volume, published by Enterprise Publishing, Inc., Wilmington, DE, lays out in a very practical manner the real-life problems and rewards of striking out on your own.

Other Traps

There are other, more subtle traps. An example is the hypothetical estimate of the money you can earn at a certain pursuit. It's easy to write down figures such as: "With a purchase price of $1 each, and a selling price of $2, selling one thousand units a day will get you a gross profit of $1,000!"

That's perfectly true, but it's based on a hypothetical numbers game, not a real case, or a real volume of sales. How do you know that you'll sell 1,000 units per day? What will your advertising costs be?

Another trap is an overly conservative estimate of the amount of work required. Many businesses, especially franchises, are of the type that require the operator to put in twelve to fourteen hours per day, more than five days per week. Many people, seeing a business opportunity for the first time, see only the potential profits, and not the problems that require them to put in prodigious amounts of time.

In fact, some seemingly lucrative businesses do provide good incomes, but if you calculate the hourly wage, the picture is quite different. The small entrepreneur often becomes a slave to his business, and wishes that he were back working for a wage because a regular job wouldn't consume so much of his time.

Deep Inside the Underground Economy
How Millions of Americans Are Practicing Free Enterprise in An Unfree Society

224

Beware of Brokers

There's a plethora of books advising readers on "sure-fire" ways to get rich in real estate or the stock market. These books emphasize the positive aspects, some to the point of dishonesty. Some never mention the drawbacks and risks involved in their money-making plans.

The biggest drawback in real estate or stock market schemes is the broker. To buy or sell anything in either field, it's necessary to deal through a broker. The broker doesn't work for free. He gets a commission on every sale. This brings out one of the outstanding and annoying characteristics of brokers — they encourage people to buy and sell, giving them "tips" about hot new properties, and other inducements. Their money is not at risk. They gain from each deal.

Some brokers carry this to an extreme, operating "boiler rooms" filled with telephone sales people to generate business for them. Anyone considering dealing in real estate or the stock market should keep this in mind before making any deals.

The media, spoon-fed information by stockbrokers, perpetuate the myth that an active market is a sign of economic health. In one sense, it is. An active market, with many people buying and selling, is very healthy for the brokers. The traders, however, all have to pay commissions on whatever they earn. In one sense, commissions are worse than taxes. The IRS only taxes income, and someone who loses money on a deal doesn't have to pay taxes on it. But the broker collects his commission, win or lose, rain or shine. An investor with a stock holding that takes a catastrophic downturn probably will hear his broker advise him to dump it immediately, and cut his losses. Of course. The broker earns himself another commission while the investor takes a bath.

A major disadvantage of the broker system is that all transactions are documented. This shuts out people in the underground economy. While many investors deal in stocks or real estate as tax dodges, exploiting the many loopholes, they can't hide a cent of any income, but must find ways to shelter it to avoid taxes. This massive documentation is a horror to the guerrilla capitalist. Most prefer to avoid it.

Traps to Avoid: "Make Money At Home" Schemes

You may have noticed advertisements urging readers to send for details of various methods that promise hundreds of dollars a month in extra income. The ads are aimed at housewives and retirees, and don't give a hint of the difficulties involved.

Some of these are for "pyramid selling" schemes, in which the person starting out is required to buy large stocks of items to sell door-to-door, or by mail. The alleged large volume comes only if you can recruit other people to buy from you and sell the items retail themselves. These schemes are not necessarily frauds in themselves, but the potential for profits is limited.

There are a number which are out-and-out frauds (see *The Rip-Off Book*, by Victor Santoro, 1984), and the Postal Inspection Service has been prosecuting some of them. These usually involve addressing envelopes or manufacturing small items at home. The way they work is to require either a deposit from the victim, or the purchase of supplies with which to run the business. If the scheme requires manufacturing small items, supposedly at a tremendous profit, the company will reject all of the items on the grounds of "defective workmanship," thereby leaving the victim holding the bag. In other schemes, for a fee the victim receives instructions on how to run the business and how to make the product, but he soon finds out that he has to dig up customers on his own, and this proves very difficult indeed.

If you're tempted to answer such an ad, the most important question to ask yourself is: "Why, if this is such a good way of making money, isn't this guy doing it himself instead of sharing his secret with others?" You'll find a common thread running through all these schemes. The ads promise "instant millions" and "sure-fire results," and it is easy to wonder why the advertiser isn't doing it himself and getting richer instead of offering to help others get rich.

One type of ad is the "address envelopes" ad, which promises you an attractive rate of pay for addressing envelopes. This is very appealing and attracts a lot of suckers. These ads have been running for decades, which means there's some money in this business for the person running the ad. The problem is that the outfit running the ad doesn't actually provide work, but merely a set of instructions on how to address envelopes and perhaps a list of direct-mail companies to contact. Unfortunately, envelope addressing by machine is far cheaper than with human labor, and there's very little market for this service for the person working at home. Another drawback is that companies usually pay by check, which brings a problem to the undergrounder.

Some of the ads are unbelievable in their tone. One ad showed the president of the company as an altruistic character. He had discovered the basic secret to making big bucks and wanted to share it with his fellow suffering humans before departing from this earth, but the ad required you to send him a deposit to find out how he did it.

At your local post office, you'll find leaflets put out by the Postal Inspection Service, explaining exactly how these frauds work, and why people who respond to them don't make any money, and lose the deposits they send in. If you see an offer that seems so good to you you're afraid of passing it up, phone the postal inspector in your area before mailing off your money. You might be surprised at what he has to say about it, and the price of the phone call will be much less than what you risk losing if the ad is fraudulent.

More Warnings

Another enticement is the "blind ad" that often appears in the classified section of the newspaper. This sort of ad doesn't specify the type of work, and often doesn't even list the company. It promises a high rate of pay for anyone who responds, and specifies that no experience is required. It might even specify that there's no selling.

The first and most obvious problem with this sort of ad is that if the offering were really as lucrative and easy as it promises, there'd be no need to advertise. They'd have no trouble finding and retaining people. What the ad doesn't say is always as significant as what it does. There's usually a cash investment required, and the business is merely the bottom end of a pyramid selling scheme, in which whoever answers the ad is really the ultimate customer, and buys a large inventory which then sits unsold in his garage.

Another possibility is that such a blind ad is a come-on for an unattractive door-to-door selling scheme. In one instance, an ad for a "Part-time Personnel Manager" was a come-on for a vacuum cleaner sales company.

Such jobs are not really jobs. In every instance, even with the large and reputable direct sales companies such as Fuller Brush, the applicant signs a contract which states that he's an independent dealer, and buys the products at a discount and sells them to the customers. "You eat what you sell" is the principle, as the dealer's income is by direct commission, and dependent on how much he sells.

Summing up, we see that these blind ads are enticements for "jobs" that are so undesirable that nobody would respond if the ad stated the offering outright.

Dead Ends

Here are some ways NOT to earn hidden income, because you can waste a lot of time pursuing these dead ends. Some of these are superficially very attractive, but require so much work that they're essentially losers.

This quick survey of impractical methods of getting into the underground economy gives you some guidelines as to why some businesses are suitable, and why others fail the purpose. The reasons are very simple:

☐ Method of payment
☐ Local laws
☐ Additional licenses and paperwork required
☐ Infraction of criminal codes.

Animal Breeding

A good backyard business, it requires an investment in expensive breeding stock. Pedigreed cats or dogs are simply not cheap, easily costing hundreds of dollars apiece. There's the cost of food and veterinary care, and the need for national advertising in animal magazines. The paperwork required for the pedigreed animals creates a trail, as does payment by check, the most common way in which customers will pay.

Diploma Mills

There are some enterprising business owners selling college-level diplomas by mail from states with loose laws. These have created a slight scandal, and a crackdown is overdue.

This is a mail order business, and the need for advertising is a serious weakness, which can bring the postal inspectors (you don't mess with those boys) down on the backs of diploma millers.

The biggest problem with this business is that payment is not in cash. Again, that paper trail.

Deep Inside the Underground Economy
How Millions of Americans Are Practicing Free Enterprise in An Unfree Society

226

Drugs

Although this book is not a guide to criminal activities, it's necessary to mention briefly illegal drug dealing, since this has proved profitable for some. Be warned that drug dealing can land you in very serious trouble, a good reason for earning tax-free money another way. Dealing in illegal drugs, like prostitution, is a classic underground business, but it has risks for anyone in it, especially for the big dealers and wholesalers. However, on a very low level, it can earn a modest profit for the part-timer.

Jack lives in the East Village in New York, sharing a "pad" with his girlfriend. Like some of the other tenants in his walk-up apartment house, he grows a few marijuana plants in window boxes. This is a relatively safe sideline, because:

1. He runs a small operation, and doesn't threaten any of the big dealers.
2. The small size of his trade makes him an unprofitable target for the "narcs," who have more serious "clients" on their minds.
3. He sells only to long-time friends, thereby avoiding undercover narcs who otherwise might trip over him.
4. Many people, even police officers, feel that marijuana is a relatively innocuous recreational drug, and some go so far as to feel that it should be decriminalized. Even the most hard-core police officer has to recognize that the "hard drugs," such as heroin and other opiates, are more serious problems.

Employment Agency

This is an excellent example of the type of business you can't work underground, and it's included here to show you some of the problems. While superficially, starting an employment agency can be written up in such a way as to make it seem attractive, the obstacles are too many to work this as an underground enterprise.

First, in most states employment agencies must be licensed. Failure to do so can easily result in prosecution, and there's every chance of getting caught. Licensing requirements are often onerous, requiring a certain amount of experience in the field and the posting of a bond.

The mainstay of running an employment agency is advertising in the classified section of the local newspaper. This puts your business out for the world to see. You can be sure that operators of other agencies read each other's ads. If they see a newcomer, they'll turn him in if he's not licensed, thereby eliminating a competitor.

Also, to advertise jobs it is necessary to find out about positions that are open. For this you need contacts inside the various companies in your area. The other agencies will already have these contacts locked up tightly. They do this by a system of kickbacks, offering part of the high fees they collect to the person who lists the jobs with them. This is the real reason why employment agency fees are so high. They are state-regulated, but are high nevertheless.

Operating an employment agency is an unethical and cut-throat business, and few people feel comfortable with it. For the undergrounder, it's an impossible situation, because the business is necessarily out in the open, the only underground aspect being the payments he has to make to the people who list openings with him.

Hustling Discount Coupons

Some hustlers, sharp-talking salesmen, have persuaded merchants to subscribe to their coupon mailing services. To stimulate sales on slow days, the merchants offer discounts, two-for-one deals, etc., which are printed in coupon form on cheap paper and mailed in bulk by the hustlers. This was a successful idea several years ago, but enough merchants have been burned by now to make this a dying craft. It's also not tax-free, since these merchants pay by check, to have a permanent record for their tax returns, and this creates the old paper trail again.

Importing Mexican Fuel

Because Mexican gasoline and diesel fuels are quite a bit less expensive than fuels sold in the United States, there's been some fuel smuggling across the border. To make it pay, it's necessary to deal in volume, not a couple of liters that will fit in the bottom of a suitcase. Smuggling a thousand gallons across the border is not as easy as smuggling a couple of pounds of dope. It's also an affront to the U.S. Border Patrol, who take smugglers very, very seriously.

Mercenary

This is another excellent example of what to avoid. While there is a slew of "armchair macho" magazines on the racks glorifying mercenaries, the reality is far different than the image.

A mercenary is not a regular soldier. He's hired only when there's fighting to do. The hard fact is that you can lose your life, which you may consider the highest rate of taxation possible. The money won't do you any good if you're dead.

You may read that mercenary work is worthwhile for some people. The trouble is finding it. Some of the "merc mags" are full of ads for mercenaries that are simply rip-offs. They promise "job listings" to the reader who sends his ten or fifty dollars. Many of these are located in foreign countries, and recourse for the person who's been ripped off is difficult.

It's necessary to have practical experience to become a merc. Even armed forces experience is not enough, in many instances. The real mercenary jobs depend a lot on personal contacts. The real professional soldiers for pay want men whom they know to be reliable, not flakes. That's why they tend to pick men they've served with in one force or another. Occasionally, they may need more men than they can find, and have to choose among some unknown quantities.

This is where the well-known ruthlessness of the professional soldier shows. They'll organize their force into two units. The first will be the reliable men, who are often also their friends. The second one will be the strangers, whose prowess they doubt. The second unit will get the dirty jobs, the suicide attacks, the diversionary roles, while the real professionals take the attack which offers the best chances of survival.

Some who find merc work attractive are those who don't like discipline, and who resent the formal organization of regular units. However, discipline is a necessary part of any armed force. The French Foreign Legion, which is a true mercenary force, is famous for its discipline, more rigid than that of the French and many other armies. They wear uniforms, have to salute, obey regulations, and anyone who fails to maintain discipline faces strict punishment.

The occasional merc force that has little discipline is likely to be a collection of flakes. The leaders are likely to be simply incompetent. The uniform does not make the soldier, and a pair of paratrooper boots and cammos do not make a merc. These are the people who are likely to get you killed.

Getting paid is often a serious problem in merc work. It's necessary to scrutinize the employer carefully, to rate his ability to pay. The employer may be a penniless revolutionary party, without the funds to pay the troops. The party officials may yet try to re-cruit mercs, calculating that most of them won't live to collect their pay. If the employer is a foreign government, its currency may not be worth the paper on which it's printed.

You, as a merc, owe no loyalty to your employer, except to fight his battles. You may not even have to take an oath of allegiance, just sign a contract. In return, he owes you no loyalty. If you're captured by the enemy, he will not try to free you, or negotiate for your exchange or release. You will simply find yourself in front of a firing squad if you're caught. Enough mercenaries have been executed out of hand for this to be a well-established procedure.

Another aspect of this is the possible abandonment of your unit by the employer, if he feels it expedient.

The only attractive part of merc work is that money you earn outside of the United States is not taxable if you spend a certain period of time away. For the IRS, it's untraceable, even if you are away for only a few weeks. Unfortunately, it may be heavily taxable in the country where you "work."

This is a risky, overglamorized occupation. While some do find it lucrative, because they have the background and the contacts, most seekers of merc work find only disappointment.

Motocross Speedway

Superficially an attractive idea, because it's a cash business, the need for licenses make it impractical as a tax dodge. There's also the problem of liability insurance.

Painting House Numbers on Curbs

In new developments, this can work, but these days most builders paint the house numbers on when they build the houses.

Porno Film Developing

A quick look through any of the "men's" or porno magazines will reveal that "confidential film processing" is a business for some. However, the advent of digital cameras and camcorders has cut sharply into the porno film processing business.

There's also an extra hazard in this business. Postal inspectors are very aggressive in pursuing child porn purveyors, and you may find a 35mm cassette full of kiddie porn sent to you by a postal inspector. You develop it, and next day the postal inspectors are at your door with a search warrant. It's enough of a task managing an underground business without this problem.

Deep Inside the Underground Economy
How Millions of Americans Are Practicing Free Enterprise in An Unfree Society

228

Real Estate

This field is full of big promises and false hopes, as well as some opportunities to avoid taxes. A close examination will give you a chance to see some of the traps inherent in this field, and exactly why it's unsuitable for the underground worker.

There are many store-front "schools" that teach real estate law and practice, and they all claim that they can instruct you well enough to enable you to obtain your broker's license, and make big money. These schools seem to have no shortage of students. Also, real estate agencies often advertise for salesmen, citing encouraging examples of huge earnings possible by selling real estate.

However, look at the realities.

- Real estate schools and agencies are constantly teaching and hiring new people because there's a catastrophically high turnover rate in this field. This tells you that there's something seriously wrong, even without seeking further.
- The main reason for the high turnover rate is that, although a few elite salespeople do earn large amounts, most real estate salespersons starve and are forced to get out of the field quickly.
- The basic reason for lack of earnings is that this field pays on commission, not salary. In other words, you eat what you sell. This is very hard on the beginner.
- The heavy investment in education required taps the wage-earner's finances heavily, and reduces his financial reserves. This means that if he doesn't start making a living quickly, he'll have to seek something else.
- Another investment usually required is an expensive car. Many real estate agencies feel that it's important to project a picture of opulent success, and one way to do this is to use an expensive car to ferry potential clients when surveying property.
- Since income depends on commissions, the real estate person usually sees feast or famine. Sales are irregular, and the most successful brokers have months during which they earn fabulous commissions, and relatively dry months.

The main reason why real estate sales is unsuitable for the underground worker is that possibly no other field is so wrapped in paperwork. To buy or sell real property, it's necessary to have it appraised, recorded, inspected and approved, etc., etc. This entangling documentation makes it impossible to conceal income.

Finally, there are some minor advantages. Almost any sales job offers opportunities to take extra deductions on tax returns. "Padding" the expense account is common in many fields, and the cunning real estate salesperson may pad his. For example, it's common to take clients to lunch, and all the documentation the IRS requires is a receipt. The tax examiner has no way of knowing if the salesman really entertained a client, or a spouse.

Restoring Old Houses

For the handy person with little money, buying an old house and rebuilding it to almost new condition is one way of getting a home cheaply. It's even possible to sell it at a profit, and not pay capital gains tax by buying another home within a year. However, the paperwork involved in a real estate transaction is such that it's impossible to escape scot-free, and it'll be impossible to sell that last home without paying taxes.

Rubber Stamps

You'll often see ads claiming that there's big money to be made in the rubber stamp business, and offering you a kit of tools and supplies to set up. While it's true that it's easy to learn to make rubber stamps, and that the margin of profit is high, you'll be disappointed in how it works for you.

The major rubber stamp makers sell either directly or through dealers, such as stationery stores, at a discount to the dealers. They have a central plant, and picking up the work from the retailers and delivering the stamps is economical, because they're usually multiple orders.

Setting up a plant, no matter how small, requires at least a store front and the various business and tax licenses that go with it. You, working out of your home, will not have a network of dealers getting the business for you. You'll have to advertise directly, not only putting your head above water, but soliciting orders that may cost you more to fulfill than you can earn from them. You'll have to pick up and deliver them yourself, and this can consume enough time to wipe out your profit.

Realistically, these rubber stamp making ads are just come-ons to sell you the materials, and not pathways to easy money.

Selling Food and Drinks in Traffic Jams

This can and does work, but only if you have a convenient traffic jam close by. Motorists, tied up for hours and unable to leave their cars, will pay outrageous prices for sandwiches and drinks. Don't depend on it as a steady source of income. It's either feast or famine.

Sexual Phone Call Service

This service, while catering to a definite and ineradicable need, consists of placing ads in sexually-oriented magazines and taking calls. When the customer calls, the seller asks for his (or her) bankcard number, and if it checks out, calls the customer back to provide a telephoned masturbation fantasy. Some people earn a lot of money doing this, but it's not tax-free, because the bankcard transactions are conclusive evidence of income, down to the last dollar!

Shooting Ranges

This is a possible moneymaker, especially in areas where access to safe shooting spots is limited, but it's definitely not tax-free. Some people make it sound simple, but there are complications. It's not a matter of simply buying or renting a piece of land and installing targets. There's a need for liability insurance, if ever an accident happens, the resulting lawsuit can wipe the owner out. There's also a need for a business license, and perhaps a special permit in some jurisdictions.

Another economic fact about shooting ranges is that only part of the profit comes from renting space. More comes from having a shop on the premises to sell ammunition, accessories, and even rent guns to shooters. Any business concerning firearms and ammunition requires a dealer's license from the Bureau of Alcohol, Tobacco, and Firearms. All of this paperwork entangles the free enterpriser in an escape-proof net. The only possibility of earning tax-free money from a shooting range is by "skimming," as in any other business.

Taking People's Pictures on the Street

This used to be a street trade, but with the advent of instant-picture cameras, this business has died. How many do you see working the street these days? There are night-club photographers, but they are successful only in that limited environment, where judgment is affected by alcohol and the need to show off.

Tattooing

Forbidden by law in some areas, this is a means of extra income for some enterprisers. In places where it's permitted, tattoo artists have their own shops, which they prefer to call "studios." It's difficult to compete with them. Another problem with operating a clandestine tattoo service is that many people are concerned about catching a serious disease from unsterilized needles.

In areas where it's forbidden, there's not only a problem with concealing income, but one with the Board of Health. Finding customers is difficult, since any advertisement is visible to the police, and word-of-mouth is chancy with such a business.

Appendix Three
Striking Back at the IRS

If you're not satisfied with the extra earnings from safe and modest underground activities, you can try some bolder steps, such as bilking money directly from the Internal Revenue Service. This has become a cottage industry since the 1990s.

One way is to file fake income tax returns. A totally imaginary Form 1040 can net you several hundreds of dollars a pop in "refunds." However, keep in mind that this is a felony, and getting caught can have severe consequences. Unlike private concerns, the IRS does prosecute.

Guerrilla Warfare against the IRS

The IRS has been making a supreme effort on several fronts to track individuals and their money. Other agencies of the government have aided and abetted the IRS, not only to extract taxes, but to gain more control over individual lives, beginning literally at birth. As we've seen, children now must have Social Security numbers to be listed as exemptions on their parents' tax return. Bank accounts are monitored and large-scale financial transactions are reported to the IRS.

As well as obtaining more information about individuals, the IRS has been making a supreme effort to process this information, to build up as complete a picture as possible of each individual of interest to the agency. Powerful computers cross-check a huge number of records and forms to detect discrepancies, something that would be impossible to do manually today. (See Henry H. Philcox, "Modernizing the IRS," *The CPA Journal*, 60, no. 11, November 1990, p. 16)

However, the most powerful computer is no better than the information fed into it. The principle of "Garbage in, garbage out" (GIGO) is the key to degrading the effectiveness of the IRS's system.

A Steady Diet of Garbage

Feeding false information to the IRS computer system can produce severe problems, because a contradictory report requires a human operator to track down and correct the error. Let's note an important warning here: Don't do this with your own forms, because it's a federal crime to put false information down on an IRS form. Instead, send in totally false returns and forms. Several possibilities are obvious.

1. Totally fabricated Form 1040s for imaginary people. These, which you can generate with a computer program of your own such as "Turbo-Tax," and "Tax Cut," choke the system because they don't match with anything else, such as W-2s and Form 1099s.

2. False forms for real people. If you have a short list of enemies, people you'd like to harass but never found the time to make their lives miserable, send in fake returns in their names. The result will be a lot of confusion, especially if the return you mail in the name of "James Festerman" contains exemptions for twice as many children as he really has.

3. False W-4 forms and faked Form 1099s. To enter these into the system, you need only the names of some genuine businesses to use as payees. These fakes will have IRS paper-pushers chasing down imaginary people who haven't reported their incomes.

4. While it takes time to generate paper forms, and you have to handle them with plastic gloves to avoid leaving fingerprints, electronic filing is faster and easier. Naturally, don't do it from your home phone.

Deep Inside the Underground Economy
How Millions of Americans Are Practicing Free Enterprise in An Unfree Society

232

Fake Informers

Another way to waste the time of IRS personnel is to pretend to have tax fraud information for sale. This is possible by mail or by phone. Using a copy machine, it's easy to produce forgeries of invoices, canceled checks, and other documents that lay out a pattern of tax fraud. These forgeries won't stand up in court, or even to a close professional examination, but they don't have to be that good, only good enough to begin an investigation that wastes a special agent's valuable time. Remember, while he's on a wild goose chase, he neglects his regular work.

Obviously, you cannot use the name or paperwork of a totally imaginary person or company for this game. The discrepancy would show up too quickly. Instead, select an individual or business you dislike as long as there's no personal connection. It would be clumsy to use the name of an employer who just discharged you, because you'd be a prime suspect upon discovery of the scam. Instead, choose a company promoting a product or cause you dislike, such as tobacco, wood pulp, contraceptives, etc. A business that makes regular contributions to a civil rights group or to the gun control lobby are other possibilities, if you're against these causes. Think of this as killing two birds with one stone. You simultaneously hamper the IRS, and use harassment tactics against someone you dislike.

You can play telephone games with the IRS as well. Keep in mind that "Caller I. D." is common in most of the country, so don't play telephone games from either your home or work phones. Using a pay phone in the financial district, call the IRS and ask to speak with a special agent. Don't give your name, but say that you have documents proving that your employer has been defrauding the IRS. Ask for a face-to-face meeting with an investigator in a public place the next day, or whenever you can arrange an appointment, then don't show up for the rendezvous.

If you have time to spare and want a little extra fun, tell the investigator you're to meet how to recognize you, giving him a totally false description. Ask him how you're to recognize him. Then go to the meeting place and remain in the background, watching the fun as the investigator waits, and waits, and waits, until he's convinced that you're not going to appear.

If you feel like twisting the knife, telephone the investigator just before he leaves for the meeting, canceling the appointment on the excuse that something urgent is forcing you to reschedule. Arrange another meeting for the following day or week. Then go to that one and watch the fun.

Going All the Way

Some enterprising people have obtained refunds from the IRS by filing totally false returns. Although this becomes more difficult every year as the IRS's computer cross-checking system improves, a new twist is the spurious electronic form. The IRS, in an effort to be more accommodating to taxpayers and generate favorable PR, assigns higher priority to electronically filed forms, often sending the refund within two weeks.

The IRS electronic filing system is so vulnerable that rings have sprung up to generate spurious tax returns wholesale. In some cases, prison inmates have filed returns, arranging for friends and relatives outside the walls to cash the checks.

Other Books of Interest:

☐ **10048 THE BIG BOOK OF SECRET HIDING PLACES, *by Jack Luger.*** The biggest and best book on concealment of physical objects ever printed! This huge book tells how searchers find hidden contraband and how to hide your stuff so it can't be found. Topics covered include: Hiding places in the home, on your person, and in automobiles; The different types of searchers you may encounter, and the intensity of the searches they may conduct; Tools and techniques used by searchers; Two sure ways of foiling search dogs; The tools you will need to build your own secret hiding places and where to get them; And much, much more. *1987, 8½ x 11, 124 pp, soft cover.* $14.95.

☐ **55085 HOW TO DETERMINE UNDISCLOSED FINANCIAL INTERESTS.** If you think there is such a thing as financial privacy in America, this book shows you how wrong you are. This IRS manual reveals the exact methods used by government agents to snoop into private financial records in search of unreported income. Sensitive transactions can be discovered without even notifying the subject of the investigation. This is the single most revealing book on financial investigative methods we have ever seen. Highly recommended. NOTE: This is the same material previously found in *Advanced Investigative Techniques for Private Financial Records. 1983, 8½ x 11, 86 pp, illustrated, soft cover.* $15.00.

☐ **61139 METHODS OF DISGUISE, Revised and Expanded Second Edition, *by John Sample.*** Here is an incredible illustrated book on how to disguise yourself! Covers everything from "quick change" methods to long-term, permanent disguises. Includes: how to assemble a pocket disguise kit you can carry with you and use at any time; ways to change your face, body shape, voice, mannerisms, even fingerprints; mail order sources for make-up, wigs, elevator shoes, fake eyeglasses, and much more. This is the most comprehensive guide to disguise ever compiled! *1993, 5½ x 8½, 258 pp, soft cover.* $17.95.

☐ **13077 HOW TO MAKE CASH MONEY SELLING AT SWAP MEETS, FLEA MARKETS, ETC., *by Jordan L. Cooper.*** You can make money selling at swap meets, flea markets, etc. — once in a while as a part-time income, or as a full-time business. After years of making good money at flea markets, the author lets you in on the secrets of success. His tips and how-to's were learned from the School of Hard Knocks and can save you some hard knocks of your own. Topics covered include: what to sell; how to display your wares; pricing; the IRS; and much, much more. A low initial investment is all that's required. You can still hold your regular job while getting started, and you will be your own boss. *1988, 5½ x 8½, 180 pp, illustrated, soft cover.* $16.95.

☐ **64167 SECOND-HAND SUCCESS: How to Turn Discards into Dollars, *by Jordan L. Cooper.*** This is the story of successful people who turn discards into dollars. Jordan L. Cooper reveals the tricks used by dozens of clever entrepreneurs to turn trash into treasures. Learn where to find all kinds of used merchandise and where to sell it for top dollar. From recycling to foraging in grandma's attic to making art from junk, this is the best resource of its kind. Topics covered include: sources of supplies; swap meet survival; used clothing; small appliances & household goods; seasonal merchandise; antiques & collectibles; arts & crafts from junque; handling problems; and much more! *1995, 5½ x 8½, 196 pp, illustrated, soft cover.* $14.95.

☐ **64145 $HADOW MERCHANT$, Successful Retailing Without a Storefront, *by Jordan L. Cooper.*** How to make money in low-overhead, street corner-style operations by someone who's been there. Covers: swap meets; flea markets; street corners; arts & crafts shows; mall kiosks; fairs & carnivals; gun shows; special interest events; and much more! Also includes valuable advice on pitfalls to avoid. Shadow businesses are highly mobile, low-cost, low-risk operations that can be started without giving up your regular job. Many of the world's most famous businesses started out this way. The next success story could be yours. *1993, 5½ x 8½, 152 pp, illustrated, soft cover.* $12.95.

☐ **64210 THE TEMP WORKER'S GUIDE TO SELF-FULFILLMENT, How to slack off, achieve your dreams, and get paid for it!, *by Dennis Fiery.*** Temporary employment, or "temp work," can be a treasure trove of opportunity for the dedicated practitioner. Rather than being a series of dead-end meaningless short-term jobs, temp work offers numerous advantages. This book explains how to effectively exploit and undermine the temp system. It contains all the information needed to successfully obtain steady, lucrative work as a temp, while satisfying the requirements of the employers who are seeking competent temp workers and fulfilling your own special needs.

1997, 5½ x 8½, 152 pp, illustrated, soft cover. $12.95.

☐ **64240 MAKE $$$ AS A NON-FICTION WRITER,** *by Duncan Long.* You want to write, but how do you break into the field? Author and educator, Duncan Long, who has over 30 years experience as a non-fiction writer shows you the ropes. Find out if you have the right stuff to become a writer; What are realistic expectations of income as a writer; Do you have to use an agent; Is freelancing your only option; What kind of workspace and equipment do you need; How to find those elusive writing assignments. If you've been wanting to make writing your full- or part-time career, don't put it off any longer. Let Duncan Long show you how to get started today. *2000, 5½ x 8½, 219 pp, soft cover. $14.95.*

☐ **64245 FREELANCE WRITER'S HANDBOOK, Second Edition,** *by James Wilson.* Much has changed since the first edition, and technological advancements have led to this second edition. New developments include: faster computers, digital photography, e-mail, electronic submissions, and e-publishing, to name a few. Written by an author who has made his living writing 70 books and more than 1,000 magazine articles for over twenty years. He gives you the down-and-dirty facts about writing for money. Before you quit your day job, let an old pro show you how it's done. *2001, 5½ x 8½, 222 pp, soft cover. $15.95.*

☐ **61183 THE I.D. MASTER, Identity Change Insider Secrets, Little-Known Tactics of Identity-Change Professionals,** *by John Q. Newman.* In *The I.D. Master*, identity-change professional John Q. Newman reveals little-known insider secrets of identity changing. In these pages, you will discover: Using the law to create a new identity; How to create a useable Social Security number; The delayed birth certificate; How to use fake ID in identity creation; Background investigations; How to create an employment history; New identity after 9/11; and

much, much more. *2002, 8½ x 11, 136 pp, illustrated, soft cover. $19.95.*

☐ **61168 THE I.D. FORGER, Homemade Birth Certificates & Other Documents Explained,** *by John Q. Newman. The I.D. Forger* covers in step-by-step detail all of the classic and modern high-tech methods of forging the commonly used identification documents. Chapters include: the use of homemade documents; old-fashioned forgery; computer forgery; birth certificate basics; and other miscellaneous document forgery. *1999, 5½ x 8½, 110 pp, soft cover. $15.00.*

☐ **10065 HOW TO HIDE THINGS IN PUBLIC PLACES,** *by Dennis Fiery.* Did you ever want to hide something from prying eyes, yet were afraid to do so in your home? Now you can secrete your valuables away from home by following the eye-opening instructions contained in this book, which identifies many of the public cubbyholes and niches that can be safely employed for this purpose. Absolutely the finest book ever written on the techniques involved in hiding your possessions in public hiding spots. Illustrated with numerous photographs, an index of hiding places and appendices of Simplex lock combinations. *1996, 5½ x 8½, 220 pp, illustrated, soft cover. $15.00.*

☐ **13063 SURVIVAL BARTERING,** *by Duncan Long.* What if you had no money? What if an entire society had no money due to the collapse of our banking system? Bartering will be the most important survival skill you can learn. People barter for different reasons — to avoid taxes, obtain a better lifestyle, or just for fun. This book foresees a time when barter is a necessity. You'll learn about: three forms of barter; getting good deals; stockpiling for future bartering; protecting yourself from rip-offs; and much more. Learning how to barter could be the best insurance you can find. *1986, 5½ x 8½, 56 pp, soft cover. $8.00.*

You can order the above titles through the following distributors or your favorite bookstore.

Loompanics Unlimited, 1-800-380-2230
Homestead Books, 1-800-426-6777
BookPeople, 1-800-999-4650
Baker & Taylor, 1-800-775-1100